Long Lance

the glorious impostor

Donald B. Smith

Red Deer Press

The Publishers
Red Deer Press
56 Avenue & 32 Street Box 5005
Red Deer Alberta Canada T4N 5H5

Credits
Cover and text design by Boldface Technologies
Printed and bound in Canada by Friesens for Red Deer Press

Acknowledgments
Financial support provided by the Alberta Foundation for the Arts, a
beneficiary of the Lottery Fund of the Government of Alberta, and by the
Canada Council and the Department of Canadian Heritage.

Canadian Cataloguing in Publication Data
Smith, Donald B., 1946–
Chief Buffalo Child Long Lance
Includes index.
ISBN 0-88995-197-7

1. Buffalo Child Long Lance, 1890–1932. 2. Indians of North America—
Canada—Biography. 3. Impostors and imposture—Canada—
Biography. I. Title
E90.B9S65   1999   971'.00497'0092   C99-910584-1

5 4 3 2 1

Photo Acknowledgments

Front Cover Glenbow Archives and Glenbow Archives (Canon Middleton Collection)

Page 16 Glenbow Archives/PA-2513-141

Page 17 Glenbow Archives/PA-2513-143 (Joe Bradshaw)

Page 18 Glenbow Archives/PA-2513-142

Page 25 Donald Smith, June 1977.

Page 26 Glenbow Archives/PA-2513-2 (Daisy Carson Blackburn)

Page 27 Glenbow Archives/PA-2513-4 (Newman Dalton)

Page 28 Glenbow Archives/PA-2513-5 (Newman Dalton)

Page 30 Forsyth County Public Library, Winston–Salem, NC/AO 3265

Page 31 Glenbow Archives/PA-2513-9 (Newman Dalton)

Page 32 Glenbow Archives/PA-2513-7 (Nannie Lewis)

Page 33 Glenbow Archives/PA-2513-10 (Lillian Doulin)

Page 34 Forsyth County Public Library, Winston–Salem, NC/AO 3574

Page 34 Glenbow Archives, Calgary (Lillian Doulin)

Page 35 Glenbow Archives/M6240

Page 37 Glenbow Archives/PA-2513-13 (Newman Dalton)

Page 37 Glenbow Archives/PA-2513-8

Page 38 Glenbow Archives/PA-2513-18 (Newman Dalton)

Page 39 Glenbow Archives/PA-2513-14 (Newman Dalton)

Page 40 Glenbow Archives/PA-2513-15 (Newman Dalton)

Page 41 Forsyth County Public Library, Winston–Salem, NC/AO 3958

Page 44 Glenbow Archives/PA-2513-24 (Newman Dalton)

Page 45 Glenbow Archives/PA-2513-25 (Kathryn E. Ray)

Page 46 Records of the Bureau of Indian Affairs, Record Group 75. From the *Guide to Genealogical Research in the National Archives* (Washington, DC, 1983), p.165.

Page 50 Glenbow Archives/PA-2513-26 (Newman Dalton)

Page 54 Glenbow Archives/PA-2513-28

Page 56 Glenbow Archives/PA-2513-31 (Lillian Dalton Doulin)

Page 58 Glenbow Archives/PA-2513-29

Page 59 Glenbow Archives/PA-2513-33 (Joe Bradshaw)

Page 60 Glenbow Archives/PA-2513-32

Page 64 Glenbow Archives/PA-2513-38

Page 65 Glenbow Archives/PA-2513-39

Page 67 Glenbow Archives/PA-2513-37

Page 79 Glenbow Archives/PA-2513-40 (Newman Dalton)

Page 85 Glenbow Archives/PA-2513-84 (Canon Middleton Collection)

Page 89 Glenbow Archives/PA-2513-41 (Howard Kelly)

Page 90 Glenbow Archives/PA-2513-47 (Howard Kelly)

Page 91 Glenbow Archives/PA-2513-46 (Newman Dalton)

Page 94 Glenbow Archives/PA-2513-44 (Newman Dalton)

Page 95 Glenbow Archives/PA-2513-42 (Newman Dalton)

Page 93 *Calgary Herald*, Sept. 23, 1921.

Page 97 Glenbow Archives/PA-2513-45 (Newman Dalton)

Page 101 Glenbow Archives/PA-2513-50

Page 105 Glenbow Archives/PA-2513-49

Page 109 Glenbow Archives/NA-1020-17

Page 113 Glenbow Archives/PA-2513-51 (Sophie Allison)

Page 121 Glenbow Archives/PA-2513-55

Page 122 Glenbow Archives/PA-2513-53

Page 124 Glenbow Archives/PA-2513-57

Page 126 Glenbow Archives/PA-2513-58

Page 145 Glenbow Archives/NA-1811-67 (Canon Middleton Collection)

Page 147 Glenbow Archives/PA-2513-59

Page 150 Glenbow Archives/PA-2513-63 (W.G.B. Kilroe Collection)

Page 153 Glenbow Archives/PA-2513-66

Page 154 Glenbow Archives/PA-2513-65

Page 158 Glenbow Archives/PA-2513-62 (Hugh Dann)

Page 159 Glenbow Archives/PA-2513-69

Page 160 Glenbow Archives/PA-2513-68 (Canon Middleton Collection)

Page 162 Glenbow Archives/PA-2513-73

Page 163 Glenbow Archives/PA-2513-74

Page 166 Glenbow Archives/PA-2513-64 (Canon Middleton Collection)

Page 171 Glenbow Archives/NA-1811-61

Page 172 Whyte Museum of the Canadian Rockies, Banff, Alberta/V701/LC.99

Page 173 Glenbow Archives/PA-2513-78

Page 177 Glenbow Archives/PA-2513-79

Page 179 *Toronto Star Weekly*, January 10, 1925.

Page 181 Glenbow Archives/PA-2513-81

Page 182–83 Glenbow Archives/PA-2513-83 (Joe Bradshaw)

Page 185 Glenbow Archives/PA-2513-76 (Canon Middleton Collection)

Page 187 *Maclean's*, May 15, 1926.

Page 199 Glenbow Archives/PA-2513-22 (Newman Dalton)

Page 202 Glenbow Archives/PA-2513-75 (Mike Eagle Speaker)

Page 215 Glenbow Archives/PA-2513-88

Page 216 Glenbow Archives/PA-2513-96

Page 217 Glenbow Archives/PA-2513-92

Page 218 Glenbow Archives/PA-2513-94 (Canon Middleton Collection)

Page 219 Glenbow Archives/PA-2513-93 (Canon Middleton Collection)

Page 223 Glenbow Archives/PA-2513-119 (Roberta Forsberg)

Page 224 Glenbow Archives/PA-2513-120 (Ted Blackmore)

Page 231 Glenbow Archives/PA-2513-98

Page 232 Glenbow Archives/PA-2513-97

Page 234 Glenbow Archives/PA-2513-105 (Canon Middleton Collection)

Page 235 Glenbow Archives/PA-2513-103 (Canon Middleton Collection)

Page 236 Glenbow Archives/PA-2513-110 (Canon Middleton Collection)

Page 240 Glenbow Archives/PA-2513-106 (Canon Middleton Collection)

Page 243 Glenbow Archives/PA-2513-99 (Canon Middleton Collection)

Page 247 Glenbow Archives/PA-2513-127 (Sophie Allison)

Page 249 Glenbow Archives/PA-2513-130

Page 244 Glenbow Archives/PA-2513-100 (Canon Middleton Collection)

Page 256 Glenbow Archives/PA-2513-121

Page 258 Glenbow Archives/PA-2513-118 (S.C. Burden)

Page 259 Glenbow Archives/PA-2513-124 (Sophie Allison)

Page 260 Glenbow Archives/PA-2513-125 (Lee Ash)

Page 267 Glenbow Archives/PA-2513-126 (Joe Bradshaw)

Page 274 Glenbow Archives/PA-2513-111

Page 275 United States Army Research Collection, Carlisle Barracks, Pennsylvania; and Glenbow Archives/PA-2513-123 (Canon Middleton Collection)

Page 278 Glenbow Archives/PA-2513-134 (Los Angeles Public Library)

Page 279 Glenbow Archives/M690 f.20

Page 280 Glenbow Archives/PA-2513-23 (Newman Dalton)

Page 281 Glenbow Archives/PA-2513-138

Page 284 Glenbow Archives/PA-2513-6 (Joe Bradshaw)

Page 285 Glenbow Archives/PA-2513-131 (Douglas Burden)

Page 289 Domenica Pallister

Page 290 Glenbow Archives/PA-2513-133 (Roberta Forsberg)

Page 292 Glenbow Archives/PA-2513-132 (Newman Dalton)

Page 306 Glenbow Archives/PA-2513-135 (Canon Middleton Collection)

Page 307 Glenbow Archives/PA-2513-91 (Canon Middleton Collection)

Page 322 United States Army Research Collection, Carlisle Barracks, Pennsylvania/PA-2513-137

Page 324 Glenbow Archives/PA-2513-139 (Joe Bradshaw)

For Jean Boyd and
John Caulfield Smith

Contents

Preface / 11

Prologue / 19
NEW YORK CITY, 1931

CHAPTER 1 / 22
Sylvester Clark Long
WINSTON–SALEM, NORTH CAROLINA, 1890

CHAPTER 2 / 47
The Trail Upward Begins
CARLISLE INDIAN SCHOOL, PENNSYLVANIA, 1909

CHAPTER 3 / 60
Sylvester Chahuska Long Lance
ST. JOHN'S MILITARY ACADEMY, NEW YORK STATE, 1912

CHAPTER 4 / 71
Lieutenant Long Lance, War Hero
VIMY RIDGE, FRANCE, 1917

CHAPTER 5 / 81
Long Lance, Journalist
CALGARY, ALBERTA, 1920–21

CHAPTER 6 / 97
Making a Name
BLACKFOOT RESERVE, ALBERTA, 1921

CHAPTER 7 / 110
Buffalo Child Long Lance
BLOOD RESERVE, ALBERTA, 1922

CHAPTER 8 / 123
Long Lance, Plains Indian
VANCOUVER, BRITISH COLUMBIA, 1922

CHAPTER 9 / 136
Talking to the Elders
REGINA, SASKATCHEWAN, 1922

CHAPTER 10 / 147
Long Lance, Native Rights Advocate
WINNIPEG, MANITOBA, 1923–24

CHAPTER 11 / 173
Long Lance, "Redskin Extraordinary"
BANFF, ALBERTA, 1925–26

CHAPTER 12 / 194
Long Lance, Biographer
CALGARY, ALBERTA, 1927

CHAPTER 13 / 208
Long Lance, Social Lion
NEW YORK CITY, 1928

CHAPTER 14 / 228
Long Lance, Movie Star
TEMAGAMI, ONTARIO, 1929

CHAPTER 15 / 250
The Trail Narrows
NEW YORK CITY, 1929

CHAPTER 16 / 267
"Hello, Sylvester"
NEW YORK CITY, 1930

CHAPTER 17 / 285
The Lady of the Peacocks
EUROPE, 1931

CHAPTER 18 / 308
The Trail Ends
LOS ANGELES, CALIFORNIA, 1932

Epilogue / 315
LOS ANGELES, CALIFORNIA, 1932

Acknowledgments / 324

Notes / 327

Bibliography / 380

Index / 390

Preface

J first became interested in Chief Buffalo Child Long Lance about 1970. Rummaging in a secondhand bookstore in Toronto, I noticed a small brown volume, its title firmly imprinted on the spine: *Long Lance*. For some time I had been interested in all historical and autobiographical writing by Indians, as First Nations people were termed at the time. Intrigued by what appeared to be an Indian's autobiography, I pulled it down and turned to page one: "The first thing in my life that I can remember is the exciting aftermath of an Indian fight in northern Montana." I bought the book, read it and never forgot it.

My next encounter with Chief Long Lance came in Calgary, in the heart of the Blackfoot's old hunting territory. In the autumn of 1974 I began teaching Canadian history at the University of Calgary. Fresh from eastern Canada, I knew little about the West. I made several trips to the Glenbow Archives, a rich source of Western Canadiana as well as appropriate lecture material. There, one afternoon, I found a sizable carton full of letters, articles and newspaper clippings about a Blackfoot warrior: Long Lance. The Glenbow materials had come from the estate of Canon S.H. Middleton, Long Lance's executor and the recipient of many of the chief's possessions after his death. The articles and letters told of his honors at the Carlisle Indian School in Pennsylvania, of his appointment by President Woodrow Wilson to West Point, of his distinguished service in the Great War with the Canadian Army, of his years as a reporter in Western Canada and of his incredible success in New York City as a writer, actor and aviator.

It was exciting material. Yet the file at the Glenbow contained so many inconsistencies. For example, an article published in the *Los Angeles Examiner* immediately after the chief's death in 1932 contained a curious reference to his father, who had signed himself J.S. Long. That seemed strange. Most Blackfoot Indians I had read about had names like Crowfoot, Red Crow or Shot-Both-Sides. And there was another leading discrepancy. In the articles of the late 1920s, Long Lance was described as a young man of thirty-five. Yet in his autobiography he claimed to have hunted buffalo in his youth, which, if he had been born in the early 1890s, was clearly impossible.

All that winter of 1974–75, I sent out dozens of letters trying to discover Long Lance's true origins. Hugh Dempsey, the director of history at the Glenbow, and Sheilagh Jameson, the chief archivist, had long been interested in the man. Both of them kindly put me in touch with several people who had known him in Alberta in the 1920s. In Calgary I met Howard Kelly, Hugh Dann and George Gooderham, and on the Blood Reserve, Mike Eagle Speaker. At Waterton Park near the Alberta–Montana border, I contacted Sophie Allison, the daughter of Canon Middleton. All went out of their way to help me, supplying me with articles and letters written by and about Long Lance. (I have placed copies of all the materials collected from them in the Glenbow Archives in Calgary.)

Having read in the article in the *Los Angeles Examiner* that Long Lance's father, J.S. Long, claimed to live in Winston–Salem, North Carolina, I wrote to the city's public library in late February. Ann Correll, the librarian in charge of the North Carolina Collection, provided the documentary proof of Long Lance's true origins. From his record of service in the Canadian army, I already knew that he had enlisted as Sylvester Long Lance. After I contacted her the conscientious librarian checked through the Winston city directories for the early twentieth century. Yes, she wrote back on March 7, 1975, a Sylvester C. Long appeared in the directories from 1910 to 1913. He was listed as a student, and his residence was given as 95 Brookstown Avenue, the home of Joseph S., Sallie, Abraham and Walter Long. In the directories Joseph S. Long was listed as "colored." The librarian also enclosed an article written about Abraham "Abe" Long, "longtime manager of the old all-Negro balcony at the theater." In the *Winston–Salem Twin City Sentinel* on Saturday, September 16, 1967, Abe had reminisced about the Carolina Theater of the old days. Three lines in that article especially struck me: "He is the last of the original Long family. A brother, Walter Long, a private detective, died here in 1941. Another brother, Sylvester, had died earlier in California." Chief Buffalo Child Long Lance had died in California. Sylvester Long of North Carolina and the famous Chief Buffalo Child had to be the same man.

In late June 1975 I made the first of what would become seven trips to Winston–Salem. I made a few phone calls, met some relatives and confirmed that Sylvester Long's father's ancestry was mixed: white and Indian. Joe Long himself had denied the possibility of any African ancestry. Sylvester's mother was three-quarters white and one-quarter Lumbee Indian. Each trip added to the information previously gathered. My research indicated that the man lionized as a Plains Indian by the North American

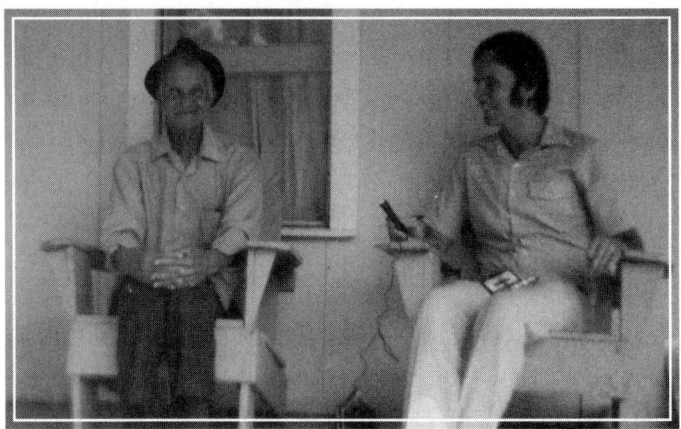

The author interviewing Charlie Carson (1887–1977), Sylvester Long's first cousin, at Carson Town, Iredell County. Charlie remembered Sylvester as a young boy.

press in the late 1920s was really an impostor. What made his story rather unique was my ability to document it and the fact that the tale involved the continent's three major racial groupings: Indian, white and black.

During my visits it was fortunate that Joe Bradshaw, a distant cousin of Sylvester's, took such an interest in the project. He generously set aside many hours of his time, locating and then driving me to see Sylvester's relatives and childhood friends. Joe introduced me to Long Lance's first cousins: Charlie Carson and his sisters Daisy Blackburn, Jency Gaither, Mammie Patterson and Nannie Lewis. I met Sylvester's half sister, Lillie Long Dalton. Her daughter, Lillian Dalton Doulin, and son, Newman Dalton, allowed me to examine Abe Long's diaries and many of the Long family's photos. Joe Bradshaw showed me Long Lance's second scrapbook that Walter Long had brought back from Los Angeles. (This second scrapbook has since been donated by Joe Bradshaw to the Glenbow Archives. The first book is also there. After Long Lance's death, his friend Clyde Fisher found it in the chief's locker at the Explorers Club in New York and mailed it to Canon Middleton.)

In February 1976 the *Canadian Magazine* published my two-part article on Chief Buffalo Child Long Lance. Thanks to

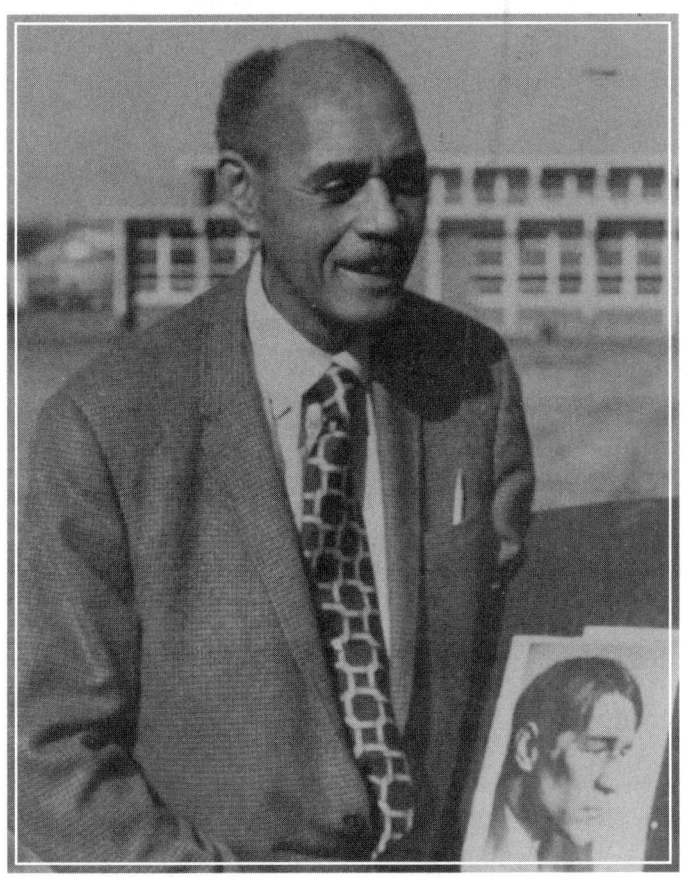

Joe Bradshaw holding one of Long Lance's scrapbooks that was given to him by Abe Long, Long Lance's brother.

the encouragement of the *Canadian*'s Alan Walker and David Cobb, who had helped me a great deal with the presentation of the articles, I decided to undertake a fuller study. Trips in Canada and the United States to interview those who had known Long Lance completed my research.

Since 1978 a number of people have read drafts of the book. My mother, Jean B. Smith, Ramsay Derry and Lovat Dickson commented on the preliminary draft. Audrey Swaffield devoted long hours throughout 1978 and 1979 reading first and second versions. Working from the comments of Jan Walter of Macmillan, I

The author with Sylvester Long's half sister, Lillie Long Dalton (1886–1978), with her descendants at Mocksville, North Carolina. Lillie's children—daughter Lillian Dalton Doulin and son Newman Dalton (1919–1984)—kindly allowed me to examine many family items and copy many old family photos.

prepared a third draft in 1980, which Judy Abel kindly read and criticized chapter by chapter. Both Professor Kenneth Porter of the University of Oregon, who has been interested in Long Lance since his graduate school days at Harvard, and filmmaker Alan King provided me with useful comments on the text. The first edition of this book, published in early 1982, owes a great deal to the suggestions and improvements of the editor, Martin O'Malley. By coincidence, Martin's father, Fred O'Malley, worked with Long Lance at the *Winnipeg Tribune* in the early twenties.

Two return trips to Winston–Salem—in June 1982 and seventeen years later in June 1999—helped clarify several issues. I have added these insights to this revised edition. I thank the Canadian Studies Center at Duke University, Durham, NC, in particular the director, Richard H. Leach, and the administrative co-ordinator, Marion Salinger, for the opportunity to return to North Carolina shortly after the publication of the first edition of my book. Special thanks to Bill Suggs for the organization of the Long Lance Festival at the Forsyth County Public Library in Winston–Salem.

For his assistance in preparing this revised edition, I once again thank Doug Cass of the Glenbow Archives. Many other staff members of the Archives assisted. My thanks to all of them. All royalties from the sale of this edition will be given to the Sheilagh Jameson Fund to assist the continuing work of this wonderful institution, the Glenbow Archives.

I am most grateful to David Smith, my fifteen-year-old son, who accompanied me to Winston–Salem in June 1999. He literally saved the research trip when he found the misplaced keys to our rented car. I also thank Anne Blackburn, Celeste Blackburn, Cheryl Bradshaw, Elizabeth Dalton, Darnell Dalton, Lillian Dalton Doulin and Esterleen Moore for their hospitality. I am also very grateful to Jerry Carroll, Molly Rawls and Bratis Roseboro for their invaluable assistance at the Forsyth County Public Library.

Unfortunately many of those who helped on previous research trips to North Carolina had passed away, but it was a special pleasure to speak on the phone with Ann Correll, now retired from the Forsyth County Public Library, whose reply to my inquiry about Sylvester Long started me on the research trail to learn more about him a quarter of a century ago.

After all these years, I am most grateful to Dennis Johnson, managing editor of Red Deer Press, for suggesting that I prepare a second edition of my book. Thanks to him, for several weeks I've relived the excitement of my early research days. Quite frankly it astonishes me now how I ever had the time (and the energy) to chase all this information down. I appreciate greatly the assistance of Dennis's colleagues at the Press, Carolyn Dearden, Amy Becker, Kristen Gough and Vicki Mix.

I warmly thank my mother, Jean Boyd Smith, to whom, with my late father, John Caulfield Smith, this book is dedicated. She and my good friend, filmmaker Bernie Dichek, have never given up on Long Lance. Their continued interest in this fascinating character has helped to maintain my own. Last and most deservedly of all, my wife, Nancy Townshend, and sons, David and Peter, are due thanks for their understanding of this and other research obsessions.

Thirty years after I first learned about him, I see Sylvester Long—Long Lance—as the quintessential twentieth-century person, an individual with several distinct identities. For reasons that are elaborated upon in this book, he chose to emphasize one racial identity over the other. Today, with the end of the Jim Crow segregationist system in the American South, he might have made a different identity choice. After all, genetically he had both European and North American ancestry; and culturally—even if there was no genetic link—he was raised in an African American society. His life provides a wonderful vehicle to tell the story of early twentieth-century racial attitudes in both the United States and Canada.

Finally, a word about terms used in this revised edition. Since the early 1980s the word *Indian* has gradually lost favor, and in Canada the term *First Nation* has gained popularity. In this text, however, I have retained *Indian* as it was in current usage in Long Lance's day. Many of the First Nations' names for themselves have recently entered English usage, such as Siksika for Blackfoot and Tsuu T'ina for Sarcee, but once again I have kept to the older terms that Long Lance and his contemporaries used.

Prologue

NEW YORK CITY, 1931

*O*n the morning of January 5, 1931, the fog in New York was impenetrable, so thick an ocean liner had collided with a dredge in the harbor. Then came the winds and an unseasonable mist, and by early evening, rain drenched the familiar thoroughfares of Manhattan, where a taxi carried two men.[1]

The cabby might have recognized one of his passengers, an unusually handsome man with high cheekbones, copper skin and straight black hair. A tailored trench coat emphasized his trim athletic body and strong shoulders. He was Chief Buffalo Child Long Lance, the newest sensation in the city of sensations. This exotic stranger was from a world inaccessible to most Americans. He attended the best parties, courted actresses and gossiped with royalty—a charismatic, accomplished, eloquent man and yet somehow self-effacing. His autobiography had been published three years earlier and had become a critically acclaimed best seller. More recently he had starred in a film, *The Silent Enemy*, which had been shot in the wilds of northern Canada and had premiered at the Criterion on Times Square little more than a year earlier. He was one of the most famous North American Indians of his day.[2]

Newspapers and magazines hungered for stories about him but kept their research to a minimum. Reporters reveled in his many achievements: athlete, war hero, journalist, biographer, full-blooded Indian chief, public lecturer, Indian rights advocate, actor, pilot. The story went that he had once trained with the legendary athlete Jim Thorpe; he had once sparred with none other than Jack Dempsey. An American president had granted him a special appointment to West Point; a grateful French nation had awarded him the *Croix de Guerre* for exceptional military valor. Born a Blood Indian in a tepee in the Sweetgrass Hills near the Canadian–American border, Long Lance had risen to celebrity through intellect, charm, courage and tremendous will. He was, one reporter claimed, one hundred percent American.

The taxi driver would not have recognized the other man — heavier, older and lighter-skinned. He was Walter Long, a private detective from North Carolina, and to him New York was foreign territory.[3] Born in a log shanty near the Yadkin–Iredell county line in North Carolina, he lived in Winston–Salem, where the air hung heavy with the smell of tobacco. As a "colored" man Walter Long could not realize his boyhood ambition of joining the local police force. Instead he took his constabulary training in West Virginia, later returning home to start his own detective agency in the black community. His celebrated Indian companion would not have been hard to track down, despite Walter Long's detective skills, for Long Lance's achievements were widely circulated in the press in Winston–Salem as elsewhere.

Had the cabby sensed the tension between his passengers, he might have put it down to the huge gulf between the two men stretching across race, class and standing in society. The two men fidgeted. They barely spoke, for there was too much to speak about. Long Lance, the celebrated lecturer and public figure, sat saying little, not even the small-talk that he used to charm New York socialites. He did not know how to begin. *Don't speak unless you can improve the silence*, he might have thought, for that was the Indian way.[4]

The taxi pushed through the wet streets of mid-Manhattan, past boarded-up stores and darkened restaurants, in this, the second full year of the Great Depression. Few people walked the streets; beggars foraged in garbage cans. From the glare of Times Square the taxi entered the garment district and headed toward the ring of skyscraper hotels surrounding the massive railway terminus at Seventh Avenue and Thirty-First Street.

The taxi pulled up at the curb of the columned entrance to Pennsylvania Station. Instantly Long Lance threw open the door and slammed it behind him. He sprinted up the gray stone steps in the rain, not looking back, hurrying across the brightly lit entrance, then inside, where he disappeared into the crowd.[5]

Walter Long followed Long Lance with his eyes, then paid the fare for this man who was his brother. He had not seen him for twenty-two years and would never see him again.

CHAPTER 1

Sylvester Clark Long

WINSTON–SALEM, NORTH CAROLINA, 1890

Sylvester Clark Long was born on December 1, 1890,[1] just after his family moved to Winston and to the little house on 4 1/2 Street behind the mansions of the rich on Fifth Street. R.J. Reynolds, the tobacco magnate, was a neighbor. In those days, before the automobile and the suburbs, black and white, rich and poor lived side by side, if not as equals at least in close juxtaposition. The whites preferred to live close to downtown with their black servants living nearby.

Sylvester's parents, Sallie and Joe Long, had farmed at Carson Town in the early 1880s and were married there in 1879.[2] Carson Town, forty miles west of Winston, lay in Iredell County in the rolling foothills of western North Carolina. It was an area of tall, magnificent trees and red clay. Winter came and stayed, but summers were long, humid and hot. Sallie had been born into slavery in the last months of the Civil War.[3] Joe came from a plantation in neighboring Yadkin County.[4]

The old graveyard just south of Carson Town. The tall headstones mark the graves of the white plantation owners and their families; the small stones, the graves of slaves.

Sallie and Joe Long lived as blacks but maintained they were white and Indian, a not uncommon occurrence at the time in the South, where racial origins were difficult to know and still more difficult to prove. Sallie's white grandfather, Robert Carson, was the son of the original plantation owner, Andrew Carson. She had seen his weathered gravestone in the cemetery just south of Carson Town: Captain Andrew Carson. Born March 1, 1756. Died Jan'y 29, 1841. He was a soldier of the Revolutionary War.[5] Robert Carson's tombstone stood in the Baptist Flat Rock Cemetery in Hamptonville, north of Carson Town.[6] Sallie rarely visited it, however, because the "colored" could not attend services there.

Robert Carson, or Bobby as he was known, was a wildcat in his younger days. A slave trader and a plantation owner, he was a reckless lover of many women,[7] practicing frequently on slave women. He was considered a small-time slave owner, his forty-six slaves being not enough to warrant inclusion in the local records of the day.[8] He settled down after he bought a handsome Indian woman at a slave auction in South Carolina. (In many of the colonies the first slaves were Indians. Occasionally they were enslaved illegally as late as 1836.[9]) He brought her to Carson Town, where he kept her as his concubine. She bore him twenty children.[10]

Sylvester Long's grandmother, Adeline Carson (1848–1932). She told Sylvester's mother, Sallie, of the family's Indian roots.

Sallie's mother, Adeline, one of the twenty children, was born in 1848,[11] when Robert Carson was fifty-six years old. By law, as children of a slave, Adeline and her fair-skinned brothers and sisters also became slaves.[12] They grew up in one of ten tiny cabins near the big house,[13] where Robert Carson lived, and they worked alongside his slaves, planting and picking cotton, the prime crop of the area. Adeline felt it her duty to tell Sallie of her Indian past, as Adeline's mother had told her, and she repeated over and over that their family was descended not from black slaves but from whites and Indians.

Sallie Long, Sylvester's mother, as a young woman, c. 1900. She was born a slave.

When Sallie was old enough, Adeline told her of her natural father, a man called Andrew Cowles of neighboring Hamptonville. It was the story of her grandmother and Robert Carson all over again: the slave girl and the plantation owner. Andrew Cowles visited Robert Carson's plantation often, and there he fathered at least two children.[14] One of them was Sallie, born in January 1865, when her mother was only sixteen.

As a girl, Sallie must have seen her father, the senator from Yadkin County in the North Carolina Senate.[15] He was a handsome man, six feet, three inches tall with black hair and brown eyes.[16]

Sylvester's father, Joe Long (1853–1932), was born into slavery.

When Sallie shopped in Hamptonville, she walked by the old Cowles mansion, a three-story building with an attached ball-room and a sunken garden on the grounds.[17] Always conscious of his image, the senator never recognized Sallie, his fair-skinned daughter.[18]

Joe Long had been separated from his mother and sister at an early age, but after the Civil War he managed to find his sister in Carson Town, married to a cousin of Sallie.[19] It is a measure of his tenacity and the racial imperatives of the South at the time that he never stopped looking for his mother. After a forty-year search he eventually found her in a small town in Alabama just before she died at the age of ninety.[20] She told him that his father was John Vestal, a white man, and that she was a Cherokee Indian.[21]

Soon after his birth in 1853, Joe had been taken into the family of the Reverend Miles Long and given the family name. Joe Long's obituary says he was "a member of the Catawba tribe of Indians,"[22] but this must be a journalist's error, for he believed his father was white and his mother a Cherokee slave.[23] Whatever Joe and Sallie believed about their ancestry, they had no clear proof of Indian forebears, so they were labeled "colored."

Joe and Sallie married in March 1879 in one of Carson Town's largest houses, owned by Joe's brother-in-law, Lee Carson. Joe was twenty-six and Sallie was fourteen. The "colored" Carsons had done well after emancipation. Segregation existed in and around Carson Town, but it was not practiced nearly as rigidly as in the more southerly cities. An outsider may not have been able distinguish between "white" and "black" among the Carson descendants, but the locals knew the rules. Blacks could not attend the school for whites or the Baptist Church at Hamptonville though blacks and whites still helped each other at harvest, and at the Carson Town Church the blacks set a bench aside for the white farmers and their families. Both communities mixed easily and comfortably every October at the week-long religious festival they called the Big Meeting.[24]

Winston was more modern than Carson Town in every way. When the Longs arrived in March 1887,[25] drawn by the prosperity of the city, Winston had telephones and soon after electric streetlights and a streetcar system.[26] Even its segregation, at least from the point of view of whites, was more up-to-date than in Carson Town. Two-thirds of the population was classified as "white" and one-third as "black," and the lines between the two were sharp and indelible. Blacks could not work as clerks in stores or attend white schools. Both communities had their own churches. Blacks and whites never worked side by side as equals. Blacks ate

Downtown Winston at the intersection of Fourth Street and Main, 1896. In the days before the automobile and the suburbs, black and white and rich and poor lived side by side, but they were anything but equals.

at their own restaurants, drank at their own water fountains and had to use separate rest rooms.[27]

Sallie's mother, Adeline, was devoutly religious. She had mastered most of the memorable gospel songs when she lived in her slave quarters and had passed them on to Sallie. Adeline and Sallie shared a strong Baptist faith and believed that their rewards, if there were rewards, lay in the hereafter. Sallie and Joe sought to instill this attitude in their children, Abe, Walter, Sylvester and Katie:[28] make faith your life's foundation and then accept the hand life has dealt you.

With the youngest son, Sylvester, the teaching went unheeded. Something in him resisted all attempts to teach him the rules of a racist society. He could not swallow the platitudes, and he could not wait for rewards in the hereafter. Doubtless he squirmed in his seat when the black preacher spoke of the coloreds' place in the world, when he rhapsodized about heaven and terrorized about hell. His parents and his brothers explained how Sylvester must show respect for the white folks, but this only confused him. His mother, his brothers and many of his Carson Town relatives all looked like white folks. Still, the family persisted.

The earliest surviving photo of Sylvester Long, taken around 1903, captioned "12 of age," one year before he first joined the Wild West Show and began to glimpse another life.

Never talk back to the white folks. Always remove your hat in their presence. Step off the sidewalk to let them pass. When Sylvester reached adolescence, they added another rule: never look a white woman in the eye.[29]

A horrific racial incident had occurred in Winston in 1895, when Sylvester was five years old. A black teenager had scuffled with a police officer after refusing to get off the sidewalk to allow a white woman to pass. The officer was shot dead by the youth. Rumors spread that the whites planned to lynch the teenager. Some three hundred to five hundred blacks gathered. When they refused to move, the militia fired point-blank into the crowd, killing an unknown number.[30]

Sylvester accompanied his family to Carson Town every October for the Big Meeting. It was at one of these gatherings that he first heard of his famous distant relative, Kit Carson, the trapper, guide, buffalo hunter and Indian fighter. Folklore held that Kit Carson had lived in Carson Town, but historians contend he

Carson Town, c. 1895–1900. The harvest festival, the Big Meeting, was the social highlight of the year.

was born in 1809, more than a decade after his family left Carson Town for Kentucky. That did not stop the locals from telling—and inventing—stories about him. There was the time Kit Carson rode by and cut the top off a young oak in Carson Town. The oak grew to a huge height and outlasted Kit Carson by many years. It was always known as "the oak Kit Carson topped."[31] Sylvester hungered for this sort of a life and fantasized about the Wild West. One day he or his mother drew a simple sketch of a cowboy riding a bucking bronco in a scrapbook she kept. At the bottom of the drawing he or she carefully inscribed his initials: SCL.[32]

The Longs, Joe and Sallie, and their children—Abe, Walter, Sylvester and Katie—were one of the few in-between families in Winston. Clearly the family's identity was racially ambiguous. The city directories of the period included colored residents separately or indicated race or color by a symbol when there was no racial division. All male members of the Long family appear as colored in the volumes for 1902–03, 1904–05 and 1906. In 1910 all male members of the Long family, then living at 95 Brookstown Avenue, are listed as colored, with the exception of Walter. In 1911 Abe M. appears as Miles A. in the white section. The following year Abe and Walter are listed as white and Joe as colored—very bizarre.[33]

From an early age Sylvester was fascinated by the myths of freedom and self-reliance of the West. Either he or his mother drew this cowboy on a bucking bronco and labelled it "SCL"—Sylvester Clark Long.

Apparently both the African American and white communities agreed that the Long family had some Indian background. The white community regarded Sallie Long as Indian but differed on the genetic background of Joe. Some whites believed that Joe, so much darker than his wife, had some African ancestry.[34] That suspicion was enough to place the family in the colored community. As Gunnar Myrdal would write in his classic study of race relations in the United States, *An American Dilemma* (1944), "Everybody having a *known* trace of Negro blood in his veins—no

White students before the West End Graded School, 1890. Joe Long worked for many decades here as the school's janitor, but his children could not attend.

The Depot Street Grade and Industrial School, where Sylvester received his earliest elementary education.

matter how far back it was acquired—is classified as a Negro. No amount of white ancestry, except one hundred per cent, will permit entrance to the white race."[35]

But that classification having been made, the white community regarded the Longs as a special kind of Negro because of their European features and Indian background. Joe worked as a clerk and later as a janitor at the whites' West End School. Sallie was employed by both white and black families as a nurse and midwife. These were considered good jobs, and both Sallie and Joe could read and write, a combination that made them aristocrats of the black community.[36]

When he was six years old, Sylvester walked two miles to the Depot Street School for Negroes even though the family then lived very close to the West End School. Sylvester could help his father clean the school, but he could never hope to attend it as a student.[37]

He earned good marks at school[38] and obtained his grade six before he left at age thirteen.[39] At school and on summer holidays, besides assisting his father, he worked with Felix Graves, his first cousin, doing odd jobs at O'Hanlon's Drug

This unidentified newspaper photo in one of Long Lance's scarpbooks was captioned, "Long-Lance at Thirteen." It reveals some of his first inklings of the life he hoped to fashion away from Winston–Salem.

Store.[40] But in 1904 he jumped at his first chance for adventure — he ran off with a circus.[41]

The turn of the century was the heyday of the American circus. Customers thrilled to gymnasts and trapezists, to wild animal acts and to sideshow freaks who tore the heads off live chickens. By the 1880s, as an extra attraction, the Wild West Show was added. How could a boy like Sylvester resist? Doubtless he performed the menial chores, feeding the horses and carrying pails of water to the elephants, but he loved it. He met Arab tumblers, Mexican wire walkers, Japanese acrobats and American cowboys and Indians. There was little discrimination within the tight-knit family of the traveling circus behind the scenes, but African Americans were barred from performing in any of the major acts.[42] Here, in the exotic atmosphere of the circus, where the stories of the West were reinvented, Sylvester Long surely received his first compelling insight into the future that might be his. With his straight black hair, high cheekbones and copper skin, he was easily mistaken for an Indian. The experience of a complete transition from one world into another changed him forever.

When Sylvester returned home he was lucky to get a job as the janitor at the new public library in Winston.[43] The months on the road with the circus, which took him throughout the South, ignited a curiosity that led him to more discoveries. During every break from floor mopping at the library, he pulled down books from the shelves.[44]

The daily humiliations now annoyed more than puzzled him. He did not want to be called "boy" the rest of his life. And it was not just riding at the back of the streetcar or watching movies high in the gallery that upset him. It was not that he had to know his exact shoe size when he bought shoes because he would be allowed to try only one pair on. It was knowing that no matter what, the lowliest white would always be considered superior to even the most accomplished black.

In early October 1908, with these frustrations bristling, Sylvester again rode out to Carson Town with his parents for another Big Meeting.[45] It was a crucial month for the young man, a turning point. He had quit his janitor's job at the library and returned to school to pick up his grade seven[46] at a small private school for blacks, using his earnings to pay the enrollment fees. All he might hope for thereafter was to enter one of the South's colored colleges, such as Slater Normal (Teacher Training) School in Winston, to prepare himself for a career as a teacher, lawyer or journalist in the

Sylvester's brothers Walter (second from right) and Abe (sixth from right) worked one summer as waiters. This was the life Sylvester fled from.

Hauling cotton to the mills in Winston, c. 1900, from an illustration pasted in Sallie Long's scrapbook. Sylvester's mother chose to record the very things her son dreaded.

black community. His first attempt at advancing toward his dream, however, did not work out. The age gap between him and the other students was three to four years, and no doubt he found it embarrassing to be among so young a crowd. He dropped out just before the annual reunion at Carson Town.

The Big Meeting was held on the first Sunday of October,[47] when the cotton was ready for picking, the sugar cane was being ground and the late corn was ready for husking. The Longs left

Abe Long's wife, Aurelia (on the right), and his sister, Katie Long, c. 1920.

early Saturday, taking the train to Statesville, where they rented a team of horses and a large wagon to carry them to Carson Town, the row of old houses strung out along the road to Hamptonville. The family rode over gently rolling ridges, past the ripe tobacco and cornfields and the rich, uncut stands of tall oak and hickory in the browns, reds and rusts of autumn. The air was crisp, invigorating, and when they arrived in Carson Town their clothes were covered with fine red dust. There were seven Longs on the trip to the Big Meeting that year, for Sylvester's oldest brother, Abe, had brought along his fetching young wife, Aurelia.[48]

Joe Long, now fifty-five, had straight black hair. His face was light brown with finely chiseled features. Standing beside Aurelia, his dark daughter-in-law, he looked Portuguese or Italian or Greek. Sallie, now forty-three, was big-framed and milk white. Their four children had the colorings of a marble cake, the darkest being Katie, nine. Sylvester looked Indian. Abe, twenty-seven, and Walter, twenty-two, were fairer. Like their father, they looked southern European.

Big Meeting week officially began with Sunday morning service at the Mt. Pleasant Church in Carson, followed that afternoon by a mammoth Sunday picnic. Most people stayed on for a week, but the Longs had to return to Winston early, Joe to his janitorial job, Abe to Max Kobra's Saloon, where he worked as bartender, and Walter to his salesman's job.[49]

Sylvester was not as gregarious as his brothers, and as a boy he mostly kept to himself.[50] Besides, after traveling with the circus and becoming disaffected upon his return to school, he was preoccupied with his future. His mind kept returning to the Wild West Show. It was his out, his trump card.

When they arrived at Carson Town, the men were away working in the fields, but the women and children rushed out to meet

Sylvester's oldest brother, Abe, when he, like his father, worked as a school janitor.

them. Sylvester's observant eyes could not fail to notice the straight hair, blue eyes and otherwise white features of many of his relatives. He spotted a tall, slender, Caucasian woman, and when he recognized her as Adeline Carson, his grandmother, he ran to her. The Longs always stayed with Adeline in her little cottage close to the church, and it was she who told the old stories and filled in for Sylvester the gaps of the past. She told him about slavery and how the master used to put the light-skinned kids out in the sun to darken them and make them look like slaves.[51]

The next day, Sunday, they arrived at the church in mule-drawn buggies and oxcarts. The men struggled into unfamiliar suits and ties and starched collars. The ladies wore Sunday bonnets, button shoes and dresses that swept the ground as they walked. From miles around came the famous colored preachers, the shouters, the hell-raisers and the healers. They exhorted all sinners to come to the center of the church to the "mourners' bench," there to cleanse their immortal souls. Up walked big, strapping farmers, trembling and weeping, to kneel at the tiny

Walter as a young man. The caption reads, "To his mama from her son Walter Long."

bench. There were hymns and wailing, mournful spirituals. Sallie Long usually led the singing of "Steal Away to Jesus," "Swing Low, Sweet Chariot" and "Go Down Moses."[52]

The young Sylvester sat on the hard wooden bench, brooding. All around him burst those ecstatic, rhythmic exclamations of "Yes, God!" and "Jee–sus!" and "Bless the Lord!" What did he feel? Disgust? Pity? Boredom? All evidence suggests he was terrified—terrified of becoming one of them, terrified of the religious half-life and the deadening slave mentality of his relatives with all its distant, hereafter rewards. With the circus he had broken away briefly and had tasted what life could offer. He did not want to have to die to taste it again.

When the church service ended, the picnic began: baked country hams, fried chicken, deviled eggs, home-baked bread, homemade pickles, orange sponge cake, pound cake and great stacks of apple pies still warm from the oven. When all this was wolfed down, when all the games had been played and all the pleasantries had been exchanged, the Longs loaded their wagon and said good-bye for another year. They reached the train station in two hours, then rattled along for another hour in the Jim Crow car back to Winston. Another Big Meeting had passed and with it came a short-term solution. Sylvester would rejoin the circus and Wild West Show and learn more about Indians and the West.

Once more passing easily as an Indian, Sylvester joined

Wagons carrying tobacco to the market on Trade Street, Winston, c. 1890, the year of Sylvester Long's birth.

Robinson's Circus, worked with the horses and learned to ride so well that some thought he had been born on a ranch.[53] He became friends with Allen Whipporwill, a registered Eastern Cherokee, ten years his senior.[54] From Allen, Sylvester picked up some useful, if rudimentary, Cherokee—the names of the months, the days of the week, the numbers up to ten. At night he memorized simple words and phrases—*si yu,* "hello," and *o gi na li i,* "my friend."[55] Eager, bright and determined, Sylvester soon mastered a workable vocabulary that helped to solidify his new Indian persona.

He returned to Winston in the summer of 1909, when the smell of tobacco was everywhere, thickest downtown by the warehouses and brick factories. African Americans from the surrounding areas flocked to Winston ("The Tobacco Center of North Carolina") to work in the newly mechanized tobacco plants. In ten years Winston's population had grown from ten thousand to nearly seventeen thousand,[56] but Sylvester wanted no part of it, nor did he want a career in the black community as a teacher or lawyer or doctor.

One of those critical boyhood incidents that could have gone either way led to a way out of his dilemma. One day he borrowed the keys to the white West End School, where his father worked, and slipped into the main office, there to clack away on the typewriter. The principal caught him, but instead of calling the police, he summoned Sylvester's father. If your son is so anxious to learn typing that he would risk reform school, he told Joe Long, then he deserves more schooling. Aware of the family's Indian background, the principal suggested that he apply for Sylvester's entry to Carlisle.[57]

The Carlisle Indian Residential School in Carlisle, Pennsylvania, was the most famous Indian school in the United States. Every year it accepted a thousand children from ninety different tribes across the country and provided them with a basic trade school education. The boys were trained as carpenters, shoemakers, tailors and printers; the girls learned homemaking skills. Carlisle also had a national reputation as a hotbed of sports, and by 1909 the Carlisle football team was known throughout the continent. In 1907, led by the mighty Jim Thorpe, one of the greatest athletes in the United States, the Carlisle Redskins defeated Chicago and Harvard. In 1908 the Redskins won ten games, lost only two and tied one.[58]

On August 10, 1909, Sylvester applied for admission, committing his first serious deception. The Carlisle form clearly stated that candidates be within the preferred age of "fourteen to eighteen." To pass as eighteen rather than nineteen, which he would be on his next birthday, Sylvester chopped off a full year, making his birth date December 1, 1891.[59] His parents, although they accepted their personal fate behind the South's color barrier, supported his efforts to find a better life.

The application asked that the candidate's parents state their tribal affiliations, a near impossible task for the tens of thousands of people of mixed origins on the Eastern seaboard. Tribal groups along the Atlantic coast had been splintered beyond recognition after the massive arrival of Europeans. Smallpox and typhus, against which North American Indians had no hereditary protection, cut terrible swaths through the Native population. They, along with slave hunts, reduced entire tribes to insignificant pockets, and by the early twentieth century only two discernible Indian groups remained in North Carolina: the Cherokees and the Lumbees.[60]

Sallie Long identified with the Lumbees, or Croatans. After the Europeans arrived and nearly obliterated the tribes on the coast of the Carolinas, many of the survivors intermingled with the first settlers, losing their ancient languages and customs. The descendants adopted the tribal name Croatan to embrace all such peoples. Joe Long regarded himself as a descendant of the Eastern Cherokee, a tribe that had suffered horribly at the hands of European settlers. He had no doubt heard of the events of 1838, when federal and state governments removed at gunpoint twenty thousand Cherokees from Alabama, Georgia, Tennessee and North Carolina. The governments wanted the rich Indian land and sent the Cherokees west of the Mississippi on a forced march known as the "Trail of Tears." Four thousand Cherokees died on the way. A small group known today as the Eastern Cherokee escaped by hiding in the mountains of western North Carolina. In the late nineteenth century, federal and state authorities recognized their right to remain and allowed them to settle in the southwestern section of the state, several hundred miles west of Winston. Joe Long had no legal proof of his mother's Cherokee origins, and since the Cherokees themselves owned slaves, including blacks, possibly that she was one of them. To be a recognized Cherokee, Joe Long would have to have been registered on the Eastern Cherokee tribal rolls, and he wasn't.

This did not deter him from writing on the Carlisle application that Sylvester was "half Indian of the Cherokee Tribe located at Cherokee County, NC." His wife, Sallie, he wrote, was "half Indian of the Croatan Tribe located at Robeson Co., NC." In fact Sallie was one-quarter Indian, as her mother, Adeline, was half-white. These distortions lifted Sylvester well above Carlisle's stip-

Sylvester Long (on left) and his brother Walter, shortly before Sylvester left Winston for Carlisle Indian School in 1909.

ulation that candidates be "at least one-fourth Indian, preferably full Indian."

The application asked for vouchers from two "disinterested persons" testifying that the applicant "is known and recognized in the community in which he lives as an Indian." The Longs decided to solicit vouchers from a black and a white. G. Hamilton Willis, one of Sylvester's former teachers at the Depot Street school, and more recently the black principal of the private school Sylvester attended for a month in September 1908, signed one voucher. He wrote, "I am acquainted with Sylvester Long; that he is known and recognized in the community in which he lives as an Indian; that in my opinion he cannot receive proper and adequate schooling at home for the reason that the public schools do not now receive pupils of Indian blood and parentage."[61]

Obtaining the endorsement of a member of the white community was trickier. Joe Long approached John Wesley Harrison, a friendly merchant who had founded and operated the Winston Clothing Company. Harrison had known Joe from childhood days in Yadkin County, and he had heard stories of Joe's mother being a Cherokee. Harrison was respected publicly in the white community as a teacher of the men's Bible class at the North Winston Presbyterian Church. Privately, fellow members of a secret organization, the Ku Klux Klan, respected him as one of their officers. He signed the voucher.[62]

The Longs appeared before William E. Franklin, president of the Winston Realty Company, who was also a public notary. With Principal Willis and Abe Long as witnesses, Joe Long testified to the accuracy of the application, then mailed it.[63] In the last week of August, Sylvester was officially invited to visit Carlisle. Undoubtedly, his family and his girlfriend, Lovie Galloway,[64] would have gathered at the railway platform to see him off. Lovie

Lovie Galloway as a young woman. When she saw Sylvester to the train, she could not have known he would never return.

Galloway was pretty and bright and devoted to Sylvester. If he had been less ambitious, less determined to break out, perhaps he would have married her, but he left Winston and by all accounts never saw her again.

After kissing his mother and Lovie good-bye, Sylvester climbed aboard the Jim Crow car, and the train pulled away in the stifling ninety-degree heat. The train passed through Virginia and Maryland, leaving behind the dank smell of the decaying vegetation. Sylvester liked the cooler weather and felt invigorated by it and the old euphoria of travel. On the hoardings he studied posters in German, Russian and Italian, all part of the rapid industrialization of the northern states in the first decade of the new century, when more than seven million immigrants arrived to find work.[65] The white-skinned foreigners were encouraged to come and were made welcome, while he, the grandson of a North Carolina senator, had to lie about his ancestry.

All went well at Carlisle—for a while. The two vouchers

The individual history card for Sylvester Long at the Carlisle Indian School records his first deceptions. His Indian blood is noted as "1/2" and his age as "18."

signed by the black principal and the white merchant showed that he was accepted as an Indian in Winston, but alone they were not enough. Linguistic proof of his Cherokee heritage was required. James Henderson, one of the Carlisle teachers examining the three hundred incoming students that autumn, suspected that Sylvester was not what he claimed to be and he challenged him to speak a few words in his native tongue. No doubt Sylvester initially froze. But then it all rushed back, and he spoke in phrases and sentences, confidently, coherently. Allen Whipporwill's circus lessons had paid off. Sylvester also absorbed another lesson that would serve him well later: the burden of proof is always on the accuser. It was too late for any teacher to travel three hundred miles back to North Carolina to investigate his vague tribal origins. Carlisle's admissions committee accepted him.[66]

What exactly played through Sylvester's mind at this point?

One clue exists. Years later a reporter asked him what books had influenced him. He replied: "There was one I remember, particularly when I was going to college . . . *Ben Hur* . . . that was a favorite of mine. . . ."[67] One can understand why. Sylvester identified with Ben Hur, the son of a noble Jewish family, seized and condemned to be a galley slave, where men rarely survived for more than a year. He toiled for three years until his fortunes turned. His ship, the flagship of the fleet, was sunk. Miraculously Ben Hur escaped from the hold and on the open water saved the life of the Roman fleet commander. In gratitude he made Ben Hur his son and took him to Rome and to fame and fortune. Like Ben Hur, Sylvester wanted to rise up and escape his persecution. His "trail upward" was to begin at Carlisle.

JOE LONG'S FAMILY TREE

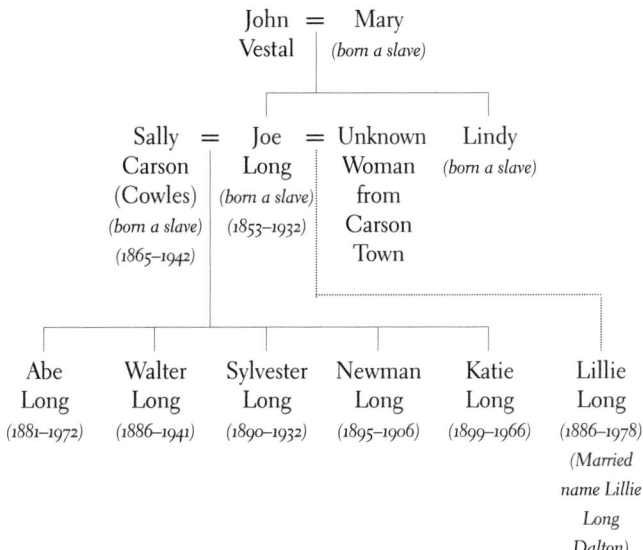

SALLY CARSON LONG'S FAMILY TREE

CHAPTER 2

The Trail Upward Begins

CARLISLE INDIAN SCHOOL, PENNSYLVANIA, 1909

*T*he Carlisle Indian Residential School was a school with a purpose: to give the Indian "a white man's chance." Those were the words of Moses Friedman, a thin-faced man with a goatee, the superintendent of Carlisle when Sylvester Long arrived in the autumn of 1909.[1] For the young men and women who sought that opportunity, Carlisle was hugely successful, and it mattered not if, for Sylvester Long, it also worked to give him an Indian's chance in a white man's world.

Early in October, Superintendent Friedman called the new students to an assembly and told them about hard work and perseverance, using the unlikely example of the Netherlands to inspire them. Through industry and determination, he declared, the people of the Netherlands transformed a barren, marshy wasteland into a country of opportunity and prosperity. He exhorted his students to stick to the rules, to resist temptation and to overcome hardships, frustrations and homesickness. "Waste nei-

47

Sylvester Long at Carlisle Indian School, c. 1910.

ther your time nor your opportunities," he cautioned them.[2]

Carlisle, founded in 1879 by Richard Henry Pratt, an idealistic American army officer, operated on rigid military discipline. Every morning Sylvester rose at 5:30 A.M., ate breakfast at 6:15, then spent half the day at studies and the other half working in the shops.

Pratt's contact with Indians had begun just after the Civil War, when his unit, the 10th United States Cavalry, was posted to the West. In Texas he commanded his regiment's Indian scouts in fierce clashes with the Kiowa, Comanche, Cheyenne and Arapaho. When, after seven years of fighting, the 10th Cavalry captured the Indian leaders, the army entrusted them to Pratt. He took them to Fort Marion in St. Augustine, Florida, and set about to "reform" them. His methods proved so successful in "lifting up" and "civilizing" the Indians that he dedicated his life to the task.

When his prisoners' terms expired, Pratt managed to convince twenty-one of them to stay in the East for further education. In 1878 he enrolled them in Virginia's Hampton Institute, an elementary school founded a decade earlier by former slaves. The experiment, though, was not entirely successful. As the great African American educator Booker T. Washington, then an instructor of the school, wrote, "The average Indian felt himself above the white man, and, of course, he felt himself far above the Negro, largely on account of the fact of the Negro having sub-

mitted to slavery—a thing which the Indian would never do."
(The fact that the Indian students did not know that Indians had
been frequently enslaved in the early colonial period indicates
their distance from African Americans in the late nineteenth century.) Later that same year Pratt asked the army for a new home
for the school. To his joy he was given the century-old Carlisle
Barracks in the Cumberland Valley, a lush farming region in
southeastern Pennsylvania, just north of the site of the historic
Battle of Gettysburg.[3]

Pratt ran Carlisle like a military outpost for twenty-five years
until he retired in 1904. Besides the unyielding discipline, he
emphasized the mastery of English. He assigned students of different tribes and languages as roommates in the dormitories so
they would have to speak English to communicate. Once they
learned the basics of the language, the students studied a trade.
Carlisle taught boys carpentry, blacksmithing, printing, harness-
making, wagon-making, painting and plastering. They also kept
the school in good repair, cleaning the grounds and tending the
furnaces. Girls were trained in general household duties such as
washing, ironing, sewing and needlework. They kept the dining
room in order and helped prepare the meals.

Anglo-Saxon Christian names, the first step in giving students "a white man's chance," replaced Indian names. Upon arrival
at Carlisle, students were scrubbed, their hair was cut and they
were issued the mandatory uniforms. They were soon made aware
that their Indian identity was something they would have to overcome along with homesickness. They marched in companies to
the classrooms, to the shops, to meals, to chapel and back to the
dormitories.[4] The Carlisle Indian Residential School gained an
international reputation, and other schools in the United States
and Canada were modeled on it.[5] But after Pratt retired in 1904,
his influence slowly waned. Carlisle operated until 1918, fourteen
years beyond Pratt, but it was still very much inspired by him
when Sylvester Long was a student between 1909 and 1912.

Sylvester's first months at Carlisle were exciting and challenging, and he immersed himself in the experience, but he had it tougher than the others. He sensed hostility from some of the students for the reason he most feared: they suspected he was black. In the dining hall, classrooms and shops, the tension was palpable.

The Western Cherokees from Oklahoma were antiblack, and they were not subtle about it. A number of their families had been slave holders, had mixed racially with whites and had even fought on the side of the Confederacy in the Civil War. When the Eastern Cherokees at Carlisle told other students that they had never heard of a Sylvester Long, or of his family, suspicion mounted and the rumors became uglier. One day a delegation of Cherokees confronted the superintendent to protest against Sylvester's enrollment as an Eastern Cherokee. One of them called him a "Cherokee nigger."[6]

Sylvester refused to be intimidated. Acceptance at Carlisle was his ticket out, his escape, and so he fought back by working hard and winning approval from his instructors. One of the stories, which may be apocryphal, is that a sympathetic instructor tried to make him fit in more easily by calling him "Long Lance" on the drill-hall floor. In any event, within a year of his graduation from Carlisle, he was calling himself Long Lance, or, more properly, Sylvester Chahuska Long Lance. The "Clark" never appeared again.[7]

His first close friend at the school was Emma Newashe, a Sac and Fox girl from Oklahoma. Her mother had carried her on a brightly decorated papoose board, taught her the tribal customs and raised her to speak the native language. Her parents died when she was nine. Three years later, as an orphan, she was sent to Carlisle from a Quaker-run school in Oklahoma. She came to enjoy the school, but, like Sylvester, found the early months difficult. She applied herself to her studies with the same vigor, learning English, history, art and music.

Emma noticed how shy and self-contained Sylvester was when he arrived at Carlisle. When she came to know him, however, she found "there was no limit to his loyalty." She admired his sense of honor, his sincerity, and she loved his sense of fun.[8] He amused her by imitating bird calls. He was strong, even as a young man at Carlisle, and took it upon himself to protect weaker, slower classmates against the bullies and hecklers.[9]

Sylvester stood by his claims of Cherokee and Croatan ancestry, and instinctively knowing that the best defense was a good offense, he contributed articles to *The Carlisle Arrow*, in which he demonstrated his knowledge of Cherokee traditions. In one of them, published in November, 1910, under the title "Origin of Names Among the Cherokees," he told how the Cherokees named their children after birds and animals. The school authorities liked it enough to include it in *The Red Man*, the school magazine that was circulated all across the country.[10] The next year *The Carlisle Arrow* carried another Sylvester Long by-line, this time an account of "Virginia Dare, or the White Fawn," a Lumbee tale of the first English child born in North America.[11]

Eventually he won acceptance by dint of what Superintendent Friedman called hard work and perseverance. In time the other students regarded him as the son of a Cherokee father and a Lumbee mother. A prominent Cherokee, a female student named Iva Miller (she later became Jim Thorpe's first wife) accepted him without question as a member of her tribe. The Carlisle students kept "character books," listings of classmates' names, tribes and pet expressions, and in Sylvester's book Iva Miller identified her tribe fondly as "same as yours."[12]

Still, rumors persisted,[13] and even if Sylvester was regarded as part Cherokee, his part Croatan tribal origins left him open to suspicion of some African ancestry. Barely two months after he entered Carlisle, *The Carlisle Arrow* published an article on the Croatans. Fannie Keokuk, a Sac and Fox Indian, wrote that the Croatans were "a mixed race" in eastern North Carolina, where

The printing class at Carlisle Indian School, 1909–10. Sylvester Long appears fifth from the right in the back row. Suspicions surrounding his claims of Cherokee ancestry when he entered did not prevent him from graduating as class valedictorian.

they had "separate schools and churches and are given privileges which are not granted to the Negroes." She said they were "a peculiar people," descended from native tribes, white sailors, early settlers—and blacks.[14]

The rest of his life, Sylvester reacted badly to this sort of talk. If he did not always openly deny it, his behavior served to put him squarely on the side of the Indians or even the whites, and some evidence suggests he may have acquiesced in antiblack bigotry and even taken the initiative. Certainly he had a quick temper, and that temper could be easily ignited by accusations that he was black.

Edgar Miller, the school printer, doubted Sylvester's Indian background and years later said quite openly that Sylvester was "a half-blood," by which he meant half black. Miller then softened his opinion by adding that all Indians from the area around Winston "look more or less that way and I may be mistaken on that point."[15]

Miller's attitude doubtless disturbed Sylvester, but he would not shrink in the face of innuendo; indeed, he selected printing as his trade with Miller as his instructor. He worked with forty other students printing the *Arrow* and *The Red Man*, as well as various printing jobs for the school. Miller recognized Sylvester's skills and came to rely on him heavily. On Sylvester's first report he noted that the young man's conduct was excellent and that he was "a promising student." Within two years Sylvester had so impressed Miller that the teacher put him in charge of all the printing machinery.[16]

Carlisle was mainly an elementary school with two years of high school for senior students.[17] Sylvester entered grade six on his arrival in the fall of 1909, but the teachers quickly accelerated him when they saw evidence of his abilities. He had no problems with English or in motivating himself, and he meticulously completed all his assignments. He excelled in the classroom, particularly in English and history, and in the autumn of 1911 he entered the tenth and final grade with Mrs. Emma Foster as his English teacher.

Mrs. Foster, one of the school's best educators, had taught at Carlisle for ten years and before that at several Indian schools in the West. She knew how to use imaginative techniques to get her lessons across. If she sensed the students were confused about, say, Shakespeare, she stopped everything and asked them to try to interpret the more obscure passages in everyday English. She encouraged them to ask questions, to probe, to search for meanings in Robert Louis Stevenson, Longfellow and Mark Twain. More importantly she cared and the students knew it.[18]

Emma Foster found in Sylvester the energetic and sensitive type of student a teacher treasures. He did more than was expected of him, submitting extra book reviews and assignments for her comments. Years later she could still recall the day, in one of those impromptu classroom exercises, when Sylvester played Shylock in *The Merchant of Venice*. "Shylock reminds me of the Indian race," he told her after. "When cornered he showed only his worst side to a world that misunderstood and misjudged him cruelly." Mrs. Foster thought it an unusually perceptive remark. Sylvester read all that was expected, and much more, in order to improve himself and develop his vocabulary. He found especially

A postcard Sylvester sent his mother after visiting the state capitol with the Carlisle school band.

rewarding Benjamin Franklin's *Autobiography*, and he soaked up all the great man had to say about pulling oneself up by the bootstraps, about rising from obscurity to "a state of affluence and some degree of celebrity in the world."[19]

At first everyone looked the same in his eyes, but gradually he perceived the differences and learned. He found the Indians from Alaska very hidebound and antisocial, doubtless intimidated by the foreign surroundings of the South. He noticed the peculiar tribal animosities that kept students apart and alienated one from another, such as those between the Sioux and the Chippewa.

There were Carlisle students from such isolated settlements that they never handled English with any confidence, and signs in the printing shop sometimes catered to a backwoods mentality: DO NOT SPIT ON THE FLOOR.[20] At Carlisle there were sons of Iroquois steelworkers, daughters of wealthy Indian farmers, awkward rustics from isolated settlements, dandies who knew about clothes and style, and gentle people like Emma Newashe, the orphan who befriended him and made him feel less like an outsider. Only when he realized that he was not the only shy and awkward one at Carlisle did Sylvester begin to relax and extend himself.

In his first year Sylvester joined the Invincibles, the boys debating society, and by December had been elected secretary. In his second year he was winning debates. He joined the Carlisle YMCA, and his experience at the Carson Town Big Meetings prepared him for the religious activities. In a fine bass voice he sang the old hymns "Rock of Ages" and "What a Friend We Have in Jesus" at the Bible study meetings.[21] He sent postcards home. In 1911 he was elected president of the Carlisle YMCA.[22]

Sylvester also joined the Carlisle school band, proudly donning the blue and red uniform for concerts at special school days and in the town of Carlisle, when the band performed in the public square. He played the E-flat clarinet, a treacherous little instrument.[23]

Carlisle students spent their summers living with families in central Pennsylvania, honing the skills they learned in the school shops. In the summer of 1912, Sylvester worked in a printing office and played his E-flat clarinet in the Pennsylvania Railroad Band at Tyrone, a thriving railroad town one hundred miles west of Carlisle.[24]

Sylvester never made the famous varsity football team at Carlisle, the one led by Jim Thorpe, but he played on the intramural football teams. His best sport was long-distance running, and he made the school's track team — no mean feat, for the competition was stiff. Thorpe, everyone's all-round athlete, was also

Sylvester Long (right) never played for the famous Carlisle varsity football teams, but he was a member of the intramural football squads.

on the track team. Recognizing Sylvester's talent he chose him as a training partner. In the 1912 Olympics at Stockholm, Thorpe won the pentathlon and decathlon, and when he returned home he was hailed as the world's greatest athlete. Jim Thorpe and Sylvester Long remained lifelong friends. Among Sylvester's treasured souvenirs was a picture of Thorpe wearing his New York Giants baseball uniform, bearing an inscription in Thorpe's hand, "Remember the mile runs, was great training for the Olympics."[25]

Sylvester learned as much from friends and classmates at Carlisle as he learned from his teachers, listening intently to the

The legendary Jim Thorpe sent Long Lance a momento he always cherished, reminding him that Thorpe had chosen him as a training partner before going on to Olympic and professional sport glory.

legends, customs and folklore of his new acquaintances. Besides Thorpe and Emma Newashe, there was Joe Ross, a Pueblo from Cubero, New Mexico, who played with him in the band. Wesley Two Moons, son of Chief Two Moons, who had commanded the Cheyennes in the fight with Sitting Bull at Little Big Horn, told him of the battle. From the Sioux he learned the details of Wounded Knee, the massacre in December 1890—almost to the day of Sylvester's birth—when the U.S. cavalry killed hundreds of

Sylvester Long was a member of Carlisle's graduating class in 1912.

defenseless Indians. All around him at Carlisle were the sons of the great chiefs, such as Robert Geronimo, who arrived at the school in 1911.[26] As many of the others struggled to shed their Indian identity, Sylvester absorbed their stories, seeking to become all that they were being taught to deny.

He was not above a little grandstanding. In late May 1911 there was a hunt for a four-year-old girl lost in the Tuscarora Mountains, some thirty miles north of Carlisle. Sylvester joined the search party and reveled in the attention he garnered as a "genuine Indian." He told Robert Gorman, a reporter for the *Harrisburg Telegraph*, that he arrived at Carlisle "from the plains and forests of the West."[27] The subsequent newspaper reports quoted his words exactly, just as he had told them, and he discovered how easy it was to bamboozle the press. He cut out the most complimentary stories and pasted them in his growing scrapbook, where he assembled the evidence for the past he was inventing.

As one of the top students in his graduating class, Sylvester was chosen by Superintendent Friedman to address the school at its commencement exercises in the spring of 1912. He stood at the podium in the Carlisle gymnasium in front of a thousand Indian students and three thousand guests.[28] Sylvester, now twenty-one and self-assured, cleared his voice and began, "Ladies and gentlemen, fellow students, and instructors . . ." He reviewed his years at Carlisle, then looked to the future:

> When we have gone through, for the last time as students, the brick portals of this institution, into the great world of competition, we do not wish to be designated as Cherokees, Sioux or Pawnees, but we wish to be known as Carlisle Indians, belonging to that great universal tribe of North American Indians, speaking the same language and having the same chief—the great White Father at Washington. . . .[29]

His address then turned to the goals of "true character" and "manhood." Sylvester Long's tribal origins were obscure and rumor may have haunted him, but he was becoming more secure in his new identity. He was a Carlisle Indian.

The twenty-one-year-old Sylvester accepted his teachers' suggestions and applied to the preparatory school of Dickinson College in Carlisle. If Lovie Galloway were waiting for him, she would have to wait awhile longer.

Chapter 3

Sylvester Chahuska
Long Lance

St. John's Military Academy, New York State, 1912

*A*s far back as Sylvester could remember, a Republican had been president of the United States. When he attended the Depot Street School for Negroes in Winston, it was McKinley, next, Roosevelt, then, during his years at Carlisle, Taft. In November 1912, when Sylvester attended Conway Hall, the preparatory school for Dickinson College, Woodrow Wilson came to power.

Wilson was a Democrat, a Virginian and a former president of Princeton University. Throughout his campaign he championed a "New Freedom" and talked of returning the government to the people and of introducing in Congress tariff reform and antitrust legislation. The change could hardly have been symbolized more vividly than at the 1913 inaugural ceremony when Taft and Wilson stood side by side. Taft—all three hundred pounds of him—represented the old order of well-fed, unresponsive Republicans, and beside him, Wilson—tall, lean, scholarly—the embodiment of the hungry reformer.

During Sylvester's boyhood the United States had moved from a rural, farming nation to an industrial world power. Railways snaked across the country, tying together its disparate regions, opening new markets and encouraging the standardization of products that could be mass produced. At the time of Sylvester's birth in 1890, the Union's population was sixty-five million, most of it on farms and in villages. By 1913 the population had neared one hundred million, and nearly half of the nation's citizens lived in cities. For twenty years the new wealth had been monopolized by a privileged few who were protected by the Republicans.

President Wilson introduced many progressive reforms. The Underwood Tariff, passed in October 1913, instituted the lowest tariffs since the Civil War. Another progressive measure provided for a graduated federal income tax designed to lift the tax burden from the back of the common man.

The "New Freedom" had its limits, however, and along with the reforms, President Wilson pushed for formal and official segregation. During his first months in office, the federal government extended segregation in Washington to nearly all departments. In the Bureau of Census, the Post Office and the Bureau of Printing and Engraving, workers were segregated in offices, shops, rest rooms and restaurants. Anyone opposed was fired. Widespread downgrading and firing of black postal and treasury employees followed in the South. Thirty-five African Americans were discharged in Atlanta, and the Collector of Internal Revenue in Georgia declared, "There are no government positions for Negroes in the South. A Negro's place is in the cornfield."[1]

Southerners took over in Washington, and their racial policies gained ascendancy in congress, which heightened public service segregation in all quarters. But Sylvester managed to escape

At St. John's Military Academy, Long Lance (on right), as he now preferred to be known, became a member of the track team.

the tide. He was at Carlisle, and he was safe in his new identity as an Indian.

Sylvester registered at Conway Hall on October 14, 1912.[2] Though his adventures were not as wild as he imagined them, certainly they surpassed the experiences of his contemporaries. He had known poverty, had traveled with a circus as far as Cuba,[3] understood what hard work and bluff could do, had felt the sting of being called "nigger," and had known the lynch mob fear felt by anyone not entirely white in the South.

On registering, he rearranged his birth date again, this time stating the truth—December 1, 1890—but he shifted his place of birth from Winston to Cherokee County, 150 miles to the west, where the Eastern Cherokees lived.

He felt old and world-weary. The juvenile atmosphere at Conway Hall embarrassed him. He had to abide by the freshman rules, which meant enduring the customary small indignities: meeting visiting athletic teams and carrying their bags from the railway station, wearing a derby hat on Sundays, observing a ban on colored socks.[4]

Sylvester Chahuska Long Lance was ready to advance his identity another step. One of many fanciful stories he would later

Sylvester Long Lance (seated immediately to the left of the conductor) played in the St. John's Band.

tell about his young days provides a glimpse of his fantasies. The story, "My Trail Upward," appeared in *Cosmopolitan* in June 1926:

> Since the day back in Wyoming when I had lost my temper and popped poor old Curly on the head, I had had two dangerous fights, both before I entered school. In one of them a friend had knocked me senseless with a six-shooter to prevent me from driving a knife into a fellow being on whose chest I sat. Two weeks later a six-shooter leveled at this same fellow being was knocked out of my hand just as I was pulling the trigger. It was only necessary to say that a feud existed between us, and he had sworn to get me.[5]

The tale was pure fiction, and Conway Hall was no match for this sort of imagination. Sylvester could not wait to get out.

Nevertheless, he did well academically in what today would be the equivalent of grade ten, his best subjects being English and ancient history. He joined the W.A. Hutchinson Literary Society, made the Conway Hall track team and appeared to fit in well. But he was unhappy.[6] When the school year ended, he worked another summer with the railroad band at Tyrone.[7]

The summer of 1913 found Sylvester again agonizing over choices. He knew he did not want to return to Conway Hall, but he also knew he did not want to choose a railroad career, working sixty hours a week in the yard office at Tyrone with only the band concerts as a weekly diversion. That summer he made friends with E.A. Wall, who had once played in John Philip Sousa's band. It was Wall who suggested that Sylvester apply for a band scholarship to St. John's Military Academy, one of the most exclusive military schools in New York State.

Sylvester mailed the application forms early in the summer, and on July 9 the director of the St. John's Cadet Band wrote to Moses Friedman, the superintendent at Carlisle, asking for a letter of reference on Sylvester's behalf. Friedman replied that Sylvester was "a splendid young man in every way" with an entirely satisfactory record at Carlisle. When St. John's Military Academy approved Sylvester's application, *The Carlisle Arrow* rejoiced. "We know he will be successful," the newspaper editorialized, "as he has the energy, stick-to-it-iveness and character."[8]

By 1913 St. John's had been under the strong hand of General William Verbeck for twenty-five years, and under his leadership St. John's had become one of the country's top military schools. He had spent the first seventeen years of his life in Japan, where his parents were missionaries, and there, growing up with Japanese boys, he had learned something of the Samurai tradition and its code of honor. He was unusually open-minded on racial issues at a time when bigotry was the norm at other northern schools and universities. (African Americans, for example, were not permitted in the dormitories at Harvard until the late 1920s.[9]) Students at St. John's came from far and wide, from all across the United States and from Canada, Mexico and occasionally even from Cuba. General Verbeck patterned St. John's on the great English schools of Harrow, Rugby and Winchester, even borrowing Winchester's ancient motto, "Manners makyth man."[10] General Verbeck admitted Sylvester as the school's only Indian.

Under the leadership of Headmaster General Verbeck, St. John's Military School, modeled on the great English schools, became one of the country's top military schools. Here Long Lance acquired some of the social graces that would later make him a much sought-after guest in society circles.

At St. John's, Long Lance, as he now preferred to be known, acquired some of the polish he later displayed to good effect in drawing rooms and on the lecture circuits. He managed to rid himself of the gawky mannerisms of his upbringing; he learned how to start a meal with the fork on the outside and work in, how to break the roll into pieces, then butter it. He learned proper enunciation, biting off the syllables, pronouncing each vowel distinctly and correctly.

Discipline at St. John's proved much stricter than at Carlisle, where the older boys had frequently slipped into town to meet women and visit the bars.[11] Long Lance, with the others at St. John's, woke up to reveille at 6:30 A.M., ate breakfast at 7:00, said his prayers at 7:30, attended school from 8:00 to 1:00 P.M., ate lunch at 1:00, attended guard mounting at 2:00, military drill at 2:30, recreation at 3:30, parade at 5:45, supper at 6:00, prayers again at 6:30, study from 7:00 to 9:15, military tattoo at 9:30 and taps at 9:45. Bugle calls regulated Long Lance's life for his three years at St. John's Military Academy.

He usually stood third or fourth in class in what today would be roughly equivalent to grades eleven and twelve. As the only Indian at the Academy, Long Lance was soon nicknamed "Chief." He joined the dramatic society, the Punchinello Club, and again made the school track team. In return for board and tuition, he played clarinet in the band under principal musician Edmund Wall, E.A. Wall's oldest son.[12] When Edmund Wall met Long Lance upon his arrival in the autumn of 1913, he rated him "acceptable, moderately good" on the clarinet.

Long Lance found St. John's much different from Carlisle. Here students warmed to him immediately. One day Ed Wall's brother discovered that his clarinet had been stolen from the school's rehearsal room. At the same time one of the workers at the school had quit. Long Lance obtained a pass a few days later, went into Syracuse and by chance happened to encounter the former worker. He chased after him, dodged passing cars, grabbed him in the middle of a street and had him arrested. Long Lance told the police to search the man's home. They did not find the clarinet,[13] but the incident bolstered Long Lance's reputation as a loyal friend.

Long Lance, although at first shy and quiet, loved attention and always had an instinct for center stage. On Circus Day at St. John's on June 9, 1914, he shone, using all the tricks he had picked up while traveling with the circus. Nearly seven hundred people from Manlius and Syracuse converged on the St. John's football field that day to watch the military academy's Wild West Show, complete with cowboys, Indians, soldiers and clowns.

Long Lance, the "Chief," stole the show, wearing flaming red blankets and a headdress, leading a party of Indians through a war dance, then running into the bushes to lie in wait for the unsuspecting palefaces. At exactly the right moment, out he leaped with his whooping followers, surprising a wagon train—according to a report in the *Syracuse Journal*—"in true professional style."[14]

Long Lance enjoyed St. John's. Barely two months after he enrolled, he wrote Superintendent Friedman at Carlisle to say, "The instruction both military and academic is of the highest quality. Both cadets and instructors are in uniform at all times, and the regulation army rules are carried out in detail. The discipline that they have here is remarkable for its realness."[15]

But soon enough he was back to agonizing over his future. What next? What would he do in the spring of 1915 with what would amount to a high school diploma? He wanted to continue his studies, and he thrived in the quasimilitary atmosphere of St. John's. In March 1915 he settled on a plan both simple and audacious. He would write a letter to the president himself, to Woodrow Wilson, requesting an appointment to the United States Military Academy at West Point.

There was, however, a major hurdle. West Point candidates had to be at least seventeen years of age but not yet twenty-two.[16] In 1915 Long Lance was twenty-four. He would have to lie again, this time to President Wilson. It was a bold move, not merely because he was lying to the president, but also because West Point was not known for its enlightened racial policies; in fact, between 1802 and 1915, only three African Americans had graduated from the academy, the last in 1889.[17] After much writing and rewriting, Long Lance sent the letter, telling President Wilson,

> I am graduating from St. John's Military Academy this spring, and am desirous of entering West Point next fall. . . . Knowing that you have the power of appointing a limited number of students to this institution each year, I wish to ask your assistance in securing an appointment for me this year. . . .

He reviewed his achievements at Carlisle and St. John's, then, marshalling his courage, came to the part about Indian ancestry and age. By now Long Lance had become an habitual liar, daring fate to catch him at the game. Sometimes it seemed almost a challenge. And so he wrote the president of the United States:

> I am of Indian ancestry, being a member of the Eastern Cherokee tribe. I shall be twenty-one the first day of next December. I stand five feet, nine inches in my stocking-feet and weigh one hundred and sixty-eight pounds in the same condition. . . .[18]

President Wilson, of course, probably never saw Long Lance's application, but the adjutant general of the War Department certainly did. Upon receiving this engaging request—an Indian applying for West Point?—he immediately conducted an inquiry. On March 18 he wrote Oscar H. Lipps, Carlisle's new superintendent, enclosing Long Lance's letter, requesting information about him. Lipps replied the next day that he had been an excellent student and noted that on his application to Carlisle, Long Lance had stated his father was half Cherokee and his mother half Croatan.

After mailing his letter to President Wilson, Long Lance spoke to General Verbeck at St. John's, telling him of his plans and asking for a letter of reference, one which he knew would carry much weight. General Verbeck was always taken seriously on these matters, for he had a considerable reputation, having served as a brigadier general in the New York National Guard and as one of the first three commissioners of the newly formed Boy Scouts of America. The general was only too pleased to help, for he encouraged his best students to apply to West Point. On March 31 he also sent a letter to President Wilson, recommending Long Lance's appointment in the highest terms. He reported that Long Lance had been an excellent student and a fine soldier and had "all the essential qualities to make an officer in the Army."

In early May the War Department contacted Long Lance with the happy news that he had been granted the appointment, meaning he could enter the competitive exam the following spring for one of the vacancies at West Point. Long Lance wrote another letter to President Wilson, thanking him for the honor and assuring him that he would "strive earnestly to justify it."[19]

When the press learned of the appointment in June, it treated it as a major story, especially welcomed in the troubled world of the time. The previous summer Franz Ferdinand, the Austrian Archduke, had been murdered in the obscure Balkan town of Sarajevo, plunging Europe into war. Earlier in the year Germany had unleashed unrestricted submarine warfare in the North Atlantic. On May 7, about the time Long Lance's appointment was approved, a U-boat sank the liner *Lusitania* off the coast of Ireland, killing 1,200, including 124 Americans. The incident nearly brought the United States into the war, just as Long Lance was completing his final exams at St. John's.

Newspapers across the country picked up the fascinating story of the handsome Indian boy selected by the president to attend West Point. It was too good to ignore. On June 16, 1915, the *Washington Post* commented in an editorial,

> The appointment by the president of a full-blooded Cherokee to a West Point cadetship comes as a recognition of educational qualifications in the appointee that promise to do further honor not only to his own race, but to the country as well. Sylvester Long Lance has already attained a high mark in a long course of scholastic training, besides having a record in athletics. True to the hint contained in his name — and a name means much with an Indian — he early determined in favor of a military career, which the kind offices of the president have now made possible.

Other metropolitan dailies carried the story, and it eventually filtered down to the hinterland and Long Lance's hometown on June 24, 1915. The *Twin City Daily Sentinel* carried a photograph of "Sylvester C. Long-Lance" on the front page under a headline that read, "Full-blooded Cherokee to Enter West Point." The caption for the photograph added, "He is a full-blooded Cherokee Indian, and the first of his race to become a student at West Point."[20]

If anybody in Winston–Salem knew otherwise, and some obviously did, nobody betrayed the native son. Young Sylvester Long, the boy from 4 1/2 Street, had somehow escaped and was doing well on the outside. More power to him.

Sylvester regularly mailed home letters, postcards and clippings during his first years at school.[21] Although her letters have not survived, one can be certain that Sallie wrote to him frequently in her large-letter script, telling him about his father, his sister and brothers, and the state of affairs around Winston–Salem. The family was proud of him, but protected him with silence. Joe still worked as a janitor in the white school system. Walter married his black girlfriend. Abe and Aurelia had a daughter, Vivian, who turned five during Sylvester's last year at St. John's Military Academy. Abe ran a small smoke shop for African Americans in the city. Walter sold newspapers at a downtown newsstand.[22] Lovie Galloway, Sylvester's girlfriend in Winston six years earlier, attended the Hampton Institute, became a teacher and married a black druggist.[23] The Longs officially remained "colored," and Sylvester's success did nothing to alter the family's status. He could not return home, of course, for that would undermine the person he had invented.

On July 3, 1915, the adjutant general of the War Department wrote again to Oscar Lipps at Carlisle, this time to request more information about the candidate's "alleged Indian ancestry." All that Lipps could do was forward a copy of Sylvester Long's original application, saying in his reply of July 6 that it was "all the information they had on his Indian ancestry." James Henderson, who had left Carlisle in late 1912 to become the superintendent of the Cherokee Indian School at Cherokee, North Carolina, was then asked to investigate Sylvester's family background among the Eastern Cherokees. When Henderson's search proved fruitless,[24] the investigation was halted. At the time, the optimistic Long Lance, who now had his "white man's chance," could not have known that the investigation would never truly close.

CHAPTER 4

Lieutenant Long Lance, War Hero

VIMY RIDGE, FRANCE, 1917

*A*ll winter, while the war raged in Europe, Sylvester prepared for the West Point examinations. He took special courses in algebra, plane geometry and military science at St. John's Military Academy, where his instructors were anxious for him to succeed. When the time came, he chose to write the tests at the examination center nearest to St. John's, which was Fort Slocum, a large army recruiting depot on David's Island, off New Rochelle, New York.

Early on the morning of March 21, he took an army ferry across to the island under a dark, overcast sky that threatened snow. He read in the morning newspaper that the French had checked the German offensive at Verdun and that American troops had advanced deeper into Mexico in pursuit of the elusive border raider, Pancho Villa. Forty thousand American suffragists planned to demonstrate at the national Republican and Democratic Party conventions in June in support of the vote for women.[1]

He headed for the examination center across an immense parade ground on David's Island, and on the way he noticed a group of black recruits for the regular army. They were assigned to a separate company, lived in segregated barracks and all their noncommissioned officers at Fort Slocum were white.[2]

There were two parts to the West Point examination, the physical and the mental. Sylvester was in excellent shape with a rugged, medium build. He was a solid twenty pounds heavier than when he had entered Carlisle seven years earlier. He passed the physical easily. Then came the written exams in algebra, plane geometry, English grammar and composition, literature, geography and history. The six papers were to be written over a three-day period, each paper four hours long, with the exception of plane geometry, which was only three.[3]

The unthinkable happened—Long Lance failed. He scored only forty-five in algebra and, incredibly, only thirty-seven in geometry. At St. John's that winter, he had demonstrated his mastery of both subjects, scoring averages of ninety-five. And for all his reading and love of the written word, he managed only a disappointing fifty-five in English composition and literature.[4] Had he panicked under the pressure of the examination schedule? Was the preparation at St. John's simply not up to the standards of West Point? This was unlikely because St. John's had established an enviable reputation for standards across the country, and he had been one of the school's top students. What happened on David's Island?

A clue might be found in the autobiographical story he later wrote for *Cosmopolitan*, in which he described bashing poor Curly on the head and nearly driving a knife into a fellow being. He explained in the article why he enlisted with the Canadian forces in the Great War. In the story he said that he "purposely 'flunked'" the entrance examinations at Fort Slocum, having "decided that the best place for a chap who could not keep from disgracing himself and his friends was fighting under the colors of an army that was upholding a world cause."[5] Perhaps, but why, if that was how he felt, did he not simply refuse to take the examinations and announce that he was going to Canada to join the army to uphold a great world cause? Why even bother to write the exams, and why bother spending most of a winter preparing for them? He could have done all he intended to do without the stigma of failure.

A likelier explanation for Long Lance's failure is that he deliberately scored poorly on the exams not because of a desire to fight for a larger cause but because he was, for the first time, in fear of discovery. All along, Long Lance had kept in touch with his former teachers at Carlisle,[6] and he must have known of the War Department's investigation into his "alleged Indian ancestry." If he had learned of James Henderson's inquiries,[7] it would certainly have unnerved him. By then he prized his identity as an Indian more than any future stature as a West Point graduate. Possibly Long Lance also realized that if the War Department received a copy of his application to Carlisle, it would reveal that he had lied about his age, which was now three years over the maximum age for West Point.

Whatever the reason, he failed three of the six tests, and he was out. And he was in no great hurry to head north to Canada to join the army. He waited nearly five months to do that, spending most of the time in New York.

To make some money he entered wrestling matches at the athletic clubs and did quite well, putting to good use his training at St. John's. Long Lance was not easily intimidated, and one day he took on a brute named Frank Leavitt, who called himself Man Mountain, and who outweighed Sylvester by a good seventy pounds.[8] After the bout Leavitt gave his picture to Sylvester, and it was faithfully pasted in his growing scrapbook.

How and when Long Lance decided to enlist with the Canadian armed forces is not known, though it is reasonably certain that he would have admired the Canadian war effort, as did his alma mater, St. John's. The school newspaper, the *Windmill*, praised Canadians for their bravery in the face of the chlorine gas attacks at Ypres in late April. An editorial in May 1915 declared, "Canadian soldiers at the front have set the real Canada before the eyes of the world, and we Americans, your neighbors, are proud of you." The adventure of war, the appeal of a cause and the glamour of the military would have attracted Long Lance. Since the odd wrestling bout did not bring in much money, he would find the security of army pay quite tempting.

In early August he took the train north to Canada and in less than a day arrived in Montreal, then Canada's largest city, with a population of five hundred thousand, the majority of them French-speaking. He asked for the nearest recruiting station and was directed to an office on Sainte Catherine. There he enlisted[9] and, as he explained later in the *Cosmopolitan* article, "three weeks after I had coughed and said 'Ahh' for the medical officer, I was on my way to France. . . ."[10]

The Canadians were glad to see him, for the casualties at the front had been staggering. Canadians distinguished themselves at Sanctuary Wood, but in that bloody twelve-day battle eight thousand Canadians were killed. The supply of recruits was drying up, having fallen from thirty thousand in January to a mere eight thousand in July. Canada lowered its medical qualifications and no longer insisted that a married man needed to have his wife's consent to enlist.[11]

French Canadians were hardly enthusiastic about the war effort. They did not see the war as their struggle, and they resisted serving in English-speaking regiments under English-speaking officers. And just when French Canadians were being asked to fight in Europe, the provincial government in Ontario was eliminating French-language instruction in its schools, a controversy that excited the Quebec press more than distant heroics in Flanders.[12]

Long Lance enlisted on August 4, 1916, two years to the day that Britain had declared war on Germany for invading neutral Belgium. Britain's declaration brought Canada into the conflict. At his enlistment Long Lance gave his father as his next of kin and listed him as "Joseph Long-Lance." He provided his family's correct address in Winston–Salem, 95 Brookstown Avenue, but then he allowed his imagination to run rampant. He lied again about his birth date, stating that it was December 1, 1891. He listed West Point in the space marked "previous military experience." His height was measured at five feet, eight and one-half inches, his chest at thirty-six inches breathing out and forty-one inches breathing in. The form mentions his complexion ("dark"), eyes ("dark brown") and hair ("black"). It also noted a tattoo on his right forearm, a tattoo of his initials on his right hand and a scar on his back.[13]

In his first month in the Canadian Expeditionary Force, Long Lance belonged to the 237th Battalion of the American Legion, a unit comprising American enlistees. Later he was transferred to the 97th Battalion, crossed the Atlantic on the troopship *Olympic*, and arrived in England on September 25, 1916. Immediately his unit headed for the Shorncliffe training camp near Folkestone and Dover on the English Channel. In October, Long Lance learned the basics: route marching, entrenching, musket practice, grenade throwing, bayonet fighting. In his company of green, untrained recruits, he was a man of considerable experience, having participated at St. John's in mock battles that included assaults on trenches protected by barbed-wire entanglement and wooden abatis. He also won respect as an Indian, for hundreds of other Indians in the Canadian army already had shown great skill as snipers. (One Indian sniper, Henry Norwest, a lance corporal from northern Alberta, was credited with 115 observed "hits."[14])

Long Lance's superiors quickly promoted him to acting corporal on October 6, then to acting sergeant on October 22. Three days later, however, he sprained his right knee in training, preventing any speedy departure to the battlefields of Europe. He recovered in hospital for two weeks, then was transferred to the Royal Canadian Regiment and the crack Princess Patricia's Canadian Light Infantry depot at Seaford, near Brighton, fifty miles to the east. There he remained for three months.

While waiting for the call to France, Long Lance could not resist the opportunity to impress old friends back in America. He mailed a Christmas card to his Carlisle acquaintances, including the superintendent. Under the message, "Kind Remembrance and Best Wishes for the New Year," he included a poem of sorts in which he promoted himself to lieutenant and talked of life in the trenches:

I've just come out of the trenches
Where we made the Germans dance,
And I'm sending this Greeting to let you know
That he is still alive, Yours Truly, Lieut. Long-Lance;
Alive and fit as fit can be,
Though fighting's not all sport,
And manners "made in Germany"
Aren't quite what you and I were taught.[15]

The poem was a hit at home. One of the teachers at Carlisle, sensing good publicity for the school, and with the United States relentlessly moving toward war, sent the Christmas card to the press. For the second time in less than a year, Long Lance made the papers. "American Indian is Fighting for Allies," the headline in the *New York Sun* read on February 12, 1917. "Lieut. Long Lance of Carlisle Surprises Teacher with Note from Trenches." The day the story appeared, Long Lance and the 38th Battalion at last shipped out for the front. On arrival he reverted to the ranks and remained a private for all of his four months in France.

For two years Allied and German armies had been locked in battle along the Western Front, which stretched from the North

Long Lance in uniform, taken while he served in the 38th Battalion, Canadian Expeditionary Force, 1917.

Sea to Switzerland. By early 1917 the war had deteriorated into an endurance test. Who would crack first? Millions of men had died in suicidal attacks trying to dislodge the enemy. In the four-month Somme offensive of 1916, British forces suffered 420,000 casualties (including nearly 25,000 Canadians) and the French more than 200,000 — all for a gain of some seven miles.[16]

The Allies wanted to capture a strongly fortified escarpment four miles long, commanding the flat plains around Arras. The Canadian Corps had been withdrawn in October from the Somme area to take over part of the Vimy Ridge front. Considering the ridge a menace to the Allies' position in northern France, Sir Douglas Haig, commander of the British forces, ordered the four Canadian divisions to take it.

Once at the front Long Lance's enthusiasm for the war quickly waned. The winter of 1916–17 was brutally cold, the cruelest in twenty-two years. The trenches at least were dry, but when the Canadians lined up for their food, the temperatures were so low that by the time they ate, the hot rations had frozen at the edges of their mess tins. Long Lance endured lice—"itchie-coos," the soldiers called them—and the enormous rats that ate on the human remains littering the battlefield. And always he lived with the din of artillery, mine charges and machine-gun fire.

After extensive preparations the attack on Vimy Ridge began at four o'clock, Easter Monday, April 9. Every battalion was in place, some not more than one hundred yards from the enemy. All night it had rained, and now the rain had turned to sleet and snow. From dugouts, shell holes and trenches, the Canadians surged forward. Amidst a heavy artillery barrage, the infantrymen rushed up the sleet-drenched hillside. All around, gun flashes lit up the sky. The 38th had a particularly difficult time. The ground they had to cross was so pocked and scarred by continuous shellfire that the men could not keep up with the artillery barrage. Some of the wounded drowned after falling into water-filled shell holes.

Vimy's German defenders emerged at unexpected places and put up a spirited resistance. But by the morning of the tenth, the summit had been cleared. On the eleventh the Germans pulled back two miles to a defensive line outside the western suburbs of Lens.[17] The Canadians had scored a striking victory. The French gratefully termed the feat, "an Easter gift from Canada to France."[18]

Long Lance emerged from Vimy unscathed, but as he later wrote, he had become accustomed to seeing men "gutted and lacerated day in and day out," to being choked with the stench of blood, iodine, cordite, burnt flares and mud. He got hit a month later, on May 22, and from a field bed in France he wrote,

> I am in a field hospital, convalescing from a wound in the head received a couple of weeks ago. Nothing serious; only a piece of shrapnel in the back part of the head and a broken nose — the latter sustained in falling on my face, I presume. I came through [Vimy Ridge] without a scratch . . . only to get hit a month later on one of the quietest days. . . . Such is war![19]

He was hospitalized for two weeks and rejoined his unit on June 4. Three weeks later he was hit again in an attack on Lens, and this time shrapnel in both thighs put him out of the war and back in England. He rested a month at a military hospital in Oxford and several weeks more at the Canadian Convalescent Hospital at Woodcote Park, Epsom, south of London. Only his excellent physical condition, he felt, saved him from having both legs amputated.[20]

When he was in hospital in England, Long Lance read another story about himself and his scrapbook grew again. An American reporter had interviewed him at the front, and in mid-July 1917, newspapers across the United States carried a long, illustrated article on "The American Full-Blooded Indian Who Fought at Vimy Ridge." This time the hyperbole ran wild, as captions of a *New York World* article revealed:

> Fenimore Cooper's Romances Have Nothing on the Real Life Story of This Full-Blooded Cherokee From Kit Carson's Country — Trick Rider, Fistic "Meeter of all Comers," All-Round College Athlete, Prize Debater and Literary Essayist, Musician . . . Carlisle and St. John's Graduate, President Wilson's Appointee to West Point Cadetship. He Now Turns Up as First Lieutenant of Princess Pat's Crack Canadian Regiment.[21]

Following his release from hospital, Long Lance was posted as a clerk to the headquarters of the Overseas Military Forces of

Canada in Argyll House on Regent Street in London. Appointed acting staff sergeant, he served from April 1918 to April 1919 in the Intelligence Section of the Canadian General Staff. He sailed for Canada on July 3, and as his point of discharge he asked for the last Canadian province to be settled—distant Alberta and the Rocky Mountains of Western Canada. Alberta seemed ideal for Long Lance, removed as it was in time and distance from his true origins and all that he was trying to deny and escape.

Long Lance had no doubt read reports in Canadian newspapers of the continuing racial strife in the United States. Thirty-eight African Americans were lynched in 1917 when he was fighting in Europe. Fifty-eight more were hanged in 1918 when the Great War ended. Seventy African Americans were lynched in 1919, the year Long Lance arrived in Canada.[22]

With the war over and thousands of southern African Americans heading to the northern cities for work, more racial violence threatened. In the "red summer" of 1919, twenty-five race riots erupted in American cities, and the year before that even Winston–Salem was not spared. In November 1918 a mob of two thousand whites stormed the city's jail, trying to lynch a black man charged with raping a white woman. The home guard fought back with fire hoses, then shooting broke out. Five whites were killed and estimates of the number of blacks killed ranged as high as fifty. The black prisoner was later found to be innocent.[23]

Sylvester Chahuska Long Lance boarded a train at Halifax and headed west across a wide, rough country to Alberta, far from the racial strife of the American South and far from questions about his racial origins. In Alberta he would start all over. Again.

CHAPTER 5

Long Lance, Journalist

CALGARY, ALBERTA, 1920–21

The troop train pulled into Calgary on Friday, July 18, 1919.[1] For the soldiers who stepped off the train and into the arms of loved ones, that was the moment when the war ended. They marched one last time, ten blocks to Mewata Barracks, there to pick up their discharge papers and back pay. Then they were civilians again.

Calgary was a young, vibrant boomtown. In just ten years its population had grown to sixty thousand from six thousand.[2] Calgary was as keen and ambitious as Long Lance, and nearly as young, having been founded only fifteen years before he was born. There were biases and prejudices, to be sure, but Long Lance did not feel the weight of them as he did in the South. The brash young city felt as exhilarating as its dry, fresh air.

Nobody rushed to greet Long Lance at the train station. After the backslaps and farewells, he was on his own. As always he loved to be the center of attention, and while rattling across the country in a train packed with soldiers ready to believe anything, he was in his element. Without much prompting, he could tell them about his friend Jim Thorpe, the man he had trained with in preparation for the 1912 Olympics and who was hitting .411 for the Boston Braves in the major leagues that season.[3] Long Lance knew boxing, too, and could describe in graphic detail how Jack Dempsey had won the heavyweight championship two weeks earlier in Ohio, beating Jess Willard, who outweighed Dempsey by fifty-five pounds. Long Lance liked to act out these bouts, and he especially liked Dempsey's crouching, aggressive style and his vicious, compact, eight-inch punches. Long Lance looked like a boxer, and he even sported the broken nose that goes with the territory.

If asked why he chose Alberta, he could answer that his spirit needed a frontier. By now he had moved his birthplace to eastern Oklahoma, some fifteen hundred miles from North Carolina, and he could complain that he wanted something less settled, less predictable, less rooted. His past was like a child's slate board, and anytime he felt like it, he could erase it and start clean again, becoming anything he wanted to be.

Long Lance left the barracks with his back pay and set out to find a room. Certainly he could not afford the big new hotels, such as the gleaming Palliser, next to the Canadian Pacific Railway station, which by Alberta standards in 1919 was a skyscraper at nine stories. He walked by the new Alexandra Hotel and the King George Hotel on Ninth Avenue and probably settled for cheap, fleabag accommodation.

While strolling about the city, he would occasionally see brown faces like his own. Perhaps at the train station, he would encounter a woman in an ankle-length, shapeless dress and a head scarf, a papoose on her back. Beside her might be a man with braided hair, wearing rumpled store-bought clothing.

He found his way around the city easily, for all the streets ran north and south and all the avenues east and west. After New York and London, Calgary was small, manageable, but colorful: cow-

Though Long Lance was short of money upon reaching Calgary, he nevertheless would not allow himself to be less than immaculately attired. So he soon purchased a new Palm Beach suit and Panama hat.

boys in ranch gear, Chinese in quilted satin jackets, Englishmen in tweed caps and knickerbockers, and hundreds of soldiers in khaki. The women looked sassy and boyish in the styles of the day, their arms and legs bare, and Long Lance watched the young ones hurrying by on their lunch hours. He looked them in the eye and heard no thunderclaps from the heavens.

He stopped at a clothing store and bought a lightweight Palm Beach suit,[4] one that sat well on his body, then selected a fine soft Panama hat. Outside on the sidewalks again, he could see the foothills in the distance and beyond them the great saw-toothed, snowcapped Rockies eighty miles away. The Blackfoot Indians called them "the backbone of the world."[5]

The streets were jammed because the next day, Saturday, July 19, was Peace Day, when the entire country would celebrate the end of hostilities. Prohibition had been in effect since 1916, however, and there was not a bar or saloon to be found. By nightfall Calgary's Eighth Avenue and Centre Street became as congested as Piccadilly Circus in London with streetcars clanging and the automobile horns *ooga-ooga*-ing. He dodged the ubiquitous Model Ts and the Maxwells, the McLaughlins and the Hudsons. Men and women walked arm in arm in the evening under the electric lights downtown.

The next day Long Lance spotted an old army friend in the crowd, Major Carlyle William MacInnis, one of his officers overseas. Long Lance rushed to him, pumped the major's hand and was delighted to find him as chipper as ever despite wounds suffered in France. MacInnis was secretary and treasurer of Alberta's Great War Veterans' Association.

"What are you going to do now, Chief?" he asked Long Lance.

Sylvester told him he planned to get a job in Calgary.

The major laughed and poked him under the arm. "I'll give you one year to go back to the blanket, Chief," MacInnis told him. "You may think you are going to stick it out in this civilized life, but you're not. I know you better than you know yourself. You're going back to the blanket—a squaw and a papoose."

It was a challenge Long Lance could hardly resist.

"I'll bet you a hundred dollars you're wrong," he shot back.

"Taken," MacInnis said, then walked away, chuckling.[6]

Long Lance searched for work all summer. At times he must have felt that he was back in the South, but despite rejections he recognized a difference. Many Albertans despised the local

Sarcee (Tsuu T'ina) Indians and regarded them as dirty and lazy. He learned that farmers paid Indians $2.50 a day for harvest work, while European immigrants were offered $4 a day.[7] And yet, when he had a chance to speak of his military record in his clear, concise English, he won respect. He also noticed that the prejudice in the foothills city was not insurmountable, not as indelible as back home. There was Lady Lougheed, the wife of Senator Sir James Lougheed, and she was of mixed ancestry. Brigadier General H.F. MacDonald, commanding officer of the Alberta Military District, had Indian ancestry. In the adjacent province of Saskatchewan, James McKay, a judge of the Supreme Court, was part Indian.[8]

Before moving on to another town, Long Lance left his name with the Soldiers Civil Re-establishment Office on the first floor of the Lancaster Building on Eighth Avenue in case something turned up.[9] He may have tried his luck elsewhere, or he may have holed up somewhere in or around Calgary (there are inexplicable gaps), but he did relate in the piece he did for *Cosmopolitan* in 1926 that he chased a dream in Los Angeles about this time. His "autobiographical" articles, even if fanciful, say much about what he wanted to do or at least what he thought he could do:

> With the war over, eventually I was sent home and demobilized as a captain. And then I had to begin all over again. At twenty-five, I had adopted the white man's customs, comforts and ways of thinking—and yet I had no way to earn a living commensurate with these newly acquired tastes.
>
> Some friend suggested I go to Los Angeles, where two professions might open for me—moving picture acting or professional boxing. In France, I had been Canadian light-heavyweight champion, and I had been told that I could go to the very top of the heap if I continued fighting.

Almost immediately after I landed in California, I was offered $500 to fight—and the heavy barred doors into the movies were opening to me.

Then, according to the *Cosmopolitan* story, he received two offers: a two-year army scholarship to study journalism and a reporter's job on the *Calgary Herald*. "That night," he wrote, "I wired the *Herald* to hold that thirty-dollar-a-week job":

That was six years ago—and never for a day have I regretted my choice. Had I taken a different road, I might have been light-heavyweight champion of the world—Jack Dempsey told me he would make me that in six months—and I might have been a movie star.[10]

One fact is certain. By October, Long Lance was in Calgary.[11] Charlie Hayden, managing editor of the *Herald*, was impressed by the application that the Soldiers Civil Reestablishment Office had forwarded to him. He hired Long Lance as a reporter, and for the next year he constantly encouraged him. Long Lance's first by-line appeared after an unusually long preamble to the story. Long Lance himself supplied the information, and, given that freedom, did what he loved to do best: invent. The preamble said that Long Lance, "an officer on the intelligence staff of General Plumer's forces in Italy during the latter part of the war," enlisted as a private in the Canadian Expeditionary Force early in 1916. It continued:

Although an American citizen, born in Oklahoma and educated at St. John's Military Institute, Carlisle University and West Point, the famous military academy of the United States, he came to Canada during the war and signed on for overseas service. He served in the field as a private and NCO, receiving the *Croix de Guerre* for bravery when a sergeant, and afterwards being promoted to the rank of lieutenant. He also served in France as

In Calgary, Long Lance further reinvented himself.

an officer before being elevated to a staff appointment in Italy. Captain Long Lance was wounded twice in the course of his war service. When the Canadian forces were demobilized, he returned to the United States, and after a brief stay there came to Western Canada and joined the staff of the *Calgary Herald.* In both his college and army careers, Captain Long Lance has been noted as an athlete and is well known as a boxer, wrestler, footballer and all-round track man.[12]

Long Lance (second from the left) shares a lighthearted moment with Howard Kelly (bottom left) and friends in Calgary.

It was an astounding example of reckless lying, lying for the sake of lying, lying as adventure. Any of his "facts" could easily have been checked. He had not fought in Italy, nor had he been born in Oklahoma. He had never been a lieutenant or a captain. Carlisle was not a university. He did not attend West Point. He did not win the *Croix de Guerre*. No matter—the next day it was all there in print for everyone to see, while he sat at his desk in the newsroom behind a bulky typewriter. And the clippings, the "proof" would then go into his scrapbook.

Long Lance's best friend in the newsroom was Howard Kelly, who at twenty was one of the youngest sports editors on a daily newspaper in Canada. Both men were sports-minded and attended all the football, baseball and boxing matches, and they kicked up their heels at the local dances. Kelly's mother cooked meals for Long Lance, or "the Chief," as he once again became known. Howard Kelly and other members of the *Herald* liked Long Lance's sense of humor. The younger staffers hero-worshiped him.[13]

For nearly three years Long Lance worked at the *Herald*, covering every beat from sports to city politics. He learned how to

Another photo Long Lance sent home in the early 1920s. Again he seems to want to tell his family of his freedoms—to ride anywhere in trains, to date white women. The caption, carefully typed on the back reads, "Stanley Park, Vancouver, B.C., August 1920. Young lady from Calgary, whom I met there and spent the day with."

write fast, how to write running copy, and he rarely worked only eight-hour days. Colonel Woods, the publisher, ran a tight ship and expected mileage from his reporters. He refused to allow reporters to use taxis in the city and once ruled that pencil stubs be saved and joined together as an economy measure.[14] The *Herald* made money. And Long Lance was a natural. The words seemed to flow from his typewriter though he was a stylist and worked hard at it, finding that the harder he worked, the more effortless the writing appeared.

He boarded with the Vahey family on Sixth Avenue, only two blocks from the *Herald*. The large white frame house with the white picket fence and the veranda, where everyone gathered on warm afternoons and evenings, became a comfortable retreat. "The spirits were friendly," Long Lance liked to say of the Vahey place. He lingered after many dinners, telling them of his travels, Carlisle, West Point and the war. Long Lance was the perfect boarder (he did not smoke or drink then), but he could be a prankster. One evening while the family was sitting down to dinner, the door to the dining room slowly creaked open and a hand holding a gun appeared, then a masked face with grotesque false teeth. "Hold up!" the intruder shouted to the startled group. Then Long Lance pulled off his disguise and the laughter bounced off the walls.[15]

It is probable that, in Calgary, Long Lance was as relaxed with himself and with the world—especially during his time with the Vaheys—as he ever had been before or would be again. He had a job with a future, friends, a home and youth, which he thought important, for about this time he lopped three years off his age, making his birth date 1893.[16] He started to date women, white women. He certainly had no difficulty winning their attention or affections.

Long Lance shunned the baggy, unkempt look then popular among the gentlemen of the press. He abhorred sloppiness and usually stood ramrod straight, shoulders back, chin up, hands at his side or clasped behind his back. He preferred clothes that accentuated his athletic body. Ralph Wilson, a fellow reporter, remembers him as "a dashing, handsome Indian who always ended up with the most beautiful girl."[17]

About this time he became involved, briefly but thoroughly, with a wealthy married woman who arrived in Calgary in one of the first Rolls-Royces ever seen in the city. They picnicked in the countryside and drove everywhere in the cushioned Rolls.[18]

The exuberance felt following World War I brought a decade of outrageous stunts. On the right Bill Strother, the "Human Spider," climbs the Calgary Herald building. On the left he stands on his head on the top of the Hudson's Bay Company building.

Long Lance realized, however, that in Calgary there were limits beyond which he could not go. The rules regarding race relations might be relaxed on the frontier, but they were there nonetheless. He knew he could never marry the women he courted, and sometimes he confided in Howard Kelly and Hugh Dann, another Calgary friend, about his predicament. They could only suggest that he travel to Oklahoma and seek out and marry an educated Cherokee girl. Such well-intentioned advice merely heightened his inner frustration.[19]

He immersed himself in the life of the city, officiating at amateur boxing bouts, joining the militia and signing up with the local Elks Lodge. Long Lance often went flying with Fred McCall, one of the great aces of the war, and in 1921 the two men edited an eighty-five–page aviation manual titled *Devoted to Flying in Alberta.* He coached football for the Calgary Canucks Football Club and was elected to the executive.[20] When Bill Strother, the renowned "Human Spider," came to Calgary and climbed the nine-story Palliser Hotel — blindfolded — Long Lance somehow managed to greet him on the roof, while fifteen thousand Calgarians whooped and

Soon after being discharged from the Canadian army, Long Lance headed west, moving farther from his North Carolina past, to Alberta, where he continued to fashion his new identity. Soon after arriving in Calgary, he sent his parents a photo showing him in his Canadian militia uniform.

cheered on the street below. Bill Strother's accent sounded famil-iar—he was from North Carolina. Carefully Long Lance, the "Okla-homan Cherokee," kept his memories of his home state to himself.[21]

No matter how late he stayed up the previous night, Long Lance always rose at six o'clock the next morning and did an hour's calisthenics and gymnastics,[22] a regime that paid off when the rough-faced "Manassa Mauler," Jack Dempsey, the heavy-weight champion, visited Calgary on March 23, 1921. Dempsey

In Calgary Long Lance developed the passion for flying that would eventually lead him to the mansion of one of America's richest women. The caption reads, "Just Landing—Calgary."

was on a cross-country tour of the Pantages Vaudeville Circuit, making some extra money. He had been a copper mine mucker, lumberjack and dance-hall bouncer and, although he went on in the next twelve years to earn $4 million in the ring, he had pocketed only $21.50 from his first professional bout in 1915.[23]

When Dempsey was in Calgary, Harry Wills, an African American contender, had challenged him for the heavyweight title. In boxing circles this was an explosive issue. Doc Kearns, Dempsey's manager, advised his man to ignore the challenge. The *Albertan* quoted the champ as saying, "I will never accept a challenge from a colored man. I absolutely draw the colored line."[24] Wills would have to wait, but Long Lance, as an Indian, would not. He showed up with his press credentials the next day to observe a demonstration with a sparring partner of how Dempsey defeated Willard to win the championship. After this Long Lance showed his pass and was allowed to visit Dempsey in his dressing room. The fighter's mother had some Cherokee ancestry, and the two men got along well. They met for breakfast the next day at the Palliser, then sparred a few rounds at the Pantages. The next morning they met again, boxed and wrestled and went for a swim at the YMCA. Dempsey was a few inches taller than Long Lance and twenty-five pounds heavier, but they resembled each other in many remarkable ways. Both had taut, well-muscled bodies, broad facial features and dark skin. Dempsey later remembered Long Lance as fast and "light on his feet."[25]

Any reference to his Indian background pleased Long Lance. One of his friends on the newspaper, a fellow militia officer, was Lieutenant Douglas Cunnington, who worked in the *Herald*'s advertising department. During the war he had won the Military Cross for capturing a machine-gun nest. In the officers' mess one day, Cunnington said to Long Lance, "Chief, there is one thing I always admired about you. Though for years I have seen you mingle with every rank of officer from General down, I have never seen you try to be anything but an Indian." Long Lance wrote in one of his later articles that this was his "most appreciated compliment,"[26] and he went out of his way to link his name with Indian subjects.

In June 1920 Long Lance met Ormer Locklear, an American stunt flyer who performed every day at the Calgary Exhibition. Before crowds of thousands the Texan pilot changed biplanes in midair and executed other thrilling maneuvers. Calgarians were shocked to learn a month later that Locklear had crashed to his death near Los Angeles. In the obituary that Long Lance wrote for the *Herald*, he included this story:

> Few, if any in Calgary or elsewhere, knew that Locklear was a quarter-breed Indian, of the Croatan Tribe, the oldest known tribe in the southwestern United States. . . . This story was brought forth when the *Herald* representative asked him if he were any relation of an Ormer Locklear from North Carolina, with whom he had attended college. Locklear recognized him as a cousin on the instant for he knew that his grandfather's brother in North Carolina also bore his Christian name.[27]

Long Lance (seated second from the left) mailed this and other photos like it home in the early 1920s. At first glance it seems a unusual choice, but his family would have appreciated its significance. As "coloreds" they could not ride in the company of whites in Southern railway cars.

While continuing to enhance his Indian persona, Long Lance doubtless winced at the "nigger jokes" that were heard in the city. Calgary had only a few black citizens, and they were seldom seen away from the shoeshine stands and railways. The respected *Beaver* magazine, published by the Hudson's Bay Company in Winnipeg, included in the March 1926 issue several such barbs. One was titled "Genealogy":

> Two negroes were standing on the corner discussing family trees.
>
> "Yes, suh, man," said Ambrose, "Ah kin trace mah relations back to a family tree."
>
> "Chase 'em back to a family tree?" said Mose.
>
> "No, man! Trace 'em! Not chase 'em."
>
> "Well, dey ain't but two kinds of things dat lives in trees—birds and monkeys—and yo' sho' ain't got no feathers on yo'."[28]

An awkward time of year for Long Lance arrived every fall when Calgary's Rotary Club presented its annual minstrel show, which included nearly a hundred blackfaced club members "forming a burnt-cork background five rows deep." The evening of song and dance included dialogue with racial humor and dialect jokes. Among the "Krazy Koons" was Long Lance's direct boss, Charlie Hayden. C.O. Smith, the *Herald*'s editor, joined the 1921 production. The very popular show played several nights at the Grand Theatre in the Lougheed Building, right next to the *Herald*.[29]

Long Lance hated to be mistaken for an African American, and there is evidence that he went along with the humor when it served to take the heat off him. He could be pushed only so far, however, and one night in Calgary he reached his breaking point. Fred Kennedy, a popular Calgary journalist, was covering a regimental dinner at the Palliser Hotel and sat at a table with Long Lance. After dinner Kennedy, Long Lance and two other companions walked across the street to McCrohan's Restaurant and sat at the horseshoe counter. Ten minutes later two men entered, and when the waitress motioned them to the stools next to Kennedy's group, they moved forward, then abruptly stopped. "I am not sitting alongside any nigger," one of the men told the waitress. Long Lance ignored the remark, so the same man repeated it, louder. "*I am not sitting alongside any nigger!*"

Long Lance politely excused himself, turned to the man, who by now was glowering at him, and asked, "Were you addressing me, sir?"

"I sure as hell was," the man said.

The way Kennedy remembers it, "Long Lance's left didn't seem to travel any more than eight inches, but when it connected with the man's jaw, he went out like a light."[30]

Chapter 6

Making a Name

Blackfoot Reserve, Alberta, 1921

O n the morning of May 27, 1921, when a late frost had covered the green lawns of Calgary with a haze of frozen dew,[1] Long Lance headed off by train on his first out-of-town story. He enjoyed the ride eastward through the small station stops with grain elevators marked Indus, Dalemead, West Carseland and Carseland. It was Long Lance's assignment to go to Gleichen, sixty miles east of Calgary, to report on the Blackfoot Indian Reserve.

While on the train he had time to scribble a letter or postcard to his family. He wondered about them often when he was alone. Over the past year he had mailed many letters and photographs from Calgary, each photograph bearing a carefully typed caption on the back: "The big parade in honor of the 250th anniversary of the founding of the Hudson's Bay Company," "Long Lance climbing out of the cockpit of a biplane," "Long Lance with Howard Kelly and other Calgary friends on a prairie picnic," "the national parks at Banff and Jasper."[2]

At Gleichen the train jolted to a stop. Gleichen was a busy little distribution center with four grain elevators. There were buckboards at the station and a few cars. Long Lance observed the ranchers, homesteaders and some distinctively dressed men in dark suits and black hats, accompanied by women in bonnets and plain dresses. These were the Dunkards, the German Baptist Brethren, who were much like the Amish of southeastern Pennsylvania near Carlisle. The Dunkards lived close to Arrowwood, just south of town beyond the Blackfoot Reserve.[3]

He walked from the station toward a cluster of white frame buildings on the reserve side of the tracks. On a fence post he saw a meadowlark; its song reminded him of spring despite the cold weather. He moved quickly to keep warm and soon came upon the Indian agent's office, where a few Indians stood on the steps, chatting among themselves and using expressive hand gestures as they talked. The men wore their hair in braids, some with wide-brimmed "Indian Joe" hats, colorful handkerchiefs tied under their chins, buckskin coats and store-bought shirts and trousers. The women were clad in blankets with bright handkerchiefs over their heads.

Long Lance approached them and said hello in English. The men stopped talking; the women did not look up. The response did not surprise him, for he knew from Carlisle how wary Plains Indians were of strangers.

Inside the building a fire burned, and one of the clerks directed Long Lance to the largest office, where he saw a man about his own age dressed in a jacket and tie, working at his desk. The agent, George Gooderham, looked up, listened to Long Lance explain his assignment, then suggested he come back after lunch. "You can join Corporal Harper of the Mounted Police and myself on an inspection of the western end of the reserve," he said.

In the early afternoon Long Lance returned, and soon the three men rattled off in Gooderham's new black Ford, dust billowing behind them. At the first stop, the Anglican Residential

The Blackfoot Indian Agent George Gooderham speaking with Boy Chief, a Blackfoot, at Brooks, Alberta, in the early 1930s. The tone of Long Lance's stories about the Indian reservation system would change throughout the years from wholesale approval to gentle criticism to stinging condemnation.

School, Gooderham read out the Truant Act, warning the children that they must attend school. (The year before, the federal Department of Indian Affairs had made school attendance compulsory on all reserves in Canada.)

Driving around the reserve, Gooderham instructed Long Lance on what to write about, what points to include. The Indians were having great difficulty adjusting to the new economic conditions, he emphasized. Only forty-five years ago they had lived off the buffalo, but since the great herds no longer roamed the prairies, the Indians were in distress. After ten thousand years of nomadic life, they could not be expected to settle down easily in a single generation. Gooderham spoke to the reporter as if he had never seen an Indian before. Long Lance grew restless and soon put away his notebook.

As they bumped over roads that were little more than wagon ruts, the men could see flocks of migrating birds of every size and color flying to their nesting grounds in the North. On the green hillsides were cattle, thin from the long winter, moving out to pasture with their calves. They saw small herds of Indian ponies, cayuses. All along Gooderham continued his narrative, explaining that the Indians first obtained the cayuse after the arrival of the Spaniards. Runaways were traded north from Mexico and had reached the Blackfoot some two hundred years earlier.

Finally Long Lance could take no more. "I am a Cherokee from Oklahoma and a graduate of Carlisle Indian School," he told Gooderham, who had been too preoccupied to read Long Lance's references. He had assumed from the stranger's dark complexion that he was West Indian. It was an awkward introduction, but Gooderham and Long Lance quickly warmed to each other. Long Lance did the talking now, telling the agent about the Cherokee, the Carlisle Indian School and his friend, the great Jim Thorpe. As they passed some Indian women on the road, Long Lance asked Gooderham to stop. He tried some of his rustic Cherokee on the Blackfoot women, who seemed startled and baffled. They could not understand a word Long Lance spoke.[4]

The party visited several farms after the tour of the reserve. At the 160-acre operation of Harry Red Gun, they found the proprietor in his field with a team of horses, busily plowing and seeding. Long Lance always traveled with a camera, and he snapped a picture of Harry to accompany his article. Gooderham explained how the Indians with cattle worked from sunup to sundown, branding the animals in the spring, castrating the males, segregating the dry cows. Long Lance knew enough about the operation from his trips to Carson Town to make pleasant conversation.

The Indian agent wielded immense power under Canada's Indian Act, the federal legislation that governed all aspects of a native's life. Even to leave the reserve, an Indian had to obtain a pass from the agent, stating where he was going and the purpose of the trip. Gooderham and his staff of about a dozen looked after the Blackfoot's land sales and leasing, housing, health, livestock— everything and anything from bookkeeping to directing the sowing of the crops. The Blackfoot Reserve, Gooderham explained, was the richest in Canada, nearly half of its 450 square miles having been sold to the federal government in 1910. Money from the sale enabled the Blackfoot to buy plows, reapers, binders and harrows.[5]

Gooderham and Long Lance talked about the war, too. Gooderham had joined the Imperial army in Britain, and as a lieutenant he had commanded a battery on the Passchendaele front in 1918. Long Lance told him that he was a captain and described Vimy Ridge and Lens. Long Lance and Gooderham became friends, and over the next five years Long Lance came to know the Gooderham family well. George's wife, Mary, had been the first woman to attend the School of Practical Science and study architecture at the University of Toronto.

Gooderham's father had been an Indian agent in Saskatchewan and later among the Blackfoot in Alberta. His family belonged to the temperance branch of the Gooderham family; the other branch owned Gooderham and Worts, the old Ontario distilling firm. George had been born in 1889 on Poor Man's Reserve in central Saskatchewan, and since he grew up there and later at neighboring Piapot's Reserve, his first friends were Indian children. He had learned Cree from them and often ate in their rough log huts along the flats of the Qu'Appelle River. His friends' mothers fed him bannock and, as a treat, tea. He had observed Indian rituals and ceremonies.

His parents had sent him east to Ontario for his education, but he always returned to the plains in summer. While visiting the Blackfoot at Gleichen after the war, his father suffered a sudden and fatal heart attack. Pressed by his father's friends, George applied for the position of Indian agent in January 1920. When Long Lance arrived in Gleichen, Gooderham had been the agent for only a year and a half,[6] yet his early years among the Indians gave him an air of maturity and long experience.

George and Mary Gooderham were much impressed with Long Lance. Mary remarked that Long Lance's vocabulary and turn of phrase were infinitely better than most southern Albertans. From the first meeting they saw in Long Lance a man with a "burning ambition to make a name for himself."[7]

Long Lance also called on Canon Stocken, the resident Anglican missionary with the Blackfoot, whose rectory was not far from Gooderham's office. Stocken had come to the reserve from England in 1885 as a young man of twenty-seven and had served nearly forty years in Indian missions in southern Alberta.[8] He was able to tell Long Lance what the reserve had looked like in the mid-1880s. By then the Indians' large skin tepees were gone. Their clothing was no better than cotton sacking from the ration house. In 1879 the last of the great buffalo herds had been exterminated on the Canadian side of the border and four years later on the American side as well. Deprived of the mainstay of their way of life, the Indians tried to adjust both to poverty and to the confinements of the reserve. They also had to cope with tuberculosis and scrofula that ran rampant.[9]

Long Lance wrote down uncritically what he was told by the missionary, which doubtless reflected a lack of confidence in his own observations and judgments. At the Carlisle Indian School he had been taught to respect the pious, unselfish character of the Christian missionaries and the humanitarianism of Indian agents. In his first article he praised the "broad educational system" of the Anglican church and the work of the "paleface missionary" who

Long Lance on one of his visits to the reserves around Calgary in the early 1920s. Here he absorbed Plains Indian culture, which gave him confidence to pass himself off as a full-blooded Blackfoot chief when he returned to New York.

he predicted would "always be a perpetual monument of self-sacrifice." He described Canon Stocken as "the most honored and respected white known to the Blackfeet of Canada," and he referred to Canada's Indian policy as "clear-sighted" and administered by "a group of self-sacrificing employees."[10] He tried to please everyone, and the result also pleased the city editor at the *Herald*, who thought the article was uplifting and asked Long Lance for another, this time on the Sarcee.

A June provincial election prevented Long Lance from visiting the reserves for a while. For years the farmers of Alberta had felt themselves the victims of an eastern Canadian oligarchy, one that sold them high-priced farm machinery and at the same time allowed the railways to charge excessively high freight rates, all of which conspired to keep the farmers impoverished. A growing resentment against old party lines nourished a backlash against the Liberal party in Alberta. On June 17 a new agrarian party, the United Farmers of Alberta, pledged to liberating the province from "eastern domination," won a resounding victory. Long Lance had exercised his franchise since he joined the Canadian army,[11] and he voted this time though he kept his political preference private.

With the election over, Long Lance headed off on his next out-of-town assignment to the Sarcee Reserve, south of Calgary. He enjoyed these excursions, seeing new places and meeting new people, escaping the routine and the predictable in the city. His boredom threshold was low. Thanks to Canon Stocken of the Blackfoot Reserve, he had a contact with the Sarcee, Archdeacon John Tims, who had been the first Anglican missionary with the Blackfoot from 1883 to 1895 and the resident missionary at the Sarcee Reserve since 1895. Tims was the father of Anglican Indian missions in the Calgary area in the late nineteenth century. A strict and efficient administrator, he had acted for years as the secretary-treasurer for all Anglican schools and missions in the diocese.[12]

Long Lance borrowed a friend's roadster this time for the short trip — ten miles south of the city — up Fourteenth Street, past the large elevated water tank, across Weasel Head Bridge. It was a bone-dry summer with the green grass of May now burnt and brown. The midday heat reminded Long Lance of North Carolina, but without its oppressive humidity. On a rough gravel road he approached a cluster of houses, barns, cattle sheds and granaries surrounding a church, mission house, hospital and school. Each Sarcee family, like the Blackfoot, sited their stables a hundred yards behind their homes. In all directions he saw the small frame houses of the Sarcee, painted white with red trim, dotting the rolling upland around the mission.[13] He parked the roadster and walked to the rectory, where Archdeacon Tims greeted him at the door. An elderly man who always wore his clerical collar, the archdeacon had lost most of his accent but none of his formally polite English manner. He invited the young reporter into the parlor.

Long Lance studied the room and made notes he thought would be helpful. He noticed dozens of silver cups standing on the mantelpiece, each one dutifully inscribed. When asked,

Archdeacon Tims gladly told of his rowing days in England, where he had won his first silver cup at the age of eight for coxing the winning four in the Oxford Royal Regatta of 1865. He won other silver cups for rowing, canoeing, coxing and boating of every description.

Immigrant missionaries were numerous in Canada. Although many Canadian-born clergy shunned the Indian missions, preferring instead to travel to distant corners of the world, French and Belgian Oblate Fathers served in the Roman Catholic stations and self-sacrificing, middle-class Englishmen, like Stocken and Tims, in the Anglican missions.

Archdeacon Tims originally intended to work in Uganda, where Anglican missionary work had just begun, but there was an urgent appeal for missionaries in the Canadian Northwest. In 1883 he was sent to establish an Anglican mission to the Blackfoot. At age twenty-five he sailed from England to New York, took the Northern Pacific Railway to Helena, Montana Territory, then a stage to Fort Benton, Montana, and finally an express wagon to Blackfoot country on the Bow River at Blackfoot Crossing. He arrived just weeks before the Canadian Pacific Railway construction crews and found the Indians in a pitiable condition. "The buffalo had disappeared and they were just settling down to reserve life," he said. "They did nothing except dance and attend the ration house. Morally they had descended to the depths of iniquity. Gambling, thieving, lying and adultery were common." The young missionary watched his first Sun Dance that July and wondered what, in God's name, he was doing here. "The fantastic costumes of the people, the paint and feathers, the . . . foreign tongue made my heart sink within me, and if ever I felt the hopelessness of a task . . . it was then."

He suffered a nervous breakdown, and two attempts were made on his life, the last in 1895, which resulted in his departure from the Blackfoot mission and his replacement by Canon Stocken. When Long Lance arrived to interview him, however, great progress had been made, and Archdeacon Tims was in good spirits and fine health as his burly frame and barrel chest attested. "Our adherents are not all of them what we would wish," he admitted, "but comparing them with the average white congregation, I think their attendance at Divine Service and on the Means of Grace generally is good." Their material lives, too, had improved. "Many of the natives have good floors and good roofs overhead, whilst their walls are covered with pictures and ornaments, clocks stand on shelves, cupboards hold crockery and tables, chairs and cooking ranges are found in nearly all."[14]

The archdeacon's daughter, Winnifred Tims, was a teacher at the Sarcee Anglican School. At her father's suggestion, she took Long Lance on a tour of the school. Long Lance also met Doctor Thomas F. Murray, a friendly twenty-eight-year-old Indian agent and medical doctor who had recently arrived from London, Ontario. Dr. Murray told him of the terrible mortality rate among the Sarcee. Three out of four died before reaching the age of twenty. The Sarcee population had fallen from more than three hundred when the treaty was made in 1877 to 155 at the beginning of 1921. To combat tuberculosis Dr. Murray explained how the Anglican school would become a sanatorium and government school later that year.[15]

Long Lance's article on the Sarcee was much tougher than the puffery he had written about the Blackfoot. The thought that kept running through his head was that the Indians had surrendered their land in return for tuberculosis. "The plight of the Sarcee is a real tragedy," Long Lance wrote. "Little do the people of Calgary realize that they are daily witnessing the passing of a nation as dramatically as any that have been depicted by the pen of J. Fenimore Cooper."

Through Archdeacon Tims, Long Lance met Jim Starlight, the Sarcee chief. Chief Starlight owned the reserve's largest farm, on which he raised wheat and oats and some of the best stock. Educated at the mission school, he spoke excellent English and

In the early twentieth century, tuberculosis devastated the Sarcee community. Among this group of students in the Sarcee school in 1912, two wear bandages to cover open tubercular sores.

played a strong game of chess. Long Lance and Chief Starlight liked each other from the start. Three years later the chief loaned Long Lance his white buckskin costume for the Calgary Stampede.[16]

Long Lance did not attempt any in-depth investigation of the Sarcee. He talked to the missionary and the agent, toured the school and talked with the chief, then hurried back to Calgary to write his story. Another visitor to the same reserve that summer worked much differently, and Long Lance happened to mention him indirectly in his story, published in late July. Describing the Thunder Dance performed by the "pagans" in the spring, Long Lance wrote, "A government ethnologist has just bought the tribe's entire outfit for the pipe dance, to be kept in the government museum as a historic relic of the aborigines of this country." The government ethnologist was Diamond Jenness, soon to become one of Canada's best-known anthropologists.

Jenness spent two months on the Sarcee Reserve, arriving each day by horse and saddle to talk to some of the older Indians, to learn of the early organization and history of the community.

He was a government employee, determined to gather as much knowledge as possible about the Indian people at a time when they were rapidly dying off. Using skills he acquired in fieldwork in New Guinea and the Arctic, Jenness cross-checked all the facts given him through his interpreter. Their paths might have crossed the day Long Lance visited the reserve.

There were similarities between Jenness and Long Lance. Both were of medium height, strong and wiry, and nearly the same age. They were recent immigrants to Canada, Jenness coming from New Zealand and England, Long Lance from the United States. Each man wrote extensively in the 1920s on Canada's Indians.[17] But here the likeness ends. Long Lance wrote in a light, breezy style, capable of such analogies as "Buffalo was to the Indian what roast beef is to the white man." In his governmental reports Jenness confined himself to strict, balanced, academic prose. Long Lance brightened his writing with anecdotes and never shied from using himself in his stories if it helped to move them along. In his article on the Sarcee, he told of Chief Bull's Head, who had been a great Sarcee warrior in his youth and who had gone on many war parties against the Cree to the north. One day Chief Bull's Head unexpectedly encountered a Cree chief whom he had fought years earlier. The Cree simply poked his head into Chief Bull's Head's tepee, and the old Sarcee, as Long Lance put it, "almost jumped out of his skin."

"I thought I left you dead on the battlefield," Chief Bull's Head exclaimed.

"You thought so, but you didn't," the Cree replied, smiling.

The next Sunday, according to Long Lance's account, the two old warriors attended church together at the suggestion of Archdeacon Tims. Long Lance remarked in his article that the incident reminded him of an event he had witnessed at Carlisle (which he called in his story an Indian university). This was the meeting at Carlisle of the famous Chief Joseph of the Nez Percé and the elderly American army general who had chased him for thousands of miles in the Nez Percé War of 1877. On the commencement platform, Long Lance wrote, the two men met for the first time since the war. "The one-armed general and the blind chief stood motionless for a moment; then they grasped each other's hands and turned and faced the audience." They could not speak, these "two men of iron, who had maimed each other in a terrible massacre years before." For the remainder of the commencement, Long Lance concluded, the two men stayed close by each other "and the general became the blind chief's guide."

It all made for a well-rounded tale, long on drama and short on facts. Long Lance became better at this through the years, but it was not the sort of account one might expect from someone as exacting as Diamond Jenness. Chief Joseph and General O.O. Howard did meet at Carlisle, but Long Lance could not possibly have been there. The encounter occurred at the commencement of 1903,[18] when Long Lance was at his desk at the Depot Street School for Negroes in Winston.

George Gooderham, the agent with the Blackfoot, recognized that Long Lance knew little of the Plains Indians, but he also perceived the man's talent for conveying the sense of a story and writing it in a way that would appeal to a large audience.[19] He encouraged Long Lance to write more stories on the Indians, as did his editor at the *Herald*. Long Lance's next assignment was the Blood Indians, who lived one hundred miles south of Calgary. Here Long Lance met another Anglican missionary, the Reverend S.H. Middleton, who would teach him more about Indians than he ever expected to know.

Chapter 7

Buffalo Child Long Lance

Blood Reserve, Alberta, 1922

Samuel Henry Middleton, or "S.H." as he was known, met Long Lance at the train station in Macleod and drove him to St. Paul's Blood Indian School, located on Big Island in the middle of the Belly River, fifteen miles south of Macleod.

The Blood Indian Reserve was beautiful and easily the largest in Canada, some fifty miles long and thirty miles wide, just north of the Montana border. All around him Long Lance saw fields under cultivation, hundreds of thousands of acres as far as the eye could see. The Indians were horse and cattle ranchers as well, and they built their own homes on the grasslands. With the money they made, many of the farmers purchased the newest, most efficient farm implements, and the reserve thrived.

Middleton liked what he saw in Long Lance, and what he saw was his model of the ideal Indian, one who could measure up to any white man. On the drive to the school, the two men talked politics, discussing Arthur Meighen, who had just replaced

The Reverend S.H. Middleton became the closest thing Long Lance would know to a lifelong friend and confidant. Middleton found in Long Lance the vision of the noble red man.

Robert Borden as prime minister of Canada, and the new American president, Warren Harding. They touched on sports, as the Anglican missionary, although considerably slighter and less robust than Long Lance, loved to hike, ride, climb mountains and play soccer. Long Lance also was drawn to Middleton. He listened for hours to stories of the Blackfoot language and Blood legends. Unlike Archdeacon Tims, who was appalled at the brutality of the Sun Dance, Middleton explained that in fact the Sun Dance grew out of a longstanding worship of the Great Spirit, whom the Indians believed to be identical to the Christian God.

All his life Samuel Middleton had fantasized about the "Red Indians." He was an orphan and a romantic. He lived with his grandparents in Burton-on-Trent, a crowded English industrial town in the western Midlands and, like thousands of English boys, he thought of North American Indians as brave and noble savages who roamed never-ending plains and brandished tomahawks against their enemies. Children's books and magazines, the penny dreadfuls, were crammed with stories of Indians and the Wild West.

When Middleton graduated with a Bachelor of Science degree in agriculture from Kingston College in 1904, he declined an offer from his grandfather to join the family firm of carriage makers in Derbyshire and decided instead to go to Canada for the challenge and adventure. He set off for Brocket in the Canadian Northwest and the North Peigan Reserve in early 1905.[1] The North Peigan were the smallest of the three Canadian Blackfoot-speaking tribes, which included the Blackfoot, Blood and Peigan. About five hundred North Peigan lived north of the 49th parallel, while some three thousand resided in the United States, where they were called the Blackfeet.[2]

Young Middleton bought a small ranch near Brocket, some work horses and fifty head of cattle. He hired Indians to help him put up fences and buildings, and he came to know them well. They assisted him through difficult times. Terrible blizzards struck that first winter. In summer, hailstorms pelted his crops. During the autumn of 1907 half his stock froze to death.

The Peigan ranchers did not have life any easier. They were confused and demoralized, suffering through what anthropologists would later call culture shock. The former buffalo hunters and their sons failed at farming, and now their attempts at ranching were floundering. Few could read or write or understand English. Middleton volunteered his services to the Anglican Diocese of Calgary, offering to help in any way to bring the Indians into the twentieth century.

These were boom years in Western Canada, and the Anglican bishop in Calgary needed all the help he could get. As the Indian population dropped, sodbusters increased a hundredfold. In 1895 the District of Alberta had contained thirty thousand inhabitants; by 1905 the new Province of Alberta boasted nearly two hundred thousand inhabitants. By 1911 the population had doubled to four hundred thousand.[3] The bishop asked Middleton if he would work as a lay reader for the Reverend R.W. Haynes, an Anglican missionary at the Peigan Reserve. Middleton agreed and loved the work. Two years later the bishop asked him to give up his ranch to become the principal of the St. Paul's Boarding School on the reserve. In 1909 he sold the ranch and his stock, and, like the early Jesuit missionaries who worked and lived among the Hurons and Iroquois in Eastern Canada, he devoted his life to the service of the Indians.

Middleton spent his first days with the Bloods, patiently traveling by saddle horse over the vast open grasslands of their reserve. Thousands of horses and cattle grazed on the unbroken prairie, and scattered along the streams and in isolated spots in the uplands, he found small family groups of Bloods. He loved to visit the old Indians in their tepees and crude log homes, smoking with them the *kinnikinic*, an Indian tobacco made from the bark and leaves of sumac and willow.

To the west the imposing Rockies stood always in view, in particular a lone citadel of rock that stood apart from the rest like a fortress. The Blackfoot called this peak, which rose nearly a mile above the surrounding plains, Ninaistoko ("Chief Mountain") because it stood out like a brave leader. When Middleton lived near the North Peigan at Brocket, the Indians honored him by calling him by the same name.

Middleton started to learn the Blackfoot language that winter during his free hours at St. Paul's. He studied Archdeacon Tims' and Canon Stocken's translations of the gospel, and from his students' parents he learned rudimentary pronunciation. Soon he managed a basic vocabulary and acquired a rough command of the language's sound and intonation. For Christmas 1909 he attempted to preach in Blackfoot, and from then on he held a regular Sunday service in the language of his congregation. The Blackfoot admired his courage (all his predecessors had used translators for their sermons) and encouraged him to continue. He began putting prayers and hymns into Blackfoot, and the congregation grew.[4]

The center of Middleton's life now was Big Island. He repaired the dilapidated buildings as much as the mission's small budget allowed. For eleven years he pleaded with the Department of Indian Affairs for new quarters, but to no avail. The response was always the same: "The Government will consider your proposals and you will be favored with an answer in due course."[5] He found that a fresh coat of white paint could make the mission look as if it had had a complete face-lift, at least from a distance.

Progress was slow but steady. At the entrance to the school campus, on the left of the driveway, stood the hospital and gymnasium; on the right was the girls dormitory, which also served as the school's dining room and kitchen. Farther on was the boys residence, the rectory, the church (used as a schoolroom on weekdays), stables, a granary and outbuildings. It was a problem to obtain enough firewood for the hot-air furnace, and Middleton worried that the use of so many coal-oil lamps for lighting posed a fire hazard to the old frame buildings. He installed additional fire extinguishers, axes and fire pails, then worried that he had overextended the school's budget for the sake of fire safety.

When Middleton became principal, St. Paul's had thirty students from six to eighteen years of age. The enrollment rose to fifty in a few years, and to sixty-five by 1917. He believed that agriculture would be the salvation of the Bloods, and he modified the school program to emphasize it. The boys worked on the farm in the morning and spent the afternoons in the classroom, following the government-approved curriculum for Alberta's public schools. Middleton conducted a special evening class on modern methods of farming and care of livestock. The boys farmed forty acres and cultivated a four-acre kitchen garden. It proved such a success that within a few years the school sold surplus farm produce to neighboring settlers. While the boys worked in the fields, the girls learned cooking, needlework and general housekeeping. Middleton insisted that only English could be spoken in the classrooms and on the school grounds. Indian music and dancing were forbidden.[6] He reasoned that however cruel the regulations seemed, they were necessary if the Bloods were to compete with their white neighbors. He also included an hour of daily religious instruction, and every morning and evening he led the students in prayer.

It was hard to attract good teachers to the school, for the church could pay them only half of what the best city school board offered.[7] When Middleton arrived at St. Paul's, he met Katherine Underwood, a teacher he regarded as a perfect candidate. She was a young mission worker from Norwich, England, who had come to St. Paul's to teach in 1905. She was quiet, hardworking and greatly respected by the Bloods, who named her Sipistaki ("Owl Woman") because she kept such a good watch over their girls. In time Middleton and Miss Underwood fell in love, and on April 19, 1911, Archdeacon Tims officiated at their marriage. They had four children, but even with family duties, Katherine continued to work as the school nurse.[8]

Bishop Pinkham ordained Middleton a minister in 1913, and he dropped his first name, Sam, in favor of the initials S.H., which he thought was more befitting a minister and a school principal. Every week S.H. instructed the advanced students for half an hour on "the duties of British citizenship" and strongly encouraged patriotism among the Bloods. Portraits of King George V and Queen Mary were hung in the school's big dining room, and the Union Jack was flown every Sunday. S.H. even taught his students to eat as they did in the "Old Country." "Stay with your British teaching," he told them. "The fork is a left-hand instrument." He organized St. Paul's like his old grammar school at Ashby-de-la-Zouch in England with school uniforms, a prefect system and an Old Boys Association.[9]

Early on Middleton tried to establish a Boy Scout troop, but the boys showed little interest. Appealing to the Bloods' old warrior spirit, he then organized a cadet corps, which the sons and grandsons of the last great plains warriors welcomed with great enthusiasm. In no time Corps Commander Reverend S.H. Middleton had his unit in competitive trim, and in 1920 it won the R.B. Bennett Shield Trophy for the best all-round cadet corps in Alberta, beating sixty white units in the province.[10] Middleton made no secret of his admiration for the Carlisle Indian Residential School that Long Lance had attended. He tried to duplicate it on a very reduced budget and considerably smaller scale. He especially admired General Pratt, the founder of Carlisle, and in a letter to Pratt's daughter in 1935, he admitted that "for years I have eulogized his memory, and quoted him time and again."[11]

What infuriated Middleton was the government's stingy financial support. By treaty, the Dominion of Canada had promised the Blackfoot education, but then had failed to provide it by making inadequate grants to the churches to cover the expense of teachers and school facilities. When Long Lance arrived in August 1921, Middleton bitterly poured out all his grievances.

Long Lance's published story championed the Bloods and took on the government, much to Middleton's delight. Long Lance wrote that the Bloods were the most progressive tribe in Alberta.[12] The Blackfoot had sold nearly one half of their reserve, and the Sarcee leased a third of their land to the government, all to obtain the necessary farm equipment and housing that the Department of Indian Affairs had refused to provide. The Bloods, however, held on to every acre that was theirs. Without government money, they built their own houses and bought the farm equipment they needed. Somehow, Long Lance wrote, "they seemed to have acquired a desirable kick in their make-up that is not enjoyed to the same degree by their two brother bands." The Bloods refused "to lie in the feathered nests that most Indians like to wallow in, under the protecting wings of the government."

Long Lance described the Indians out haying, "hundreds of them, old and young . . . working silently on immense stacks of the golden stems, mowing and cutting, or turning over the summer fallow." The rye crop, even though the harvest was several weeks away, already reached one's chest. Long Lance knew about horses from his days with the Wild West Show, and he was impressed by the quality of the animals he found on the Blood Reserve. He noticed a few pintos, but "none of the ordinary cayuses, so commonly owned by Indians."

He gave Middleton most of the credit for the success of the Bloods, calling him "a powerful stimulant to character building among the younger Indians . . . a remarkable power for good among this tribe." He had scribbled his notes furiously while talking to Middleton, and inevitable errors crept in. Middleton told him of an old Blood warrior, Mountain Horse, and Long Lance recorded that he was the head chief of all the Bloods and not just one of the minor chiefs. Long Lance also ignored, in his enthusiasm for Middleton and the Anglican operation, the work of the Roman Catholic mission on the reserve. The Roman Catholic residential boarding school for the Bloods had roughly the same enrollment as St. Paul's.

When Long Lance's article appeared in the *Herald* on August 27, Middleton read it carefully. He was fascinated and puzzled by the man. It surprised him that Long Lance referred to a young Indian as a "buck" and quite bizarrely described a group of St. Paul's girls he met at Waterton Park as "a group of dusky daughters of the plains, not yet one generation away from savagery. . . ." He considered Long Lance extraordinary but also at times demonstrably non-Indian in his ease with strangers, his command of English, his firm handshake, his smartly tailored suits. Middleton reconciled this with the fact that, as a Cherokee, Long Lance indeed had been "civilized" for more than a century and was easily a couple of generations ahead of the Canadian Plains Indians. Still, the conundrum remained. Years later, Middleton would write of Long Lance, "He was an interesting personality, sometimes Indian, ofttimes white, but the two together — never. They did not blend. He was inwardly torn by strange conflicting emotions."[13]

Long Lance sent thirty copies of his story to St. Paul's and warmly thanked Middleton for his help.[14] A few months later Middleton wrote Long Lance to invite him to speak at the annual school reunion in mid-February, a big event that was attended by the graduates and friends of St. Paul's.[15] Long Lance accepted, and in a cheery note on January 15, he thanked Middleton "for the boosting which you have given me." He added, "I hope the Bloods will not be disappointed when they see what sort of an article you have been praising."

He arrived in Macleod for the second time on the noon train from Calgary on Saturday, February 11. Middleton met him at the depot and drove him to the mission on Big Island. This time the prairie was covered with drifts of snow.

All day the following Monday, St. Paul's prepared feverishly for the 9th Annual Re-Union of the Old Boys and Girls Association, which was to commence at six-thirty that evening. The girls cooked roasts in the kitchen and cut up potatoes, carrots, turnips and onions by the sackful. They baked fresh bread and prepared pies and cakes. The boys hauled in dry wood for the fires and scrubbed and decorated the school dining hall, then set freshly laundered sheets on the tables.

At dusk the wagons, drawn by frost-covered ponies, began to pull up at the school. The visitors thawed out in the hall, removed their coats and greeted one another. As the hall filled, Mr. and Mrs. Middleton entered with the five teachers and instructors and the distinguished visitor, Long Lance. They took their places at the head table directly under a huge Union Jack flanked by the portraits of King George V and Queen Mary. Throughout the dinner the older people, like Mountain Horse, spoke Blackfoot, but the younger Bloods talked among themselves in English.[16]

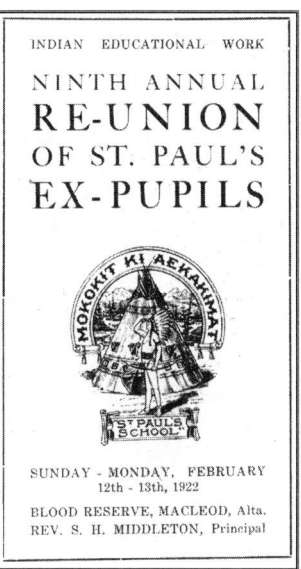

INDIAN EDUCATIONAL WORK

NINTH ANNUAL
RE-UNION
OF ST. PAUL'S
EX-PUPILS

SUNDAY - MONDAY, FEBRUARY
12th - 13th, 1922

BLOOD RESERVE, MACLEOD, Alta.
REV. S. H. MIDDLETON, Principal

The program for the reunion of St. Paul's alumni, 1922, when Long Lance was adopted by Chief Mountain Horse as "Buffalo Child."

When the dishes were cleared and tea was served, Middleton tapped his water glass, cleared his throat, and in a deep, commanding voice proposed a toast to His Majesty, King George V. Then, with everyone seated, he introduced the honored guest, "Captain Sylvester Chahuska Long Lance, Cherokee Indian . . . brilliant student and athlete at Carlisle, war hero in the Great War, distinguished journalist . . . all male students at St. Paul's would do well to try to imitate his outstanding career." Long Lance stood, resplendent in his blue Carlisle uniform, and proposed a toast to the former pupils of St. Paul's.[17] Then he spoke.

"The average Indian walks daily among worlds unrealized. He sees the pleasures and advantages of the white world in a sort of haze that forever denies them to him." Echoing General Pratt, he emphasized the message that "the pleasures and advantages of the white man [are] with a dash of initiative, grit and determination . . . as available to you as they are to him."[18] One of the St. Paul's graduates who had served overseas, Mike Mountain Horse, replied to the toast.[19]

Mike Mountain Horse's father, Old Mountain Horse, a man

Mountain Horse, Blood Indian chief, photographed during the annual Sun Dance ceremony in 1925.

in his midsixties, was given a quick translation of Long Lance's speech. He probably did not agree with everything Long Lance said, especially when he exhorted the Bloods to adopt the ways of the white man, but as an old warrior and as the father of three sons who had seen action with the Canadian Expeditionary Force, he admired courage. For his generation courage was still the most valued quality of a man's character, and he knew of Long Lance's war record.

Middleton hoped to present Long Lance as a role model for the young Bloods. He recalled that the elder Mountain Horse had helped with the ceremony by which Edward, Prince of Wales, was adopted by the Bloods during his Royal Tour of Canada in 1919.[20] Middleton asked Old Mountain Horse to give Long Lance, the Cherokee war hero, a Blackfoot name, and he gladly consented.

When the toasts and speeches ended, Mountain Horse motioned Long Lance to step forward and kneel with him on a buffalo robe in the center of the dining hall. Long Lance came forward with his usual assurance; then the Indians surrounded them. Mountain Horse, wearing an eagle-plume headdress, began the ceremony by taking from one of his sons a long, forked stick, which held a hot coal. He placed it on a metal pan and covered it with sweet grass. A pleasant fragrance wafted over the room. Mountain Horse held his hands in the smoke of the sweet grass, then stroked his arms and his chest to purify himself with its essence.

After a Blackfoot prayer Mountain Horse took red clay from a buckskin bag and carefully painted Long Lance's face with the sacred paint, which the Blackfoot believed had the power to ward off sickness and bring long life. As Long Lance knelt before him, the old Indian daubed his forehead, chin and both cheeks to represent the sun's daily course through the heavens, the forehead signifying the rising and the left cheek the setting sun.[21] After this Mountain Horse raised Long Lance to his feet and prayed again. In the old Indian mission building, two thousand miles from his home, the man born Sylvester Long in Winston–Salem had his wildest dream made real: spiritually he was being reborn a Plains Indian.

Mountain Horse placed his war bonnet on Long Lance's head. Then he and his wife chanted the war song of Buffalo Child, the Blackfoot gutturals giving the war cry a ferocious sound. The new Buffalo Child was to sing this song at all times of danger.

The ceremony over, Mountain Horse turned Long Lance around and abruptly pushed him away. In Indian society all stand at the same level. Having honored one with an adoption, the Bloods, aware of the perils of vanity, quickly cut him down to the status of every other warrior.[22]

Middleton explained later the exact words Mountain Horse had used when he gave Long Lance his new name: "Buffalo Child's bravery is talked of daily among the Blackfoot, Blood and Peigan Indians of these plains, and as you must henceforth be known by this honorable name among these tribes, you must ever endeavor to be the great Indian whose spirit now comes back to earth and enters your body."[23] Among the Bloods, Long Lance now replaced the warrior Buffalo Child.[24]

Long Lance probably posed for this photo the morning after his adoption as Buffalo Child at the Blood Reserve. It was subsequently used as an illustration in Maclean's in 1923.

The rest of the evening was given over to fun, with a "white" dance following the speeches and ceremonies. Long Lance loved to dance, and he sat out few of the waltzes, polkas and fox-trots that night. St. Paul's Old Boys and Girls rhythmically stepped around the newly adopted Blood, and he reveled in their attention. Before he left the next morning, he asked his missionary friend to photograph him in a Blood war bonnet and a Hudson's Bay Company blanket.[25] A new batch of clippings featuring Buffalo Child Long Lance would soon be pasted into his scrapbook.

Chapter 8

Long Lance, Plains Indian

Vancouver, British Columbia, 1922

By the end of the winter of 1922, Long Lance was ready to move on. By the spring, he was restless, even a little bored. For months he had been assigned to City Hall, trying to find some challenge in yet another debate on mill rates, snow removal or storm sewers. He was reckless enough to decide to try to liven things up. On the morning of March 29, Long Lance left his rooming house carrying a large paper bag containing a mask, matches and a fuse. When he arrived at City Hall, he went straight to the city engineer's office, where he was known, and without any trouble managed to obtain a gas inspector's bag and a large pressure gauge, which he took to the men's washroom on the main floor.

He spread out his paraphernalia on a wash basin, attached the pressure gauge to one of two leather handles on the outside, then attached the fuse to the gas inspector's bag. He stuffed all this back into the paper bag and walked upstairs to the mayor's office. From the anteroom he heard Mayor Sam Adams and the

Calgary City Hall, 1922, where Long Lance performed the prank that cost him his job at the Calgary Herald.

commissioners heatedly discussing what Long Lance had come to regard as "the totally unexciting question of city finances."[1]

Long Lance slipped the gas mask over his face, then ignited the fuse to his homemade "bomb" and opened the door to the meeting. He pushed the black satchel with the rapidly burning fuse just inside the doorway. Mayor Adams, facing the door, yelled and fled the room, colliding with his secretary on the way out. One commissioner dove under the conference table, while another, watching the fuse burn down, clenched his fists and smashed through three layers of glass in one of the office's west windows. He plunged ten feet to the ground, his feet running before he landed.

It was the biggest prank in Calgary in years, and two days later a rival newspaper, the *Albertan*, printed a poem to honor "the scheme of Lance's":

> Come, gather round my trusty friends
> And hear the ghastly tale;
> Whilst the world in laughter bends,
> The city hall doth wail. . . .[2]

The bomb prank once again shone the spotlight of celebrity on Long Lance. This cartoon, inaccurately depicting the scene, later appeared in the Toronto Star Weekly.

"Tellum Bigley," the *Albertan's* resident humorist, loved the prank. "Commissioner Samis wasn't scared when he saw the bomb," he wrote. "He merely ducked under the table so as to give the rest of the crowd room to get to the door."[3]

Colonel Woods, the *Herald's* strict, no-nonsense publisher, knew that Charlie Hayden, the kindhearted city editor, would not give Long Lance the punishment he deserved, so he called in C.O. Smith to act as hatchet man. When Long Lance arrived in the newsroom, Smith motioned him to his office, where he delivered a tongue-lashing and a stern lecture on the proprieties and responsibilities of a *Herald* reporter. Long Lance had disgraced his newspaper and insulted the city's elected officials. Abruptly and coldly Smith fired him.

In that evening's edition Colonel Woods and C.O. Smith apologized for the prank. "The *Herald* deeply regrets this occurrence and that this indignity to His Worship Mayor Adams and to the commissioners and other officers of the city was suffered by them through the act of a member of its staff, and tenders its sincere apologies to Mayor Adams and to the other City Hall officials affected by his conduct." Long Lance had already apologized to

Mayor Adams, and the mayor was good-spirited enough to see the fun of the joke. The mayor refused to accept the newspaper's apology and intervened on Long Lance's behalf,[4] but Colonel Woods would not relent. Long Lance was out.

He left Calgary in April and went by train to Vancouver, where he was welcomed by the mild, nearly summer weather of the Pacific Coast. Vancouver, with a population of two hundred thousand, was three times the size of Calgary. Downtown Vancouver was built at the base of a short peninsula that ended in the city's famous Stanley Park. To the northeast lay the section of Burrard Inlet known as Vancouver Harbour, protected by Stanley Park from the Gulf of Georgia. Three small Squamish Indian reserves—Capilano, Mission and Seymour Creek—faced the harbor on the mountainous North Shore.

Long Lance took a room at 906 Howe Street,[5] a block from busy Granville, one of the major shopping districts. Immediately south of his rooming house lay the industrial area of False Creek and beyond it the residential areas of Kitsilano, Point Grey and Shaughnessy. The tall burners of nearly a hundred sawmills on the north shore of False Creek and Burrard Inlet belched smelly pollution into the Vancouver sky.

Vancouver was not yet forty years old and owed its prosperity to its selection in 1886 as the western terminus of the Canadian Pacific Railway. A second transcontinental line was built to the year-round, ice-free port just before World War I.[6] The local newspapers had shared in the boom times, swelling on weekends to fifty or more pages. In 1922 the leading paper was the evening *Province*, with a circulation of sixty thousand, about three times that of the younger morning *Sun*.[7]

Long Lance decided, rightly, that the more sensationalist *Sun* would likely be interested in his Indian stories. He went to see Bert Stein, the city editor,[8] and brought out his scrapbook with his of articles on the Blackfoot, Sarcee and Blood Indians. He impressed Stein with his stories and dazzled him with all that

Chief Buffalo Child Long Lance—which was how he introduced himself when he arrived in Vancouver—had accomplished. The *Sun* agreed to buy a series of stories on the Indians of British Columbia for their Sunday edition.

The editor, basing his introduction on Long Lance's scrapbooks, glowingly presented his first story, which appeared in the *Sun* on May 7:

> Here's a regular story from a regular Indian. It was written by Chief Buffalo Child Long Lance of Calgary. He is one of the few outstanding figures of his race. He is a graduate of Carlisle Indian School and of St. John's Military Academy of Manlius, New York. He is the only Indian to be appointed to West Point, the United States Military Academy, by a president of the United States. Appointed by President Wilson in 1914. Relinquished this appointment one year later to go overseas with the Canadian troops. Went overseas as a private, was commissioned and rose to the rank of captain. Twice wounded and decorated with the *Croix de Guerre*.

Long Lance's warm reception in Vancouver was unusual, especially as it was afforded by the *Sun*, which had been fueling the fire of racism for months. A wave of "yellow peril" fear had washed over the province about this time. One out of fourteen of British Columbia's five hundred thousand inhabitants was of Chinese or Japanese descent. As if to sound the alarm, the *Sun* published *The Writing on the Wall* in August 1921, a tract urging vigilance against the Chinese and Japanese. To believe the author, Mrs. Glynn-Ward, the Chinese were repulsive characters, opium smokers who lived in filth, and the Japanese were agents of Imperial Japan, who were furiously buying up property at strategic locations on the coast. After the book appeared, the *Sun* praised the work as serving "to awaken those unbelievers in eastern Canada who still wonder why the West is crying out on its knees for new immigration legislation."[9] The sly reference to Long Lance being "one of the few outstanding figures of his race" was indicative of the newspaper's attitude.

Diamond Jenness, who regularly traveled throughout British Columbia after World War I, observed the ugly racial situation on the Pacific Coast. Jenness found that British Columbia Indians suffered the same invective as the Chinese and Japanese. The whites, he wrote, "spoke of the native population as 'Siwashes' and, for good measure, they occasionally added the epithet 'dirty.'" He wrote that everywhere on the coast, whether they worked as stevedores, fishers or cannery workers, "it was said that the Indians were shiftless and unreliable." Jenness noted that in the interior of the province, one or two villages even enforced their own Jim Crow system. In the town of Hazelton, for example, which had a population of three hundred whites and four hundred Indians, "no Indian might walk beside a white man or woman, or sit on the same side in the village church."[10] The situation was all too familiar to Long Lance.

Racial hate existed on the Indian side as well. In 1922 many Indians refused to speak to journalists in British Columbia. Franz Boas, the distinguished American anthropologist, discovered this animosity when he made his first field trip there in 1886. As one Cowichan Indian on Vancouver Island told him, "Whites look upon the Indians not as humans but as dogs." As a result the Indian said his people "did not want to explain their culture to outsiders, as they might laugh at things that were their laws, such as painted houses, and articles used for celebrating their festivals."[11]

Long Lance, as an Indian journalist with splendid credentials, broke through this barrier of distrust. One of his first contacts was Andy Paull, an articulate thirty-six-year-old Squamish Indian leader. He had attended a Roman Catholic residential school for six years on his home reserve of Mission. Paull had also spent two years learning the traditional ways of his elders in the Squamish settlements on Burrard Inlet and Howe Sound. The elders encouraged him to study the white man's legal system, and from 1907–11 Paull worked in the law office of Hugh St. Quentin Cayley in Vancouver. The young Indian had a fine, retentive mind, and he acquired a good general knowledge of Canadian law and legal procedures, and memorized substantial sections of the statutes relating to Indian affairs in British Columbia.[12]

When Paull was growing up, British Columbia Indians felt the full weight of the provincial government's injustices against them. In Ontario and the prairie provinces, first British and then Canadian authorities claimed absolute sovereignty over all the land but still recognized that Indians had certain land rights on the principle of prior occupancy. Through the numbered treaties on the prairies, the Crown officially "extinguished" native title by an exchange: the Crown promised the Indians reserves, varying from one-quarter to one square mile per family of five, and specified trapping, fishing or farming equipment, annual treaty payments and schools. In return the Indians gave up their land claims, retaining only their fishing and hunting rights in the surrendered territory.

In the 1850s the Indians on Vancouver Island were approached to cede lands, but when the economy-minded colonial legislature refused to make any further payments after 1859, the surrenders ceased. Successive British Columbia governments (even after the province entered Confederation in 1871) held for over a century to a simple premise: the Indians have no justifiable land rights. Without negotiation the provincial government, on its own authority, took Indian lands and then assigned small tracts to the respective bands as their reserves.[13]

The Indians' small numbers enabled the British Columbia government to proceed as it wished in the late nineteenth century. At the moment of European contact about a third of all Canada's native people lived along the Pacific coastline and along the major western rivers flowing through it. Here the climate was mild with rich and easily available food resources. The natives had no agriculture and depended on abundant wild roots, berries, salmon, halibut and eulachon (candlefish, prized for its oil) as their staples. The settlement of the area by outsiders forced them from their traditional lands, however, and, as happened on the plains, diseases against which they had no natural immunity devastated the tribes, reducing their numbers by as much as ninety percent.[14] As the nineteenth century ended, many lost hope and self-respect. They could not speak English and had no grasp of the British legal system. The government could ignore them.

Long Lance met Andy Paull ten years after the young Squamish had returned from his four years of study with Hugh Cayley, the Vancouver lawyer. On his first visit Long Lance took the ferry across to North Vancouver, then walked to Mission. He could see in the distance the silver-painted towers of the reserve's Roman Catholic church. Soon he reached the white picket fence that set off the thirty acres left by the provincial government to a band of about one hundred Indians. He walked along a graveled street lined with small houses, and in the yards he noticed the Squamish's dugout racing canoes. Finally he reached the small frame building that was Andy Paull's house.[15]

Paull was smaller than the average Blackfoot. The Pacific Coast Indians had the dark eyes and black hair of the Plains Indians, but they were built entirely differently, more compact and powerful, with large shoulders and small legs. Their physique, it was said, came from centuries in canoes.[16] At school Paull was nicknamed "white boy" for the way he easily mingled and sometimes imitated those of the dominant society around him. He was an extrovert and, like Long Lance, loved sports. He played and coached baseball, lacrosse, boxing and canoe racing.[17] Long Lance talked of his days at the *Calgary Herald*, and Paull would have remembered the name of the newspaper. Cayley, the lawyer he worked for in Vancouver, had been one of the *Herald*'s first editors during the time of the Riel Rebellion of 1885.[18]

Long Lance wrote to his friend the Reverend S.H. Middleton and described Paull as "one of the smartest Indians I have ever met."[19] He was impressed by Paull's familiarity with the legal aspects of the Indian situation in British Columbia, and he was intrigued by the political organization of the British Columbia Indians, for which Paull was the provincial secretary. In 1915 the coastal tribes under the leadership of Paull and the Reverend Peter Kelly, a Haida minister, established the first province-wide native organization, calling it the Allied Tribes.[20] In his letter to Middleton, Long Lance expressed surprise at finding such a well-developed sense of organization among the British Columbia Indians. "You can tell the young fellows there that they are way ahead of us on the plains."[21]

On Sunday, May 21, the *Sun* carried Long Lance's story on the Squamish. Long Lance had relied on Paull, Chief Mathias of the Capilano Reserve and what he called "representative members" of the tribe. Paull, who strongly distrusted Indian agents and the Department of Indian Affairs, greatly influenced Long Lance, who a short year earlier had written that Canadian Indian policy was "clear-sighted." This time Long Lance gently criticized the federal Department of Indian Affairs, questioning such actions as the outlawing of the Indian potlatch.

For years the Department of Indian Affairs and the missionaries had tried to destroy Indian society and culture. The missionaries spoke against totem poles and traditional carvings. They wanted Indians to work, dress and pray like Euro-Canadians. Then in the 1880s, they attacked the famous potlatch ceremony of the Pacific Coast Indians. The potlatch was a great event at which the host gave away huge amounts of food and valuable gifts to all his guests. In its various forms the potlatch validated the transfer of property, recognized the change from adolescence to adulthood, recorded marriage arrangements or settled personal quarrels. The government and the missionaries disapproved of this "wasteful, heathen" custom, and in time the holding of and attendance at a potlatch was made a criminal offense. Since November 1921 a number of indictments had been secured against Indians for participating in potlatches. In early May 1922 twenty-three of those convicted, including a grandmother, were serving prison sentences of not less than two months each in the Oakalla Prison.[22]

Paull and other Squamish Indians explained the age-old potlatch custom to Long Lance, and in his story for the *Sun*, Long Lance wrote, "The potlatch does not entail the giving away of anything. The Indian who holds it is either paying a debt to his guests for some material kindness which they have rendered him or for a similar potlatch rendered to him in the past, or is simply giving away what he knows he will get back."[23]

During Long Lance's first month in Vancouver, the Methodist Church was fighting a campaign to convince a local service club, the Gyro Club, to drop the word potlatch as the name of its week-long summer carnival. In defense of both the name and "the respected custom," Long Lance wrote a forceful article that appeared in the *Sun* on Friday, May 19. He argued that "the law governing the Potlatch is at once oppressive and antagonising." The law was so loosely worded, he wrote, that "an agricultural show or an exhibition may be held as a Potlatch in the eyes of the law." He asked why the Indian was "compelled to throw aside every native custom that formerly gave him self-respect . . . why cannot he be allowed to remain a decent Indian instead of being forced into a ragged nondescript?"

The whole potlatch issue and his association with Andy Paull led Long Lance to reassess his views of the Indians' future. Until that summer he usually repeated General Pratt's assimilationist goals, a philosophy that had been thoroughly drummed into his mind at the Carlisle Indian School. After a month in British Columbia, he began to see things differently.

From May to July, by steamer and train, Long Lance traveled hundreds of miles, visiting bands along the coast. He produced feature stories for the *Sun* every Sunday. They read well. He knew how to collect information quickly, how to use a telling anecdote and how to make the story vivid and appealing to his readers. When he interviewed old Indians who spoke little or no English, he used young graduates of the Indian residential schools as interpreters. He did his homework, too, reading all the standard books available, including John McLean's *The Indians of Canada* (1889) and *Canadian Savage Folk: The Native Tribes of Canada* (1896) and a recent study by Franz Boas, the American anthropologist.[24]

On June 4 the *Sun* carried Long Lance's account of the Nanaimo Indians on Vancouver Island. The next week it featured his story on the peoples of the Lower Fraser Valley ("Chilliwack Indians Possess Richest Store of Folklore"). On June 18 he reported on the Haidas, the Indians of the Queen Charlotte Islands to the north of Vancouver Island ("Name of Haida Struck Panic to Indian Heart"). In late June and July he sent in stories from the interior of British Columbia on the history, legends and current state of the Kootenays, Lillooets, Thompsons and Shuswap.[25]

As he traveled throughout the province, Long Lance increasingly became aware of the untenable position in which the Indians of British Columbia found themselves. On the mainland, apart from a large tract of land in the northeastern corner of the province, included in Treaty Eight in 1899, there had been no attempts to buy Indian land. Even their rights to the small land areas arbitrarily allotted them as reserves were not always respected. When Long Lance visited the Shuswap Reserve at Kamloops, he reported to S.H. Middleton that "the Western Canadian Ranching Company [is] pumping water right off the reserve, while the Indians' crops are literally burning up for lack of moisture." And, he added, "I meet many cases of this sort every day."[26]

At Nanaimo, Long Lance met the most influential Native leader in British Columbia, Peter Kelly, chair of the Allied Tribes. Kelly had been born in 1885 in a Haida longhouse on the Queen

Charlotte Islands. His parents, of noble Haida lineage (and by 1885 both Christian converts), sent him to Coqualeetza Institute, the Methodist boarding school for Indians at Sardis, just outside Chilliwack, sixty miles east of Vancouver. At Coqualeetza he attended an elementary school before becoming a teacher among his people at Skidegate in the Queen Charlottes. He was the first Indian teacher among the Haida. Gifted, energetic and determined to succeed, Kelly studied long and intensely. Through home study he qualified for entrance to the Methodist Columbian College at New Westminster. Here, with four nonnative students, he studied for three years. Upon his graduation in 1916, he was ordained.

Kelly became known among his people as Klee-Als, "the Orator" and as the driving force behind the Allied Tribes. He proved himself a capable and popular minister both to the Nanaimo Reserve and to the neighboring communities of Cassidy, Cedar, Extension, Chase River and South Wellington.[27]

Long Lance described Kelly in the *Sun* as "a man of commanding appearance. . . . Barely more than thirty, he possesses the strong, athletic build of the Haida, plus their strong facial characteristics. . . ."[28] He found Kelly more restrained and aristocratic than Andy Paull, who was immensely likable and down to earth.

In the summer of 1922 Long Lance had an opportunity to see Kelly and Paull in action. The Allied Tribes staged an important meeting in Vancouver, where fifty chiefs met with Charles Stewart, Prime Minister Mackenzie King's minister of the interior and of mines, and superintendent general of Indian Affairs; and Duncan Campbell Scott, the deputy superintendent general, the most senior civil servant in the Department of Indian Affairs. The seven-hour meeting took place on July 23 in the Vancouver Post Office building. As Long Lance reported in the *Sun*, the Allied Tribes asked for "full title to their reserve lands, as enjoyed by the other tribes of the Dominion, and for better education facilities and medical attention for the natives of this province."[29] To Long

Lance's delight, Stewart and his cohorts met the most spirited delegation of Indians they had ever seen. "There were no folded-arm, dignified speeches by ex-warriors and chiefs," he wrote to S.H. Middleton, "but instead, there was a superb firing line of brainy, quick-witted young men who knew the Indian Act and all its tangents as well as the Honourable Dunk [Duncan Campbell Scott] himself."[30]

Long Lance's association with the *Sun* ended with his final submission in late July. He had never intended to stay long in British Columbia, the agreement with the newspaper having been only for the weekly series. In May, when he was in the midst of his travels throughout the province, he had written to Middleton to tell him of his next project. "If things work out right," he wrote on May 11, "I am planning to go from here to Regina and write up the Saskatchewan Indians for the *Leader*, and on to Winnipeg, for the Manitobans—and so on down the line, finishing up with a book."

In the summer of 1922 it was time to move on, time to reinvent himself yet again. The public knew the "real Indian" as a mounted horseman in beadwork, moccasins, embroidered jacket and feather headdress. Through movies, stage productions and the rotogravure sections of the weekend newspapers, they had been conditioned to recognizing the plains warrior as the genuine article. If he advertised himself as a Cherokee, he knew his writings would have little impact. The Cherokee of Oklahoma, his current tribal designation, had already adjusted to the white man and wore business suits or workman's overalls. This did not sell. It made more sense to become a Plains Indian. Though his induction into the Bloods of Alberta had been purely ceremonial, he would make the title real.

Before Long Lance left Vancouver, he wrote in his last article in the *Sun*, on August 27, of his "fellow-tribesmen, the Blood Indians of Alberta."[31] Taking out his now extensive scrapbook, he carefully removed all references to Cherokee and wrote Blackfoot or Blood in pencil over the blank spaces.

Chapter 9

Talking to the Elders

REGINA, SASKATCHEWAN, 1922

A few days before Long Lance arrived in Regina, the capital of the province of Saskatchewan, hundreds of local citizens had gathered at City Hall to hear their city's first radio broadcast, which beamed a quavering "Rule Britannia" to the city of thirty-five thousand people.[1]

He checked his bags and, as in the other cities, walked first to the local newspaper office, that of the *Regina Leader*. As was often the case, he needed money. Long Lance was not one to hoard his hard-won income; he spent it on clothes, food, entertainment, women and travel. He liked to live well. He produced again his scrapbooks with articles on the Sarcee, Squamish, Haida and a dozen other groups for the managing editor, who was suitably impressed. Journeymen reporters with this flair for feature writing did not come by often, and Long Lance's ability to handle a story was quickly apparent. He was no cub reporter anymore, but an experienced professional who knew how to read unfamiliar situations, how to ingratiate himself, how to get the "goods" and how to make sense of it all — and he knew what editors wanted.

The managing editor of the *Leader* sensed immediately the news value of a series of articles on the Indians of Saskatchewan, especially after studying what Long Lance had produced in British Columbia. He told him that in Regina one hardly ever saw Indians,[2] yet they were all over, out there in isolated corners of the province. He told Long Lance that the *Leader* would be happy to buy four feature articles for the Saturday edition.

But where to go in this huge province that started in the south at the American border and pushed all the way up to the subarctic? Saskatchewan had sixty-eight Indian reserves,[3] and Long Lance could not visit all of them, not in a province this big and this sparsely populated. He went to see Bill Graham, the Indian commissioner for Western Canada, who worked out of an office in the Canada Life building. Graham, a short man in his midfifties, was a pudgy fellow with a peg leg, the result of a boyhood accident, but he was an energetic, no-nonsense administrator. He had joined the Indian Department when he was eighteen, and by 1922 he had served thirty-eight years. He had risen from a lowly agency clerk in Manitoba to the Indian agent of the File Hills Band in Saskatchewan in 1896 to inspector of all the Indian agents in southern Saskatchewan in 1904. Finally in 1918 he became Indian commissioner for Western Canada. During the war he organized nonnative farmers to work twenty-one thousand acres of reserve land under what was known as the Great Production Movement, and he nearly doubled the acreage under cultivation by the Indians themselves.[4]

Graham's secretary was his wife's cousin, Alice Tye,[5] an attractive woman who took to Long Lance immediately. She had never encountered an Indian quite like him, never one quite so sophisticated and well-spoken. He seemed to have been everywhere and to have done everything.

Commissioner Graham got down to business with Long

Lance in short order, starting with his two favorite subjects: Indian education and Indian farming. For twenty years he had worked to develop a model Indian agricultural settlement in the File Hills, about sixty miles northeast of Regina. With help from the principals of the neighboring Protestant and Roman Catholic residential schools, he had personally selected Indian graduates for the program at the Peepeewesis Reserve. If the young men agreed to join the agricultural colony, he had them placed on their own farms. The Indian Department laid out roads running north and south every half mile and east and west every mile. The young Indians built their own houses of whitewashed hewed logs and covered the one-and-one-half-story buildings with red painted shingle roofs. Within ten years twenty-five heads of families lived in the colony.

File Hills was Commissioner Graham's answer to "the Indian problem," he proudly informed Long Lance. He believed that Indian graduates, under strong management and control, could become good farmers. At File Hills he constantly brought in agricultural experts to lecture on new farming techniques. During the first year or two of an ex-pupil's life on the reserve, the farm instructor visited him nearly every day. Commissioner Graham boasted that he ruled File Hills with an iron hand: fiddle dances, powwows and all tribal ceremonies that he considered to be a hindrance to progress were forbidden.[6]

Long Lance listened politely, but he must have been appalled. Peepeewesis sounded more like an Indian prison camp than a new Native paradise on earth. Always curious, he announced that he would like to see File Hills first. On August 8, suitcase in hand, Long Lance set off by train for Balcarres to visit the four File Hills reserves: Little Black Bear, Star Blanket, Okanese and Commissioner Graham's beloved Peepeewesis. He enjoyed traveling through the rolling country interspersed with beautiful small lakes and groves of cottonwood trees.

At File Hills Long Lance could see for himself that Graham's claims were exaggerated if not false. And he claimed to have uncovered a scandal, the story of how Graham had "pulled the wool over" the eyes of Charles Stewart, superintendent general of Indian Affairs. On his way back to Ottawa in midsummer, just days before Long Lance's visit, the influential federal minister had stopped in Saskatchewan to check out Commissioner Graham's showpiece operation. Graham, anxious to impress the new Liberal appointee, went out of his way to convince Stewart that all was well on the western reserves. On September 10 Long Lance wrote to S.H. Middleton:

> The agent had received instructions from powers above, situated not far from here, to keep the fact that the minister was to come through, from all Indians. Hence, when the royal car rolled through, the Indians, the few who happened to see it along the trail, thought it was a party of tourists. The route of the car naturally led through a beautifully "prepared" route; that is, one which had been planted very carefully with wheat and oats—and to add the desired kick of nonchalance, nice little patches of summer fallow were very studiously perfected here and there along the chosen trail. All of which goes to show what a great, self-supporting man we have made out of the Indian during the past few years. . . .

Commissioner Graham's decoy worked, and his job (Graham was a Conservative appointee) was safe. Stewart returned to Ottawa convinced of the "splendid results" achieved at File Hills. He told the House of Commons that he found young Indian people "were making as great a success of farming as were their white brothers in the surrounding territory."[7] For the next eight years Stewart continued to cite File Hills as a great success story, heaping most of the credit on Commissioner Graham.

Of all his portfolios, which included Interior, Mines and

Immigration, the Indian Department seemed the least of Stewart's worries. Statistically it could be proven that the number of Indians had declined. In Stewart's own province of Alberta, the Indian population had fallen from about eighteen thousand in the 1870s to less than six thousand by the 1920s.[8] The federal government's own experts, the Oxford-trained anthropologists Diamond Jenness and Marius Barbeau, confirmed that the Indians were a vanishing people. In 1931 Barbeau wrote, "At present the indications point convincingly to the extinction of the race."[9] The following year Jenness commented in his *Indians of Canada*, "Doubtless all the tribes will disappear. Some will endure only a few years longer, others, like the Eskimo, may last several centuries." Duncan Campbell Scott, the Indian Department's senior civil servant, questioned the expenditure of monies to provide medical and social services to a "dying race" of one hundred thousand people, who constituted only one percent of Canada's population.[10]

Long Lance liked Stewart, a plain man brought up under pioneer conditions in Alberta who had earned a reputation as one who brought common sense to the solution of public problems.[11] In a letter to Middleton, however, Long Lance astutely observed,

> I think he is sincere and that he is a darned sight better specimen than many who are under him. But—I am afraid that these underlings are going to succeed so completely in pulling the wool over his eyes as he goes about, that, in the end, all of his apparent pep and good intentions are going to be dissipated by much misunderstanding of true facts.[12]

Commissioner Graham was one of these underlings. Duncan Campbell Scott was another, and he was by far the more damaging and dangerous of the two. Scott, the distinguished poet and intellectual,[13] was the tactician, always searching for answers to the "Indian problem." In 1919 Scott enthusiastically identified what he saw as "the millennium of those engaged in Indian work":

. . . all the quaint old customs, the weird and picturesque ceremonies, and the sun dance and the potlatch and even the musical and poetic native languages
shall be as obsolete as the buffalo and the tomahawk,
and the last tepee of the northern wilds [will] give place
to a model farmhouse. In other words, the Indian shall
become one with his neighbour in his speech, life and
habits, thus conforming to that worldwide tendency
towards universal standardization which would appear
to be the essential underlying purport of all modern
social evolution.[14]

Long Lance's prediction that the underlings would succeed
in pulling the wool over Stewart's eyes proved entirely correct. In
1927 the government denied the Indian claim to British Columbia and further expanded the Department of Indian Affairs'
restrictive controls. In 1930 in the House of Commons, Charles
Stewart energetically defended the "poolroom amendment" to
the Indian Act, a law that made an Indian liable to a fine of up to
twenty-five dollars or imprisonment of up to thirty days merely for
frequenting a poolroom.[15]

All his life Long Lance had been taught the superiority of
the white race and the need for the white man to direct and guide
the "lower" groups. Yet now he wanted to help the Plains Indians
fight back, to resist their subjugation. He traveled from File Hills
to other reserves in the Qu'Appelle Valley: Piapot, Muscowpetung, Pasquah, Standing Buffalo. He visited the Assiniboine
Reserve at Sintaluta. He tried to spread the idea that the Plains
Indians must organize to protect themselves against the likes of
Graham and Scott.

In some respects it was worse to be an Indian in Western
Canada than "colored" in the South, and nobody was more aware
of it than Long Lance. A band member required the Indian
agent's permission to travel off the reserve. Before he could sell

his hay, grain or livestock, he needed a permit. Even holding a traditional Indian dance required the agent's consent. Writing in 1923, the Reverend Edward Ahenakew, a Plains Cree minister, summed up the situation: "We have been brought up as children, treated as children, made to act according to rules and regulations that are not our own, and at the command of officials whom we do not always respect."[16]

Traveling throughout Saskatchewan, Long Lance became convinced of the need for the Indians to do something. He pointed to the treaty promises and showed how the government had reneged by not providing adequate education and medical care. From Muscowpetung Reserve, just north of Regina, he wrote S.H. Middleton on September 10, "I am getting each chief and each leading young man on every reserve in touch with the secretary of the Allied Tribes of B.C., so that he can explain the workings of their organization and help them out in details of a more intricate nature. In other words I am trying to get everybody in touch with each other."

During his youth in the South, Long Lance learned how to hide his true feelings. When he met Commissioner Graham, he knew enough not to volunteer any information concerning his political work with the Indians. He even used Graham's office as a mail drop, swapping jokes with him and using Alice Tye's typewriter to type up his articles.[17] He worked silently, confiding only in Middleton and possibly in George Gooderham of the Blackfoot Reserve, who likewise regarded Commissioner Graham as "dictatorial."[18]

At a dozen reserves in Saskatchewan, Long Lance ate bannock with the Indians in their homes and smoked *kinnikinic* with the old men. He interviewed elders, such as seventy-year-old Night Owl on the Starblanket Reserve near Regina.[19] The old people had confidence in their values and were passionate about passing them on to their children and grandchildren.

On every visit, Long Lance picked up more stories of resent-

Long Lance interviewed and photographed Night Owl and his wife in autumn 1922 at the Starblanket Reserve near Regina. Such interviews fueled Long Lance's sincere desire to become a spokesperson for Plains Indians.

ment against the white man. In the Qu'Appelle Valley, the older Cree told him of their bitter disappointment at the Canadian government's failure to enact the provisions of the treaties. They recalled what the late Chief Piapot, one of the major leaders of the Plains Cree, had said. Until his death he had been intimately involved in the treaty process and in its aftermath. "The white people are using our wood, our hay and killing our game," he said. "In order to become sole masters of the land they put us on small reserves as big as my hand and made promises as long as my arm, but the next year the promises were shorter, and they get shorter every year until now they are about the length of my finger — and they keep only half of that."[20]

Probably the most articulate of the Indian leaders that Long Lance met was Dan Kennedy, or Ochankugahe, "the Pathmaker." He belonged to the Assiniboine Band at Carry-the-Kettle's Reserve, about fifty miles east of Regina. Born in 1874 Kennedy had known the last days of the Assiniboine's free way of life before they settled on their reserve in 1882. He had been sent to a residential school and, as one of the most promising students, had gone on to study at St. Boniface College in Winnipeg.[21]

Long Lance met the Pathmaker in the autumn of 1922, when the air was sharp and chill and the poplar leaves were turning to gold. From the railway station at Sintaluta, where the grain elevators hovered like skyscrapers, he walked along the straight dirt road toward a substantial-looking farmhouse that he had been told was Kennedy's. It was conspicuous among the one-room log cabins, all nearly hidden by stacks of split wood piled up by the doors. The Indians' dogs barked as he entered the yard, then playfully romped about him as he shut the gate.

Kennedy looked remarkably like Long Lance himself. He was forty-seven, but appeared as young as Long Lance, who was thirty-one. The Pathmaker was handsome and powerful, and despite certain warriorlike features, his smile was kindly and warm. He invited Long Lance inside and told him he had just finished his harvest of three hundred acres of grain using his own threshing machine. Kennedy also owned forty head of cattle.[22] As they talked Kennedy explained the frustrations of living under the Indian Act and the resident agent's strict supervision. In his youth the Indian agents had made life on the reserve "a veritable concentration camp."[23] Things had improved, he said, but much of the government paternalism remained. Kennedy agreed with Long Lance that Indians needed political organization. Long Lance reported to S.H. Middleton that, for his efforts to spread the

Long Lance's photo of Chief Carry-the-Kettle and his wife was selected as one of the illustrations in his fabricated autobiography Long Lance, *published by the Cosmopolitan Book Corporation in 1928.*

idea, Kennedy presented him with a gift of a beautifully decorated firebag.[24]

Long Lance's special gift as a journalist was his ability to draw people out. He knew how to interact with Native people, particularly the mission-educated. With their help as interpreters, he could contact the older men who were eager to tell their stories of the "buffalo days." Through Kennedy he met the oldest Plains Indian warrior left in western Canada, Chief Carry-the-Kettle. At that time, the aged chief wore the coat given to him by the Canadian government. How incongruous to see the ancient

145

Assiniboine leader wearing what was essentially a mercantile marine officer's coat in the middle of the Canadian plains. Inmates of the Kingston federal penitentiary in Ontario made the blue serge coats and trousers that the western treaties stipulated be given to chiefs and headsmen.[25]

Chief Carry-the-Kettle, believed to be 107 years old in late 1922, had been on war parties when Sitting Bull and Crowfoot were infants. Long Lance talked to him through an interpreter and gained even greater respect for the wisdom and integrity of the elders.

Later, Long Lance wrote,

> Though Chief Carry-the-Kettle had killed more than a hundred men on the war path, there was something in his face that was truly spiritual—a remarkable gleam of human goodness that made him bigger in my eyes than any man I have seen. When he had to refer to his killings on the war path, he did it with a whimsical air of apology which made it evident that it was distasteful to him. In spite of his destructive record, Chief Carry-the-Kettle was one of those men in whose fearless hands a person would gladly place his life, if it depended on a matter of fair judgment and the kindness of human nature.[26]

By the end of autumn, Long Lance was acquiring a more accurate grasp of Indian life past and present. He felt at ease on the reserves. Throughout December Long Lance summarized in the *Leader* his interviews with the Cree, Sioux, Ojibwa (Chippewa) and Assiniboine. As the distinguished Western Canadian historian Hugh A. Dempsey has written, in these articles (and others he would write in Western Canada), Long Lance "was carrying out valuable field work at a time when few ethnologists, and even fewer journalists, were concerned about the history of the Indian."[27]

CHAPTER 10

Long Lance, Native Rights Advocate

WINNIPEG, MANITOBA, 1923–24

*L*ong Lance felt awkward and insecure in his new Plains Indian identity. While in Saskatchewan he sought to solidify it. On February 4,[1] in Regina, Long Lance had two photographs taken of himself in his "tribal regalia."[2] Not wanting to leave any possibility of doubt about his plains origin, he appeared in buckskin pants and vest, wearing a tobacco pouch and a headdress. He even borrowed a wig with two long braids to cover his cropped hair.

To the old Indians, of course, these portraits must have looked ridiculous. In the 1920s the tribes' distinctive styles of dress had not yet blended. In the photographs, however, Long Lance wore a Blackfoot vest, a Blood tobacco pouch, Crow Indian pants—worn backwards—and a headdress used in the Chicken Dance.[3] To anyone not familiar with Indian dress, doubtless he looked authentic.

Long Lance in full festive regalia. The pants probably came from the Crows in Montana, the tobacco pouch from the Bloods, the vest from the Blackfoot. On his head Long Lance wore a wig and the headdress used in the Chicken Dance.

In early November, Long Lance justified his decision to assume a Plains Indian identity to S.H. Middleton. He explained that he had not lived with his own people since he was sixteen and that he now knew more about the Indians of Western Canada and the Pacific Coast than he did of his "own progenitors." By presenting himself as a Blood, he could, he added, give his writings "an additional touch of interest." He concluded, "Furthermore, I believe that as a Canadian Indian, which I have become in toto, I can do more for Indians who need something done for them."[4]

Middleton was perplexed, and he took nearly three months to reply to Long Lance. The decision upset the missionary though he could understand how Long Lance would enhance his credibility if he wrote on the Indians of Western Canada as one of them, instead of as an American Cherokee. Middleton rationalized that Long Lance, through his writing and personal contacts, could help change negative views of Indian culture. After some apparent hesitation, the missionary accepted Long Lance's new literary identity. When he replied in early February 1923, he ended his letter, "Write soon, the longer the letter—the better."[5]

Long Lance also told Commissioner Graham of his decision, but there was not the slightest problem in this quarter. Commissioner Graham already idealized Long Lance as the Indian athlete, the Indian war hero and the successful Indian writer. He invited Long Lance to Regina's Armistice Ball. Years later Long Lance recalled the "look of pride on his face as he took me from guest to guest, introducing me as Captain Long Lance."[6] The fact of the matter was that Commissioner Graham was delighted that Long Lance chose to present himself as a Western Canadian Indian, as, in a sense, one of his own.

When Long Lance arrived in Winnipeg early in 1923, he followed his usual routine. After selling himself to the editors of the *Tribune*, the newspaper agreed to buy a series of stories on the Manitoba Indians. That winter he crossed the province by train from the Sioux Reserve at Oak River, in the southwestern corner, to the Peguis Saulteaux (Ojibwa) Reserve immediately north of Winnipeg. By dogsled he visited the Crees on the southwestern shore of Lake Winnipeg.

The *Tribune* liked his work and asked him to become a regular contributor. One of the two photographs he had brought from Regina graced his first article, and the *Tribune* captioned it, "Arrayed in the full regalia of his tribe, Chief Buffalo Child Long Lance . . . presents a picturesque and striking appearance."[7] Luckily for him, few Indians then lived in Winnipeg, and there were fewer students of native culture. His bizarre, pan-Indian costume escaped comment or criticism.

During his first winter in Winnipeg, a more cosmopolitan city than Regina, rumors of Long Lance and his accomplishments raced through the city, and he did not discourage them. In May 1923 the *Tribune* described him as "the youngest chief west of the Great Lakes and one by blood inheritance." Garnett Clay Porter, another journalist working in Winnipeg at the time, understood that Long Lance held two university degrees. Long Lance managed to convince Professor W.T. Allison of the Department of English at the University of Manitoba, and the *Tribune*'s literary editor, that he had won the Italian War Cross as well as the *Croix de Guerre*.[8]

Inevitably Long Lance received numerous invitations to speak, and he accepted nearly all requests. He was at ease at the podium. His favorite topic was "The Red Man, Past and Present." Through experience Long Lance had mastered the basics of public speaking—voice modulation, gestures, humor, maintaining eye contact with the audience. He spoke to gatherings of authors, to church and local service clubs.[9]

Winnipeg served as his home base for the next four winters. While the Panama Canal had hurt the city by allowing Vancouver to take over the western markets it had once supplied, Winnipeg still remained the most important city in Western Canada in the 1920s. "The Chicago of the North" had great railway marshalling yards, repair shops, roundhouses and grain-handling facilities. Downtown Winnipeg was the financial heart of Western Canada, home to the head offices of the chartered banks and the trust and insurance companies. From 1901 to 1911 a million immigrants passed through Winnipeg's gates, many staying. The population rose from 42,000 in 1901 to 140,000 by 1911 and to 180,000 by 1921.[10]

Of all the Canadian cities in which he had lived, Long Lance found Winnipeg the most European. In the streets he saw Mennonite and Hutterite farmers in their Old World dress. He

Photo momento given by Long Lance to his "old friend," Fred O'Malley of the Winnipeg Tribune. *Signed, "Chief."*

mingled with men and women with broad Russian, Greek and Slavic faces. In spite of their ever-increasing numbers, a strict quota system ensured that all but a small number of Jews and Slavs, regardless of their academic standing, were kept out of the Manitoba Medical College.[11] Discrimination against Jews and foreigners in the job market was nearly universal. The ethnic division between North and South Winnipeg had increased during the thirty-seven–day General Strike of 1919, when the strikers of the northern working-class area were pitted against the middle and upper classes of South Winnipeg.

Long Lance duplicated one of the Human Spider's feats by standing on his head on the parapet of a skyscraper in Winnipeg. The photo appeared in the Toronto Star Weekly.

As an Indian and as a successful journalist, Long Lance escaped much of this abuse and strife although on his first visit to the Fort Garry Hotel, a doorman refused him entry. When his friends at the *Tribune* privately complained, the hotel management promptly apologized to him.[12]

Reporter Allan Bill, then in his midtwenties, stayed in the same rooming house as Long Lance, which was close to the *Tribune* at Smith Street and Graham Avenue. Bill got to know him as well as Long Lance would allow. He regarded Long Lance as "a good-natured soul . . . built like a wedge" but a man "who never harmed anyone."[13] Always Long Lance was out for good times, and rarely could he resist a dare. Once a fellow reporter challenged him to duplicate one of the feats of Bill Strother, the Human Spider. Long Lance responded immediately by standing on his head on the parapet of what was then considered a sky-scraper in Winnipeg.[14]

After work Long Lance and Charles L'Ami, one of the *Tribune*'s editorial writers, walked to the local YMCA and boxed. After this, still with energy to burn, Long Lance ran the indoor track and vaulted on the parallel bars. He was invited to all the newspaper parties and never played the wallflower. When the "black bottom" dance rage hit Western Canada, Long Lance was one of the first Winnipeggers to try it.[15]

Again, still somewhat insecure in his new identity as a Plains Indian, Long Lance overdid his performances. One New Year's Eve, the *Tribune*'s editor, Wilfred (Biff) MacTavish, invited the staff to a gathering at his home on Oak Street. Long Lance was there, too, and after some coaxing he announced that he would do a war dance, right there in the dining room. L'Ami imitated the sound of tom-toms on the keyboard as best he could and out came Long Lance, "the chief," wearing a headband and two towels as a breechcloth. He began slowly, and, with sweat gleaming on his powerful torso, his feet made intricate patterns on the polished floor. He danced faster and faster, and for a moment his frenzy convinced even the most skeptical onlookers that he had indeed reverted to some wild, distant state of mind. He had "gone Indian" some remembered years later. The dance became so frenetic that Long Lance had to be forcibly stopped.[16]

Sometimes, too, for effect, he let out his war whoop. Professor Allison's son, Carlyle, then a student at the University of Manitoba, once invited Long Lance to join a group of his friends at a university dance at the Royal Alexandra Hotel. That night he made himself the hit of the evening. All the young, pretty coeds clamored for his attention. Enjoying the spotlight, Long Lance asked Carlyle as they were walking to a restaurant after the dance, "Did you ever hear an Indian war whoop?" Carlyle replied that he never had, and so Long Lance, at the corner of Portage and Main, let go with his best effort, one that split the night and turned heads for blocks in all directions. Carlyle remembered it as sounding "like several fire sirens and air-raid warnings lumped into one . . . blood curdling and exciting. . . ."[17]

For all his exuberance and flamboyance, Long Lance acquired a reputation as a warm, generous friend. Vernon Knowles, the managing editor, told of the evening when his daughter was very sick and Long Lance "left the office after a terrific day's work, and spent a large part of the evening sitting by her bedside, regaling her with Indian stories."[18] He often took the time to tell Indian stories to his friends' children even when they were not sick.[19]

Long Lance liked the *Tribune*. After three years of newspaper work, he had developed a smooth and popular style, and that winter he started selling some of his Indian stories to other magazines. *Maclean's* summarized his articles from the *Regina Leader* in a two-part series that appeared on February 15 and March 1, of 1923. The *Toronto Star Weekly* bought his *Tribune* article on the refugee Sioux Indians in Manitoba who had come north in 1862. (When the American government failed to observe the terms of its treaty with the Sioux, they rebelled in Minnesota, killing five hundred settlers.) Two American newspapers, the *St. Paul Pioneer Press* and the *Chicago Herald*, bought the same story.[20]

In the summer of 1923, Long Lance, encouraged by his success, returned to the field. He traveled to the Duck Lake area of central Saskatchewan, the site of the Rebellion of 1885. There he researched two stories, one on the rebellion, the other on the last stand of Almighty Voice, a young Cree who in 1897 with two other Indians managed to hold off an attacking posse of one hundred men for three days.

Father Henri Delmas, the local Roman Catholic priest, arranged for accommodation at the Duck Lake boarding school.

Long Lance and Father Delmas got along well, and Long Lance described the priest as "an all-round good fellow with a fine sense of humor, and hospitable to a fault." In a postscript to a three-page letter to S.H. Middleton, written while he was staying at the school with Father Delmas, Long Lance explained, "If this letter seems somewhat jerky, put it down to the fact that I have had to turn around and talk or laugh with somebody at the end of every sentence."[21]

After his research in Saskatchewan, Long Lance took a detour through his old haunts in Alberta, where he looked up his friends Howard Kelly and Hugh Dann. For a lark the three of them decided to go down to neighboring Shelby, Montana, for the world heavyweight boxing championship. As a promotional stunt, the tiny town, then in the midst of an oil boom, decided to host the championship on July 4. Some twenty-five thousand boxing fans descended on Shelby, which had a population of only five thousand. With no hotel rooms to be had, Long Lance and his friends spent the first night in a big tent and the second sleeping on unironed clothes in a laundry.[22] It was worth it, for Long Lance watched from the grandstand as an old acquaintance, Jack Dempsey, defeated the challenger, Tommy Gibbons, in fifteen rounds.

After returning from Shelby, there was more excitement. In 1923 the Calgary Exhibition added bronc riding, calf roping and bull riding to its events, and it became known as the Calgary Exhibition and Stampede. To add a frontier touch, Blackfoot, Stoney and Sarcee Indians were given passes and encouraged to set up an Indian tepee village on the Stampede grounds.

When the Exhibition and Stampede board heard Long Lance was in town, its members sought him out and asked him to help with a publicity stunt. Unlike the Indian elders, who spoke little English, Long Lance spoke it fluently and articulately, and knew how to hold the attention of a large audience. This time, instead of dropping a fake bomb in a door at City Hall, Long Lance agreed to organize a kidnapping of the mayor.

Long Lance (center), Howard Kelly (to his immediate left) and C.O. Smith (to his immediate right) at the Dempsey–Gibbons fight, Shelby, Montana. Although Smith had fired Long Lance from the Calgary Herald *in late March 1922, they became friends once again.*

At 10:15 A.M. on the morning of July 12, Long Lance, Running Rabbit, seven chiefs and a healthy assortment of Blackfoot, Stoney and Sarcee warriors, all painted and feathered and mounted on war ponies, charged down Seventh Avenue to City Hall. They hastily dismounted and, led by Long Lance, who knew the way, crowded into the mayor's office. Swiftly Long Lance ordered Mayor Webster to vacate his official chair, then installed Running Rabbit, who spoke not a word of English, as mayor. Photographers scrambled to record the "kidnapping" as the war party took the mayor, dressed in chaps, blue silk shirt, pink handkerchief and huge Stetson hat,[23] to the steps of City Hall. There they tied Mayor Webster to a horse and rode him to the center of the city at Eighth Avenue and First Street West. In the hot July sun the Indian mayor officially adopted the captive as a Blackfoot, naming him Chief Crowfoot, and then returned charge of the city to the white chief, who was now one of them.

The stunt made a great splash in Eastern Canada. According to the *Herald*, several Eastern Canadian reporters covering the Stampede "declared the ceremony the most striking and pic-

The "kidnapping" of the Mayor of Calgary at the Stampede. He stands between Long Lance and Chief Running Rabbit after taking part in the publicity stunt.

turesque they had ever seen."[24] Long Lance never forgot it. As a memento he had a photograph taken of himself at the tepee village in his white buckskins, moccasins and war bonnet, mounted on an Indian pinto. The Stampede board rewarded him with an official medal and made him a publicity agent and Indian committeeman for the 1924 Stampede.[25]

In late July 1923, Long Lance spent about two weeks with the Stoney (Assiniboine), speaking at the Stoney Reserve, thirty miles west of Calgary. With an interpreter he went directly to the old Indians and sat with them at a campfire, collecting their stories. In an article on the Stoney for the *Herald*, Long Lance skillfully introduced Stoney viewpoints. He quoted at length, for example, the comments of Hector Crawler, a traditionalist leader, on native religion: "If the ministers knew what our Sun Dance and religion are they would help us. If there is but one God, and we should all follow Him, should we not all work for each other's religion?"[26]

Despite all excesses in his presentation of himself as a Plains Indian, Long Lance truly wanted to explain their society and culture to others. He particularly wanted to make known the strengths of their age-old religious traditions. After visiting the Stoney he traveled to the Blackfoot Reserve for their Sun Dance.

Long Lance had himself photographed at the Calgary Stampede's tepee village.

Back in the days of the buffalo hunt, the Blackfoot always gathered after the long winter to give thanks to the Creator. Through the medium of the Sun Dance, they sent their prayers to the Great Spirit. They prayed for the animals, for the grasses on which the animals fed and for all the peoples who lived under the mercy of the sun, without whose life-giving rays nothing could endure. Half a century after the plains buffalo were hunted to extinction, the Sun Dance remained a great spiritual celebration.

Long Lance returned to Gleichen, Alberta, on August 3, 1923, and headed for the Sun Dance flats on the north bank of the Bow River. By wagon and buckboard, some seven hundred Blackfoot converged on the site, carrying tepee poles and canvas covers. Their colorful green, red, blue and yellow tepees with boldly painted designs rose in a large circle. Gates to the east and west marked the sun's path across the sky.

At the encampment the large lodge in the center had the same significance to the Blackfoot as any cathedral has to Christians. During the Sun Dance ceremony, the Blackfoot used the leafy branches of the poplar tree to build the Sun Dance, or medicine, lodge. It stood in the center of the camp, and from a distance looked like a grassy hillock.

The Blackfoot Indian agent, George Gooderham, arranged for Long Lance to stay with Joe Calf Child for the week before the Sun Dance and for the four days of the actual ceremony. Long Lance found his tepee accommodation surprisingly comfortable. Joe's wife had constructed embroidered backrests made of willow, and from the tepee poles she hung a variety of attractive objects: bags, belts, pipes, shawls, rattles and headdresses. At night he fell asleep to the sound of drums throbbing outside, and in the morning he awakened to the smell of burning sweet grass and his host singing his medicine song.[27]

Apart from his visit with the Stoney, Long Lance had never stayed long on a reserve, perhaps a few days at most. Also, he had never been entirely on his own. He had worked through intermediaries—Indian agents, missionaries or residential school graduates such as Andy Paull and Dan Kennedy. This time, alone among the people to whom he had begun telling his readers he belonged, he did not find it easy. The Blackfoot received him politely, but it was obvious they did not regard him as one of their own. His easy friendliness and his enthusiasm to write about the sacred ceremonies made the Blackfoot suspicious, and they kept their distance.

Long Lance knew something about the Indian way of life, but he did not know enough to stay out of trouble. He knew nothing about tepee etiquette, and inevitably he made mistakes. It unsettled the old people when he walked between his host and the fire. He did not know where to sit, unaware that male guests always sit on the host's immediate left. And when he was introduced, Long Lance always gave his own name, which the old Indians never did.[28] To the Blackfoot he talked and behaved like a white man.

The elders eventually objected to Long Lance's presence. Although they had agreed to allow him to visit the camp and to stay with Joe Calf Child, they had insisted to Gooderham that the stranger stay away from the inner circle containing the Sun

Joe Calf Child at the Blackfoot Sun Dance camp in early August 1923.

Dance lodge and the tepee of the Sun Dance Woman.[29] They did not want their sacred rites to be publicized, especially by someone they considered—for good reason—an outsider unfamiliar with their language and the religious significance of the event.

Long Lance talked as much as he could with Joe Calf Child, his host. He peppered him with all sorts of questions on the Sun Dance. After a few days he also made another friend, an attractive young woman, Mary Only Owl. Shunned as he was by the Blackfoot, he appreciated her company. She was extremely friendly, but that was her profession, as the lonely Long Lance soon discovered.[30] His already shaky image plummeted still further by being seen constantly with this woman, whose easy charms made her one of the community's fallen women.

Long Lance had difficulty in arranging suitable photographs to illustrate his article. He could not photograph the Sun Dance Woman, Mary Wolf Leg,[31] the virtuous maiden who had organized the ceremony and who stayed fasting in a tepee. The Sun Dance Woman was as sacrosanct as the Virgin Mary in Christendom. Long Lance neatly sidestepped all obstacles by photographing another Blackfoot woman, Mary Only Owl! He boldly captioned it in his first article, "Cat's Woman, the Blackfoot Virgin, who Bought and Put on the Sun Dance this year."[32]

Long Lance later used this photo of Mary Only Owl at the Sun Dance camp to illustrate his article "The Sun Dance," published in Good Housekeeping. *He had earlier used Mary's picture to illustrate his "Secrets of the Forbidden Sun Dance," published in the* Toronto Star Weekly. *In that article he captioned the shot, "Cat's Woman, the Blackfoot Virgin who bought and put on the Sun Dance this year," but in* Good Housekeeping, *he gave her a more exotic name. She appears as "Miss Ghost Skin."*

Whatever his tribulations in covering the story, Long Lance's glimpse of the ritual provided enthralling copy for more than one future article. In a piece published in *Good Housekeeping* in 1927, he offered a convincing eyewitness account of "our Blackfoot Sun Dance." With the best instincts of the magazine free-lancer, Long Lance devoted nearly the entire *Good Housekeeping* article to the role of Indian women in the ceremony. Again he used the photograph of Mary Only Owl, introducing her this time as "Miss

Ghost Skin, the Blackfoot girl who 'put on' the 1926 Sun Dance."[33]

His rebuff at the Sun Dance hurt, but Long Lance did not dwell on it. He knew he could trust Gooderham, and he knew that few outside would ever hear of his rejection by those he called his "own people." When John Murray Gibbon, the Canadian Pacific Railway's general publicity agent, approached him that autumn to write up several Blackfoot tales for use on CPR menu cards, he eagerly accepted.

During the winter of 1923–24 Long Lance, from his Winnipeg base, prepared brief stories about "The Indian Scout," "Blackfoot Travois and Cayuse" and "Indian Medicine Practices."[34] In the summer of 1924 the handsomely printed cards appeared in the CPR's luxury dining cars, placed on the white linen tablecloths between the monogrammed china and the cut flowers that were part of first-class rail travel in the 1920s. At the bottom of each card was a short note explaining that, on application to the dining car steward, extra cards could be obtained in envelopes ready for mailing. Soon they were being sent out across the continent, nicely publicizing both the railroad and Chief Buffalo Child Long Lance.

After the Blackfoot Sun Dance, Long Lance wrote his articles on the Rebellion of 1885 and Almighty Voice. In his haste to convert his notes to stories and make money to pay his bills, Long Lance sacrificed accuracy. When his article on the Rebellion of 1885 appeared in the *Saskatoon Daily Star*, a local historical society strongly complained that he had taken severe liberties with the facts. In a letter to the newspaper in early November, two executives of the Prince Albert Historical Society said that while the story was "quite entertaining," it contained "many errors regarding the participants and actual happenings."[35]

Long Lance often erred in small ways, for he knew little of Canadian history and was more interested in the color of an event. He was one of those journalists who fancied himself more a writer than a reporter, one of those who never let the facts ruin a good story. In his article on the Stoney for the *Calgary Herald*, for instance, he reported that the French *coureurs de bois* Radisson and DesGroseilliers reached the foothills of Alberta around 1800. Even if the claim were true (most reputable authorities believe they never traveled farther west than what is now Minnesota), the dates are totally inaccurate. By 1800 Radisson and DesGroseilliers had been dead for nearly a century![36] Long Lance also frequently confused Indians of the same or similar name. In his *Maclean's* article he referred to the great Blackfoot warrior "Running Rabbit, who took a prominent role in a raid on the Assiniboine in 1863." Long Lance wrote that Running Rabbit "was still living, well and hardy, the last time I heard of him." The original Running Rabbit had died in 1918, three years before Long Lance had visited the Blackfoot Reserve, and the well and hardy Running Rabbit that Long Lance mentioned was the great warrior's son.[37]

The hundreds of thousands of newcomers who settled on the Canadian prairies in the early twentieth century knew nothing about the Native population, and even those who should have been vigilant did not always spot Long Lance's errors. John Hawkes, the librarian of the Saskatchewan Legislative Library, wrote in 1924 in *Saskatchewan and Its People*, "The Chief is a highly educated man who . . . has had considerable press experience, and his bright literary contributions to the lore and history of the tribes are not only interesting and well written but are valuable because of their authenticity."[38]

To his credit Long Lance never hesitated to travel great distances from his new home in Winnipeg to achieve a rapport with the characters of his stories. He was never content to pick up material from secondary sources. In late May 1923, for example, he went out of his way to visit Almighty Voice's parents, Sounding Sky and Spotted Calf, who still lived only four miles from the bluff where their son had fought to his death.

Long Lance was blessed, or cursed, with the novelist's imag-

*Long Lance photographed Spotted Calf and Sounding Sky, mother and father of
Almighty Voice, who would figure prominently in Long Lance's autobiography.*

ination. He knew how to inflate a story to make it read well and
enhance its sales potential. He embellished upon the known
details when he sat down to write his version of the last stand of
Almighty Voice, going so far as to invent dialogue and to include
scenes that cannot be confirmed.[39] It was, nevertheless, a compelling story of a young Cree who killed a Mountie and then
evaded capture for two years. Long Lance sold the story to the
Winnipeg Tribune, the *Montreal Family Herald* and *Maclean's*.[40]

When Almighty Voice was finally cornered, it was, Long

Lance said, because he wanted to be found.[41] Joined by his cousin Going-Up-to-Sky and his brother-in-law Topean, he had decided to die in a last, defiant stand. They chose a thicket in a half-mile clump of bush growing on rolling, open prairie. According to Long Lance's version, which was cited into the 1970s as an accurate account,[42] the large force of Mounties and volunteers charged the Indians' position twice. Topean was killed, but Almighty Voice and Going-Up-to-Sky killed two Mounties and the postmaster of Duck Lake. The police called for reinforcements, and more Mounties and volunteers arrived from Duck Lake, Prince Albert and Regina. That night Almighty Voice shouted from the bluff to his attackers, "We have had a good fight today. I have worked hard and I am hungry. You have plenty of food; send me some, and tomorrow we'll finish the fight." All during the night his mother chanted to him from a nearby hill, urging him "to die the brave that he had shown himself to be." Throughout the night Almighty Voice yelled back in the darkness, "I am almost starving. I am eating the bark off the trees. I have dug into the ground as far as my arm will reach, but can get no water. But have no fear—I'll hold out to the end."[43]

That night Almighty Voice's mother changed her chant to a lament—a death song for her son. The next morning field guns were positioned, a nine-pounder and a seven-pounder. As Long Lance described it, "At six o'clock the next morning, the big guns began belching forth their devastating storm of lead and iron in deadly earnestness. It was obvious that no living things could long endure their steady beat. At noon the pelting ceased." Almighty Voice was dead. The bluff where he and his two companions died, Long Lance continued, "marks the spot where the North American Indian made his last stand against the white man."[44]

After the summer of 1923 Long Lance headed back to Winnipeg, and the *Tribune* sent him to New York to cover the Dempsey–Firpo boxing match. On the evening of September 14, a crowd of eighty thousand—more than the entire population of

Calgary—gathered at the Polo Grounds, the home stadium of the New York Giants of the National League. Long Lance followed the fight blow by blow. Firpo, the Wild Bull of the Pampas, stormed into Dempsey, knocking him clear out of the ring. Fortunately reporters at ringside pushed Dempsey back through the ropes at the count of nine, and the champ rallied and went on to knock out Firpo. It was one of the classic boxing fights of all time, and Long Lance was there. He wrote back to the *Tribune*, "There may have been a fight more savage, spectacular and brutal than the slugfest here Friday night between Jack Dempsey and Louis Angel Firpo, but it must have been back in the dark ages when men wore leopard skins around their loins and wielded tree stumps instead of eight-ounce gloves."[45]

The *Tribune* loved his report and later sent him to cover other fights. In May 1924 he left Winnipeg for Michigan City, Indiana, to cover a bout between Georges Carpentier and Tommy Gibbons. In September 1924 the *Montreal Star, Edmonton Journal, Calgary Herald, Saskatoon Star, Regina Leader* and *Winnipeg Tribune* all carried his story from Jersey City on the fight between Firpo and Harry Willis, the "Black Panther." A fellow journalist described Long Lance's fight stories as "virile, red-blooded, graphic."[46]

Long Lance stayed at the Commodore Hotel on Forty-Second Street and Lexington Avenue, right next to Grand Central Station. The Commodore was the largest of the Grand Central hotels, twenty-eight stories high, with more than two thousand rooms, but it was dwarfed by other skyscrapers in central Manhattan.[47] Long Lance stayed an extra three weeks in New York, and from there he wrote again to S.H. Middleton to report that he was getting around and meeting people worth knowing. "Have been out to dinners, theaters, ball games, and have had several good motor trips and games of golf," he wrote in a letter dated October 8. He loved (as he would write after a speaking tour to Columbus, Ohio, the next year) being looked after "as though I were really somebody."[48]

Introducing himself as "a full-blooded Indian, a chief of the Blood tribe of Alberta,"[49] he arranged to write a story of the Indians of the Canadian Plains for *The Mentor,* a small American educational magazine. On his way back to Winnipeg, he stopped in Toronto and called on Herb Cranston, the editor of the *Star Weekly,* who had bought his article on the Manitoba Sioux that spring. Cranston was anxious to meet and discuss work with Long Lance. He wanted light human interest stories, and Long Lance's Indian pieces were exactly what he wanted for the *Star Weekly.* As Cranston was fond of saying, "We seek to entertain rather than to instruct."[50] Using this formula Cranston had managed to raise the circulation of the *Star Weekly* to more than 150,000, making it the largest periodical in the country.[51] He bought Long Lance's article on the Sun Dance and asked for more.

Long Lance returned to Winnipeg in November and became a full-time reporter again. On weekends he assisted with boxing programs in the city, helping to judge the City Amateur Boxing Championship in mid-February. He dated many women and paid much attention to a particularly striking piano teacher.[52] When summer arrived, like a migrating bird, he returned to Alberta. In late June he set off for the Macleod Jubilee, the Calgary Stampede and his new summer job as a CPR public relations representative at the company's famed Banff Springs Hotel.

Fort Macleod, founded as a North-West Mounted Police post in the fall of 1874, was the oldest white settlement in southern Alberta, older by a year than Calgary. To help the town celebrate its fiftieth anniversary, twenty-five hundred Blackfoot, Bloods and Peigan and fifteen thousand tourists joined the two thousand citizens for the Jubilee. Long Lance moved easily from the townsite to the Indian village, keeping fellow reporters abreast of the powwows and contests among the Indians.[53]

He worked hard to improve his image with the Blackfoot, for the rebuff at the Sun Dance still smarted. This time he looked for ways to forge stronger ties with the Blackfoot nation that had adopted him, the Bloods. At the Indian village he approached old Eagle Speaker, the veteran of several Blood war parties against the Cree. He had corresponded with his son, Mike, whom he had met on his first trip to the reserve in August 1921. Mike had recently become the first Blood to enter agricultural college, and S.H. Middleton suggested that Long Lance write to encourage the young Indian in his studies. Long Lance approached Eagle Speaker and asked if he and his son could adopt each other. To his joy the old man said yes.

The ancient ritual took place in Eagle Speaker's tepee in the Indian encampment. Three Blood elders—Spear Chief, Morning Bird and Mike Oka—joined Eagle Speaker. Spear Chief led the ceremony. He took a piece of rawhide, tied Mike's and Long Lance's hands together as they knelt, then painted their faces with the sacred red paint. After raising them up, he asked them to walk four times around the fire. When this was done, Spear Chief untied the rawhide, and the two were blood brothers. They would remain close for life.[54]

Despite becoming a blood brother, Long Lance never won full acceptance from the Bloods. As part of his adoption ceremony at St. Paul's in February 1922, Old Mountain Horse had pushed him away, reminding the new Buffalo Child of his place among them, but now some of the Bloods were shocked to see photographs of Long Lance in "tribal dress" splashed across newspapers and magazines. It appeared that he was consciously using his adoption by the Bloods for personal publicity. On July 30, a month after the celebrations at Macleod, Middleton wrote Long Lance to say that some of the leading Bloods felt he was "using" his "Blood Indian name and tribal connections to commercial advantage."

Long Lance knew that by flaunting his false credentials he was upsetting, even antagonizing, the Bloods, and he knew he had reached another turning point in his life. Five years later he

At the Calgary Stampede in 1924, Long Lance helped with the ceremony to make F.M. Johnston, manager of the Hudson's Bay Company store in Calgary, an honorary Sarcee chief.

would tell a reporter that his dream was to "find a young Indian girl, and settle down on the reserve."[55] In 1924 he might still have done this. Using Middleton's good offices, he could have visited the Bloods and apologized to those he had offended. The missionary would have been delighted to introduce him to suitable female graduates of St. Paul's, and he could have married. But this he rejected. He wanted more — more fame, more recognition.

Long Lance was beginning to feel let down by the Indians, whom he thought he had helped by promoting a better understanding of their culture among his readers and by helping them politically. He could not understand why the Blackfoot did not appreciate his efforts, and something in his spirit seemed to sag.[56] He became a little more hardened, a little more cynical. Although he had encouraged the Blackfoot nations to hold a political meeting that autumn, which they did, he did not attend.

After the Calgary Stampede in July, in which he headed the Indian contingent,[57] Long Lance took up his new job for the rest of the summer at Banff. His responsibilities included writing publicity, entertaining VIPs and accompanying trail rides of guests staying at the Canadian Pacific Railway's luxury hotels at Banff and Lake Louise.[58] When he received his next invitation to lec-

Yoho Camp, near Field, British Columbia, 1924. Left to right: Long Lance, Jim Brewster, Tom Wilson, Jonas Benjamin, Jake Two Youngmen.

ture as an Indian chief at the fourth annual Ohio History Day in Columbus, Ohio, he accepted without hesitation.

In Columbus, officials of the historical society reserved the Governor's Suite at the expensive Chittenden Hotel for him, and everywhere he went he was treated as a distinguished visitor. In early October he spoke at length of "his people" to the local Chamber of Commerce, the State Archeological and Historical Society, and the Exchange Club. Over radio station WEAD, a woman sang "The Song of Love" in honor of Long Lance.[59]

The highlight of his visit was his address on Ohio History Day to an audience of six thousand. He spoke at Logan Park, about twenty-five miles south of Columbus in the Pickaway Plains. At this same site, exactly 150 years earlier, Chief Logan had given one of the most famous speeches in North American Indian history. After frontiersmen had massacred his entire family, Logan took up arms against the white man. Under a tall elm tree, he defended his stand, saying, "There runs not a drop of my blood in the veins of any living creature. This called on me for revenge. Who is there to mourn for Logan? Not one."[60]

The small elm of 1774 had grown to an immense girth of 25 feet and a height of over 150 feet.[61] When Long Lance spoke,

Long Lance with youthful admirers at the Logan Elm, Circleville, Ohio, in the autumn of 1924.

though, not a single reservation remained in all of Ohio. The Indians had been expelled a century earlier, driven west of the Mississippi or murdered like Chief Logan's family. Long Lance spoke beneath the same elm, and his words hit their mark, reminding his audience of the injustices of years past.

He spoke for half an hour on the North American Indian, past and present. His eloquence stirred the crowd. When he reached the end, they surged forward so enthusiastically that the platform collapsed just minutes after Long Lance and the others had climbed down. For another half hour Long Lance shook hands with hundreds of well-wishers until the organizers whisked him away.[62]

Although he well realized that a number of Blackfoot and Bloods disapproved of his masquerade, Long Lance, the consummate showman, would not abandon it. He wanted to help the racial group to which he wanted to belong, but at the same time, he had lost control—he had become addicted to fame and public notoriety. In November 1924, as a Blackfoot, Long Lance addressed the Canadian Club in Montreal, then the Women's Canadian Clubs in Toronto and Hamilton. His press clippings grew, including a feature article in the *Toronto Star Weekly* that carried a full-page caption: "Redskin Extraordinary is this Indian Chief."[63] He might have found being a "professional Indian" repugnant, and in his letters there is evidence to support this,[64] but it did not stop him from exploiting the role.

CHAPTER 11

Long Lance, "Redskin Extraordinary"

BANFF, ALBERTA, 1925–26

*W*hen he covered the Dempsey–Firpo fight in New York in September 1923, Long Lance got a taste of the gratuitous publicity that can suddenly bring an unknown to center stage. He was at the Polo Grounds covering the fight for newspapers in Western Canada. Although ringside was studded with celebrities, Long Lance managed to attract notice when a journalist covering the fight dropped into his story a reference to this conspicuous young Indian, who happened to catch his eye as blows were exchanged in the ring. He wrote,

> Among the newspaper men at the ringside of the Dempsey–Firpo fight in New York sat a young chap of athletic build. The casual observer might have thought this fellow had acquired a healthy tan at one of New York's popular beaches. Looking him over more care-

fully, the observer would have noticed that this individual's skin was copper-colored, that his hair was jet black, that his cheek bones were prominent and that he had an unflinching eye. Inquiry would have brought out the fact that it was Chief Buffalo Child Long Lance, a full-blooded Indian chief representing a syndicate of newspapers in the Canadian Northwest.[1]

Long Lance dutifully pasted the reference in his scrapbook, already bulging with other clippings and photographs.

Long Lance excelled in sportswriting, especially in covering boxing, and it did not have to be a world championship fight staged in New York City. He had immersed himself in the amateur sports of Winnipeg when he worked for the *Tribune*, and at several other points in his life he could have chosen to make it his career. He might have been one of the very best, filing vivid copy on boxing, such as when he wrote, "where crushing blows are swishing through the air like nine-pounders, where bulky frames are tottering like giant buildings in an earthquake."[2]

During the winter Long Lance worked as a free-lance writer for the *Tribune*, another indication of how highly he was regarded as a sports and general features writer. He could be assigned, or assign himself, to just about any location in Canada and usually be assured that his stories would be bought. He covered the ski championships at Mount Revelstoke in British Columbia,[3] then returned to Banff to welcome New Zealand's "All Blacks" rugger team. The New Zealanders, having completed a twenty-eight–game exhibition tour of Britain, were returning home. The team of thirty included several Maoris and others of mixed Maori and European ancestry. Most noticeable to Long Lance was the utter lack of discrimination among them. They were a fun-loving crew who went up and down the toboggan slide at Banff at all hours of the night. Often during their two-day stay at Banff, they performed Maori dances to a drum and native chants. The All

Long Lance (at center) at the Banff Winter Carnival. Second from the right is a Maori with the visiting "All Blacks" rugger team from New Zealand.

Blacks took to Long Lance as easily as he took to them, and before they left Alberta, the New Zealanders made "Chief Buffalo Child" an honorary member of their team.[4]

By the 1920s the Banff Springs Hotel had become something of a Canadian legend. The gigantic hotel–castle lay anchored to the base of Sulphur Mountain on a pine-covered bank above the swift-flowing Bow River. Here, every summer, came the rich and powerful with their huge steamer trunks and servants. They came for the peaks and valleys and the stunning, blue-green lakes of one of the last great wilderness regions of North America.

Long Lance's job as the CPR assistant press representative at Banff was to make sure influential guests had a pleasant stay. With his wide range of conversational topics and his warm and friend-ly manner, he performed his duties with ease. After a visit to Banff in the summer of 1924, the English journalist Eldred Walker included a sketch of Long Lance in his book *Canadian Trails Re-Visited*. What Walker remembered vividly was a chance meeting with Long Lance on the hotel's veranda. The immaculately attired Long Lance approached the portly, elderly Englishman, introduced himself and asked what he thought of the Rockies. Over drinks the two men had a lengthy conversation, discussing art, literature, journalism, agriculture and science. Walker was impressed to find someone in such an unlikely place to whom no topic seemed foreign. He could compare the delights of Banff with those of New York and London. The Englishman was impressed. Suddenly, as Walker describes in his book, this dark-skinned stranger stopped talking, paused and bluntly asked, "You are looking hard at me. Can you tell to what nationality I belong?" Long Lance waited, and seeing that the Englishman was baffled, told him, "I am a full-blooded Blood Indian. I am Chief Buffalo Child Long Lance of the Blood Tribe."

"Had the heavens opened," Walker concluded in his book, "I could not have had a greater surprise."[5]

Long Lance enjoyed his work at the hotel, for it allowed him to play his favorite role of "noble red man," freely rubbing shoulders with the wealthy and socially prominent of the continent. In these, the hotel's golden days, many of the visitors arrived with letters of credit worth fifty thousand dollars, all earmarked for a stay of two or three months in Banff. It was a make-believe world of which an old Banff banker observed, "The men would fish and play golf, and the women would change their clothes."[6] Long Lance cut an imposing figure on any dance floor, and at the Banff Springs Hotel he became a much sought-after partner.[7]

The summer of 1924 ended quickly enough. In late August Long Lance was on his way east again, this time at the request of the hotel management to accompany a visiting party of British scientists heading to Toronto. Long Lance was the ideal host. During the two-day journey across the prairies and down through northern Ontario, Long Lance spent much of his time with Sir Richard Paget, a famous English voice specialist. Long Lance told him what he knew firsthand of various Indian songs, and Paget was fascinated. In a fine bass voice, Long Lance chanted the songs as the train rattled on through the country. According to Long Lance's later comment to a reporter from the *Toronto Star*, Sir Richard caught on quickly: "Many of the Indian songs I talked to him about and illustrated for him were most difficult. They were in a very minor key with all sorts of peculiar Indian inflections graded down from ordinary sounds to a grunt. It is next to impossible for anyone except an Indian to pick them up. It was astonishing . . . before he left the train at Toronto he was singing them as accurately as a native Indian."[8]

Long Lance provided this photo of his "father" to illustrate Fred Griffin's article, "Redskin Extraordinary is this Indian Chief" that appeared in the Toronto Star Weekly. *The photo was captioned, "Old Chief Long Lance, father of Chief Buffalo Child."*

Long Lance pushed his Indian identity whenever and wherever, becoming increasingly bold and even reckless. To help Fred Griffin of the *Star Weekly* with his feature story on "The Redskin Extraordinary," Long Lance supplied him with his two clippings books and actually gave him a photograph of an old Plains Indian in a war bonnet and said it was his father. In due course the photograph appeared with the article, captioned, "Old Chief Long Lance, father of Chief Buffalo Child."[9]

When summer arrived, Long Lance returned to Calgary and Banff. The Stampede board had invited him months earlier. The official guests in 1925 were Long Lance's commander in chief in World War I, Field Marshal Earl Haig, now nearly seventy, and the Countess Haig. Haig was touring Canada in his official role as Grand President of the British Empire Service League.[10] He was a somber Scot with a full mustache, bluish gray eyes and a handsome face. He walked with the rangy, swinging stride common to men who ride a great deal.[11] At the request of the Stampede board, the Sarcee chief, Joe Big Plume, was to adopt Haig into his tribe with Long Lance acting as the interpreter.

On that fine July day the weather was perfect. After the field marshal had led the Stampede parade through the heart of the city, mounted cowboys and cowgirls, Indians and chuck wagons rumbled to a stop at the corner of First Street West and Seventh Avenue. Thousands watched as Chief Big Plume, in buckskin and full headdress, conducted the ceremony. As instructed, Haig knelt on an Indian blanket, and Long Lance began translating the Sarcee chief's words into English:

> Field Marshal Earl Haig, I am going to make you a chief of the Sarcee Indians. The Sarcees had a great warrior killed one hundred years ago. He was the greatest warrior that the Sarcees ever had, and you are Great Britain's greatest warrior. . . . The name that the Sarcees are giving you is Big Chief Akahtse, which means Chief Bull's Head.[12]

Not knowing any Sarcee, Long Lance's interpretation was loose and free. Improvising, he said that the original Bull's Head had died a hundred years earlier, in 1825, when actually the old Sarcee warrior had died in 1911.[13] But the error was not detected. Unlike Chief Big Plume, Long Lance's narrative was smooth and polished, in the finest English he could muster. He knew what to deliver, and it worked.

After Long Lance placed an eagle-plume headdress on Haig's head, he carefully adjusted it, as if he had been doing this sort of thing all his life. When the ceremony was over, Long Lance extended his hand, broke into a wide smile and welcomed the newest Chief Bull's Head into the tribe.[14] The performance was such a success that the Stampede board invited him back for the following summer.

After the Stampede, Long Lance returned to the Banff

Long Lance adjusts Field Marshal Earl Haig's headdress after his ceremonial adoption by the Sarcee tribe. Long Lance spoke no Sarcee but translated anyway.

Springs Hotel, where his public relations job awaited him. Again, in return for his room, meals and a modest salary, Long Lance eased into his role as the resident Indian at the hotel. This time during his stay at the Banff Springs, he appeared in a comic strip, "Cicero Sapp," published in the *New York Evening World* on August 18, 1925. In the comic strip the visiting Mr. Cicero Sapp is told by the manager of the Banff Springs Hotel that he will introduce him to a real, full-blooded Indian chief. Not wishing to meet him looking like a city slicker, the bourgeois Mr. Sapp dresses up in a ten-gallon hat, cowboy duds, and a gun and holster. He is

Long Lance's notoriety rose another notch when he was the subject of "Cicero Sapp," a cartoon strip appearing in the New York Evening World.

astonished when the hotel manager presents a handsome Indian wearing a dinner jacket, looking as much like a real Indian chief as a Broadway dandy.

When his duties at Banff were over for another summer, Long Lance rejoined the lecture circuit. In the early 1920s public lectures were a popular entertainment. Movies were new and popular, to be sure, but until 1927 they were silent. Through his article in *The Mentor*, Long Lance had gained an audience in the United States, and after the Ohio History Day speech, other requests came in. A suave, well-spoken Indian chief was a great novelty, and Long Lance took full advantage of it. In the autumn of 1925 he went to New York, then lectured at a dinner of the British Empire Club in Providence, Rhode Island.[15] After that he went back to New York and spoke at the Dutch Treat Club, whose membership consisted of the editors of many of the leading newspapers in the United States.

At the Dutch Treat Club, Ray Long, editor-in-chief at *Cosmopolitan*, then a general interest magazine, and vice-president of Randolph Hearst's magazine chain, introduced Chief Buffalo Child. Long Lance gave one of his best talks, prompting applause that rang out for five minutes. Long, a director of the club for ten years, said he had "never heard a more interesting address before this club than that given by Chief Buffalo Child Long Lance."[16] Afterward he invited his guest to visit his home at Greenwich, Connecticut,[17] and there he suggested that Long Lance use his lecture notes for an article for *Cosmopolitan.*

Ray Long had expensive tastes. The short, dapperly dressed man with a sporty, upturned mustache was the proud owner of some forty suits—all custom-tailored in London—and shirts and pajamas made in Paris. At forty-seven Long was reputedly the highest-salaried editor in the world, earning $180,000 a year. He was a prodigious worker, and a typical weekend's work involved reading thirty-three short stories, two novels, four or five magazines, several trade papers and all of the New York Sunday newspapers, which he clipped, sending pertinent items to his assistants. *Cosmopolitan* received some three thousand manuscripts a month, of which it accepted between twenty-five and thirty.[18] Ray Long wanted Long Lance's article to be one of these in a magazine that could boast ten times the circulation of the *Toronto Star Weekly.*

Long Lance stayed a month in New York. He loved dropping names, and in his letters to Canon Middleton in Alberta, he told of the famous writers he was meeting. Twice he had met Sinclair Lewis, who had just published his two devastating reviews of American middle-class life in his novels *Main Street* and *Babbitt*. He also had talked with Kathleen Norris, the popular romantic novelist, and Peter B. Kyne, the writer of westerns. He spent many hours with Vilhjalmur Stefansson, the Arctic explorer and lecturer.[19]

Between the parties and the hobnobbing, Long Lance managed to line up work. The American Bureau of Commercial Economics invited him on a lecture tour of the American Midwest. The bureau was a private, nonprofit organization sustained entirely by memberships and voluntary contributions. In cooperation with President Coolidge's national outdoor recreation program, the bureau sent lecturers and films throughout the United States, urging Americans "to take a greater interest and part in outdoor life." The bureau paid all expenses, plus an honorarium, and secured passes for Long Lance on nineteen American railways. The tour started in Washington, where the organization's headquarters was located, and it continued on to Illinois, Michigan, Wisconsin, Indiana, Iowa and Missouri.[20]

One of Long Lance's first lectures was to the University Club in Evanston, Illinois, just north of Chicago. For forty-five minutes, as a Blackfoot chief, he told of his people's origins, language, customs, sports and religion. He concluded his talk with slides and a question period. Dr. James Washington Bell, an economics professor at Northwestern University, later remarked on how much he enjoyed Chief Buffalo Child's answers, when his "ready wit and native point of view quite captured the hearts of his listeners." In a thank-you letter to the bureau, one Charles MacConnell wrote, "His talk was crammed with interesting information—just the sort of things we have asked over and over about the Indians since we were children."[21]

Always impeccably attired, Long Lance traveled across the continent many times in the mid-1920s on the lecture circuit.

In all six states where Long Lance lectured, the treatment of the Indians remained a sensitive issue, and Long Lance attracted large crowds. The Indians had been killed off or brutally exiled from Illinois, Indiana, Iowa, Missouri and from most of Michigan and Wisconsin. As Long Lance traveled through Illinois to Alton, Champaign, Chicago, Greenville, Moline, Normal, Peoria, Springfield and Urbana, and to dozens of other centers in other states, he knew he could expect waves of sympathy from his audiences. He spoke to business groups, service clubs and college students. At Eau Claire, Wisconsin, he addressed fifteen hundred people at the Opera House. In Milwaukee he stood before two thousand at the auditorium in Juneau Park.[22]

In another letter to Canon Middleton, this one on February 18, Long Lance described the details of his tour and concluded by saying that he would "probably go down into Oklahoma for a few days before returning up west." He told Middleton about all his railway passes, and how easy it was to make "jumps" from train to train. Yet, although he had the railway passes, and a trip to Winston–Salem would hardly have cost him a penny, he resisted the temptation.

By 1926 Long Lance had been separated from his family for seventeen years, nearly half his life. He knew the risks of returning home — the risk of being exposed, the risk of succumbing to the warmth of family and old friends, the risk of the ghetto. With this far-ranging lecture tour, and with his assignment for *Cosmopolitan*, he felt he was on his way up at last, and the easy accessibility of Winston–Salem could not have come at a worse time. It had been so long since he had been accountable to those who knew who he really was and where he really came from that he had grown accustomed to living a fictional life. Sylvester Long had lived in one realm, and Chief Buffalo Child Long Lance lived in another.

His lies were becoming more compulsive and more outrageous. In March 1926 he was interviewed by the *Minneapolis Sunday Tribune*, and the story that appeared on March 7 concluded, "To the Plains Indians, Chief Long Lance is 'Big Boss' — all their tribes, in addition to the Blackfoot Indians of Alberta, are said to look upon him as a leader." In the winter of 1925–26, Long Lance pushed his "Indianization" yet another step. He resolved to erase his past completely by trying to forget it himself. In June 1926 Ray Long published the autobiographical article Long Lance had worked on over the winter. It was titled "My Trail Upward," and in it Long Lance wrote, "I took [the trail] because I, a Blackfoot Indian, wanted to live like a white man." He sum-

---

MacLean's Magazine   **May 15, 1926**

I Wanted to Live Like
the White Man

By CHIEF BUFFALO CHILD LONG LANCE

Chief Long Lance, an Indian, has run the gamut from cowboy to college student, to soldier, to boxer, to newspaper and magazine writer. They told him that he could never "live white," that sooner or later he would go back to the feathers. They were mistaken, and in this article he tells why.

In articles such as this, which ran in Maclean's, *Long Lance presented himself as the model red man — noble but tamed.*

marized the story that he had recently been telling in New York, Washington and throughout the Midwest. He wrote of his Blackfoot boyhood, his years on western cattle ranches, traveling with Buffalo Bill's Wild West Show, Carlisle, his service in the Canadian army in France and his career as a writer in Western Canada. He cleverly blended fact with fiction, and the whole story fit neatly within the bounds of credibility. It was great reading. *Maclean's* printed an expanded version in Canada in May 1926. *McClure's*, a widely circulated American magazine, carried the story in July 1927.[23] Selling the story three times brought Long Lance much-needed income.

When the *Cosmopolitan* article appeared, Long Lance hastily wrote Canon Middleton, urging him to buy a copy, but warning that the magazine's editor had taken liberties with the "facts." He claimed it was the editor's idea that he had attended "a mission school in southern Alberta," instead of "at Wind River, Wyo., where it should have been."[24] Middleton again was puzzled, for Long Lance earlier had told him that he had attended a mission school in Oklahoma. Nevertheless, Middleton kept silent about his doubts. Even with his best "white" friend, Long Lance could not be honest.

Six months later Long Lance wrote Middleton again, this time to tell him "it is good for a globe-wanderer like me to have one good confidante like you; one whom I can be myself to, always, and speak what is in my mind. . . ."[25] Even with Middleton, Long Lance could only tell of the ripples on the surface of the pond, not the turbulent waters below and never the muddy bottom that gave the pond its color.[26]

"My Trail Upward" begins,

> Missionaries on a Blackfoot Indian Reservation in southern Alberta taught me my ABC's—but an old-fashioned bartender out in Laramie, Wyoming, first thrilled me with the idea that I might become educated and really make something out of my life.
>
> This man was a Pennsylvania Dutchman and so he happened to know about Carlisle Indian School. He asked me one day when I was in the old Central Bar with a crowd of cowboys why I did not go there and become educated. He explained that it was free for Indians.
>
> "But I can't even speak good English," I told him.
>
> "Well," he said, "you can educate yourself for entrance to Carlisle by reading. Read, read all the time—anything and everything you come across."
>
> I think that bit of advice changed the trend of my whole life. I was at that time sixteen years old and a full-fledged cow-hand. I could break and ride bucking horses. I could barely sign my own name and spell out words; but I could ride almost anything that stood on four feet. I was proud to be a cowpuncher; that was doing pretty well at that for an ignorant, half savage young Indian buck.
>
> A few days before I met this old bartender—I'm ashamed that I've forgotten his name—I had been fired from a ranch fifteen miles west of Laramie. At that time my temper was as wild and unbridled as a wolf's, and this was the cause of the trouble.

This all happened in 1907, and I'd come down from the reservation to follow the round-ups. I had made this step on my own initiative, because I was curious to know about this Pale Face who had conquered my people and compelled us to live on comparatively small reservations. Up to this time I had never done anything but follow the Indians' line of least resistance—hunt and fool around with horses. I always went on the trail alone and I thought a lot. Finally one day I made a resolution; I was going out to meet the white man on his own grounds, study him and find out just what sort of fellow he was. . . .

Long Lance described in rich detail a series of adventures as he went about studying the "Pale Faces." When he arrived at Carlisle, he wrote, "my brain was as tough as raw buffalo meat. . . ." It was when he was traveling with Colonel Cody and the Wild West Show that, he says, he got his first good opportunity to study these white people at close hand.

One afternoon the chiefs and some of the older Indians were taken out to a wealthy American's home and served with refreshments; and some of us youngsters were taken along. This chap had a lot of friends in to meet us, and he introduced us as "real Americans. . . ." [These people] were different from any I had ever met. They had the dignity that the Indian likes, and they did not *yapiota*—talk too much. An Indian distrusts anyone who talks a lot. These people so impressed me with their bearing and their environment that I decided on the spot, "I am going to be like that."

Finally, the *Cosmopolitan* article ends:

Two or three times a year I go back to my Indian reservation, where I spent my boyhood and where my people still live. I was proud when they elected me a Chief. I had won my spurs fighting side by side with the white men—and my tribe had recognized this.

I'm proud to be as much like a white man as I am—but I'm proud, too, of every drop of Indian blood that runs through my veins.

I'm proud of my Indian heritage—and I'm proud, too, of the land and people of my adoption.

I have reached no dizzy heights of material success, but I have succeeded in pulling myself up by my boot straps from a primitive and backward life into this great new world of white civilization.

Anyone with determination and will can do as much.

Shortly after the *Cosmopolitan* and *Maclean's* articles appeared at the end of May 1926, Long Lance spoke in Vancouver on Indian history at a North American railway executives convention at the Hotel Vancouver. He then returned again to Calgary for the opening of the Stampede. Mounted on an Indian pony, he wore white buckskin and a full eagle-plume headdress in his usual place at the head of the Indian section.[27] After the Stampede he took the train to Banff for his last summer in the Rockies.

Evidence exists from the summer of 1926 of the human cost to Long Lance of his continued deceptions. The trail of lies from Winston–Salem to the Canadian Rockies was costing him his sanity. Morley Roberts, a well-known English novelist and journalist, participated in the week-long "trail ride of the Canadian Rockies" that July. Perceptively he noted an unstable aspect about Buffalo Child Long Lance, whom he described in his *On the Old Trail: Through British Columbia After Forty Years*, published the following year. He began by introducing his fellow trail-rider as "a full-blooded Indian, said to be a chief," "a captain in the War," "a good horseman." But the Indian dances he performed were bizarre:

One was a kind of sex dance after the manner of the prairie chicken and the other a very exhausting and almost horrible war dance. This, he told us, was danced by a war party just before they went out for scalps. I do not know how they preserved enough energy to lift a wig from a barber's block if they kept it up all night as he said they did. All this was quite interesting, but I remembered long years ago meeting two fine old chiefs of the Blackfeet and I wondered what they would think of an Indian, chief or not, dancing in this way for the entertainment of a crowd of pale-face girls.[28]

A messy—and nearly fatal—incident that summer, involving a married woman, also hints at the mental ground Long Lance had lost. In Banff, Long Lance met Florence Sheridan, a vivacious young woman married to a man twenty years her senior. She and her husband had come up from Chicago for the summer, renting the old Dawson house on Banff's Buffalo Street. The wealthy Chicago lawyer's first wife had died in 1917, and on September 10, 1924, at the age of fifty-six, he married the former Florence K. Donovan of Aberdeen, Washington.[29] After thirty-one years of heading a busy and important law firm in Chicago, John Jay Sheridan was exhausted and weak. He came to Banff for rest. To ensure that their vacation would be comfortable, the Sheridans brought along their black butler, Athay MacFarlane.

Long Lance met Florence on a trail ride.[30] Soon they became constant companions, and they were together on the night of September 9, the eve of the Sheridans' second wedding anniversary. That night, feeling "indisposed," John Jay went to bed early, and Florence and Long Lance were left alone. They made a fire in the living room to break the cold of a chilly autumn night. The time passed quickly. About eleven o'clock Florence left the living room to ask Athay, the butler, to prepare drinks. Unfortunately he was inebriated and loudly refused. Hearing the noise from the kitchen, Long Lance rushed to the lady's assistance.

The butler, drunk and resentful of Long Lance's affair with his boss's wife, pulled out a razor and angrily struck Long Lance on his front right thigh, making an eight-inch gash. Long Lance chased him out of the kitchen, but, hurt and bleeding, could not catch him. He limped to the living room, there to be comforted by Florence. After a few moments there was a crash in the kitchen, and the butler rushed into the room, thrashing the air with his razor, determined to finish Long Lance once and for all. Long Lance seized a heavy iron poker from the hearth and smashed it over the butler's head, knocking him senseless. Neighbors heard screams from the house, hurried in and found blood splattered on the furniture, a body unconscious on the floor, a badly wounded Indian and a hysterical woman. The next day Florence's husband told the Banff newspaper that he had not heard a sound.[31]

For two days Athay MacFarlane's life hung in the balance. He survived and Long Lance escaped a murder charge. But he lost his job. John Murray Gibbon, fearful of publicity surrounding CPR employees who became involved in scandalous affairs, dismissed him without delay. Through it all, public opinion sided with Long Lance. The *Fort Macleod Gazette* commented that Long Lance lost his job "by taking a lady's part against a 'nigger.'" The *Banff Crag and Canyon* joked, "Anyone in future employing negro servants should keep them supplied with safety razors."[32] The *Calgary Herald* on September 10 said that "only the thickness of the negro's skull saved him from instant death as the poker was almost double with the force of the blow."

At the hearing held a month later in the Banff police court, Athay MacFarlane testified that Long Lance had caused "grievous bodily harm," but as MacFarlane could not recall the details — because of drink and the knock on the head — the charge was dismissed. The court also dismissed a charge by Long Lance against the butler.[33]

When Long Lance ran into Fred Kennedy, one of his Calgary newspaper friends, he explained how he had been attacked and slashed and how he had nearly lost his manhood. Kennedy could not resist. If Long Lance had lost his manhood, he later wrote, it would have been "a fate worse than death so far as the gregarious Indian was concerned."[34]

Long Lance already had a substantial assignment, a story that he had been working on for four years. In early October he left for New York to see Ray Long at *Cosmopolitan*. (Never a man to miss an opportunity, he stopped off in Chicago to see Florence one more time.[35]) When he arrived in New York, he took a small apartment at The Clarkson, a huge Victorian building on the Upper West Side, near the northwestern corner of Central Park.

Ray Long was still enthusiastic about Long Lance's work and encouraged him to write a story about General George Armstrong Custer. By now, Indian life and experiences were becoming distant for Long Lance. It had been four years since he had had any real contact with Plains Indians. When asked to give a Blackfoot name to the baby daughter of a friend with whom he boxed at his athletic club, he could think only of Napi ("Old Man"[36]), the name of one of the most significant mythic figures in Blackfoot folklore. Napi was the Blackfoot's "trickster," a spirit who had helped to create human beings and who had made many of the rivers, mountains and grasslands. It was hardly appropriate for a baby girl.

During the winter, Long Lance worked on his story of the Battle of Little Big Horn for the June 1927 issue of *Cosmopolitan*. Long Lance's first sketch of the story had appeared in the *Winnipeg Tribune* on February 24, 1923. It was a fantastic tale, stretched to the limits by Long Lance's ever-expanding imagination. Based on what he learned at Carlisle, and from interviews with old Sioux warriors in exile in Western Canada, Long Lance claimed that Custer had not been killed by Indians. He had not died spectacularly with pistols blazing in both hands, besieged by thousands of Sioux. According to Long Lance there had been no last stand at all. At the end of the battle the man generally acclaimed as one of America's bravest military heroes had committed suicide.

In "The Secret of the Sioux," Long Lance said he first heard the real story of Custer's death "whispered around the Indian campfires of the Montana prairies when I was a boy." More accurate is his second statement that "years later, in 1910, while I was attending Carlisle Indian School, I heard more from Wesley Two Moons, son of Chief Two Moons, who commanded the Cheyennes who were with Sitting Bull in the Custer Massacre." (Long Lance was safe here, for Wesley Two Moons had died of pneumonia in 1911, when Long Lance was in his third year at the school.[37])

Even if Long Lance had not heard the story directly from the young Cheyenne, other Indian students could have told him, or he might even have read it in *The Carlisle Arrow*. During Long Lance's time at Carlisle, the rumor of Custer's suicide was widely circulated. On October 21, 1910, the school newspaper published an Indian version of the Battle of Little Big Horn. In the article, Moses Friday, an Arapaho, stated that when the Indians located Custer's body they "discovered that he was not scalped or mutilated in any way." All they found was a bullet hole in his head. Friday suggested that Custer had killed himself rather than be taken by the Sioux, for "Indians never scalped the bodies of persons who had taken their own lives."

When Long Lance visited the Sioux near Moose Jaw, Saskatchewan, and at Oak Lake, Manitoba, in the winter of 1922–23, the elders confirmed the story. Even so, Long Lance was not satisfied. He wanted still more drama. In "The Secret of the Sioux," he added the bizarre twist that Sitting Bull wanted to save General Custer because he considered Custer to be his blood brother.

According to Long Lance's story, the Sioux medicine man had met Custer at West Point in 1859. After discussing Sioux land rights in Washington, D.C., Sitting Bull and his party were escorted to the United States Military Academy "and shown the young embryo officers who were later to come out onto the plains and help establish peace between the Indians and pioneers." Having taken a liking to the young cadet who had shown him and his party around the grounds, Sitting Bull called young Custer *Weh-hunka-wanzi*, "blood brother." Seventeen years later, just before the Battle of Little Big Horn, Sitting Bull warned his followers to spare his *Weh-hunka-wanzi*. His warriors carried out his orders. At the end of the battle, Custer was standing alone, the only survivor of his command. Before the Indians could give the peace sign, Custer put his gun to his head and pulled the trigger.

The story is incredible. Long Lance alone—of all Custer's biographers—states that Sitting Bull met Custer previously in 1859. Even accepting this unlikely event, how could Sitting Bull have ensured that his message was relayed to everyone before the battle? There would have been many Sioux and Cheyenne who could not have known him by sight, let alone pick him out amidst the smoke and dust of battle.[38]

In an era of wonderful nonsense, "The Secret of the Sioux" attracted widespread attention. In the 1920s Americans turned for an entire decade to many lighthearted diversions—a heavyweight boxing match, a craze for the Chinese game *mah-jong*, the Charleston. It was the Age of Ballyhoo. After the war they wanted to be entertained, and the times were uncritical. Even the sober *New York Times* was smitten by Long Lance's yarn, commenting that, if true, "then the mystery surrounding the death of General George Custer in the Battle of Little Big Horn is a mystery no longer."[39]

The article distressed others. Long Lance later told his friend Howard Kelly in Calgary that Mrs. Custer, the general's eighty-four-year-old widow, threatened court action. In Norfolk, Nebraska, a reunion of renowned frontiersmen protested against the inaccuracies.[40] In the long run, however, the publicity worked in Long Lance's favor. It won him instant fame in New York City, which is exactly what he wanted.

Long Lance, Biographer

*A*mong Ray Long's responsibilities in William Randolph Hearst's organization was the Cosmopolitan Book Corporation, the book publishing arm of *Cosmopolitan*. Founded in 1914 the Corporation had published several popular authors, and each year the firm released some forty-five titles.[1] After seeing Long Lance's articles, Ray Long knew that Long Lance had a book in him, and he wanted it for the Cosmopolitan list.

In late March 1927 the two met in Long's large, luxurious office in New York. The editor's enormous desk and chairs were carved from heavy oak, as was an ornate and richly paneled chest. Behind the desk rose shelves of books, and directly in front of him, on the opposite wall, hung a portrait of the conglomerate's monarch, the king of sensationalism, William Randolph Hearst.[2] The imposing painting showed a smiling Hearst, the owner of twenty-two American dailies, fifteen Sunday papers and seven magazines.[3]

The busy editor came straight to the point, telling Long Lance that there was a market for a boy's adventure book on Indians, and Long Lance was the man to write it. Long Lance contained his excitement with some difficulty, for this was the chance he had been waiting for. He accepted the proposal and asked Long the expected professional questions, as if he considered such offers every day. How long a book? The editor suggested seventy thousand words. When? Long told him he wanted *The Story of an Indian Boy* by the end of the year. Editing, layout, printing and promotion would take eight months. Long would schedule the book to appear in the autumn of 1928.

Long Lance signed a contract at the end of March, the terms being those of a standard literary contract: a ten percent royalty on the list price of the book, an advance of $500 against royalties, half to be paid on submission of a first draft and half on completion.[4] If the book sold, as planned, for $2.50,[5] Long Lance would make twenty-five cents on each copy. Just before the contract was completed, Ray Long, with Long Lance's consent, made a critical editorial suggestion.

For his articles and books, Long preferred a personal, or confessional, style.[6] It helped keep circulation and book sales mounting by injecting an easily identifiable narrator. Instead of *The Story of an Indian Boy*, Long suggested *Long Lance*.[7] It should be Long Lance's own life story along the lines of all that he had written and spoken of in earlier articles and on the lecture circuit. It should begin in the 1890s, when he was growing up.

Long Lance knew as a journalist that telling the story in the first person would considerably enhance it and give it more impact. He wanted to reach the largest possible audience, but he also realized that to write his life as if he had been born a Blackfoot involved enormous risk. But who would expose him? Both his autobiographical article and his story of Custer had been heavily embellished with fiction, and no one had unmasked him, so what could stop him now?

Before plunging into the project, Long Lance decided to contact his family because any disclosure on their part would end his masquerade forever. Sometime in the spring of 1927, he became Sylvester Long again and met Abe, his oldest brother, in Philadelphia.[8] He had not seen his brother in eighteen years. Abe had aged; there were wrinkles at his eyes, flecks of gray in his side-burns and he had a slight stoop to his shoulder. When Sylvester had left for Carlisle in 1909, Abe, then twenty-eight, had recently married. Now he was forty-six. His daughter, Vivian, of whom he had written so proudly, had died at the age of eleven in 1919. His wife, Aurelia, however, was in good health, and she and Abe were happy. To help with expenses, she had started a hair-straightening shop in the basement of their home in Winston–Salem.[9]

As Long Lance listened to Abe's news, ghosts of the past rushed back at him. For Abe, as for their parents, religion and the activities of the First Baptist Church were the universe. Abe was intelligent and hardworking, but his horizons were limited. He spent his days directing patrons up the stairs to the colored gallery of the Auditorium Theater, and he thought that the world was being good to him.[10]

Everyone at home still lived on top of one another in the lit-tle house on Brookstown Avenue. Walter still operated his own detective agency in the black community. Joe, their father, worked into his midseventies as a janitor, and each Thanksgiving the students at West Winston School expressed their gratitude to "Uncle Joe" by presenting him with a live turkey.[11]

Long Lance showed Abe his extensive scrapbooks. He explained that he had managed to obtain a complete secondary education. In the Canadian army he had risen to become an offi-cer. As a Plains Indian, his articles were published in the big mag-azines, and now he was being asked to write a book. The contrast between their lives could hardly have been greater. Any assur-ances Sylvester requested must have been provided, since no fam-ily member in his lifetime gave away his secret.

Sylvester's grandmother, Adeline Carson (left); his mother, Sallie, and father, Joe (center), and brother Abe (kneeling) at the Big Meeting at Carson Town, c. 1930.

In the summer of 1927 Long Lance returned again to Alberta to do his research in Calgary at the public library and to consult some of the local Indians. To pay his expenses in crossing the continent, he first completed several sportswriting assignments. Earlier in the year he had written an article for the *Winnipeg Tribune* on Gene Tunney, the ex-marine who in September 1926 had outboxed a weary Jack Dempsey to win the world heavyweight crown. Before leaving New York, Long Lance covered the Sharkey–Maloney heavyweight fight at Yankee Stadium on Friday, May 20,[12] but that night the fight was of secondary importance.

That morning, *The Spirit of St. Louis* had lifted off a muddy runway at Roosevelt Field on Long Island bound for Le Bourget Airport near Paris. During one of the preliminary bouts, the fight announcer broke in to report that a ship three hundred miles off the Atlantic coast had sighted Charles Lindbergh's plane. He asked the crowd to pray for the daring flyer. The response was immediate and electrifying: as one, the thirty thousand fight fans stood and bowed their heads to pray for the aviator's safe passage over the ocean. The next day the first reports of Lindbergh's successful arrival in Paris reached the United States.

Long Lance traveled to Calgary by train, paying his own way this time, the Canadian Pacific Railway having withdrawn his pass after the fracas at Banff the summer before. He brought with him his huge trunk and a wooden box containing a typewriter. Finances, as always, were tight. Fortunately he managed to sell three major articles that summer. One was a reworked version of "My Trail Upward," which he sold to *McClure's* in July. He rewrote his *Toronto Star Weekly* article on the Sun Dance and sold it to *Good Housekeeping*. The third was a lively, well-written story about the Prince of Wales and other European aristocrats who had recently bought ranches in Alberta. It was titled "Princes Go West, But What of the Young Man Without Money?" It appeared in *McClure's* that November. The fees from the three articles covered his summer and autumn expenses until his return to New York in December.

In Calgary he took a room next to the Vaheys' home on Fourth Avenue, where he had last stayed in 1921–22. It had been six years since he spent a full summer in Calgary, and much had changed. Many of his friends of the early 1920s had married and were starting families. Howard Kelly, still sports editor of the *Herald*, was studying for a law degree at the University of Alberta. Hugh Dann was well launched on a new career with the John Deere Plow Company, making frequent trips across North America.

Long Lance was left on his own for the first few weeks. He went for long walks, watched baseball games at Mewata Park and St. George's Island, and worked out often at the YMCA, where he became good friends with Maurice Fidler. Fidler, a strong, husky man of twenty-one, had been in Long Lance's boxing class at the YMCA in 1921–22. During the summer of 1927, they met daily and boxed, wrestled and played handball. Fidler was perceptive and could see behind Long Lance's easy, happy manner. He found him a "warm-hearted, wistful, lonely man." He recognized in Long Lance a sensitive man in whom lingering discrimination was taking its toll. After a workout one day, Fidler and Long Lance walked over to Rosie Helmer's poolroom two blocks away, but Long Lance could not enter. Large signs on the poolroom walls declared NO INDIANS ALLOWED. As an Indian, Long Lance could not step into a tavern or buy liquor at the government-owned vendors.[13]

That summer Long Lance, freed for several months from his obsession with publicizing his Plains Indian identity, drew closer to the local Indians and tried to help their children. He put his embarrassment at the Blackfoot Sun Dance behind him. Once a week he visited the reserve at Gleichen, where he conducted boxing classes for the boys, always urging them to take pride in their race. Every so often he brought the boys to Calgary to let them practice in the gymnasium at the YMCA.[14]

In his book, Long Lance, as he later stated in the introduction, wanted to relate "the experiences of our old warriors who are still living, but who cannot tell their own stories because they do not speak the white man's tongue." He worked on his manuscript all summer, writing most of it at the Vaheys' next door to his rooming house. He seemed always to be at the Vaheys' at mealtime. The Vaheys' oldest daughter, Jean, devoted most of her summer to his project. She proofread and corrected his text, and kept a pot of strong coffee on the stove.[15] Long Lance still found the spirits friendly at the Vahey house.

Long Lance often told Fidler of the effort, self-discipline and concentration the book required. By his own admission he was a slow writer. Once, at the YMCA, he admitted to Fidler, "What I write is well-written, but it takes so long to get it out."

Fidler knew the area that Long Lance was describing in the book. His grandfather and two uncles had a ranch at Boundary Creek, four miles north of the Montana border and just southwest of the Blood Reserve. They had arrived in Alberta in 1883. When

Mike Eagle Speaker as a young man. His life supplied much of the inspiration for Long Lance's autobiography.

he had spent the summer of 1917 at the ranch, Maurice had learned much about the history of the area. Once, after asking Fidler to review parts of the book, Long Lance asked him what he thought of it. Fidler tried to be encouraging and supportive, but pointed out a discrepancy: in the 1890s his father had played minor league baseball and his grandfather had a fully operating ranch in the area that Long Lance described in his manuscript as Indian and buffalo country. Without explaining why, Long Lance simply told him that this fictional touch was necessary for the book. Fidler let it go at that, but it troubled him.[16]

Long Lance incorporated many of his Indian interviews of the early 1920s into the manuscript along with several of his published stories, such as those about Chief Carry-the-Kettle and Almighty Voice. He also used information supplied by his "brother," Mike Eagle Speaker. And, when it served his purpose, Long Lance did not hesitate to invent.

In the early, stronger chapters of *Long Lance*, he relied heavily on what he learned from Eagle Speaker. Since their first meeting at St. Paul's mission in August 1920, Long Lance had kept in touch with the young Blood Indian. When Mike left the reserve to study at Claresholm Agricultural College in 1922, Long Lance encouraged him, sending him letters as he traveled across Canada writing for the western dailies. In 1923 he spent a weekend with Mike at the school, which was sixty miles south of Calgary. They met again after their adoption as brothers at Macleod in 1924. When Mike came up to Calgary in 1926 to enter the rodeo events at the Stampede, he met with Long Lance, and in the summer of 1927, Long Lance invited him to Calgary.[17]

Mike respected Long Lance. He looked up to him as a great warrior, an Indian hero in the Great War, and also as someone like himself who left his tribe to acquire a white man's education. Blood brotherhood in Plains Indian society meant a perfect sharing, and when Long Lance asked about the Bloods' customs, Mike eagerly told him all that he could.

Mike's great-grandmother had raised him after the death of his mother and grandmother. She was born in the 1820s, half a century before the buffalo disappeared. In 1914, before Mike was sent to St. Paul's Mission School at the age of ten, she had told him and his brothers all that she knew of the Blood ceremonies and culture. Their father, Eagle Speaker, who had trained under some of the best-known medicine men in the Blackfoot Confederacy, also taught him much. Mike was a curious student, a keen observer, and during his childhood many of the old customs were still practiced. Everyone had horses, and the travois was still used.

Few adult Bloods in the years before World War I could speak English, and few had joined the Christian church.

Mike Eagle Speaker and Long Lance spent two weeks together in the summer of 1927. They stayed in Calgary for a week, in Banff for four days, then traveled to Golden, just across the Alberta border into British Columbia, where they spent another four days. Long Lance questioned Mike on the Blackfoot language and Blood customs. Mike soon realized that Long Lance really knew very little about Plains Indian life.

Long Lance's opening chapter began with an arresting scene: "The first thing in my life that I can remember is the exciting aftermath of an Indian fight in northern Montana. My mother was crying and running about with me in my moss bag-carrier on her back. I remember the scene as though it were yesterday, yet I was barely a year old. . . ." He remembered that his mother's hand was bleeding, and years later, he wrote, his aunt confirmed this "startling impression":

> One day, when I had grown into boyhood, I asked my aunt about it. I described the scene to her and told her the position in which she was standing in relation to the pony, where my mother was standing and how she handed me to her; I gave her a word-picture of the whole circumstance, as it was so indelibly inscribed on my memory. As I talked, I could see my aunt's features taking on a gradual look of wonderment. And when I was through, she looked at me in great surprise and exclaimed:
>
> "Can you remember that! You were only fourteen months old then. It was when your uncle, Iron Blanket, was killed in a fight with the Crows—and your mother had cut off one of her fingers in mourning for him, as the women used to do in those days."

After that, Long Lance writes that he relapsed "into the mystic sleep of infancy again" until he was four, from which age he could remember things distinctly. The colors he remembers from those early years were "a dull, deep bluish gray":

> Everything I saw was tinted with this mystic grayness. It represented danger, mystery, and distance. We were not yet entirely at peace with our ancient enemies, the Crows, the Assiniboines, the Sioux, and the Crees; and stories of a new peril which might spell our doom—the White Man—were being whispered about our camp fires. Danger lurked everywhere, even in the animals from which we secured our food.[18]

Having drawn the reader in, Long Lance then makes Mike Eagle Speaker's childhood his own, pushing it back into the late nineteenth century and grafting onto it stories that he had collected from the old Plains Indians. He did a skillful job of it.

Early in the book Long Lance explains how Indian children were taught to ride horses soon after they learned to walk. He relates how the fathers hardened their sons to make them "brave and stoical, and good and courageous fighters." Every morning, summer and winter, they were taken down to the river for a plunge in an icy stream or a roll in the snow. From their mothers they learned the moral teachings of the tribe. Lying was severely punished. "We had a legend for everything that was good, and the more we youngsters lived up to the legends which our mothers told us, the more highly respected we were in the tribe."

Such insights into Plains Indian life were accurate, and through them the book manages a strong and legitimate Indian flavor. Short references to aspects of Plains Indian culture keep appearing, such as the Indians' ancient courtesy of not interrupting anyone while he is talking and their respect for old people "so deeply bred into us that to this day I have not the courage to dispute the word of an old person."[19] Mike Eagle Speaker's finest reminiscences are scattered in the book like raisins in the dough, all carefully selected by a gifted journalist who knew how to use anecdotes.

When he went beyond Mike's reminiscences, it was always to make a point. While among the Lillooet Indians in British Columbia in June 1922, Long Lance heard of a fascinating whipping custom. To toughen the children's bodies, the men whipped them each morning with fir branches. Anxious to emphasize the hardiness of Blackfoot youth, Long Lance simply added this practice as another feature of Blackfoot culture, even though it had never occurred among the Bloods.[20] Nor did they burn dry fir needles on the backs of their hands to see who could endure the torture the longest.[21] Still, the essence of what Long Lance wrote was true: the Blackfoot insisted on a harsh, rigorous upbringing to make their sons warriors who were tough enough to withstand the elements.

Long Lance relayed numerous colorful incidents from Plains Indian life, some of which he had heard from the elders, some of which he had read and others which he made up. He described the Indians' domestic life, the Sun Dance, the awesome powers of the medicine men and the band's desperate search for the vanishing buffalo. A book reviewer commented that "Inevitably one is reminded of Hiawatha and Fenimore Cooper's adventure tales . . . startling accounts of dances, rites, famous medicine men of the past, battles, pony raids, great hunting expeditions in the Rockies—all told with verve and remembered with clarity."[22]

Long Lance also borrowed ingeniously from his own childhood. Throughout *Long Lance*, his mother, not his father, is the dominant figure. In North Carolina it was his mother who had attended church every Sunday and who insisted on a strict religious atmosphere in the home. There is an element of truth in the statement that his Blackfoot mother "trained us to live right."[23]

After wild adventures in the Rockies, where his band hunted mountain sheep and goats, and captured a large herd of wild horses, they returned to the plains only to find that their fellow Blackfoot had signed treaties with the governments of the United States and Canada and "were living on reservations and getting along well." Under Crowfoot, their tribal leader, members of the last roving Blackfoot band decided it was time to lay down their arms, take up their reserves and send their children to the missionaries' schools "that they might learn to work with their hands and become as white men":[24]

> Our day as free rovers of the open plains had ended. A few years later we boys were in mission schools, learning our ABC's and how to hoe with our hands. How this shamed us: to have to work like women, when we had thought that we were going to be warriors and hunters like our forefathers. This manual labor so humiliated us that whenever we looked up and saw any of our old warriors passing the school, we would lay down our hoes and stand still until they had passed.[25]

Long Lance's conclusion, however poignant and evocative, was historically inaccurate. Crowfoot was not living "on that bright day in 1897."[26] He had died in 1890. Nor could the Blackfoot band have been roaming freely over the prairies and into the Rockies in the mid-1890s because they had made treaty in 1877 and were settled on their reserves in the early 1880s.

Long Lance completed the first draft of his book by late November, then checked some of the spellings of Blackfoot words with Canon Middleton before heading back to New York. Three weeks later, the final draft was ready.[27] The day after he submitted the manuscript, it was being circulated around Ray Long's office, page by page, avidly being read by half a dozen people at once.[28] After final editing the book was printed to be ready for August and the autumn book trade. Cosmopolitan liked the book so much that it decided on a first run of ten thousand copies instead of the usual three thousand.[29]

Long Lance dedicated the book to Canon Middleton and Commissioner Graham, the inclusion of the latter a sign of his growing cynicism. The inscription reads, "Dedicated to the two White Men who have guided and encouraged me most since I have taken a place in civilization." To be safer still, he included a thank-you to Duncan Campbell Scott, the Deputy Superintendent of Indian Affairs in Ottawa, whom he termed "a friend of the Indian." He then signed it, two thousand miles from the site,

BUFFALO CHILD LONG LANCE
Blood Indian Reservation
Cardston, Alberta
July 1, 1928

When *Long Lance* was published in August 1928, the international press praised the book extravagantly. The *Philadelphia Public Ledger* called it "a gorgeous saga of the Indian race." From the south, the *New Orleans Times–Picayune* hailed it as "by all odds the most important Americana offered this year." In Britain, the *New Statesman* wrote, "This book rings true; no outsider could explain so clearly how the Indians felt. . . ." Ernest Thompson Seton, the distinguished naturalist and student of the North American Indian, called the book "one of the best pictures ever offered of the old-time Indian at his best."[30] Dr. Paul Radin, the well-known anthropologist, went even further, giving it his academic stamp of approval in a review in the *New York Herald Tribune*.[31] A year earlier, Dr. Radin had published *The Story of the American Indian*, an exhaustive study of all the major native groups in the United States. Dr. Radin had received his doctorate in anthropology from Columbia University in 1911 and had devoted his life to the study of what was then called "primitive man." For years he had worked with the Winnebago tribe, a small Siouan-speaking group in the Midwest, publishing ten good-sized monographs and several articles about them.

In his review of *Long Lance*, Dr. Radin began by commenting on the tragedy that so few biographies and autobiographies existed of the first Americans. One was forced to learn about them, he wrote, from works written by sophisticated Europeans and Americans "who, no matter how detailed may be their knowledge, can never properly understand the workings of a society so utterly alien to them as is that of so-called primitive man." For this reason he welcomed the appearance of such an "authentic" autobiography. He praised the book as an "unusually faithful account of [Long Lance's] childhood and early manhood. . . . I cannot think of any work that could act as a better corrective of the ridiculous notions still prevailing about the Indians than this autobiography of Long Lance."

Dr. Radin, however, expressed one reservation. While Buffalo Child had described the "external side of the Blackfoot culture" with "remarkable realism," the anthropologist felt that he had done very little to illuminate the Indian mind, since he "consistently refuses to reveal much about his inner self." He forgave this, though, explaining that in fact it serves to establish the book's authenticity, for "no Indian talks much about himself."

Long Lance was a success and sold well across North America and Europe. The first printing nearly sold out by the end of 1928, and Cosmopolitan ordered a second printing. In England a publisher printed a special British edition, and in 1929 German and Dutch translations appeared.[32] Long Lance was about to become one of the most famous Indians of his day.

CHAPTER 13

Long Lance, Social Lion

NEW YORK CITY, 1928

*I*n January 1928, in the Crystal Room of the Ritz Hotel in New York, Ray Long gave a luncheon to honor Emil Ludwig, whose popular biography *Napoleon* had been riding the best-seller lists for nearly a year. As Ray Long's latest prodigy, Long Lance was a special guest at the luncheon. Sipping a cocktail before the event, he heard a drawling voice behind him. "Chief Long Lance, I've been wanting to meet you for a mighty long time." He turned to find that the voice belonged to Irvin S. Cobb, the writer and humorist, then at the height of his fame.

"Well," Long Lance replied, "you don't have to tell me who you are."

Ray Long, ever the opportunist, rushed over and said to Long Lance, "Chief, why don't you make Irvin write a foreword for your book?"

Cobb puffed on his cigar. "I'd be delighted," he said.

The deal was made on the spot.[1]

Over the next few months Long Lance and Cobb saw a good deal of each other. Cobb and his wife, Laura, invited Long Lance to their attractive white house at East Hampton, on the eastern tip of Long Island. It was a pretty two-story home with green shutters, festooned in summer with rambler roses.[2]

Cobb and Long Lance were exact opposites. Cobb liked to hunt and fish, but that was the extent of his sporting life. He was a bulky man with heavy jowls and a triple chin. He loved to eat and it showed, but he made light of it, once describing himself as "an ugly-faced old man, with beetled brows and a big 'bay' window."[3] Thanks to his amusing tales of Judge Priest, a wise old southern judge fond of mint juleps and helping innocents in trouble, Cobb had become the most widely read and highest paid short-story writer in America.[4] He had come a long way from his first job as a reporter on the *Paducah Daily News.*

Cobb never forgot his Kentucky roots, and Judge Priest always described the South in the most affectionate terms. His father had been a Confederate army veteran, and Irvin himself had proudly joined and become a colonel in the United Confederates organization, always championing the cause of the soldiers who marched in gray. Cobb loved to tell "darkie" stories. His friend Bob Davis of the *New York Sun* once wrote that from 1918 to 1928 he had listened four or five hundred times to Cobb's "one hundred Southern Ethiopian classics."[5] Cobb's first novel was about Judge Priest's servant, Jefferson Exodus Poindexter, or as Jeff called himself on a visit to Harlem, "Col. J. Exeter Poindexter, Esq. (the 'Col.' standing for 'colored')." Still, Cobb was fascinated by the North American Indian. Once, in Oklahoma, a magazine had reported that he "is said to have declared himself to have a small strain of aboriginal blood."[6]

Since his boyhood in Kentucky, Cobb had collected Indian artifacts. He decorated his study with Navaho rugs, Plains Indian war bonnets and Flathead buffalo spears. One of his most prized possessions was a good-luck necklace worn by Chief Joseph of the

Nez Percé, whose famous 1877 retreat from the U.S. Army had been called by General W.T. Sherman one of the finest pieces of military strategy he had ever known. Cobb loved Indian legends and traditions. For years he had studied their sign language and had mastered much of it. In 1925 a band of South Peigans in Montana (where they are known as Blackfeet) formally adopted him and humorously named the roly-poly Kentuckian Piitaohpikis, or "Eagle Ribs."[7]

Long Lance endured Cobb's darkie stories, and Cobb never suspected that Long Lance was an impostor. Instead, in an enthusiastic foreword, Cobb praised the book and the author in the fullest terms, telling of how he emerged from the war "as a captain of infantry, his body covered with wounds and his breast glittering with medals bestowed for high conduct and gallantry." Again it was Long Lance who provided Cobb with all the details.

The foreword continues:

> . . . sinking his own engaging personality, his own individual achievements into the background, he depicts graphic phases of a life which has altogether vanished, of a race which rapidly is vanishing. I know of no man better fitted than Chief Long Lance to write a true book about the true American Indian, and I know of no book on the subject which better reveals the spirit of the Indian in the years that are gone and the spirit of times the like of which will never be seen again.
>
> I claim there is authentic history in these pages and verity and most of all a power to describe in English words the thoughts, the instincts, the events which originally were framed in a native language.
>
> And I claim the white man will owe him a debt for this work of his and that his people the Indians already owe him a debt for having performed it.[8]

Several days after meeting Cobb at the luncheon at the Ritz, Long Lance attended a glittering cocktail party at Cobb's Park Avenue apartment. Long Lance had invested in a finely tailored $180 tuxedo, one that showed his athletic body to advantage.[9] The men arrived in full evening dress and the women in stylish, long-waisted gowns with strings of pearls circling their necks. Long Lance reveled in the chitchat, telling the guests stories of the Navaho, the Sioux and the Cree in his soft, cultured voice. When he referred to "my people," his voice took on a sad, arresting tone. One bejeweled matron asked Long Lance if he could demonstrate the Indian sign language. Graciously, he consented.

For the sign for spring, Long Lance made rapid movements with his hands, suggesting rain, then, with a quick upward thrust of his hand, he indicated the regenerative force of the land in spring. With long, curving and flowing movements he imitated summer's gentle winds, and with more hand gestures he made the sun set in autumn and snowflakes dance in winter. He soon attracted a considerable audience and told how the Indian languages were descriptive and figurative.[10] "The Indian calls a looking glass 'He peeped into the water and saw himself.' That comes from the old days when they would bend over water and see themselves. . . ."[11]

He resurrected all the material he used on the lecture circuit. His Indian stories were not only a welcome relief from the usual cocktail party small-talk, but also exactly what the rich and powerful wanted to hear about the noble red man. Long Lance explained that Indians had no "curse" words, and that the worst thing one Indian could say to another was to call him a "bad dog." He told them that Indians had no words for "How do you do?" or "Good-bye." Instead, he explained, "When we enter another's home, we just grunt and sit down. We take it for granted. When we leave we just 'Huh.' That is all."[12] He told of how in the old days the elders never died of disease and their teeth never fell out, but after eating the white man's bread, they died of diseases and their teeth rotted.[13] And he told how Indians acquired their names. "An Indian always has more than one name," he said.

> The first name is given when he is born. Some circumstance will be noted and that determines his name. When he gets to be about six years old his playmates will give him another name, 'Crazy Horse,' 'Lazy Dog'—something like that. That name will stick until he is eighteen, and then he has to do something to earn a real name. When they were still fighting, he had to go out on an exploit and do some brave act; then they would change his name perhaps to 'Sheet Lightning' or 'Uses-Both-Arms.' These names are like medals in the army, like decorations, and that is why an old Indian will never tell you his name. If you ask him his name, he will turn to some third person to answer, because he does not want to brag.[14]

Irvin Cobb was showing off Long Lance, who proved to be the hit of the party. During the evening one of the ladies remarked to her companion, "Isn't it wonderful that a dark-skinned person can look so distinguished?"[15]

Dark-skinned persons were a rarity at Park Avenue parties in 1928. By the late twenties, blacks constituted ten percent of Manhattan's population, and Harlem was known as the "Negro Capital of the World." When the blacks moved in, the whites sold their homes and moved farther out. Many New York hotels, restaurants and theaters refused African Americans admission, and even some of the New York churches denied them membership.[16]

The North American Indians, whether dark-skinned or copper-skinned, belonged in a different category. The affluent, upper-class Americans of Park Avenue felt a certain shame and guilt about the plight of the Indian, whose land was stolen, whose numbers were receding to the vanishing point and who posed no threat to real estate values. Long Lance's listeners' knowledge of

Long Lance (left) at an "Old Boys" reunion of St. John's Military School at the Hotel Pennsylvania, New York, in the late 1920s.

the Indian came from such romantic treatments as Longfellow's *Hiawatha* and the works of James Fenimore Cooper.

The audiences Long Lance spoke to at the cocktail parties and on the lecture circuit were aware of their own shallow roots. Men such as Irvin Cobb and Ray Long had come from small towns and second-, third-, perhaps fourth- and occasionally fifth-generation immigrant families. But what were one hundred or two hundred years compared to thousands, to "time immemorial"?

Long Lance knew what they wanted to hear and he delivered. He acted the modern noble savage, the twentieth-century Hiawatha. He talked plainly and directly, and in reply to any question, he always looked the questioner straight in the eye.[17] To the women crowded around him, he seemed the embodiment of all that was free and natural and vaguely dangerous.

Long Lance stopped worrying about being unmasked and basked in the adulation. He discussed with confidence many sub-

Long Lance at a sitting with the portrait artist Brynjulf Strandenaes. The portrait was commissioned by Manlius Military Academy (formerly St. John's).

jects, even chromatic aberrations. When asked about mixed marriages and the physical appearance of the children from such a relationship, he explained that white couples might have a black baby because of "a Negro-element a generation ago." But he quickly added that this never happens to those of distant Indian ancestry. "After the fourth generation of intermarriage between white and Indian, all Indian features disappear," he said. There are no "throwbacks."[18]

    Irvin Cobb helped launch Long Lance socially in New York. Valuable contacts were made at the party and at Cobb's house on Long Island, and more dinner invitations arrived. Once, at another party at the Ritz Hotel, Long Lance met Natacha Rambova, the wife of the late Rudolph Valentino. Without hesitation Long

Lance asked her to dance, and Natacha, wearing a blood-red dress and a red turban, accepted. They fox-trotted around the floor as the orchestra played "The Sheik of Araby," the song Rudolph Valentino had inspired.[19] To onlookers Long Lance looked like a sepia version of the Latin lover himself.[20]

A drawing of Long Lance by Princess Alexandra Victoria of Schleswig–Holstein–Glücksburg.

There were many other women. That winter Long Lance dated Mildred McCoy, the actress, and Vivian Hart, the light-opera singer.[21] So successful was he with women that Cobb nicknamed him "the Beau Brummell of Broadway."[22] He became close friends with Princess Alexandra, the ex-wife of Prince August-Wilhelm, the fourth son of the German Kaiser, whom she had divorced after the war. In 1926 the redheaded princess had left Europe with her second husband, a retired German naval officer, to earn her living as a painter in New York. Princess Alexandra later drew an appealing sketch of Long Lance in his Broadway tribal costume: top hat and tails.[23]

Long Lance's name inevitably surfaced in the society columns in newspapers. O.O. McIntyre, who wrote a chatty and informal column called "New York Day by Day," spotted him first. He wrote on May 20, 1928, "A social lion of the season is an Indian — Buffalo Chief Long Lance, who has been invited everywhere." McIntyre described him as "straight as an arrow, with smoothly brushed black hair, broad shoulders and waspish waist. . . ." He called him an intellectual, who had "graduated from three universities." Across

Among the women who sought out Long Lance's company was the actress Mildred McCoy, who inscribed her photo, "To Long Lance, the Maker of Dreams."

the United States, in more than three hundred newspapers, some seven million Americans read of "Buffalo Chief," who, in the words of the gossip columnist, had become "a social wow."[24]

In mid-January 1928 Long Lance visited West Point. Through Frazier Hunt, a senior editor at Cosmopolitan, he had met Lieutenant Bonner Fellers, a West Point English instructor, and his wife, Dorothy. Lieutenant Fellers invited Long Lance to speak to his classes.[25]

Long Lance wrote to his friend Howard Kelly in Calgary to tell him about the visit to the military academy, and he included

Another companion of Long Lance's was the opera singer Vivian Hart.

in his letter the somewhat stilted remarks of a young cadet named W.D. Moore, who obviously had fallen under Long Lance's spell. "We saw in him the man developed by proper training from a people we consider far inferior," Cadet Moore said.

> He was built like an athlete; carried himself like a soldier. His lectures showed a brilliant mind for research. His clothes betrayed a fine taste, and his smooth, regular flow of language showed him a master of our language. The ease with which he took hold of his audience showed leadership. So, in this civilized savage we see an athlete, soldier, scholar and leader. He is wholly a man.

The remarks sound almost too flattering, too much of what Long Lance's self-portrait might have been. Indeed, they were, for no cadet named W.D. Moore ever attended West Point.[26]

In the same letter to Howard Kelly, Long Lance told of a practical joke he took part in on his visit to West Point. Whether the incident actually occurred or not, it reveals that Long Lance considered the details important, since he wrote about the incident at such great length. It involved "a very beautiful girl about twenty, married to an 'old major' about thirty-seven":

> For some reason or other, none of the other officers nor their wives like this particular Major very much. And since the young wife had been looking at my picture in one of the officers' suites and asking his wife to introduce us when I came up, every damned officer and his wife on the Post had conspired to get her over to their big party for me, alone. Well, it was the funniest thing you ever saw. They framed the Major with a lot of examination papers, and about four of their wives went over to their [the major and his wife's] home and, only as women can do, managed to get her over. Then my host, a captain, said: "Now, Josephine will be there by the time we arrive; she's crazy to meet you, and don't be afraid to give her a thrill. That's what she's looking for; that damned husband of hers is a dead old stick; so as soon as the party gets started, get her out into the kitchen and rub her up a little; wait until you see her— she's a beaut."
>
> When we got back to his apartment in the officers' quarters, sure enough, I got a glance of the queen sitting in the drawing room. She was so damned good-looking that I went into the bathroom with the Captain to primp up a bit. And, before I knew it, here she was in the bathroom, saying, "I couldn't wait for you to

come in." Oh, boy, what a beauty she was—exactly like Jean Gardiner—only her eyes were more beautiful than any I ever saw. A throbbing knock-out! She is what they call "an Army girl"; that is, she is the daughter of a General and was born in the army and has lived all over the world. She is quite a flash in Washington society, where she goes every two weeks for a social whirl— and she neither drinks nor smokes. What I enjoyed about the whole thing was that it was open and above board and everybody was a party to our little flirtation. I am glad that I have had the unpleasant experiences that I have; for now I can play up to a little innocent frame-up like this without any thoughts of allowing it to go too far. To the evident joy of everyone present, we had many quiet little moments in the kitchen, and it was all very nice. I think everyone of the officers and their wives was much pleased with the way I conducted myself; though we were all drinking, and now the whole post, that is, our big circle, refers to her as my "Sweetheart." As I said, Howard, thank goodness, I know what it is all about now; this married proposition, and I would never think of going any further than playing just a little before all the gang. . . .[27]

Back in New York, Long Lance pasted in his scrapbooks the documentary proof that he continued to impress interviewers, among them Gladys Baker, the New York correspondent for the *News-Age-Herald* of Birmingham, Alabama, which styled itself "the South's Greatest Newspaper." After *Long Lance* was published in the fall of 1928, Baker met the author in a small French restaurant on Eighth Avenue. The former debutante from Jacksonville, Florida, left the interview captivated by the dark, handsome stranger. In her article she described Long Lance as "distinguished looking," and added for her Alabama readers the supreme compliment: "Were it not for his straight black hair, which is cut close to his head, and his skin, which is not red but more the color of ivory-tone parchment, he might be taken for a Wall Street broker."[28]

Long Lance confided very little to his friends in his many letters, but he methodically listed all his social successes. In June 1928 he wrote to Howard Kelly in Calgary to tell him about the fabulous house parties he had attended on Long Island. "You know the kind we've often seen in the movies but never in practice," he wrote. "Well, I can tell you now that they exist." He rattled off the same superficial letter to Canon Middleton and the Fellers, telling of an evening at Irvin Cobb's, a lunch with celebrities in downtown Manhattan, a dinner party where he met Princess Alexandra, a weekend trip to Washington, D.C.[29]

By the autumn of 1929 Long Lance had at last become the celebrity he desired. Others might now boast of being at a party that he attended. He gave out opinions on everything from genetics to presidential politics. When reporters asked him about the presidential campaign building up, Long Lance urged all the chiefs of all the tribes to support the Republican ticket of Herbert Hoover and Senator Curtis of Kansas. Curtis's grandmother, after all, was one-half Kaw Indian. (The federal franchise had been extended to all American Indians in 1924.[30])

Long Lance eagerly accepted speaking invitations, which paid him honoraria of one hundred dollars per lecture, a not inconsiderable sum at a time when the average annual income was less than fifteen hundred dollars.[31] In early October he returned to Columbus, Ohio, to speak to the Chamber of Commerce and again at Logan Park on Ohio History Day. From there he went to Cleveland to speak at the Halle Brothers Book Fair. At the end of the month he was in Utah, speaking in Salt Lake City to the Bonneville Club, composed of four hundred of the state's most influential businessmen.[32]

Before leaving Ohio he stopped in Akron at the request of

the B.F. Goodrich Company. The Goodrich people wanted Long Lance to design and then endorse an improved canvas running shoe. Long Lance liked the idea and brought with him a pair of old moccasins, suggesting that Goodrich make up an experimental pair of running shoes modeled on them. When the shoes were ready, Long Lance tested them. In the words of a Goodrich publicist, " . . . not only did every bit of canvas, every stitch of thread, every ounce of rubber mean something to him, but he was able to explain it so that white men could understand."[33]

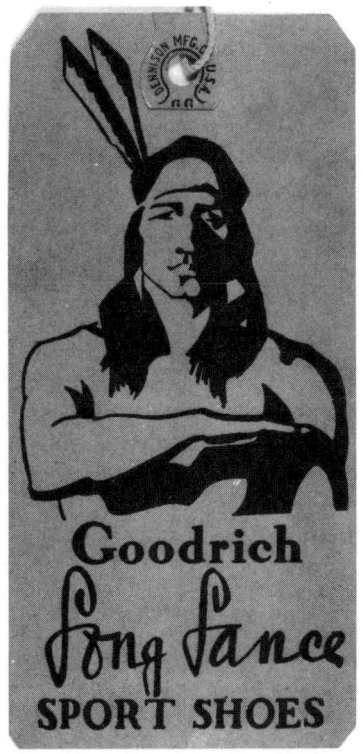

The tag attached to B.F. Goodrich's Long Lance Sport Shoes.

By the late 1920s, Long Lance, after years of pasting stories and pictures into his scrapbooks, was beginning to believe his own press clippings and to regard himself in the same heroic terms as others. In a manuscript he prepared in 1928, he called himself "a spokesman for the Indians of America" for the first time.[34]

Long Lance's previous Indian stories were written to entertain, but this one had anger and fire in it. At the time, most Americans assumed that the Indians in the West were doing well, making progress, but Long Lance wrote that they actually were doing very badly—starving, in fact. The Office of Indian Affairs held a billion dollars in an Indian trust fund, money the tribes had made through land sales, but Long Lance said the fund was not being used "to feed the starving stomachs of our old people who bore

A *poster prepared to advertise the Chief Long Lance Shoe.*

the brunt of this terrible thing that civilization has done. . . ."

This was the generation, he wrote, that had seen the newcomers "surge across the West, killing their game, raping their women, giving them diseases that they had never heard of, picking fights with them and trading bad liquor for their buffalo robes." And the government itself had interfered and "by trickery, promises and presents . . . bribed the Indians into signing away their rights to their reservations." Gone at least for the moment was the soft-spoken noble savage who was proud to tell what he had made of "a white man's chance." Long Lance's attack on the federal Office of Indian Affairs, the "Indian Bureau," is clear and direct. Few Americans, he said, realized

> . . . that the Bureau of Indian Affairs still controls both their person and their property; that the Indian tribes have no say as to whether their funds shall be used to support the government Bureau or not; that they can be declared mentally incompetent by the Bureau without resort to civil court; that the heirs of an Indian, even his own brother, can not administer his estate except through the approval of the Bureau; that the Indian Bureau can destroy the will of an Indian without having to show cause to any court.

Long Lance called for a reorganization of the Office of Indian Affairs and the laws governing the Indian.[35]

It was all true. Charles Burke, commissioner of the Office of Indian Affairs, recognized the evils of the system himself. In 1924 he told a reporter, "We are not even yet being square with the Indians. We are stealing land from some of them, depriving some of them of the water without which they must starve, making drunkards and loafers of others."[36] Burke tried to stop the abuses, but his critics charged that he had failed to do enough. He was the bureaucrat most easily vilified, the one with the highest profile, but the bureau had by this time grown to be a huge, headless monster, and any criticism of an individual was useless and probably unfair.[37]

The reformers' attacks increased when the Meriam report was released. In February 1928 Lewis Meriam and his associates of the Institute of Government Research published a detailed study of American Indian policy called *The Problem of Indian Administration*. It provided the first comprehensive description of what had happened to the Indians since the Indian wars ended. Investigators reported that living conditions in the West were wretched. General death and infant mortality rates were shamefully high. Entire communities suffered from trachoma, an eye disease resulting in blindness. Tuberculosis crippled and maimed when it did not kill outright. Reservation housing was substandard. Hunger was the common lot. The Meriam report concluded that unless drastic measures were taken immediately, the Indian in the United States appeared to be on the verge of extinction.[38]

Long Lance's outspoken manuscript, perhaps the closest thing he ever wrote to the truth, was never published, and the fault must lie with the Cosmopolitan Book Corporation. Unwittingly the corporation set in motion an investigation of Long Lance's origins, when, as a gesture of courtesy, it sent a complimentary advance copy of *Long Lance* to Commissioner Burke. An accompanying letter, dated August 3, 1928, read

Dear Mr. Burke:

Chief Long Lance recently submitted a manuscript for a book that has the makings of a standard work. We are publishing it under the title of "Long Lance."[39]

The emotional reaction of those who have read it is enthusiastically favorable. Irvin S. Cobb has dramatically expressed this feeling in a foreword to the book.

Under separate cover we are sending you an advance copy. It would interest us very much to know what you think of "Long Lance."[39]

The request was a straightforward and simple, and Commissioner Burke decided to try to satisfy it, but first he wanted to learn more about the distinguished man of letters who had attended the bureau's school at Carlisle before being accepted to West Point.

On August 29 he contacted Major General Wahl, adjutant general at the War Department, concerning Long Lance's record at West Point. Back came the surprising reply, dated August 31, that "Mr. Long-Lance" had failed the competitive examination. Burke decided to probe deeper, suspecting that the fraud might be greater. He sent off more letters in September, all of them asking, in different ways, "Who is Long Lance?"

By late November Commissioner Burke had the evidence before him. Cobb, in his foreword to *Long Lance*, said that the author was a chief of the "Northern Blackfeet." On October 4 Commissioner Graham wrote from Canada that "this designation is only conferred on him in an honorary capacity." Long Lance claimed to be a Blackfoot in his book, but on October 7 another letter from Canada arrived, this one from Percy Little Dog, the interpreter for the Blood Indian Council:

I am pleased to inform you, that we never saw or heard a thing about "Buffalo Child Long Lance" until the winter of 1922, when he attended the annual re-union of "The Old Boys and Girls" Association of the St. Paul's School, Blood Reserve. He was our guest, and there was given the name of Buffalo Child, by one of the older members of the tribe. He is not a Blood Indian, and has no tribal rights on the Reserve. We have heard he was a Cherokee Indian, but do not know definitely who he is and where he came from.

Little Dog's letter carried considerable weight with Burke, who had met the Blood spokesman in the autumn of 1927. The tall, forty-four-year-old Plains Indian had been part of a party of thirty-five Blackfoot Indians who had toured seventy cities in the United States as guests of the Great Northern Railroad. In full regalia they took part in the Centennial Railway Exhibition in Baltimore, parading every day. In New York, Percy Little Dog initiated Mayor Jimmy Walker into the Blood tribe, giving him the name "Many Rider" and painting his face with war paint. In Washington, D.C., he met Commissioner Burke, and in perfect English he laid before him the Canadian Blackfoot claim for their share of the sixty-two-million-acre lease in Montana, which by the Treaty of 1855 belonged to the Blackfoot Confederacy.[40]

Canon Middleton also wrote to the Office of Indian Affairs, and the letter, dated October 23, said that Long Lance was a full-blooded Cherokee Indian: "he received his first education at a Reservation Boarding School in Oklahoma, from there he went to Carlisle, and then proceeded to St. John's Mil. Academy, Manlius, N.Y." Other letters from Oscar Lipps, a former superintendent at Carlisle, and James Henderson, one of his former teachers, confirmed that Long Lance, or "Sylvester Long," had attended the Indian school as a Cherokee.

By the end of November, Commissioner Burke finally had enough information to reply to the Cosmopolitan Book Corporation. He wrote simply,

Gentlemen:

Through your courtesy receipt is acknowledged of a publication of fiction entitled "Long Lance," for which please accept thanks.

This book is very interesting and quite readable.

Sincerely yours,
Chas. H. Burke
Commissioner

He said no more, but by that one phrase, "a publication of fiction," he indicated that the book that had been praised to the skies by critics and by the Cosmopolitan Book Corporation was not authentic. The corporation had encouraged Long Lance to write another book,[41] but it never appeared. Nor did Ray Long ever again publish any of Long Lance's articles in *Cosmopolitan*. Commissioner Burke's short but devastating reply had undoubtedly ended Ray Long's interest in Long Lance.

When Long Lance returned to New York at the end of October, he found dead leaves on the sidewalks and the grass in Central Park turning from a lush green to a drab brown and yellow. He must have been aware of the investigation into his past and feared the worst. Evidence exists that Canon Middleton wrote to him, enclosing the letter from the bureau.[42] Commissioner Graham in Regina also may have corresponded with him on the matter of Burke's inquiries.

Long Lance decided to flee, and he had a ready excuse. A few days after he had returned to New York, he had been approached to co-star in a silent film being made in northern Canada. He bought some heavy woolen shirts, a parka, some work boots, and in a day he was gone.[43] Two days later he was five hundred miles north of New York on Lake Temiskaming, on the border of northern Ontario and Quebec. Once there Long Lance filed away his article on the Indian Bureau and hoped that the results of the inquiry would not unmask and destroy him. He knew he could not risk antagonizing the bureau now. He also knew that if he wanted to carry on the charade, he would have to concoct a new and convincing explanation of his origins.

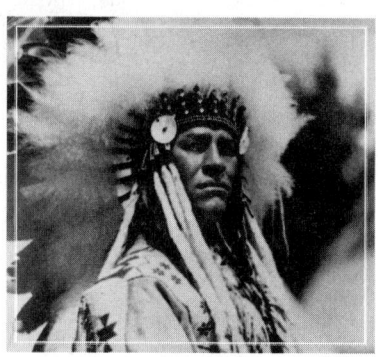

Chapter 14

Long Lance, Movie Star

Temagami, Ontario, 1929

*I*t was Douglas Burden, a young naturalist and explorer, who selected Long Lance to star in his film *The Silent Enemy*. He first thought of making the film in 1927 after seeing the Meriam C. Cooper–Ernest Schoedsack film *Chang*, a documentary that depicted a Thai family's struggle for survival in the jungles of Southeast Asia. It was shot four hundred miles north of Bangkok and included hundreds of extraordinary pictures of leopards, man-eating tigers and, in the final scene, a herd of stampeding elephants.

For years Burden had objected to Hollywood's inaccurate and demeaning portrayal of the Indian as a wicked savage of the plains. He knew the reality was different and wanted to record it on film before both the Indian and the wilderness vanished. In 1908, when he was nine years old, he had camped with his father in northern Canada and came to admire the Ojibwa (Chippewa) Indians' mastery of the woods.[1] "With an Indian you tend to be

228

silent—you speak softly, if at all," he said. "You become increasingly sensitive to your surroundings, and as a result you find yourself endlessly listening to what the forest has to say."[2] In *The Silent Enemy* he hoped to show the Indians and their traditions and customs before the coming of the white man, and he wanted to film the wildlife in northern Canada the way Cooper and Schoedsack had done in Thailand.

Douglas Burden wanted to depict early Indian life authentically and so offered Long Lance a starring role in The Silent Enemy.

By 1927 at age twenty-nine, Burden was an experienced world traveler. After graduating from Harvard in 1922, he had left on a round-the-world tour, which included hunting on the Mongolian border, in the jungles of Vietnam and in the high Himalayas. Before that, in the summer of 1921, he had mined diamonds in Brazil and had spent 1924 looking for a lost silver mine in Central America. In 1926 the American Museum of Natural History sent Burden to the isolated island of Komodo in the Dutch East Indies (now Indonesia), and there he obtained thirteen specimens of the largest lizards in the world, capturing two alive for the Bronx Zoo.

For the film's legal counsel, Burden enlisted William Chanler, a friend from Harvard. Chanler worked in a New York law firm, but the idea of making *The Silent Enemy* excited him, and he asked for and was given a leave of absence. Burden and Chanler then arranged the financing with friends and private investors, eventually bringing the script to Jesse Lasky of Paramount, who agreed to distribute the independently produced film when it was completed.[3]

William Chanler became Douglas Burden's legal counsel for The Silent Enemy.

Burden, with Lasky's backing, managed to get enough money to start work on the film. He began by reading all he could on northern Canada and the Indians who lived off the land before the Europeans arrived. He read Francis Parkman's histories of early Canada, then examined the entire seventy-three volumes of the R.G. Thwaites' edition of the *Jesuit Relations*, the records of the travels and explorations of the Jesuit missionaries in what was then New France. For more detail he studied Samuel Hearne's graphic account, first published in 1795, of his travels across the treeless Barrenlands between Hudson Bay and the Arctic Ocean.[4]

Once Burden had formulated a rough outline of *The Silent Enemy*, he looked for a capable director. He approached H.P. Carver, who had been for five years general manager of Cosmopolitan Productions, owned by William Randolph Hearst. Carver, who had already directed a film on Indians, was an excellent choice. In Burden's words, "He was somebody you could get along with; he enjoyed being away out in the wilderness. He was very fond of these people, so he could get a lot out of them."[5]

During the summer of 1928, Burden and Carver traveled by train and canoe throughout northeastern Ontario and northwestern Quebec, scouting locations and seeking out photogenic and cooperative Ojibwa. The Indians gathered in small encampments to fish in summer, where they stayed together until fall. Then they dispersed, returning to their family hunting territories. Burden spent six weeks visiting the bands along the shores of Lake Abitibi, on the border between Ontario and Quebec.

The Indians were experiencing hard times, and they were eager to work on the film. The building of the Canadian Pacific Railway, followed by two more transcontinental railways just before the war, had brought ruthless nonnative trappers into northern Ontario and Quebec. Fur was at a low point by the late 1920s, and the Ojibwa welcomed Burden's offer of employment. It would assure them of food and provisions and good wages all winter. Father Evain, a portly, white-bearded Roman Catholic priest, helped obtain Indian "extras" from his wide-ranging congregation. Most of the hundred Indians hired were Ojibwa from Lake Temagami, just west of Lake Temiskaming, but some came from Abitibi farther to the north, Kippewa to the east and Mattawa on the Ottawa River to the south.

With the Indian actors signed up, Burden and Carver selected locations for shooting. For the autumn scenes they chose Tem-Kip Camp (short for Temiskaming–Kippewa), at the mouth of the Kippewa River at the lower end of Lake Temiskaming on the Quebec side. They also chose Rabbit Chutes, halfway between Lake Temagami and Lake Temiskaming, for the Indian village and for winter scenes. The Chutes, unlike the area around Tem-Kip Camp, had never been cut over by loggers. A magnificent stand of red pine stood by the rapids, where Rabbit Lake emptied into the Matabitchewan River. The high, wooded ridge—dramatically surrounded on one side by the rapids and on the other by Rabbit Lake—was ideal for the tepee village in the film. Everything was ready for late fall shooting when Long Lance arrived on location at Tem-Kip Camp in early November.[6]

For several weeks the geese had been heading south in their flying chevrons, a sure sign of the coming winter. The robins, white-throated sparrows and wood thrushes had long since gone. The nights were cold, and the northern lights were beginning to play in the sky. The maples had dropped the last of their red

Baluk (Long Lance) speaking to the Ojibwa warriors. A still from The Silent Enemy.

leaves, the birches and poplars shed their bright yellow foliage and now only the dark evergreen of spruce and pine remained. Everywhere in the woods there was the smell of dead leaves.[7]

It was in late October that Burden and Carver decided to ask Long Lance to play Baluk, the mighty Ojibwa hunter, "the epitome of manly development," as the script said. What convinced them to select Long Lance was his arresting portrait in the frontispiece of his book *Long Lance*.[8] Burden and Carver went over the film script with Long Lance as soon as he arrived. It was getting late and the final fall shots at Tem-Kip had to be taken without delay. Throughout the film, they explained to Long Lance, hunger — "the silent enemy" — is dominant. They wanted to portray the Indians' search for the migrating caribou as a desperate struggle. Only when they are on the verge of starvation do they finally locate a herd, and the band narrowly escapes extinction. In addition to Baluk, the script included four other principal characters: Chetoga, the wise old chief; Dagwan, the medicine man, who is intense-

Neewa (Molly Spotted Elk), Chetoga (Chauncey Yellow Robe), Baluk (Long Lance), Cheeka (George McDougall). A still from The Silent Enemy.

ly jealous of Baluk; Neewa, the chief's daughter, the object of both Baluk's and Dagwan's affections; and Cheeka, Neewa's young brother. Baluk, the skilled hunter, finally finds the caribou.[9]

Over the next few days Long Lance got to know the other actors. Burden himself had selected the young Indian for the role of Cheeka. He met him and the boy's mother, who became an extra, at Lowbush on Lake Abitibi. The thirteen-year-old Ojibwa, George McDougall, who had lived all his life in the bush, turned out to be a natural actor. Paul Benoit of Golden Lake, just west of Ottawa, played Dagwan, the villainous medicine man. Benoit was a skilled bushman and contributed much to the film, including a scene where he stalks a buck deer, calling it with a bone horn, then killing it with an arrow from his bow. For Neewa, the chief's daughter, Burden and Carver chose Molly Nelson, or Molly Spotted Elk, a beautiful Penobscot girl from Old Town, Maine. She was easier to find than the others — she danced every night in New York at Texas Guinan's Night Club, a well-known speakeasy.[10]

Neewa (Molly Spotted Elk), a Penobscot Indian from Old Town, Maine, starred alongside Long Lance. Still from The Silent Enemy.

Long Lance's co-star, Chauncey Yellow Robe, a man in his late fifties, was born in the last days of the buffalo hunt, and had actually killed one as a young man. His mother's uncle was Sitting Bull himself. Carver happened to meet the Indian by chance in New York, when he was viewing exhibits at the American Museum of Natural History.

Long Lance was impressed by Chauncey Yellow Robe, a genuine Plains Indian, but he was also fearful. After all, Yellow Robe was a Sioux, born in Montana in 1870, and he had lived the experiences Long Lance had invented for himself in his book.[11]

But a more immediate danger existed. Yellow Robe had seen and possibly remembered the July 1927 issue of *The American Indian,* which had carried a story about Yellow Robe welcoming President Calvin Coolidge to Sioux country. Immediately below the photo of Yellow Robe was an article about "Sylvester Long Lance, Cherokee," whose "pen name is Chief Buffalo Child Long Lance." Again Long Lance worried that he might be exposed. But with Douglas Burden, the producer, he always presented himself as a Blackfoot chief. Long Lance knew Burden was a stickler for authenticity.

On location, first at Tem-Kip Camp, then at Rabbit Chutes, Long Lance immersed himself in the job at hand. Dressed in a breechcloth, headband and moccasins, he rescued Neewa, gone to snare partridges on a cliff, from a black she-bear. He also captured the bear's two cubs and presented them to young Cheeka as pets. Willy Chanler, the party's legal counsel and an expert archer, actually shot the arrow that killed the bear, but Long Lance did seize the cubs. It was no easy task, as the cubs each weighed a hundred pounds and fought back when Long Lance went after them. They slashed him severely, and he had scars to show for it, but he did not complain.[12]

At Rabbit Chutes the crew filmed the tepee village just before freeze-up and the first lasting snowfall. Some of the film's best scenes show George McDougall as Cheeka spearing fish from a birchbark canoe and shooting the rapids. Long Lance did not look nearly as comfortable in a canoe, but after freeze-up, when winter shooting began, he performed extremely well on snowshoes, which he attributed to experience gained at the St. Vital Snowshoe Club, when he had been a reporter in Winnipeg.[13]

After several weeks in the bush, many of the technicians grew tense under the strain of being isolated. They were becoming "bushed," to use the northern expression. In a letter to his friend Bonner Fellers on January 27, 1929, Long Lance described what was happening:

Supper and coffee was always a bright event at five, but after the first week we ran out of dirty stories with which to fill in the time from then until the late retiring hour of nine—and, as I said, the time surely dragged, with nothing to read or occupy our minds. We had not expected a second dog-team that brought in an extra load of supplies and the news that we were to stay out an additional two weeks; and so we were surprised to get a batch of mail up there—among it your letter! It made a whole evening for us—I mean your jokes. I read them all out aloud. . . .

The white fellows on this trip have to fight like hell to keep from "going bush," anyway. They are not used to being out of the world for so long, and their remedy is to herd together all of the time: the very worst thing that they could do. I keep within normal bounds by the Indian method of keeping to myself a lot, alone. And because I have a cheery smile when I do join all of them in the mess cabin, they all flock to my cabin evenings, thinking, I suppose, "Well, the old chief always has a smile; I'll go down and see how he gets that way."[14]

Burden himself had a terrible winter. In Nicaragua in 1924 he had contracted a mysterious illness that returned and struck him down again at Rabbit Chutes. For three weeks he lay on his bunk by the woodstove, surviving on cans of tomato juice. (Eighteen years later, a doctor finally diagnosed his illness as amoebic dysentery.[15])

Long Lance kept active after the day's shooting. On and off the set, Ilia Tolstoy, who acted as the assistant director of the film, became Long Lance's closest friend. He and the fun-loving Russian engaged in spirited Indian hand-wrestling contests, which Long Lance invariably won. Long Lance also put on Indian dances in the cook tent, which had a board floor. Stripped to the waist, with a full feather headdress streaming behind him, he did his war dance, while Ilia Tolstoy, grandson of the famous Russian novelist, beat on the tom-tom.

Throughout the winter, which was long and cold, Long Lance kept to a daily regimen of exercise. With Burden's cousin, S.C. Burden, he sometimes broke holes in the ice and took short dips in Rabbit Lake. On cloudy days when they did not film, he boxed nine rounds in the gym, three rounds apiece with each of the Hennessy brothers, the camp's contractors. And every day, regardless of whether or not they filmed, he chopped firewood for at least an hour with the lumberjacks.[16] After that he felt a clean, muscular exhaustion.

Doubtless he felt the tension, knowing of the Indian Bureau's inquiry and the presence on the set of a real Indian warrior in old Chauncey Yellow Robe. Once, in Temagami, his anxiety exploded in anger at a young Ojibwa girl, Agnes Belaney. She had simply remarked to him that she had never seen an Indian with such dark skin. Long Lance saw Agnes whenever the cast traveled in by dogsled to Temagami, where she worked as cook and dishwasher at the village's only restaurant. After serving him several times, the seventeen-year-old Ojibwa's curiosity finally got the better of her. She asked him where he came from, to which tribe he belonged and then said, "You must be a different kind of Indian." Long Lance's smile withered, and bitterly he told her that he was a full-blood and that all the Indians around Temagami were a bunch of half-breeds.[17] In Agnes's case, it happened to be true; her mother was Ojibwa and her father an Englishman. In a most extraordinary coincidence, her father was none other than Archie Belaney, the English-born writer who "went Indian" and later wrote under the name of Grey Owl in the 1930s. Archie lived in the Temagami area from 1906 to 1911, and again in 1925, just three years before Long Lance and the rest of the cast and crew arrived to make *The Silent Enemy.* As Grey Owl, Archie read

The Indian village of The Silent Enemy.

Long Lance in 1931 and hailed the author as a "splendid savage."[18] The two never met.

During that winter in northern Canada, Long Lance knew that he was the closest that he had ever been to exposure. The strain was becoming unbearable. On Christmas Eve, he finally decided on a course of action. He would continue his masquerade, but first he would alter his story.

In his tent-cabin, after warming his fingers by the stove, he sat at his portable typewriter and wrote a letter to Canon Middleton in Alberta. He started by telling his missionary friend about the movie, about how it would be "an all-Indian motion picture . . . to record the life of the Indians and wild animals of the north country previous to the coming of the White Man." Then he got to the heart of the matter:

> Now, here is the thing I want to talk to you about: I have several dangerous scenes to do in this picture— Well, to be exact, I have done all of them but one, but

that one will by far be the most dangerous of them all; and for that reason they are leaving it to the very last shot of the picture in case anything should happen to me. When I was down in Wyoming, I learned that my foster-parents, the only parents I have had since I was a child—Cherokee Indians who took me out of a Wild West Show when I was run over by a horse and had my hip knocked out of place, and kept me for several years—I learned that these foster-parents had died since I lost touch with them during the war.

He made his point in elliptical fashion, by rearranging the pertinent details of his roots and upbringing under the guise of telling Middleton of the movie and the fact that now he did not have an heir:

I have given considerable thought to this subject, and have decided that if I should suddenly be taken, I would want to appoint you as the Trustee of my estate, such as it would be; and would want the money I should leave, and the future royalties from my book, to be devoted to the higher education of the most promising young graduates of St. Paul's School, said graduates to be designated solely by you. I think that about covers the subject in its entirety, though, before I take the risk that I have mentioned, I will draw up a formal will, send it to my lawyer in New York and have him make it legal and send you a copy.[19]

The letter explained why Long Lance had been listed as a Cherokee at Carlisle rather than a Blackfoot. The fact that his "foster-parents" were dead made it more convenient. Saying he had fallen off a horse and displaced his hip as a boy shows how Long Lance's mind worked under pressure. He was clever enough to rely on real experiences, embellishing them with his imagination.

When he was a boy in Winston, a horse had tripped and fallen on him at the fair grounds. One of the horse's knees indeed had smashed his hip.[20] By appointing Canon Middleton as his trustee, Long Lance no doubt hoped to encourage his continuing silence.

Long Lance kept emphasizing his Plains Indian background during the filming of *The Silent Enemy*. The writing of his will in late March gave him the opportunity to stress again his Blood Indian origins. He returned to Tem-Kip Camp for the final sequence of the film involving the bull moose, which had been kept in a large natural enclosure. The script called for Baluk to spear it with a spruce lance tipped with a flint. The scene opened with timber wolves chasing the moose; then, just as the wolves closed in for the kill, Long Lance was to enter, drive the wolves off and plunge his spear into the moose. Burden waited off-camera with a rifle in case Long Lance was in danger. Long Lance took no chances, and the day before the scene he asked Burden, Ilia Tolstoy and Charlie Bonn, the film laboratory technician, to witness his will. The scene went well, however, and Long Lance managed to spear the moose.[21]

Long Lance's will, dated March 29, 1929, assigns all of his personal belongings to "my brother, Michael Eagle Speaker, Blood Indian Reserve, Cardston, Alberta," and all his "Estate and currency" to the St. Paul's Blood Indian School to be used "to send promising Blood youth through higher schools on being graduated." He named Canon Middleton as his sole executor and trustee.[22] By drawing up his will, Long Lance had made provision to repay the tribe and the Indians who had adopted him. It also served, equally importantly, to impress upon Burden and others in the film crew that he was a bona fide Plains Indian.

By April the filming was nearing completion. Its high point came immediately after Chief Chetoga's death. Just before he dies, Chief Chetoga appoints Baluk to succeed him, which greatly displeases the evil Dagwan. Baluk then leads the tribe to the Barrenlands in search of the caribou. Dagwan begins plotting

Chetoga (Chauncey Yellow Robe) greets Baluk (Long Lance) in this still from The Silent Enemy. *By the end of the filming, Yellow Robe was suspicious of Long Lance's claims to be a Plains Indian.*

against his rival. Weeks later Baluk proves unable to find the herd, and the band's survival is threatened. Dagwan convinces the others that Baluk has failed and is to blame. He must die as his punishment. Baluk chooses to perish as a warrior by fire.

The scene is Long Lance's finest. Naked from the waist up, at forty degrees below zero, a grim and silent Baluk climbs the funeral pyre. Tension rises as the flames crackle and Baluk sings his death chant. The producer and director were astonished at the intensity of Long Lance's portrayal. As the flames lick at his ankles, he beats the tom-tom, slowly at first, then faster and faster until—as one observer later wrote—"it seemed as though forty devils were contriving to make one mad."[23] Long Lance changes the rhythm, slower again, then faster, then a steady, monotonous *tom-tom-tom-tom-tom-tom-tom*, and with this an eerie, chilling chant—his death song.

In *The Silent Enemy* the death scene concludes happily. Just

A still from The Silent Enemy. *Long Lance making the sign for "a forest—many trees."*

as the fire begins to catch Baluk, a brave glimpses the thin smoke rising from the scouts' distant signal fires, and the cry comes, "Caribou!" The herd has been sighted. Baluk is taken down from the pyre, burned but alive, and like the great elephant charge in *Chang*, the film ends with a magnificent shot of thousands of stampeding caribou. The Indians survive. Baluk and Neewa win each other, and the sinister Dagwan is banished as an outcast, left to die a slow death, wandering alone on the empty barrens.

Burden and Carver were immensely pleased with Long Lance's work. He always arrived on time for a shooting, never complained, took risks willingly and, unlike many of the technicians, never asked for a leave of absence from Rabbit Chutes. All through the making of *The Silent Enemy*, he had been friendly and cooperative. Only one member of the cast remained unimpressed. Chauncey Yellow Robe was watching Long Lance with growing suspicion.

Yellow Robe had grown up on the plains in the 1870s and 1880s, learning the customs and traditions of his people. He was one of the first Sioux to attend a white man's school. When he was fifteen, General Pratt took young Yellow Robe to Carlisle, where he graduated with honors. After Carlisle he worked for twenty-five years as the boys' advisor, or disciplinarian, at the Federal Indian Residential School at Rapid City, South Dakota.

Although in the pay of the federal government, Yellow Robe remained a staunch Indian patriot. He was at Carlisle in 1890, the year of Wounded Knee, when the Seventh Cavalry attacked a Sioux camp that was flying a white flag of truce. Over two hundred men, women and children were massacred. When Buffalo Bill proposed to make a heroic reenactment of the Battle of Wounded Knee on film, Yellow Robe protested against it. It was not a glorious battle, he said, adding that "women and children and old men of my people, my relatives, were massacred with machine guns by soldiers of this Christian nation. . . ."[24]

Before he agreed to be Chief Chetoga in *The Silent Enemy*, Yellow Robe insisted that the picture be as accurate as possible. He would not participate if it misrepresented his people in any way. Burden and Carver assured him everything would be done to make it authentic, but Yellow Robe still harbored misgivings throughout the shooting of the film. More and more he suspected that Long Lance was not the full-blooded Indian he steadfastly claimed to be. He first sensed a masquerade in the mess hall, where the principal Indian actors and film crew ate three times a day. Yellow Robe watched and listened in silence. He noticed Long Lance's punctuality, itself a small point, but it surprised him. Indians rarely are punctual in this way, preferring to eat when they are hungry and sleep when they are tired. Long Lance always arrived on time. Yellow Robe was further disturbed by Long Lance's boisterousness, his "cheery smile," his bighearted, uproarious laughter and his easy small-talk with strangers—all peculiar character traits for an Indian to possess. He lacked the natural reserve of the Plains Indian. And for one who took pride in knowing Indian sign language, Long Lance often made grievous mistakes.[25] His dancing, too, though pleasing to the whites, was not the dancing of the plains tribes.[26] If Yellow Robe had read *Long Lance*, he would have known it could not possibly have been Long Lance's life story. The man playing Baluk could never have seen a buffalo hunt, for the herds were exterminated long before he was born.

The filming of *The Silent Enemy* finished in late April. When the ice broke up, the crew moved by canoe to the railway at Temagami and from there to points south. Yellow Robe headed west and Long Lance returned to New York. He felt some relief when he heard that Commissioner Burke of the Office of Indian Affairs, suffering ill health and hounded by his critics, had resigned in early March.[27] In the reorganization of the Office, Long Lance hoped that the investigation into his origins would be forgotten, but Yellow Robe had other ideas. After spending the summer in South Dakota, Yellow Robe returned to New York to lecture on the American Indian.[28] He also had more work to do on *The Silent Enemy*, recording the prologue for the silent movie. (Such sound work was necessary as the "talkies" became popular.) When in New York he made discreet inquiries about Long Lance.

Burden and Carver, meanwhile, cut and edited a quarter of a million feet of film down to eight thousand.[29] The final version would be an hour and twenty minutes, including Yellow Robe's prologue. To the completed film they added a musical score, now necessary, for the arrival of the talkies led many theaters to dismiss their orchestras. Titles for the screen were prepared and inserted. Yellow Robe wrote the prologue himself, and with great dignity and simplicity he began,

> This is the story of my people. In the beginning the
> Great Spirit gave us the land. The forests were ours and

A publicity notice for The Silent Enemy.

the prairies; the wild game was ours to hunt. We were happy when the game was plenty; in years of famine we suffered. We loved our country and our homes. Now the white man has come; his civilization has destroyed my people. Soon, we would have been forgotten. But now this same civilization has preserved our traditions before it was too late; now you will know us as we really are. . . .[30]

For foreign distribution, the prologue and the titles were dubbed by Paramount into German, French, Spanish, Polish,

Italian, Portuguese, Swedish and Dutch.[31] The evening of May 19, 1930, was opening night at the Criterion on Times Square. First-nighters included George Sherwood, director of the American Museum of Natural History; Thomas Hitchcock, the United States' top-ranked polo player; Kermit Roosevelt, the former president's son; Walter Damrosch, a leading composer and former conductor of the New York Symphony; and William K. Vanderbilt, a director of the New York Central Railroad. Long Lance invited General Verbeck of St. John's Military Academy and Commissioner Graham, but the two men could not attend. He also invited Princess Alexandra and a new acquaintance, Anne Morgan, the sister of J.P. Morgan, the famous financier.[32]

The critics loved the film. Robert Sherwood of the *New York Post* ranked it with *Chang*. *Time* wrote that "no schoolbook, museum or government bureau will ever preserve the vestigial red man as this picture does." The *New Republic*'s critic declared it "the only significant film to be produced in this country for a long time." The *Wall Street Journal* called it a "striking picture."[33]

Of the five Indian actors in *The Silent Enemy*, Long Lance won by far the most accolades. Irene Thirer in the *New York Daily News* congratulated the entire Indian cast, but added, "Chief Long Lance, who portrays Baluk, deserves mention over the rest." In the *New York American*, Regina Crewe wrote, "The hero role is taken by Chief Long Lance, a superb figure, agile as a catamount and utterly fearless." *Variety* said, "Chief Long Lance is an ideal picture Indian, because he is a full-blooded one . . . an author of note in Indian lore, and now an actor in fact."[34] Grantland Rice, the most revered sports journalist of the day, wrote in the *New York Sun* on May 22, 1930,

> Chief Long Lance, a former Carlisle star, puts on a battle with a bull moose in 'The Silent Enemy' that rivals the first round of the Dempsey–Firpo fight. Chief Long Lance nails the moose with his pre-Columbus lance

AN AUTHENTIC PICTURE

That the facts presented are faithful—not only from the Indian's standpoint—but from the more scientific angle of the White Man, is attested by the endorsement that the picture has received from the American Museum of Natural History and by the following letter from Mr. Madison Grant, President of the New York Zoological Society:

"Allow me to give you my warmest congratulations on the wonderful picture you showed last night. It is perfectly amazing in its detail, and in the exciting events it portrays. And it shows an extraordinary amount of hard and intelligent work. You have done a great service to science and to zoology in placing on record the life in the northern woods.

"I am thoroughly familiar with the country from the upper Ottawa River to the Hudson Bay region and I can testify that your pictures are accurate in every detail."

Madison Grant's endorsement of The Silent Enemy. *From the program, "How* The Silent Enemy *was Made."*

and then the moose nails him. The chief takes the first fall, but the moose stays down for the count. There is enough action through a minute here to last three or four modern fights.

To further guarantee the film's credibility, Burden and Chanler decided on a special screening of the film for Madison Grant, one of America's leading naturalists. The influential New

York lawyer had spent years traveling throughout North America to discover new animal species. In Alaska he had discovered a unique form of caribou that later was named after him: *Rangifer granti*. With Theodore Roosevelt and others, Grant also had played a leading role in the founding of the New York Zoological Society in 1895, and since 1925, Grant had been the society's president.[35]

Fortunately Grant liked the film — so much that he chattered enthusiastically all through the showing. After the scene in which the timber wolves attacked the bull moose, he leaned over to Burden and whispered, "They're really huskies with lead attached to their tails to make them look like wolves." When the caribou herd appeared on the screen, Grant exclaimed with his usual self-assurance, "It's nice to see you've really got caribou there!" Burden and Chanler smiled. Grant was wrong on both counts. The wolves were real and the "wild caribou" mainly were reindeer, a domesticated version of the caribou.[36]

Grant was wrong on a third count, too. For years "the high priest of racialism in America"[37] had researched race theory. In his book *The Passing of the Great Race* (1916), he alerted America to the danger of its "superior races," the Nordics, being submerged by inferior immigrants. In his final work, *The Conquest of a Continent* (later published by Charles Scribner's in 1933), he repeated the theme, emphasizing the peril of racial miscegenation. Because the Negro was "inferior to the Nordic in intelligence," Grant stressed that "states which have no laws preventing the intermarriage of white and black should adopt them." The Nordics also must be vigilant to unmask the "pass-for-white" mulattoes.[38] Grant failed to spot the impostor in *The Silent Enemy*. In a letter to Burden after the screening, Grant wrote, "I am thoroughly familiar with the country from the upper Ottawa River to the Hudson Bay region, and I can testify that your pictures are accurate in every detail."[39]

Despite all the work done by Burden and Chanler, and

despite Grant's imprimatur and the fine reviews, *The Silent Enemy* failed at the box office when released in August. Perhaps it was too authentic, too educational. One commentator cynically observed, "To say that this admirable production is 'educational' is to condemn it to be shown in empty theaters. There is no more demand for education among movie fans than there is among college students."[40] The film also suffered because it was a silent movie when as the talkies were beginning to sweep the market. When Paramount backed out of its promise to promote the independently produced picture, it was doomed.[41]

The Silent Enemy was among the last authentic silent movies ever to play on Broadway, and though it failed commercially, fifty years later the respected film historian Kevin Brownlow called it a "priceless treasure."[42]

Long Lance had now proved himself a gifted actor, but had his publishers and producers known his true past, they might not have been so amazed. After all, Long Lance had spent years perfecting his Indian persona. But even as his invention of himself became more polished, his increasing notoriety was making it harder and harder to prevent investigation into his past.

CHAPTER 15

The Trail Narrows

NEW YORK CITY, 1929

*B*efore returning to New York following the filming of *The Silent Enemy*, Long Lance stopped off in Toronto for an interview for the *Star Weekly*. There he talked to Wilfrid Eggleston, a young writer who had grown up in Alberta, about the film project and the North. He could still dazzle a young writer, and he impressed Eggleston, who later wrote, "Chief Long Lance is an anomaly. A Blood Indian born on the border country around Coutts, Alberta, and raised in the tribe, he is yet one of the best stylists in Canada today."

Long Lance also enlarged on the adventures of the movie project, fabricating tales of spectacular side trips to the Northwest Territories and to Alaska. "Hard times up there this winter among the Indians and Eskimos," he told Eggleston. "Trapping was very poor. Game is getting scarce, country's getting trapped out." He told of going to Windy Lake, "the geographical center of the Territories," which he said was "thirty-six days by dog team" from The

Pas, Manitoba. He could deceive as easily as breathing by now. He mentioned that he had traveled forty-eight hundred miles by airplane with a Captain Lenson of the United States Air Force, flying north and west of Nome, Alaska. All of these details—thirty-six days by dogsled, forty-eight hundred miles by airplane—were included in the *Star Weekly* story.[1] It was Long Lance's forte that he could make anyone's experience his own, for he never made either of these trips although he knew others who had. His friend Ilia Tolstoy had tried to locate a caribou herd in the Barrenlands, and when he returned, unsuccessful, two cameramen flew to Alaska and managed to find and film a reindeer herd. Long Lance himself spent the entire winter at Rabbit Chutes.[2]

Canon Middleton invited him to visit Alberta, but Long Lance, edgy about the bureau's inquiry and Yellow Robe's suspicions, declined. As a result Middleton's well-intentioned attempts to act as a matchmaker came to nothing. Earlier, he had written from the Blood Reserve, "I suppose while staying in the wilds you have many times thought of taking unto yourself a partner for life. If you fail in your endeavours, please remember that we have a delightful Blood girl here, who I am sure would make you a charming life partner."[3] Long Lance chose another season in New York instead.

Before he had gone north for the film, Long Lance had agreed to appear in advertisements endorsing the B.F. Goodrich Company's line of running shoes. As he browsed through the newsstands in New York, he saw his picture in full regalia in such magazines as *American Boy*, *Boy's Life*, *Youth's Companion* and *Popular Mechanics*. The story in one of the advertisements read,

> One winter we came near starvation. Our braves hunted over the plains for the frozen heads of buffalo they had killed early in the fall. They chopped the skin from the tops of the heads, and our mothers cooked it for food. We were saved by finding a herd of mountain

sheep which had been driven down into the foothills by the big snow. We slew the entire herd and ate them on the spot. On many occasions like this, our lives depended on the endurance of our legs and feet in hunting game for food.

In our primitive life, nothing was more important than our feet. I wonder if the white race would not be sturdier if they took better care of their feet in childhood—by wearing shoes that allow free exercise of the foot and leg muscles.

As for myself, I always wear rubber-soled canvas shoes in the stiffest climbing and the longest hiking, whenever the weather permits. They are more like moccasins in strength-building than any other modern shoe.[4]

That summer he also heard his name in Goodrich radio commercials prepared by the J. Walter Thompson Advertising Agency. Long Lance met frequently with the Goodrich people at the Thompson offices in New York, working on publicity for the Chief Long Lance Shoe. Specimens of the shoes were manufactured in late summer of 1929, when orders for fall delivery were taken.[5] The Goodrich people asked Long Lance to write *How to Talk in Indian Sign Language,* a thirty-four–page booklet designed to publicize the new shoe. It was released in 1930. In the booklet Long Lance is shown in a breechcloth and headband, his powerful torso bared to the waist, demonstrating the sign language of the Indians in eighty-three photographs. Goodrich also managed to persuade Jim Thorpe to write a glowing testimonial to Long Lance and his new shoe. It did not take much persuasion because Thorpe by this time was in desperate need of money.

By 1930, at age forty-one, Thorpe was finished as an athlete. He had played his last football game for the Chicago Cardinals in

1929 and retired from the game. Like many professional athletes he had no savings to fall back on. His first wife, Iva Miller, whom he had met at Carlisle, became fed up with his drinking bouts and divorced him in 1923. He had remarried and now had a wife and two children to support.[6] Under the title "The Greatest All-round Athlete in Modern History Adds a Word," Thorpe wrote,

> Like most Indians, I have always been a great user of canvas rubber-soled shoes. When my old schoolmate, Chief Long Lance, and I were running with and against one another on the track team of the Carlisle Indian school, I remember how we used to kick about the rubber-soled shoes we had to wear in our athletics. We spent most of an evening once discussing the kind of shoe we would like to see someone turn out.
>
> Little did I think then that Long Lance himself would some day design this shoe. I have just tried out my first pair of the new Chief Long Lance Shoe and find that they remove the last objection we had to this type of footwear.
>
> Long Lance and I trained together for the 1912 Olympics, and when the games were over at Stockholm, I told Long Lance that it was the stiff competition that he had given me in the mile run which had enabled me to win the World's All-Around Athletic Championship that year. He was always an intense trainer, using up dozens of pairs of rubber-soled shoes, and I don't know anyone better fitted than he to know what we want in a shoe of this sort.
>
> I'll go the limit in saying that in all my years of athletics, I find the Chief Long Lance Shoe the smoothest, the best natural foot and leg-muscle builder of any shoe of any kind I have ever seen. It is the shoe that I have been looking for all these years. . . .

The Greatest All-round Athlete in Modern History Adds a Word

LIKE most Indians I have always been a great user of canvas rubber-soled shoes. When my old schoolmate, Chief Long Lance, and I were running with and against one another on the track team of the Carlisle Indian school, I remember how we used to kick about the rubber-soled shoes we had to wear in our athletics. We spent most of an evening once discussing the kind of shoe we would like to see someone turn out.

Little did I think then that Long Lance himself would some day design this shoe. I have just tried out my first pair of the new Chief Long Lance Shoe and find that they remove the last objection we had to this type of footwear.

Long Lance and I trained together for the 1912 Olympics, and when the games were over at Stockholm I told Long Lance that it was the stiff competition that he had given me in the mile run which had enabled me to win the World's All-Around Athletic Championship that year. He was always an intense trainer, using up dozens of pairs of rubber-soled shoes, and I don't know anyone better fitted than he to know what we want in a shoe of this sort.

I'll go the limit in saying that in all my years of athletics, I find the Chief Long Lance Shoe the smoothest, the best natural foot and leg-muscle builder of any shoe of any kind I have ever seen. It is the shoe that I have been looking for all these years.

Though I have received hundreds of requests, I have never before given permission for my name to be used in a testimonial, which, I think, shows my wholehearted sincerity in endorsing the Chief Long Lance Shoe as the best I have ever seen.

JIM THORPE

Jim Thorpe's endorsement of the Chief Long Lance Shoe.

Long Lance spent the summer and autumn of 1929 in New York, preoccupied with Goodrich's promotion campaign. The skyscape of the city changed dramatically that October as wreckers knocked down the old Waldorf-Astoria Hotel to make way for the skyscraper to end all skyscrapers, the Empire State Building.[7]

The task of writing a booklet on the Indian sign language

caused Long Lance not the slightest qualm, even though, as old Yellow Robe had realized in an instant, he knew precious little about it. Fortunately he had other resources, such as William Tomkins' *Universal American Indian Sign Language*, which appeared in 1926. Earlier illustrated works such as Ernest Thompson Seton's *Sign Talk* were readily available,[8] and Long Lance finished the booklet in short order.

That summer, Bonner and Dorothy Fellers, his West Point friends, were on leave in New York awaiting Bonner's posting to the Philippines in the fall. In 1928, on several trips to West Point to give special lectures, to referee track meets and to research an article on the military academy,[9] Long Lance stayed at their apartment. He was always a popular house guest. When asked if he wanted breakfast in the morning, he laughed and told his hosts that he "never felt right until he had his protein." The Fellers were happy to take the chief along to West Point parties, where he chatted, danced, told old Indian tales and managed to lower everyone's inhibitions. At one of these parties Long Lance thumped on a tin wastepaper basket so loudly that people heard the noise three floors away.

One afternoon in New York, driving out with the Fellers to visit friends in Connecticut, Long Lance sat in the rumble seat of the small Pontiac with Bonner and Dorothy sitting up front. On one of the rough roads, Dorothy turned to say something to Long Lance and to her horror saw that he was gone. The rumble seat was down. Just when the Bonners feared the worst, they heard whoops of laughter and watched Long Lance pop up again, perched in the rumble seat. "I thought I'd just disappear," he told them, as the threesome bounced on to Connecticut.

But Dorothy Fellers noticed that no matter how comfortable Long Lance appeared in social situations there were times when he plainly was awkward. Once he made a well-meaning but completely misunderstood remark to a close friend of Dorothy's. The friend's scathing retort, Dorothy noted, obviously hurt and

Long Lance in the summer of 1929 with a friend of S.C. Burden, Morgan Wheelock. Long Lance spent the summer promoting the B.F. Goodrich shoe named in his honor.

angered him. But he did not reply, and "just quietly disappeared perhaps to hide his hurt or control his short-fused temper. Or maybe both."[10] His inner tension rose as the risks of his being exposed increased.

That summer, Long Lance rented a single room at the Explorers Club on Cathedral Parkway, three blocks north of Central Park. The room in the attractive eight-story building cost fifteen dollars a week, and he probably heard of it through Douglas Burden, who was a member. The Explorers Club was founded in 1904, and in twenty-five years it had become one of the most distinguished clubs in the world, organized with the objective of "uniting explorers in the bonds of good fellowship and promoting the work of exploration by every means in its power." Its members included the late Admiral Peary, Roald Amundsen, discoverer of the North West Passage, President Theodore Roosevelt, Ernest Thompson Seton and the Arctic explorers Vilhjalmur Stefansson and Fritjof Nansen.[11]

At the club Long Lance met Dr. Clyde Fisher, one of its directors and a man keenly interested in Indians. Fisher had earned a doctorate in botany at Johns Hopkins University in 1913 for his thesis on cell division in the developing seeds of various species of *Pepero-mia*, tropical members of the pepper family. He had little interest in becoming a narrow specialist in the field, however, and read widely on zoology, geology and astronomy. He was familiar with flowers, insects and birds, and could name the stars in their constellations and discuss the theory of relativity. After he joined the Department of Education at the Museum of Natural History in 1913, he went on expeditions to Bermuda, Europe and the American West. On a 1927 trip to the Standing Rock Reservation in North Dakota to photograph and study Indian cer-

THE NEW CLUB HOUSE

During the summer of 1929, Long Lance stayed at the prestigious Explorers Club in New York City.

emonial dancing, the Sioux had inducted him into their tribe.[12]

Long Lance's other friend at the Explorers Club was Seumas (James in English and pronounced sha'-mus), Chief of Clann Fhearghuis of Stra-chur and Clann Ailpein, who included among his Scottish ancestors Ferghus the Great, mightiest of the Ferguson clan's kings, and Duncan, murdered in Shakespeare's play by Macbeth. The club's most colorful member, he was known as "the wandering Scot." The tall, handsome Scot always appeared bekilted at the Explorers Club. He wore a dirk in his belt, a *sgian dugh*, or black knife, and the traditional Gaelic *sporan*, or leather purse. He was fifty years old in 1929 and claimed to have fought in armies around the world, serving in his late teens in Armenia

Seumas, Chief of Clann Fhearghuis, in the library of the Explorers Club in New York, around 1930.

and the Balkans with "the Bashi-bazouks [Irregular Horse] recruited mainly from the Hak Kari country of Kurdistan." He returned briefly to the Western Highlands, then set off for West Africa, and, when he was twenty-four, crossed the Sahara. During the Russo-Japanese War, he said he commanded seven squadrons of "Kuban Cossacks." He concluded his military career by serving seven years in South Africa with the "British Legion of Frontiersmen, Military Scouts."[13]

Not everyone at the Explorers Club believed the friendly Scot's exploits. Indeed, as his obituary in the *Explorers Journal* says, "there were often controversial discussions about the Chief among some of the members."[14] Perhaps because of this, he and Long Lance gravitated to each other and developed a warm rapport.

In late September 1929, Seamus, Dr. Fisher and E.W. Deming, the artist, proposed that Long Lance be accepted for membership in the Explorers Club. To strengthen the application, the seventy-year-old Deming, who had lived in the American West in the 1880s and 1890s studying and sketching Indians, wrote a strong letter of support. He had always believed that "the Blackfeet Indians are racially magnificent," and his paintings of the Western Indians were highly regarded. Clark Wissler, the anthropologist, told Deming in 1921, "You, above all, have been able to get inside the Indian life and to see the world as the Indians see it." In his letter Deming's praise was unqualified. "Long Lance," he wrote, "although he is well educated and has lived the life of the white man for many years, belongs to the old time Indian and has written one of the best books on the old time Indian life."[15]

On October 11, the membership committee voted into the club "Buffalo Child Long Lance . . . a full-blooded Chief of the Blackfeet Indian tribe, who has long been well known and respected in Canada and the western states, not only as an explorer, but also as a writer and lecturer on Indian experience and affairs." Induction into the club was a great honor. At the same meeting the Explorers Club elected Charles Lindbergh as an honorary member.[16]

Long Lance was the only nonwhite member living at the Explorers Club though on the streets north of the building was Harlem with a quarter of a million blacks. To the east was Spanish Harlem with some one hundred thousand Latin Americans, blacks and West Indians.[17] Long Lance even had a cousin, Felix Graves, in Harlem, but he never invited him to the Explorers Club.

Long Lance put all his energy into the masquerade at the

Explorers Club, no doubt hoping that his distinguished company might protect him from further investigation. He went out of his way to meet and talk at length with members such as Frederick Webb Hodge, Club President George G. Heye and Dr. Clark Wissler, all well-known students of the North American Indian. He became friendly with Hodge, who had edited the authoritative, two-volume *Handbook of American Indians* in 1910. Long Lance and Hodge liked to read in the club library. Hodge was sixty-five, but as a younger man he had done anthropological fieldwork among Indians in Arizona and New Mexico. Heye had spent a lifetime collecting Indian artifacts and had founded the Museum of the American Indian in New York in 1916. He was interested in Long Lance's knowledge of Indian sign language. Long Lance read Wissler's *The American Indian: An Introduction to the Anthropology of the New World* (Second Edition, 1922) and Wissler read Long Lance's autobiography.[18]

When Clyde Fisher asked Wissler what he thought of the book, the anthropologist was at a loss about what to say and somewhat embarrassed. Twenty years earlier he had done fieldwork among the Sioux and then more systematically among the Peigan nation of the Blackfoot Confederacy. Without question he knew that Long Lance's autobiography was fiction. From his own field trips at the turn of the century, he knew that the Blackfoot were not chasing the last buffalo or organizing war parties in the 1880s. By that time the Confederacy lay shattered, its member tribes in Canada and the United States ill-fed, stricken by disease and confined to their reserves and reservations. Yet knowing all this, Wissler kept his silence. When Dr. Fisher pressed him for an opinion of *Long Lance*, Wissler replied as best he could. "If you begin it," he told him, "I think you will finish it."[19]

Wissler's reaction can perhaps be explained by his humanistic outlook on life[20] and by his grudging respect for Long Lance and what he had accomplished. In an age when the Indians were viciously treated, as much by the slanderous stereotype pushed by

Hollywood as by the ruthless bullying of settlers on the plains, Long Lance succeeded at least in capturing something of the essence of the Indians' heroic and noble history. If it was fiction disguised as fact, then it was fiction done well, and in its own peculiar way, done accurately. Unlike Wissler's own dry monographs on the Blackfoot "Material Culture," "Ceremonial Bundles" and "Societies and Dance Associations," *Long Lance* reached a much wider public with an impact that caused many readers to abandon their erroneous notions about the Plains Indians.

Also, Wissler could not prove on his own that Long Lance was an impostor. Even if he could identify unmistakable Caucasian and Negroid physical traits in the man, it really established very little. Perhaps Long Lance was not full-blooded, but by the 1920s few North American Indians were. In Canada and the United States, the ancestry of many who were officially classed as Indian was, in fact, mixed. Jim Thorpe, the Sac and Fox Indian, was by his own calculation only "five-eighths Indian," and his first wife, Iva Miller, classed as a Cherokee, was at least half white. On the South Peigan or Blackfeet Reservation in Montana, three-quarters of the population under thirty were of mixed racial origin by 1930, and it was a relatively isolated reservation. Most of the racial mix had been with whites, but there had been some with blacks, too. Even among the Bloods of Alberta, there were band members descended from Henry Mills, a black frontiersman from Montana, whom the Blackfoot called Six-apekwan ("Black White Man").[21]

Culturally, too, it was becoming difficult even for anthropologists to determine racial ancestry. Neither the American nor the Canadian governments were interested in protecting the Indians' culture and religion. The Duncan Campbell Scotts and Charles Burkes partially succeeded in their attempts to eliminate the "primitive" customs and remake the Indians into red white men. In Canada, ever since the midnineteenth century, Indian women lost their Indian status when they married a non-Indian, while non-Indian women marrying Indians gained it.[22] Long Lance easily could have been born of such a racial mix. Or perhaps he had simply done so well at the reservation mission school and at Carlisle that he had lost much of his native culture, which, after all, was the objective of Indian education in those days.

Another advantage Long Lance enjoyed was his skillful use of Mike Eagle Speaker's childhood memories in his autobiography. Wissler would recognize many of the experiences in the early pages of the book as authentic even if Long Lance's description of Blackfoot history was not.

Long Lance's will, which now mentioned his "Cherokee foster-parents," explained why he might occasionally be termed a "Cherokee." As long as the results of Charles Burke's inquiry remained in the files at the Office of Indian Affairs in Washington, his true identity might not be discovered.

The fall of 1929 brought catastrophe to most Americans. The 1920s had been a decade of prosperity, when the United States moved from outdoor privies, ice boxes and horse-drawn buggies to electric refrigerators, cars, vacuum cleaners and telephones. Spending reached spectacular heights. The stock market broke in early September, recovered quickly, slid again in late September, recovered momentarily in early October, then suffered an alarming decline. Prices fell so rapidly on October 24 that panic seized the market. Overnight, hopes and fortunes vanished. As stocks plummeted, bankruptcies followed, and within two months of the crash, three million people were out of work. Factories closed, stores shut down, construction stopped and breadlines formed on the streets. November was the month of panic and December the month of melancholy adjustment.[23]

The Depression did not hurt Long Lance's lectures at first, for he offered his audiences something fresh and uplifting: "Be wise and persevere." In late November he spoke at the American Museum of Natural History on "An Indian's Story of His People."

He repeated the talk at the Explorers Club, where he was praised in the club's newsletter for his "brilliant and humorous account of the characteristics of the life and philosophy of his people of the northwestern plains."[24]

Economic hard times dampened but did not in any way end his social life in New York that winter. Long Lance, in fact, remained a much sought-after guest. Fannie Hurst, to whom Ray Long had paid seventy thousand dollars for the serialization rights to her novel *Back Street*, invited Long Lance to her New Year's Eve party.[25] At Princess Alexandra's apartment he met her cousins, Princess Nina of Russia and Princess Xenia of Greece, both nieces of the late czar.[26] His friend W.R. Edrington, the banker, included him in his theater parties.[27] Several times Long Lance lunched with Carl Van Vechten, the New York music and drama critic turned novelist.[28]

Even Walter Winchell, the famous New York gossip columnist, caught him at play that winter and once wrote in his "On Broadway" column in the *Daily Mirror*, "Chief Long Lance, the Indian lecturer, and the first Mrs. Guy Bolton are uh-huh. . . ."[29]

Seumas, the Scottish chieftain, who occupied the room next to Long Lance's at the Explorers Club, kept track of his friend's exploits. He had a sprightly sense of humor, and when women phoned for Long Lance, as they did day and night, his standard reply was, "No, this is not Long Lance. . . . I am Chief Longer Lance."[30]

Long Lance's career as Indian–lecturer–showman began to crest in the last two weeks of January 1930. He spoke on the Indian sign language to five hundred guests at the Explorers Club annual dinner at the Hotel Astor on January 18. The next day, in the Sunday edition of the *Herald Tribune*, Beverly Smith's article "One Hundred Per Cent American" appeared. Before going into detail on the man who was "Buffalo Child Long Lance, full blooded American Indian, Chief of the Blood band of the Northern Blackfeet, athlete, soldier, author, explorer and scholar," she began,

You may find him some day at the American Museum of Natural History, delivering a learned lecture on Indian archeology before the trustees and directors; or at West Point, judging a track meet; or at the Explorers Club, writing a report for the United States Bureau of Commercial Economics. He is, to use a much abused phrase correctly, a one hundred percent American.

Again Long Lance provided the research material from his scrapbooks. Then in conversation with her he raised the level of his fantasies still higher than the printed words. He told the writer that he had "played tackle on the great teams of 1910, 1911 and 1912 of which Jim Thorpe was the bright star." He said he had attended the Olympic Games at Stockholm in 1912, when Thorpe triumphed over the world's best. Instead of reporting that he had been wounded twice in France, he raised the number to eight, adding that he had been "decorated by three governments for gallantry in action."

His lies now were increasingly reckless, and could have been exposed in an afternoon of checking, but they appeared in print, as they usually did, just as he told them. He had lost his balance. He felt something closing in on him. It was as if he wanted one final fling at acceptance and acclaim—or perhaps subconsciously he wanted to be caught, wanted to lose the hand he had dealt for himself so many years before, when he had first resolved to pass himself as the Indian he believed he really was.

On the evening of January 28, Katherine Hale (the pen name of Mrs. John Garvin), the former book critic of the *Toronto Mail and Empire* and in her own right a well-known writer and poet, met Long Lance at the annual dinner of the Poetry Society of America. The Depression had entered its third month, and it was not a good time for American writers whose books, new and old, sold as remainders in the book shops and drugstores of New York.[31] Still, the dinner was a gala affair. Four hundred guests

You are cordially invited to attend

the ANNUAL DINNER *of*

THE POETRY SOCIETY OF AMERICA

BILTMORE HOTEL

Tuesday Evening, January Twenty-eighth
AT SEVEN O'CLOCK

THE SPEAKERS AND GUESTS WILL INCLUDE

JOHN ERSKINE	JULIA PETERKIN
WITTER BYNNER	CHIEF LONG LANCE
J. E. SPINGARN	HENRY GODDARD LEACH
HARRIET MONROE	KATHERINE HALE
RUPERT HUGHES	EDITH WYNNE MATTHISON
NAOMI ROYDE-SMITH	

DINNER COMMITTEE

Emma Mills, *Chairman*

Mrs. Thomas Lamont	Mrs. Edwin Markham
Corinne Roosevelt Robinson	Mrs. Frederic Edey
Marguerite Dixon Clark	Marjorie Mansfield
Mrs. Ernest Stillman	William Griffith

SINGLE RESERVATIONS ARE $3.75 (including tip)
MEMBERS ARE PRIVILEGED TO BRING GUESTS

Long Lance's invitation to the Poetry Society of America Dinner, January 28, 1930.

attended the banquet at the Biltmore Hotel, opposite Grand Central Station. Hale spotted Long Lance in the lobby and later wrote, "His clear-cut aquiline features, dark complexion and magnificent carriage set him entirely apart from everyone else in the brilliant crowd. He moved among people, everywhere recognized and smiled upon. . . ."[32]

In the ballroom that evening, Long Lance was in his glory. During the after-dinner poetry readings, he got up to demonstrate his evocative, if not perfectly accurate, Indian sign language. Then, under the huge crystal chandeliers, in a room decorated with hand-carved wood, velvet drapes and rare Venetian marble, he recited in a soft voice the "the heroic death song of his Blackfoot tribe which he had translated from their language."[33]

> Oh, look down upon Long Lance,
> Thou knowest Long Lance,
> The Sun, the Moon, the Day, the Night;
> Tell me if it is real,
> This life I have lived,
> This death I am dying.
> Ah, the clouds are leaving my door,
> The Outward Trail is no longer dark,
> I see—I understand:
> There is no life, there is no death;
> I shall walk on a trail of stars.[34]

The evening was a tremendous success, a personal triumph in every respect. But the trail was narrowing. A week after the banquet of the Poetry Society of America, Chanler, still acting as legal counsel for *The Silent Enemy*, summoned Long Lance to his office.

CHAPTER 16

"Hello, Sylvester"

NEW YORK CITY, 1930

*L*ong Lance had not seen Will Chanler for months. Then, on February 5, 1930,[1] a phone call summoned him to Chanler's office—as soon as possible. He walked west along Cathedral Parkway from the Explorers Club to the subway, deposited his five-cent fare and walked down to the Broadway level. The front page of the *Times* carried a story on former President Taft's ill health, another on New York Governor Franklin D. Roosevelt acting to end the dressmakers' strike and a human-interest item on Charles Lindbergh, who had just celebrated his twenty-eighth birthday in Los Angeles.[2] Long Lance hopped off in the Wall Street district and walked toward the Mutual Life Building, while cold wind swirled through the office tower canyons. At 32 Liberty Street he stepped inside and took the elevator to Chanler's office.

"Hello, Sylvester," Chanler greeted him.

Long Lance must have guessed that Chanler knew the truth, but he had lived with the masquerade and the fear for so long—

since 1909 when he entered Carlisle, twenty-one of his thirty-nine years. Instinctively he was on his guard. He glanced around the well-furnished law office — the walls lined with red, leather-bound legal volumes — and replied, calmly, "Sylvester? Who's Sylvester?"

Chanler zeroed in.

"You're Sylvester — Sylvester Long. You come from North Carolina, and you're not a Blood Indian."

Chanler was furious. Both he and Burden knew that the seemingly authentic, full-blooded Indian chief they had cast in the role of Baluk was a fraud. Chauncey Yellow Robe had recently contacted the Office of Indian Affairs in Washington and had informed William Chanler of his deep suspicion that Long Lance was not a Blackfoot.[3] The day before, Charles Rhoads, Burke's successor at the Office of Indian Affairs, had confirmed Yellow Robe's story. Long Lance was a Croatan, not a western Indian. He was Sylvester Long, not Chief Buffalo Child Long Lance.

Long Lance stood firm. "I've never heard of the Croatan tribe," he said, looking Chanler straight in the eyes.

"We know what the facts are," Chanler shot back, "and there's no use arguing about them."

Long Lance denied the charges. Then, appearing to crack, he confessed to Chanler that he had in fact lied. The true story, he told him, was that he was not a Blood — but a Blackfoot! He patiently explained that he had kept his ancestry a secret because his father was a renegade Blackfoot around Laramie, Wyoming. He was "a wild character and not held in very good repute," and all along Long Lance sought to hide the relationship behind a claim that he was a Blood. He was ashamed of his father, he explained. He did not want to be known as an outlaw's son.

Pressed for more details, Long Lance told Chanler that he was born in Montana and had no memory of his mother. His earliest recollections were of the days he worked as a child on white ranches in Wyoming. At the age of nine or ten he ran away with the Wild West shows. When he was with Robinson's Circus in

North Carolina, a horse fell on him and smashed his hip, dislocating it.[4] It was a convincing rebuttal, and years later Chanler remembered how sincerely Long Lance had defended himself, always with the steady gaze leveled on his inquisitor's eyes. Chanler related more of the story in a later letter to Commissioner Rhoads:

> He was taken from the circus in a buggy by a doctor and nursed by a Cherokee family; he thinks their name was Long; he lived with them for about two years, although he says he ran away from them to join a circus at some time. He does not remember whether he went to school there but knows that he could read and write a little when he was sent to Carlisle from the Cherokee Reservation. He thinks he was given the name of "Sylvester Long" at Carlisle, although he may have been given that name by the Cherokees. . . .[5]

Long Lance urged Chanler to check out his story, to write to Canon Middleton and to James Henderson, one of his teachers at Carlisle. He then opened his scrapbook and showed it to Chanler in an attempt to prove he was a Blackfoot, but here he miscalculated. Chanler noticed that "whenever the name of his tribe in the earlier clippings referring to his West Point days appeared, the printed word was erased and 'Blackfoot' was written in pencil."[6] In his second letter to Commissioner Rhoads, Chanler suggested that Long Lance "call upon your office and endeavour to straighten out the records." He also thanked Rhoads for sending information on the Croatan Indians.[7]

Chanler knew the Plains Indians well enough. An uncle who had fought in the Indian wars in Arizona and New Mexico had once sent him a full eagle headdress and buckskin suit, and he had worn it often as a boy. When he was about ten, he had read George Catlin's two volumes on his travels among the western Indians in the 1830s, Francis Parkman's *Oregon Trail* and all of Fenimore Cooper's books on the Eastern Woodlands Indians. Just five years earlier, around 1925, he had traveled west to visit the Blackfeet, or South Peigan, Reservation at Browning, Montana, in the company of James Willard Schultz, the white author who had married a Peigan woman and written many books on their old ways and customs.[8] Still, Chanler did not know of the Croatans, the tribe to which Commissioner Rhoads said Long Lance belonged.

Commissioner Rhoads had sent along an excerpt from the *Handbook of American Indians*, which was edited by Fred Hodge, one of Long Lance's friends at the Explorers Club. The entry on Croatans explained that the name was recently given to a group of people in North Carolina, previously classed as "free negroes," but who claimed to be Indians. The term, according to the *Handbook*, "serves as a convenient label for a people who combine in themselves the blood of the wasted native tribes, the early colonists or forest rovers, the runaway slaves or other negroes, and probably also of stray seamen of the Latin races from coasting vessels in the West Indian or Brazilian trade."[9]

Chanler then wrote to James Henderson, the Carlisle teacher then living in Canton, North Carolina. Long Lance had been out of touch with him for nearly twenty years—perhaps he even assumed he was dead—and he had made a grave mistake in suggesting that Chanler check him out as a reference. Henderson was retired as superintendent and agent for the Eastern Band of Cherokees, a post to which he had been appointed after leaving Carlisle in 1912.

Henderson wrote to Chanler on February 24 and repeated most of what he had reported to the Office of Indian Affairs in October 1928. He said he had once known "Sylvester Long who now calls himself Long Lance" but added that "he was never recognized at Carlisle by the Cherokees as a Cherokee Indian" and "it was alleged that he was more of negro blood than Indian." Henderson also said that, shortly after his appointment as the

Eastern Cherokee superintendent, he was asked to investigate the Cherokee background of Sylvester Long when President Wilson had nominated him to West Point. He looked into the matter, but "could find no one in the reservation who knew anything at all in regard to his life history." Later, Henderson continued, he learned about Sylvester's father from a chance meeting with a journalist from Winston–Salem. The reporter had read Long Lance's articles and told Henderson that his father worked as a janitor at the Winston–Salem high school and "often spoke of having a son at Carlisle and that he was going to West Point."

Totally bewildered, Chanler scrawled across the bottom of Henderson's letter, "Mr. Henderson was Disciplinarian at Carlisle in Long Lance's time, and Long Lance himself referred me to him to prove he really was a Blackfoot from Wyoming!"

Shortly thereafter, Chanler heard from Charlie Bonn, who worked as a lab technician on *The Silent Enemy*. Bonn's boss at Eastman Kodak was Jules Brulatour, who formerly owned a theater in Winston–Salem, one of the theaters where Abe Long had worked.[10] All indications were that Long Lance, far from being a Plains Indian chief, was, by southern racial standards, a Negro. In early March, Canon Middleton's letter arrived.

Middleton enclosed copies of the previous Office of Indian Affairs inquiry and his reply to it, stating that the alleged Blackfoot really was a Cherokee from Oklahoma. He said that the story Long Lance told of his origins is "almost identical with the version he had given me at different times, but this he always communicated confidentially, and I have always treated it as such." Middleton proved to be a loyal friend. "Knowing Indian life as I do, I know him to be of true blue," he wrote. "He has wandered over no easy road, and so far as I know, has come through unscathed and unsullied. All honour to his Indian blood, his training, his character, and his respect for those who respect him." He concluded by saying, "Shall be pleased to hear, at your pleasure, the result of your investigations."[11] And so he would.

Ilia Tolstoy (center), grandson of the famous Russian novelist, was dispatched to Winston–Salem to investigate Long Lance's claims of Indian ancestry.

Canon Middleton's letter convinced Chanler that a full investigation was needed. He contacted Ilia Tolstoy, then visiting at Aiken, South Carolina, close to the Georgia border, requesting him to go to Winston–Salem and ask about Long Lance and Sylvester Long. He wanted the whole affair cleared up and quickly, for an extensive advertising campaign was being prepared for the movie with Long Lance billed as a full-blooded Indian. Chanler wrote to Middleton in early March, saying, "Certain Indians in New York and some others are spreading around a story that Long Lance is part negro."[12]

Long Lance and Chauncey Yellow Robe at the American Museum of Natural History several months before Long Lance was confronted about his true identity.

In February and March the rumor that Long Lance had black and not Indian ancestry reached many of his friends. Irvin S. Cobb exploded in anger when he heard it. "To think that we had him here in the house," he raged. "We're so ashamed! We entertained a nigger. . . ." Others simply dropped him from their circles.[13]

Those who stuck by him included crusty old Seumas, the chief of Clann Fhearghuis, his friend at the Explorers Club. Breaking his silence at last, Long Lance admitted his mixed ancestry to Seumas and the worldly wise Scot kept the secret safe.

He told Long Lance how much the world's races had been mixed, and how, after Bonnie Prince Charles was defeated at Culloden, the Highlanders were dispersed all over the world and had mingled with many races. Many was the time, he counseled Long Lance, that part-Oriental, African and American Indian clansmen came to him "some clutching an old Bible or a piece of tartan, proud of their Scottish heritage."[14] Seumas, Middleton and Clyde Fisher of the American Museum of Natural History all stood by Long Lance. Curiously so did old Chauncey Yellow Robe.

Shortly after his interview with Chanler, Long Lance must have confessed to Yellow Robe that he was a Cherokee, born and raised in a southern town that recognized only two races: white and colored. After he was adopted by the Bloods in Alberta, Long Lance decided to identify fully with the Bloods and the Blackfoot and to use Buffalo Child Long Lance as his pen name. Once the secret was revealed, the old Sioux finally understood. Yellow Robe must have respected the courage it took to challenge the color barrier, for he apparently forgave and accepted Long Lance. When he fell gravely ill in March 1930, he agreed that Long Lance should replace him on the publicity tour to Hollywood. Chanler and Burden had no choice but to send out their other headliner and hope for the best.

Yellow Robe's unexpected death from pneumonia in early April affected Long Lance deeply. He wrote to Yellow Robe's daughter, Rosebud, and in grief and despair said, "One thing I do know: he will never die in my memory. I think I thought almost as much of him as you his own children did." Later he offered to pay for the education of Rosebud's youngest sister, Evelyn.[15]

Long Lance undertook the film promotion tour in late March. The disclosure was not yet public. He would have one more taste of celebrity status. Because Burden and Chanler sent him, and because the trip was important for the movie, he may have thought it meant that the investigation had ended or had come to nothing. Whatever it meant he loved Hollywood. Through his connections at Paramount, he met and was photographed with Clara Bow, the "It Girl" of the late 1920s, who commanded a salary of five thousand dollars a week.[16]

Thanks to a letter of introduction from Fannie Hurst, Long Lance also met Douglas Fairbanks at his studio home on the United Artists lot. The talkies had hurt Fairbanks' career, but the silent star was still at the height of his fame and the King of Hollywood. He had a proper queen, too, in Mary Pickford, the most popular female movie star in the country. In a letter to Canon Middleton, Long Lance related that Fairbanks and Pickford "are greater in person than they are even on the screen — very real people." In Hollywood he also met Charlie Chaplin, Irving Berlin and the comedian Harold Lloyd.[17]

Long Lance worked hard to publicize *The Silent Enemy* in Hollywood, where there were other Indian actors but few as articulate and faultlessly dressed as the smooth, self-styled Blackfoot. The *Los Angeles Times* described him as "a very clever young Indian of the new school, a Carlisle graduate who fought in the World War and has written things for good magazines." At a powwow held in his honor by Hollywood Indians from fourteen tribes, Long Lance danced the prairie chicken dance with a young Cherokee named Iron Eyes Cody.[18]

On March 22 Long Lance was introduced to Anita Baldwin, one of the richest women in the United States. She was in her midfifties, five feet, five inches tall with hazel eyes and a fine Grecian nose. A graceful woman of regal stature, she had been dubbed by the *Los Angeles Times* "the lady of the peacocks."[19] She was not the first woman to fall under Long Lance's spell, and when he left California to return to New York, the twice-divorced woman could not get him out of her mind.

Unknown to Long Lance the investigation into his past had continued. Ilia Tolstoy set out for Winston–Salem on his mission for William Chanler. Tolstoy had lived a rich and varied life. He

Anita Baldwin, "The Lady of the Peacocks," c. 1900. She was one of America's richest heiresses and was fascinated with Long Lance.

was born in 1903 at Toptikovo in Tula Province, south of Moscow, and on both sides of his family he boasted famous ancestors: Leo Tolstoy, the Russian novelist, was his paternal grandfather, and General Diterichs, a distinguished czarist officer, was his maternal grandfather. He had attended schools at Odessa and the Moscow School of Agriculture before serving in the Imperial Cavalry under General Kuropatkin near Tashkent in the deserts of Central Asia. A superb rider, he once traveled on horseback from Samarkand across the mountains of Afghanistan to Peshawar in northwestern India (now Pakistan). Commissioned in Her

Majesty's Leib Guard, he had fought against the Bolsheviks in the civil war, and after the defeat of the White Guard armies, he had fled to the United States.[20]

Tolstoy arrived in Winston–Salem in early April, the most beautiful month of the year. The sky was clear, the temperatures were balmy. Red, white, purple and orange azaleas were blooming everywhere. The first leaves were sprouting on the oak trees.[21]

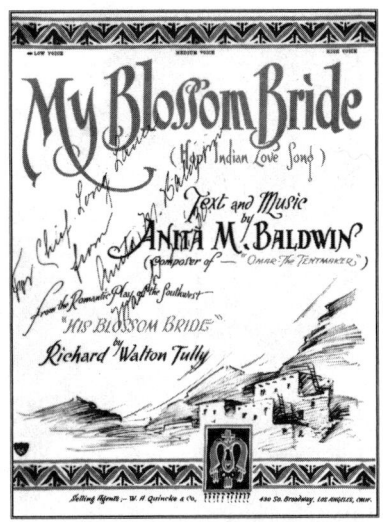

On their first meeting Anita Balwin presented Long Lance with an inscribed copy of a musical score she had composed.

Since Long Lance's departure, the population of Winston–Salem had quadrupled from nearly twenty thousand in 1909 to eighty thousand in 1930, due mainly to the good fortunes of the R.J. Reynolds Tobacco Company, the most profitable tobacco operation in the country. It employed twelve thousand local residents. The spire of the twenty-three–story Reynolds skyscraper dominated the city, and spread before it were blocks of Reynolds factories and gaudy signs proclaiming, CAMELS LEAD THE WORLD. In 1913, when Winston and Salem officially amalgamated, R.J. Reynolds introduced the cigarette that became the best-selling brand in the 1920s. In 1930 the Reynolds Company sold 38 million Camels, and North Carolina's second-largest city became known as "Camel City." The smell of tobacco was everywhere.[22]

On his first morning in Winston–Salem, Tolstoy called on the Longs at their home on Brookstown Avenue. He got the address from the West End School, where Joe had worked into his midseventies until ill health kept him from the job. Brookstown Avenue was a short, dirt road in the middle of white West Win-

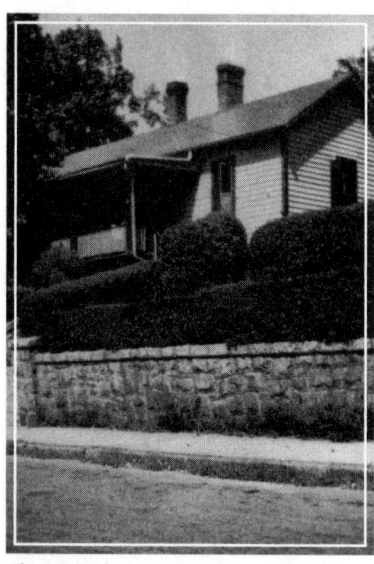

The Longs' home on Brookstown Avenue,
West Winston, where they moved in 1907.

ston. Tolstoy noted that the one-story frame house on a slight hill was "very poor, but good in comparison with the colored houses around." The Longs kept their hedge and front lawn well trimmed, and on the lot stood many good-sized trees: oak, walnut and a chinaberry tree.[23] His knock at the door was answered by a thin, elderly man, about five feet, eight inches with a mustache, straight gray hair and rather dark skin.

Tolstoy's Russian accent startled Joe and Sallie Long, but when he introduced himself as a friend of their son—he used the name Sylvester—they relaxed and welcomed him. Ilia understood Joe quite well, but Sallie's accent was much thicker, with a rollicking Deep South cadence, and he could not catch everything she said. Still, Sallie was anxious to hear all she could about her son, and she fired one question after another at their visitor. When Ilia reciprocated and began to probe into Sylvester's background and origins, Joe and Sallie became suspicious. They told him abruptly that they were Cherokee and suggested that he talk to their son, Abe, who worked at the newly opened Carolina Theater. The interview was over.

Ilia found Abe at the theater, where he managed the colored section. Prominently displayed by the side entrance to the gallery, he saw the ticket prices listed at ten and fifteen cents.[24] Ilia liked Abe at once, whom he described as "quite decent and intelligent," but Abe pretended at first that he did not know who Sylvester Long was. Joe and Sallie had identified Sylvester Long

Abe Long by the entrance of the Carolina Theater, where he spent the thirties and forties directing the flow of traffic up the seventy-four steps to the colored gallery.

as their son, so Ilia was puzzled. He persisted, and finally Abe admitted "that he had a brother by the name of Sylvester, who [had] not been home for twenty years." He said no more.

Ilia then went to see R.H. Latham, the superintendent of schools,[25] who spoke of Joe Long as an "exceptionally good man" who had never missed a day of work. He said he knew Joe was an Indian, and, yes, he would gladly have a chat with him and find out what he could.

Joe told Latham that he had been born in Yadkin County, that his father was a prominent white man by the name of John Vestal and that his mother was an Indian.[26] Latham also learned that Sallie Long's father was white and her mother a Cherokee. (From about 1913 to 1953 the Indians known at the turn of the century as Croatans called themselves Cherokee. Today they call themselves Lumbees, from the Lumber River in Robeson County.[27])

Latham referred Ilia to William Blair, president of the Peoples Bank, a man Joe said he had known since his arrival in the city forty-five years earlier. The white community held the seventy-year-old Colonel Blair in high regard. He had graduated from Harvard and from Trinity (now Duke University) in neighboring

Durham, and he had traveled widely and read far beyond the narrow confines of banking. The *Winston–Salem Journal* once said that William Blair would have been the English philosopher Francis Bacon's ideal of an educated man: "He can name the bones in the human body, enumerate all the moons of Saturn, interest the children with animal stories, and discuss philosophy. . . ."[28]

Colonel Blair, of course, was thrilled to meet the grandson of the giant of Russian literature, and he cleared his desk immediately. Leo Tolstoy's vast novels and intricate plots with their strong, bold characters epitomized in his mind the complexity of Russia. The American South was complex, too, as any native-born Yankee trying to grasp the subtleties of the racial system soon realized. Colonel Blair summarized for Ilia the basic southern rule: anyone with any known Negro ancestor was colored, even if he or she had blue eyes, blond hair and the fairest of skin. In the South an American with the same pedigree as Alexander Pushkin, Russia's greatest nineteenth-century poet, would be regarded as colored, simply because one of his eight great-grandparents had African ancestry (Pushkin's great-grandfather, Hannibal, one of Peter the Great's generals, was black).[29] It seemed ludicrous, but Colonel Blair had more surprises for Ilia when he told him all that he knew of the Longs.

He explained that Joe Long had come to Winston in the late 1880s, when the town had a population of less than eight thousand. Because of his hooked nose, tanned complexion and straight black hair, he was accepted as an Indian and treated accordingly. He even managed to get a job as a clerk at a store where all the other clerks were white. "Long was employed because it was understood he was an Indian," Colonel Blair told Ilia. It was also known in the community that Sallie Long had "only white and Indian blood with no mixture of any other." Because Joe and Sallie were "Indians," Colonel Blair recalled that they were advised to act as such. "I remember perfectly well that the white people, and perhaps I was among the number, advised

Joe not to associate in any way with the colored people, as it was understood that he was an Indian."[30]

Looking back on it all, the elderly banker realized the difficult and unenviable position in which Joe and Sallie found themselves when they arrived in Winston. If they had moved to Robeson County in the southern part of the state, where mixed bloods were numerous, they could have joined that community.[31] There were thousands of Croatans in Robeson County. No one knew for sure where they came from, but it was believed they were descendants of survivors of Sir Walter Raleigh's missing colony. Colonel Blair outlined to Ilia the abortive attempt to found an English settlement on the North Carolina coast in the late 1580s. The white survivors intermingled with the neighboring Indians and later migrated to Robeson County. In Robeson there were three racial classifications: white, colored and Indian—not just white and colored as in Winston. The Croatans in Robeson had their own schools and churches.

Joe and Sallie Long rejected that option. Instead they first tried to gain acceptance as whites of Indian background, and early on in Winston they nearly succeeded. There was already a local family in Winston, the Poindexters,[32] known to be of distant Indian ancestry. At the turn of the century, individuals of white and some Indian ancestry—like Will Rogers, the famous humorist—were treated as whites. The Virginian-born second wife of former President Woodrow Wilson never tried to hide the fact that she was a descendant of Pocahontas. Charles Curtis, the current American vice-president, was one-eighth Kaw Indian.[33]

When Joe and Sallie presented themselves at the local white church, they were admitted, but not for long. Someone from Iredell County probably reported that "back home" they were classified as "colored." When the white congregation made it known that they were not welcome, Joe and Sallie left and attended the colored churches.[34] The issue was settled, the racial barrier had surfaced once again, and the Longs forevermore were "col-

Sallie and Joe Long in their later years. They kept their son's secret faithfully. The photo caption reads, "Divorced by the Will of God after 53 Years of Happy Life."

ored." Joe's dark skin had already convinced many in Winston that he had black and Indian blood. When the Long children reached school age, they attended the black school because, as Colonel Blair explained, "the races here have separate schools." White children avoided the Long children.[35]

Colonel Blair's testimony proved so illuminating that Ilia asked him to repeat the most salient points in a sworn affidavit. He complied, and in the document dated April 9, 1930, Colonel Blair said that "it has always been my understanding that Joe

A grateful Long Lance inscribed at the bottom of this print, "For Ilia Tolstoy whom I am honored to call the best Pale-faced Friend I have anywhere in the world."

Long's wife had only white and Indian blood with no mixture of any other. . . . I have known Joe quite well through all these years and I never heard anyone in this city or state express even a doubt but that his was Indian blood."

After his lengthy talks with Colonel Blair and Latham, Ilia returned to see the Longs, and this time they received him with open arms. In his report to Chanler, Ilia wrote: "I thought they would never stop talking and telling me about their lives and showing me pictures." Sallie and Joe by this time knew Ilia was a loyal friend of their son and was on their side.

Ilia interpreted the evidence favorably, and on April 10 he telegraphed Chanler in New York, "Have full information and affidavit of him being Indian and white." When the telegram arrived, followed by Ilia's full account of his investigation, Chanler felt enormous relief. Long Lance may have lied about his past, he may have come from North Carolina and not the western plains, but at least he was Indian. Chanler told Ilia that Long Lance's Indian ancestry was "all we care about; what tribe he belongs to is entirely secondary." In a note to Colonel Blair and Latham, Chanler thanked them for their help and said he would talk to Long Lance and "see that he stops calling himself a Blackfoot."[36] As far as Chanler was concerned the case was closed.

Ilia Tolstoy and Long Lance had a grand reunion when they met in New York in late May. At first Long Lance was surprised to hear of his friend's visit to his hometown, but he was delighted to know that everyone in his family was doing well and to hear about his parents' fifty-first wedding anniversary.[37]

Just as important was the news that Ilia's report to Chanler had been favorable. Long Lance took one of his portraits as Baluk in *The Silent Enemy* and inscribed it "For Ilia Tolstoy whom I am honored to call the best Pale-face Friend I have anywhere in the world—*Netawa Hanka-wanzi* Long Lance—May 30 '30." *Hanka-wanzi* was the highest compliment Long Lance could bestow. It meant that he had taken Ilia Tolstoy as his blood brother.[38]

CHAPTER 17

The Lady of the Peacocks

EUROPE, 1931

*R*umors that Long Lance was part black cost him some society friends, but he persevered, bloodied perhaps, but not yet out. He kept up his social appearances. In the summer and early autumn of 1930, he stepped out often in his formal evening coat, tails, silk hat and patent leather shoes. He kept in trim, too, working out daily at an athletic club on the roof of a New York skyscraper.[1]

The reviews of his performance in *The Silent Enemy* continued to appear, maintaining his hard-won status as a celebrity. In September *Liberty* magazine suggested that a clever producer should schedule James Fenimore Cooper's *Last of the Mohicans* and "assign Chief Long Lance—who did such good work in *The Silent Enemy*—to the role of Uncas." *Screenland*, a movie magazine, said that Long Lance, if cast in a talking picture, would "give Gary Cooper, Richard Dix and the rest of our great outdoor heroes of the screen an awful run for their cinema money."[2]

Although he knew his days as Chief Buffalo Child Long Lance, Blackfoot, were numbered, he tirelessly continued to add to his invention. Always good for a colorful story and a lively interview, he earnestly told one journalist that every day he ate rare meat and raw eggs and drank two quarts of milk every night after his workout.[3] When the *New York Times* interviewed him, he spoke about the drought that threatened many parts of the country that autumn. Seeding clouds was not the answer, Long Lance said. He suggested instead that concentrated thought could bring on the rain to save the fall harvest. "I have no doubt that the mind of man can be brought to such a state that it can control the forces of nature," he told the *Times*.[4]

The nation remained in the grip of the Great Depression. Every day on the streets of New York, Long Lance passed beggars and panhandlers, and returning home at night he walked by homeless people sleeping in doorways and on park benches. In the poorer districts there were long breadlines.

He tried to do what he could to help, for he was essentially a generous man. In early July a former Carlisle student showed up on the steps of the Explorers Club looking for him. His name was Dan Arapaho, an Oglala Sioux from Pine Ridge Reserve in South Dakota, and he was in desperate straits with no money and clad in a soiled blue shirt and an old pair of trousers. Long Lance checked his closet and gave the man a suit, shirts, ties, socks, even some of his underwear. He also gave him money to tide him over until he found work, which he later did, driving a truck.[5]

One woman he saw frequently that summer was Te Ata, or Mary Thompson, a Chickasaw Indian from eastern Oklahoma. A striking beauty with long, black braids, she had graduated from the Oklahoma College for Women and studied theater at the Carnegie Institute of Technology in Pittsburgh. After coming to New York, she had appeared in several roles on Broadway.

Te Ata was not at all disturbed by rumors of Long Lance's background. She accepted without question his story that he was

Long Lance told Seamus, his best friend at the Explorers Club, that the painting "A Winter's Night in Lithuania" by Kowaltski was his favorite work of art. The painting, featuring a lone wold overlooking a human settlement, is a telling comment on the depth of his loneliness.

a Blackfoot who had been adopted by Cherokees before coming to Carlisle. She found Long Lance "gracious" and "very personable," and she simply liked being with him. She enjoyed his inquiring mind and found they had many common interests, among them a keen enthusiasm for new books and movies.[6]

However, the rumors persisted, gathering strength. Seumas noted their effect on Long Lance. He grew apprehensive and self-conscious at the Explorers Club, feeling he was always under scrutiny. In Calgary, he had never touched alcohol or smoked, but now he indulged heavily in both. He even attended club meetings smelling of liquor.[7] Against the rules of the club, he kept alcohol in his room in a bottle labeled "hair tonic." Seumas and Clyde Fisher stood by him, but the belief that he was a "half breed nigger" showed in others' hostile glances.[8] By the end of the summer he was ready to leave the Explorers Club.

An opportunity to move out gracefully came that autumn when he was offered free flying lessons at Roosevelt Field on Long Island. With his savings he paid for room and board at the

Long Lance proved to be a quick study in flying school. The sky, he said, was the only place he found true freedom.

Roosevelt Field Hotel. He began his training in early October under an instructor named Lester (Husky) Flewellyn, and he first went aloft in a Consolidated Fleet biplane with a Kinner ninety-horsepower engine.[9]

After only five hours of flying time, Long Lance sought more excitement. He volunteered to demonstrate a new automatic Switlik Manufacturing Company parachute at the air races at Trenton, New Jersey, in mid-October—even though he had never parachuted before. On a cold and blustery Sunday afternoon he dropped through the cabin floor of the Switlik plane. Far below, thirty thousand spectators watched him float safely to the ground.[10]

Two weeks later, ready for more thrills, Long Lance went up and executed several unscheduled stunts. On his first solo flight he took his plane up to an altitude of about three thousand feet, then nosed it down with the engine at full throttle, pulled back on the stick and executed a perfect loop. He then climbed up again and did two more loops and some rolls and tailspins, outlandish tricks for a rookie flyer on a solo flight. On October 29, 1930, in the *New York Sun*, a story appeared detailing the feat and once again repeating the accomplishments of Long Lance's career, from a famous football player at Carlisle to West Point cadet, to light-heavyweight boxing champion of the Canadian army. The item described Long Lance's aerobatics before an audience of instructors who looked on "aghast" while other students turned "a pinkish pale. . . ." The *Sun* continued:

> Chief Long Lance says there is something about the air that agrees particularly well with the temperament of the Indian. The ranginess and freedom akin to that of this continent before the advent of the white man appeals to the redskin. The Indian aviator says he hopes to interest others of his race in the game of emulating the eagle. He is very confident of his ability to fly and is completing the course at the Long Island field rapidly. A week ago Saturday he made his first parachute jump, or rather he was dumped out by Parker Cramer, who flew Sir Hubert Wilkins over the pole. . . .
>
> Chief Long Lance has always proved himself to be the master of the unexpected. Up until he was in his teens he could talk little English, could not read it at all and had never been inside a white man's house. He has since been an honor student at Carlisle, a West Point cadet, a winner of the *Croix de Guerre*. . . .[11]

At Roosevelt Field, Long Lance started dating a young woman flyer, Laura Ingalls, who came from a wealthy family and had been educated in Paris and Vienna. That same October, when Long Lance parachuted and did his solo stunts, Laura Ingalls became the first woman to fly from Los Angeles to Roosevelt Field, making the trip in twenty-five hours and thirty-five minutes.[12]

Flying temporarily revived Long Lance's flagging spirits. He seemed to brighten. He wrote to Mike Eagle Speaker in Alberta to tell him of his flying lessons and declared them "more fun than riding bucking horses." In mid-December he sent a note to Dorothy Fellers' sister, Isabel, to announce that he had obtained

Walter Long with his father, Joe, taken around late 1930, near the time of Walter's visit with Long Lance in New York.

his private pilot's license and was working on earning a commercial license. "I like it better than anything I have ever done," he told Isabel and her husband, who lived in Connecticut. "I seldom see New York anymore—thrown the old top hat into my locker at the Explorers Club, and forgot all about it."[13]

Long Lance had never experienced such freedom as when he was climbing, diving, banking, and making loops and rolls. In the air he was not a "full-blooded Indian" or a "colored," but a man alone against the elements. There was nobody to report to, nobody to prove himself to, nobody to lie to. Among the clouds his only enemy was death, and he did not fear it. He escaped all the rumors and ugliness, literally rising above it all in the skies over New York. He would soon be brought down to reality.

On December 31, New Year's Eve, his brother Walter left Winston–Salem for New York. When he arrived in the city he discreetly inquired about Sylvester and learned of his flying lessons at Roosevelt Field. On January 5 the two brothers met in Manhattan after a separation of twenty-two years. Walter told him that Joe and Sallie had been dangerously ill that autumn. Their father, now seventy-seven, had been hospitalized for five days in late November. Abe and Walter could not afford the doctors' fees and hospital bills, and they needed help from Sylvester.[14]

After his meeting with Walter, Long Lance continued to feel uneasy and could not sleep. The next morning, he poured out his anguish in a letter to his brother:

> I must have been in sort of a daze. I don't remember how I said goodbye. And it was only when I had gotten on the train and my brain had cooled a little that I remembered seeing you reaching for the taxi fare, and then realized that you, too, must have gotten out at Penn Station. I had been under the impression that you were going to take the taxi on to some other destination, and when I got out my mind was so fixed on not making a fool of myself saying goodbye to you, that my eyes actually saw things that did not register in my mind until I had gotten home.
>
> I lay awake most of the night, wishing that I could phone you . . . kicking myself because I had not stayed at the apartment all night with you, and a thousand other things that came to my mind when it was too late. I would have given anything to have seen you again. I don't think that I have ever felt the emotions that my visit with you brought into being.

> I have not yet fully untangled these emotions: my
> own darling brother whom I used to romp and play
> with, coming to me after twenty-two years, wondering
> if I were going to be ashamed of him. . . .[15]

Long Lance felt pulled in opposite directions, frustrated and
guilty. His love for his family struggled against his desire for more
weeks, months, maybe years of excitement and celebrity. In the
end, as always, he decided he would not return to the Jim Crow
car on the train pulling into Winston–Salem.

Once his flying lessons were paid for, Long Lance sent
checks home: $25 in March, $30 in April, and, when he began
working again, $100 in June, $230 in August, $50 in December and
$40 in February. He wrote to Abe to thank him for being "so kind
and sympathetic with me." He asked him to tell his father "that I
love him as I have always done—more than anything in the world
now—him and our sweet mother." But he would not come home.
He wrote, "If there is anything in the papers, Abe, you will be
careful about names, won't you. What a condition this is! Good
night my dear brother—And thanks a million times for what you
and Walter are doing."[16]

Within two weeks of seeing Walter, Long Lance was at center stage again, this time making a special appearance at a showing of *The Silent Enemy* at a theater near Roosevelt Field. At the
end of the month he spoke to five hundred people at the Hotel
Pennsylvania in New York, and in the audience were film stars
Maurice Chevalier, Tallulah Bankhead, Fredric March and
Claudette Colbert.[17]

Then, almost miraculously, a chance at a glamorous job in
California surfaced. His new employer would be Anita Baldwin,
whom he had met earlier on his publicity tour in Hollywood.
Mrs. Baldwin was fascinated by Indian culture and had written
several songs about the tribes of New Mexico and Arizona. She
had traveled among the Hopi in New Mexico to research their

music and collect artifacts. From her first meeting with Long Lance, she was impressed by the handsome Blackfoot chief, and when he left Hollywood for New York, he promised he would send her a copy of *Long Lance*. She kept in touch with him while he was in New York, and early in the spring of 1931 she wrote to offer him employment as her secretary and bodyguard on a trip to Europe in the fall.[18]

Long Lance accepted. Upon receiving his commercial pilot's license in mid-May 1931, he left for Chicago, where he boarded the Santa Fe Chief, the express train to southern California.[19] A short-term job would allow him to send more money home and provide a temporary distraction from the agonizing urge to return home to visit his ailing parents.

On his way west Long Lance looked up an old friend, Susie Curtis, at Elmira, New York. She had met him in Banff in 1926, the summer he had, in her words, a "fearful" affair with "a married woman of Chicago." Miss Curtis had corresponded with him ever since, and at her request Long Lance met her at the Elmira station. She traveled with him westward on the train for two hours until they met the eastbound train on which she returned home. They never saw each other again.[20]

As the Santa Fe Chief chugged into the outskirts of metropolitan Los Angeles, it crossed the San Gabriel Valley. From the train window Long Lance caught his first glimpse of Anita Baldwin's immense ranch of more than three thousand acres. The Santa Fe Railway had been granted a right-of-way across the estate by her father, Elias Jackson, or "Lucky" Baldwin, in return for a station on the property. Included in the deed was a provision that all passenger trains must stop on signal at the Baldwins' Santa Anita station. When the train pulled in, Long Lance grabbed his bags and stepped down onto the wooden station platform. Mrs. Baldwin's chauffeur met him in one of her three Rolls-Royces and drove him to Anoakia, the Baldwin mansion.

Anita's father had worked for years to create a great fruit and livestock farm. He had personally supervised the planting of avenues of eucalyptus and poplar and groves of fruit trees. After his death Anita kept up the work, building her own home, Anoakia, on the northern edge of the estate so that she could work at it daily. The first two letters of the mansion's name were from *Anita* and the next three from the lofty oak trees scattered over the estate. It was discovered later that *Anoak* itself was an Indian word meaning "where no harm shall befall."

To enter the estate the chauffeur first checked in at the guard house on Baldwin Avenue. A high, ten-foot concrete wall—nicknamed the "Great Wall of Anoakia"—surrounded the property, which was lit all night. A guard with a sidearm and dogs patrolled the grounds day and night. For more protection, barbed wire and six strands of low-voltage wires had been stretched along the top of the wall. If the circuit was broken, a revolving light on the roof of the mansion turned on and a system of bells, gongs and sirens was activated.

Anoakia astounded Long Lance, having come from the breadlines and panhandlers of New York. The mansion and the grounds belonged to another world. After leaving the guard house, the Rolls-Royce passed a large stable, a garage and finally came to the house itself, built in Italian Renaissance style with a balustraded terrace, a grand stairway and a loggia with Roman columns. In 1928 the building was valued at five hundred thousand dollars. It stood on two levels facing Foothill Boulevard to the south and was shaped like a half-H, with terraces spreading about it. The house looked over the San Gabriel Valley, and on a clear day one could see the ocean in the distance.[21]

The chauffeur carried Long Lance's bags to the door. Edwin, Anita's Scottish butler, answered the bell, greeted Long Lance, then told one of the Indian maids to inform "Madame" that her guest had arrived. Long Lance's bags were taken to one of the guest suites, and he was invited inside.

The living room was on the main floor, between the dining

room and the library. Through the opened doors he could look through all three rooms, a distance of more than a hundred feet. Rich oriental rugs covered the floors and custom-designed furniture filled the rooms. The oak leaf and acorn, the peacock and the California poppy—Anita's favorite symbols—appeared in the decor of all three. From where he sat, Long Lance could see the sculpted plaster oak leaves and acorns and the peacock theme in the Tiffany-designed luster glass chandeliers on the ceiling of the living room. The tiles in the fireplace were fired to a peacock hue.

When Anita arrived, she welcomed him and showed him around the house. Also on the main floor were bedrooms, the kitchen and breakfast room, and a small North American Indian Hall decorated with scenes of the Indians of the northern plains. She had commissioned Maynard Dixon, a leading western artist, to complete the murals when the house was built in 1913. Upstairs were a number of additional suites, but because of the financial pinch, which even Anita felt, they were closed. There were gas and electric fixtures in all of the rooms and a fireplace in each bedroom. The basement contained a bowling alley wide enough for two lanes, a billiard room, a "jinks," or rumpus room, and a wine cellar with two huge barrels of wine (one of muscatel, one of port) and a rack with niches for as many as 549 bottles. On the north side of the house was a swimming pool seventy-five feet long and thirty feet wide. For a bathhouse Anita had built a miniature reproduction of the Athenian Parthenon with six dressing rooms, all with private showers. There was a Greek-columned gymnasium that Long Lance was welcome to use. Throughout the grounds were aviaries with peacocks, birds of paradise and love birds.[22]

After a few days at Anoakia, Anita and Long Lance traveled to Tallac, her large, thirty-two-hundred–acre estate at the southwestern corner of Lake Tahoe, on the California side of the California–Nevada border. To the southwest of Anita's home, surrounded by massive yellow pines and cedars, Long Lance saw the mountain the local Washoe Indians called "Great Mountain," or Mount Tallac. He fit in well here, and at a party one day he demonstrated how the Indians let fly their arrows from the hip. He was an excellent shot with the bow and arrow and flung off bull's eye after bull's eye.[23]

At Tallac, Long Lance learned much about Anita Baldwin. Despite every apparent advantage, he discovered that she was a much distressed woman. At night when she could not sleep, she called Ralph Tweedle, one of her guards, and asked him to bring some Cokes to a little screened-in side porch at her lodge. There, in the dark, she talked about how worried she was about losing her property, about threats on her life and people trying to break in to see her, usually demanding financial help. It was assumed she was immensely wealthy and probably easy prey, but in fact she was property rich and cash poor, and could not even pay her taxes.[24]

Anita's life had not been happy. As a child all she had enjoyed was money. Her father had risen from humble origins to become one of California's wealthiest men, but at the expense of any meaningful family life. Born on a farm in Ohio in 1828, Eli, or "Lucky," came west by wagon train at an early age. He made a small fortune from shrewd real estate speculation around San Francisco, then invested heavily in the Comstock Silver Mine in Nevada, making millions. He used his profits to buy up land around the small town of Los Angeles, eventually accumulating more than fifty thousand acres. During the great real estate boom at the turn of the century, he sold portions for prices ten times higher than he had paid and, with his coffers overflowing, he bought a huge estate at Lake Tahoe. On his death in 1909, his fortune was estimated at ten million dollars.[25]

Unfortunately Lucky Baldwin did not have the same success with women. He had four wives and, in his biographer's words, "a well-defined but unsubstantiated rumor of a fifth, not to mention numerous sweethearts and a breach of promise and seduction suits."[26] It was said that he was so fearful of being poisoned by his second wife that he refused to eat anything she prepared until she had tasted it.[27] He had an affair with Jennie Dexter when he was in his late forties and she was sixteen, eight years younger than his daughter by his first marriage. Their child, Anita, was born in January 1876, and three years later Lucky and Jennie were married.[28]

Anita's mother died when she was five years old, and three years later her father married again, this time to a beautiful blonde named Lilly Bennett, who at sixteen was just eight years older than Anita. When she was older, Anita was haunted by her origins and undertook extensive genealogical research. She discovered that her mother was descended several generations back from a line of Flemish counts, who in turn traced their ancestry back to the Emperor Charlemagne.[29]

Anita's own experience with marriage proved to be as disappointing as her father's. When she was fifteen, she eloped with her first cousin. She gave birth to twins who died in infancy, and after seven years of marriage her husband deserted her. She then married Hull McClaughrey, the son of a wealthy northern California family, but in 1913 this union as well was terminated in the courts of law. Anita gave him three hundred thousand dollars as a settlement and won custody of their two children, Dextra and Baldwin.[30] Anita told reporters in 1914 that she would never marry again. She once explained to the *San Francisco Chronicle* that she preferred dogs to men. "They are faithful and true. They are constant. In this particular they differ most from men."[31] She changed her name back to Baldwin.

When her second marriage ended, Anita immersed herself in community work, and during World War I she placed her estate at the disposal of the government. The United States Balloon School was established on her property. Anita spent ten thousand a month on the U.S. Army soldiers until the war ended. After the war she donated large sums for the establishment of a hospital for crippled children in Los Angeles. Anonymously she gave fifty thousand dollars to an orthopedic hospital in San Francisco. She also contributed substantial amounts to establish the Anita Baldwin Baby Clinic in the city, and she was heavily involved in women's issues, upholding the right of women to vote. And she strongly supported the North American Indian. "All my life," she later wrote, "I have been interested in Indians and he [Long Lance] was only one of many whom I have tried to help."[32]

By the summer of 1931 Anita was sad and lonely. Despite all the care she had showered on them, her children's lives were in complete disarray. Dextra had married and divorced. Baldwin had recently had left his wife and two children to live in Paris with Suzanne Lenglen, the French tennis star. And there were economic problems. As she wrote to Baldwin on December 16, 1930: "Business is so very bad. . . . There are countless suicides and so much red activity." By spring, conditions had deteriorated further, and she had to cut back Anoakia's staff to a chef, assistant chef, two Indian housemaids, three gardeners, two watchmen, a chauffeur and a handyman.[33]

Anita lived in fear at Anoakia despite the elaborate security system. She was convinced each May 1 that communists would storm her home. In late 1929 she announced that she intended to sell all her property in southern California, then estimated at a value of twenty to twenty-five million dollars, and live year-round at Lake Tahoe. "For years and years I have wanted to cut away from the worries and troubles which the management of this business provokes in order that I might have time to devote myself primarily to music and travel," she told a reporter. "There are many, many places that I still have not seen and that I would like to visit."[34] Unfortunately the Depression made it impossible to find buyers, but she still insisted upon going to Europe to see her son, Baldwin, in the autumn of 1931.

Anita found Long Lance a refreshing diversion. He was the perfect choice as bodyguard and secretary for the European trip. She wrote to Baldwin from Tallac on July 6 and told him all about her new Indian employee:

I am planning some work, musically, etc., with an educated Indian, who has gone thru Carlisle, Manlius and
left West Point to join the Canadians in the World War
and returned a Captain of Infantry. He has just completed his air course, being a commissioned pilot, etc.
He had collaborated on a book and movie called *The
Silent Enemy*, a story of the Indians in the North. He is
a Blackfoot, born in Montana and must be about 35
years old. He is a gentleman and his ways are gentle,
too, so I am glad to have him in the home while I
assimilate all the knowledge he can impart of legend,
customs, etc.

She trusted Long Lance and insisted on only one precau-
tion, which was to warn Tweedle, the night guard, "to keep a special watch on the maids' quarters since Long Lance, as an Indian
Chief, might assert his 'tribal rights' if he felt so inclined."[35]

Long Lance and Anita had long talks. He spared no details
about himself. When he drew up his American passport application at Tallac in early July, he asked her to witness it.[36] He began
by stating that he was born at Sweetgrass, Montana, and again
dropped years from his age, claiming that he was born on December 1, 1896. He added that his father, Pitah, died at Sweetgrass in
1900. On Anita's advice he marked the purpose of his journey as
a "pleasure trip" to "France, Italy, Germany, Sweden, England,
Austria, Spain, Switzerland, Belgium" with his mailing address as
Tallac, El Dorado County, California.

If Anita had doubts about Long Lance's true identity, they
were removed when an affidavit from Emma Newashe, dated July 1,
arrived. In June, Long Lance had written to his old friend from
Carlisle, who had married shortly after graduation and lived in
Luther, Oklahoma. He asked her to certify for the United States
Passport Office that he was born in Montana, near Sweetgrass,
and that she had known him since Carlisle.[37] Twenty-one years

after Carlisle, Emma probably remembered him as a Cherokee, but now believed his story of being a Blackfoot adopted by Cherokees. In her signed affidavit she testified that "to the best of my knowledge and belief he was born in Sweet Grass, Montana, on December 1, 1896."

In mid-July Long Lance met with a state department official in San Francisco. He brought his application, witnessed by Anita, and the affidavit from Emma Newashe, "an old family friend." Long Lance told the officer that he had asked his brother, Eagle Speaker, who lived on the Blood Reservation in Alberta, to make out an affidavit, but unfortunately he had not done so. The agent noted in his report, "Applicant claims that his brother is rather illiterate and would not perhaps understand how to attend to this matter." Long Lance said that Emma knew Eagle Speaker "intimately" but had forgotten to state this in her affidavit.

Then came the big risk. Almost casually he advised the State Department to check the records of the Carlisle Indian School to verify his tribal identity. He gambled that it would not go to the bother of checking with the Office of Indian Affairs. All went well. The Carlisle records were not checked. Satisfied that the applicant was "a full-blooded Indian of the Black Foot tribe," and "a very high type, intelligent person," the agent recommended that the passport be issued.

The night before Anita and Long Lance departed for Europe, Elizabeth Analla, a Yankton Sioux from South Dakota living in Los Angeles, visited Anoakia. She knew the Indian maids who worked for Anita. While there she spoke with Long Lance and learned of the Sioux warrior he admired most, Chauncey Yellow Robe, who had been "like a father to him."[38] It is a revealing comment. Despite his outward confidence, Long Lance always sought an authority figure, a Canon Middleton, a Chauncey Yellow Robe, and, as the weeks passed, an Anita Baldwin.

Anita and Long Lance viewed the trip to Europe somewhat differently. Writing to Emma Newashe, Long Lance stated that it was a "vacation given me as a forerunner of some work that I am going to do for the Indians upon my return in November. . . . I am getting a four-place Lockheed plane, as my travelling vehicle, and will devote all of my time from then on to helping our people, with private backing." The understanding was that as long as he behaved himself he would be given his airplane, but, according to a later statement made by Anita, there was no such promise. He was simply hired on "a salary as secretary–bodyguard, etc." to accompany her, her daughter, Dextra, and Lowry McCaslin, the manager of her Los Angeles office, to Europe. On August 26 they sailed from New York to Le Havre on the *Ile de France*.[39]

Lowry McCaslin was a recent graduate of the University of Southern California and just twenty-three years old. At university he had been on an athletic scholarship and played on the basketball and football teams. One of his best friends was a young man with acting ambitions whose name was John Wayne. On his frequent visits to Anita, McCaslin often found Long Lance there, and the two men got along well. They boxed at Anoakia's gymnasium. It was arranged that McCaslin would leave the party in southern France, see Europe on his own, then join Anita, Dextra and Long Lance in Berlin a few weeks later.

During McCaslin's absence, Anita, Dextra, Long Lance and a hired chauffeur drove from Cannes to Nice, Monte Carlo, Monaco, Cap d'Antibes, Juan les Pins and Barcelona. In the mornings Long Lance was introduced to the skimpy continental breakfast of coffee and croissants. In the evenings came his reward: exquisitely cooked French meals and fine wines. At the villa Anita rented at Cannes, he installed a boxing ring and every day he ran along the beach.[40]

On the way to southern France, Anita visited Baldwin in Paris, where he ran a radio import shop near the Etoile. At his apartment Long Lance would have seen his collection of French impressionist works, particularly those of Henri de Toulouse-Lautrec, which Baldwin had been buying for some time. Long

Lance told Anita that her son was "a fine chap." His remarks pleased her, as he knew they would, and she passed them on to Baldwin.[41]

In October, Anita and her entourage traveled through Italy, Austria, Germany, Belgium and Holland. They stayed at the best hotels: the Excelsior in Rome, the Hotel Bristol in Vienna, the Adlon in Berlin. All the while Long Lance took notes. Years earlier he had read of ancient Rome in *Ben Hur*,[42] and many times Princess Alexandra had told him about Berlin. Now he was seeing it all firsthand. He found Spain "unsettled politically," as indeed it was, just five years before the onset of its civil war. In Rome he made no comment on Mussolini's government but wrote in a letter back to North America that the city was "far more interesting with its ruins than I had anticipated." He liked Vienna and Berlin most of all for their "cleanliness, industry and stately beauty."

Of the five countries they visited, Germany and Austria seemed to be in the most serious economic straits. In Germany more than seven million were out of work. Long Lance wrote that "no one knows what will ultimately happen to them. Hundreds of gigantic factories are closed tight, throwing the villages which depended upon them into utter unemployment."[43] The year before, a new party, the National Socialists, had won a hundred seats in the Reichstag elections. If he had inquired, Long Lance would have learned that Princess Alexandra's ex-husband, Prince August Wilhelm, had recently declared that Adolf Hitler was God's gift to Germany. The ex-Kaiser's fourth son had just joined the Nazi Party.[44]

On the European trip, clearly, something happened to unsettle Long Lance's state of mind and send him into bouts of severe depression. He was not one to reveal much of his innermost thoughts (certainly he never did so in any of his letters), but from Anita's remarks it is apparent that all was not well. Publicly she stated that he was "a man of estimable character and gentlemanly in all respects (his conduct being always of the highest type)." Yet privately she recorded different impressions. Six months after the trip, Anita reported that he had made several suicide attempts in Europe. "The first night out on the *Ile de France*," she said, "he was saved from jumping through a porthole. In Cannes and Berlin he was also saved."[45]

More evidence exists of his bizarre behavior. In Berlin in late October, Anita, McCaslin and Long Lance were invited to a formal dinner party of thirty to forty people at the Adlon Hotel, sponsored by German friends of Anita. Long Lance was late. When the dinner began his chair was the only one unoccupied. A number of the Germans had read *Long Lance* (the German translation appeared in 1929) and were anxious to meet him. When he finally did arrive, he stumbled in drunk.

The waiters had just carried in a roast pig with an apple stuffed in its mouth. They placed it at the head of the table. At that moment, and to everyone's horror, Long Lance ran to the head of the table and grabbed the huge carving knife. He hovered menacingly over McCaslin, looked him in the eyes and shouted, "I'm going to cut your heart out." McCaslin turned white. When Long Lance finally calmed down, McCaslin took him to his room. The dinner party was ruined.[46]

Anita and her party returned in mid-November from Amsterdam. She later wrote that Long Lance "was left in New York in Nov. given up as too much of a responsibility."[47] He still belonged to the Explorers Club, and he stayed there, momentarily lifted out of the inexplicable but deep depression. Through his old friend Seumas, he met Elisabeth Randolph Clapp, known to her friends as Bessie, a dancer who lived with a girlfriend in a Greenwich Village apartment.

Bessie was an unlikely candidate for the bohemian life, having come from a wealthy and influential family. She had attended the Dwight School in Englewood, New Jersey, the exclusive Ethel Walker School in Simsbury, Connecticut, the Holy Cross

Elizabeth Clapp was the daughter of a prominent and influential family. She fell immediately in love with Long Lance, who gave her the name Dakotawin. The inscription on the photo reads, "Enni-Poka from Dakotawin." "Enni-Poka" is her spelling of "Buffalo Child" in Blackfoot.

Convent in Washington, D.C. and finally the Collège Féminin in Paris. Her socially prominent grandmother, Mrs. Charles E. Clapp, was the niece of Henry Clay Frick, the famous industrialist. Her grandmother had harbored high hopes for her vivacious granddaughter, as had her parents, but Bessie chose instead a lifestyle of her own in New York and Greenwich Village.[48]

Bessie was eighteen years old and believed that she was part Indian; as a result, she "always felt drawn to them as one might be drawn towards a magnet."[49] Long Lance became an irresistible

However much Long Lance loved Elizabeth Clapp, his "Dakotawin," his only option, as always, was to run. He told her he was pledged to another.

attraction, and Bessie fell deeply in love with him. She told him all about herself. Her parents had separated several years earlier. Her father had moved to Mississippi and her mother, with a new husband, to Kinderhook, New York. Bessie's uncle worked as a stockbroker in New York.[50] Her grandmother's uncle, Henry Clay Frick, was a coal and coke baron who had ruthlessly amassed a fortune at the turn of the century. On one of their walks they passed Frick's home on Fifth Avenue at Seventy-First Street, and Bessie, laughing, told Long Lance how Frick built his five-million-dollar mansion to "make Carnegie's place look like a miner's shack." Inside the mansion were paintings by El Greco, Van Dyck, Vermeer, Rembrandt and Rubens.[51]

Long Lance warmed to her, telling her of his boyhood among the Blackfoot. They spoke a great deal about Indians and about old Seumas and his eccentricities. He mentioned Anita and the airplane she had promised him.

Bessie believed that "if a person really loves someone, no matter what nationality he is, she has a perfect right to marry him."[52] The pretty brunette wanted to marry Long Lance, who, she said, "apparently had no worries or cares in the world." He gave her the Sioux name Dakatowin, which he told her meant "Indian maiden."[53] All indications are that he fell in love as quickly and as deeply with her as she did with him.

By this time in his life, Long Lance feared aging and wanted to marry. At the Halle Brothers Book Fair in Cleveland in mid-October 1928, he had told a woman reporter that "man reaches his peak of physical prowess at thirty-four years. At thirty-eight the decline begins." He turned forty-one on December 1, 1931. In a letter written to Mike Eagle Speaker in May 1930, he had congratulated him on his marriage and added, "I am leaving it off too long. . . ."[54] But he never asked Bessie to marry him, probably still fearing the implications of such a commitment. His inevitable exposure as a fraud and an impostor, when it occurred—whether days, months or years away—would hurt this young, innocent woman, perhaps even emotionally destroy her. In any event he told one further and tragic falsehood: he claimed to be engaged to someone else. In Bessie's words, "being an Indian, he wouldn't break his promise to her."[55]

For more than twenty years Long Lance had fabricated a past in which to live. Cut off from any meaningful relationships (by this point he had not written to Canon Middleton for over a year), he now had not a soul to rely on now except his patron, Anita Baldwin. He wrote pleading letters and sent her telegrams; finally Anita, though disillusioned with him, agreed to help. She told him that "if he gave up his fast cocktail-drinking New York friends, eschewed parties and women, and left drinking alone, his tuition would be paid at an air school and an effort made to assist him in acquiring a plane."[56] Anoakia had become Long Lance's last refuge.

Chapter 18

The Trail Ends

Los Angeles, California, 1932

*I*n late December 1931 Long Lance was once again aboard the Santa Fe Chief, heading across the Midwest on his way to southern California. The lulling motion of the train did not calm his anxieties. Rumors that he was an impostor were circulating in New York again, and life at the Explorers Club had never been more uncomfortable. But he displayed none of his inner torment. After he had packed his bags the night before, he had taken the club's switchboard operator to dinner. She later reported that Long Lance had appeared happy that evening and was looking forward to his trip to the West Coast.[1] Shortly after his departure, the club secretary wrote to the commissioner of the Office of Indian Affairs to ask if Long Lance really was a Blackfoot and if, as another rumor had it, he had been expelled from West Point "for conduct unbecoming a cadet."[2] En route to Los Angeles Long Lance sent a note to Alice Tye, Commissioner Graham's secretary, to tell her, "I am on my way to the coast to resume my flying and get my Lockheed. My address will be just: Santa Anita, California."[3]

At Anoakia he was reunited with Anita, and any onlookers, if they did not look closely at skin coloring, might have thought it was a mother welcoming a returning son. Anita looked all of her fifty-five years, but Long Lance easily could have passed for thirty-five, the age he claimed to be, six years younger than his actual age. She greeted him warmly, believing that his arrival was proof of reformed behavior, and later, on December 28, she wrote, "Long Lance is here for a few days — while seeking a place to stay in or near Glendale where he plans to finish his [pilot] training as eastern weather delayed him too much. He takes some scientists up 20,000 ft. — next August — to photograph eclipse — comet or some solar event."[4]

That evening, at dinner, no doubt Anita launched into a discussion of her favorite themes. Long Lance would try to appear interested, but he had heard it all before in Cannes, Rome, Berlin and Vienna. Back in the United States, she fretted about her country being full of racketeers, kidnappers and gangsters. "At present," she said, "we are law-ed to death and taxed to death. We have no freedom, but too much license!" She attacked President Hoover, whom she believed was ruining the country. "During the Hoover administration, my holdings have shrunk in value from $35,000,000 to about $15,000,000. . . ." She feared that Japan's aggression in China would eventually plunge the United States into another world war.[5]

Long Lance stayed at a hotel in nearby Glendale but frequently visited the Santa Anita Ranch and Anoakia. Anita offered him "the use of [her] home, [her] collection of books and research information, for study and for a head-quarters. . . ." She also paid his tuition for an advanced flying course at the Glendale airfield and visited him there.[6]

As December passed into January and then into February, time weighed heavily on Long Lance. He seemed no closer to getting his Lockheed, and he heard nothing further of a previously discussed expedition to Central America to find a lost Mayan city, which he also felt he had been promised.[7] Long Lance was free to fly whenever he wanted at the Glendale field, to go riding at the Santa Anita Ranch or to read the rare books in Anita's library, but as usual he wanted something more exciting, a bigger challenge. He felt frustrated and uncertain, and he began to drink excessively with predictable results.

Iron Eyes Cody, the young Cherokee actor who had met Long Lance in March 1930 during his Hollywood publicity tour for *The Silent Enemy*, visited Anoakia several times and witnessed Long Lance's abusive behavior to Anita's guards. "He'd come up drunk and push these guys around," Cody said. "He was a husky man. When he'd started drinking, boy—he'd try to break the gate down. So they said, 'Someday we're going to put one in you.' He always told me that they threatened to shoot him."[8]

Friction also grew between Long Lance and Anita, and it got worse when she heard he had fallen in with a fast crowd in Los Angeles. Beyond that, he did small things to annoy her. Soon after he returned from New York he told her, playfully, that in a single month in New York he had slept with more than a dozen women.[9] By mid-March she distrusted him so much that she hired a detective to follow him and report on his movements.[10]

At the same time Anita was obsessed with the safety of her grandchildren, for earlier in March, Charles Lindbergh's infant child had been kidnapped from his isolated estate in New Jersey. Anita dispatched Ralph Tweedle, her guard, to stay at Dextra's to protect her and her daughter,[11] also named Anita. On March 7 she wrote to Baldwin in Paris:

> We are guarding Anita rather carefully—since the Lindbergh tragedy and am wondering if I should not write Nell [Baldwin's wife] to be cautious with the children. I can't afford to give them a watchman at present.

Could you afford $100.00 per month for a night man? I wish Nell would move to her mother's for a while.

If we could only "clean house" here—in these United States! I go about armed to the teeth like a pirate! I am wondering what awful thing will happen if this continues. We need a vigilante committee—a few lynchings, etc. God keep you, my son. . . .

By the third week of March, Long Lance became resigned to the truth that the beloved Lockheed would never be his. Then, on March 17 or 18, Bessie Clapp telephoned from New York to tell him she had married a Japanese art student named Tom Hayakawa. The news was made no less painful by her confession that she would have married Long Lance if only he had been free. She and her husband would be stopping in Los Angeles on their way to Japan—could she see him? Thinking fast, he replied that regrettably he would be leaving in three days, that he had decided to return to Canada and was heading up to Vancouver.[12]

On the evening of March 19, Long Lance finished his dinner and went to a movie. It had been a pleasant spring day with the temperature that evening a mild sixty degrees. After the movie he returned to his room at the Glendale Hotel. J.H. Williams, the night clerk, brought him a special registered letter from Bessie in New York, mailed before she telephoned him.[13]

An hour later Long Lance reported to the night clerk. Williams had warned him earlier that "his movements were being watched and that Mrs. Anita Baldwin was paying to have this done." After chatting a few minutes, Long Lance showed Williams a gun he was carrying and the police permit for it. A taxi was called, and when it arrived Long Lance took his .45 Colt revolver, climbed in and told the driver to take him to Anoakia in neighboring Arcadia. He had been drinking.[14]

Long Lance often visited Anoakia at odd hours, day and

night. When he arrived this time, about midnight, he poked his head out of the taxi and called to the guard, "It is me, Sergeant." Joseph Hannah, the watchman, nodded.[15] The gate swung open and the taxi drove up the winding driveway to the mansion.

At the entrance the taxi stopped, and Long Lance got out and walked to the door, which had an immense, three-foot peacock, the tail fully spread, etched into its glass. He rang the bell and Anita answered. Later Anita would explain that she had been reading in the library when the bell rang. Long Lance's demeanor startled her, "being quite abrupt, very depressed and non-communicative." They returned to the library together. Then, as Anita described it, "I excused myself and left for my own quarters in the house, closing the doors between the library and the back hallway to the sleeping quarters." It was when she was in her room, soon after leaving Long Lance, that she claimed she heard a gunshot from the library.[16]

Sergeant Hannah, the watchman, whose room was next to Anita's, ran to the library to investigate. He testified at the subsequent inquest that he had gone to his room to retire for the night after Long Lance had arrived at Anoakia. He had been sleeping for an hour or two when Anita knocked on his door. "She told me she had heard a shot and for me to investigate it."

Hannah testified that when he entered the library, he saw Long Lance slumped on the leather settee by the library table, legs stretched out, head thrown back, a .45 caliber pistol in his right hand. Hannah went into a state of shock at the sight of the ugly head wound. He told Anita what he had found, then rushed to call the Los Angeles and Pasadena police, only to be told that Anoakia was not in their jurisdictions. When Anita realized that Hannah was too shaken to be of any use, she called for John Gilbert, the caretaker, to take charge. Gilbert called the chief of police of Arcadia. It was 1:45 A.M.

Anita left the mansion to stay with Dextra, who lived five hundred yards away, and by the time she got there she was, she said, "nervous and unstrung." Police Chief Louis Richards, a Captain Pardue and Dr. William Heidenreich arrived at about 2:15 A.M. Dr. Heidenreich examined Long Lance and determined that he had been dead for thirty or forty minutes. A ballistics expert arrived at the mansion at 2:45 A.M. to assist in investigating Long Lance's death. The verdict came quickly: suicide. One of America's most celebrated Indians was dead by his own hand, and although many had suspected that a dark truth lay behind Long Lance's public persona, none could identify with certainty what had provoked his final act. A mystery in life, Long Lance remained a mystery in death.

When Long Lance had been at the height of his powers— when he had been hailed as Buffalo Child Long Lance, Blackfoot chief, and when rumors of his past had only begun to surface seriously—he must have wondered how long he could continue his masquerade. He had come a long way from 4 1/2 Street in Winston–Salem to the Explorers Club in New York, from the Big Meetings in Carson Town to glittering dinners in the finest hotels, from reading *Ben Hur* to writing *Long Lance*.

In him burned two fires: one the desire for boundless celebrity, the other the genuine urge to employ that celebrity in the service of Indian rights. He had first invented himself as the model of the red man that the dominant society was clamoring to see: the noble savage who had been tamed. But along the way his beliefs were being shaped as much by the people he sought to represent. On the one hand he had written in the final paragraph of *Long Lance*, "Our [Indians'] job is to try to fit ourselves into the new scheme of life which the Great Spirit has decreed for North America."[17] On the other he had his unpublished article contained a stinging condemnation of white society.

Which fire burned the brightest in the early morning hours of March 20, 1932, cannot be known. Long Lance was a complex man. Perhaps the glittering lure of celebrity had become so irresistible that he would risk confronting his lies with yet more lies, hoping that he could delay the inevitable. But surely he knew he could not finally defeat it. The opportunity for escape may have still remained feasible, but that would have meant exile from the public eye. Perhaps he knew, too, that his dream of becoming a spokesperson for Indians across North America would only provoke continued investigations into his past that were certain to uncover the truth. For whatever reason—narcissistic or altruistic—Long Lance chose death over a life that could only otherwise end in obscurity or humiliation.

In his autobiography, Long Lance's fabrications of fact were often truths of his heart, and this is almost certainly the case in his claim that he had been adopted by Spotted Calf, mother of Almighty Voice, who had fallen in a hail of police cannon fire. Wanted for murder, Almighty Voice had eluded capture for two years before choosing the place where he would make his last stand.

In Long Lance's version of the story, the wounded Almighty Voice escapes through the North-West Mounted Police lines under cover of darkness. Rather than returning to a life on the run, he fires a single shot "which clipped the hat off the head of one of the pickets while he was lighting his pipe."[18] Having proved he could have escaped, Almighty Voice creeps silently back to the thicket and soon thereafter his death song is heard. "Right or wrong," Long Lance wrote of Almighty Voice and his two companions, "they had displayed a quality which all brave men admire."[19] Then, in what could have served as an epitaph for his own life spent running from the inevitable, Long Lance concluded, "How he got away and why he returned, no one will ever know."[20]

Epilogue

Los Angeles, California, 1932

*L*ong Lance's friends were shocked and incredulous when they heard the news. Williams, the night clerk at the Glendale Hotel, could not believe that Long Lance would commit suicide. He wrote to Susie Curtis, who contacted the hotel when newspaper reports of the incident reached New York, "I cannot tell you all I know as it would bring the hotel into prominence and I would lose my job and gain nothing." On December 27, 1932, Elizabeth Analla, who worked at Anoakia, wrote to Chauncey Yellow Robe's daughter, Rosebud, to say that Long Lance's death "surely is a mystery to the friends who knew him." She asked Rosebud, who was raising her family in New York, "Are you coming to Dakota this coming summer? If you do let us plan to see each other. I have much I'd like to talk over with you. I have been home since May after spending six years in California. I feel sure your family are all his friends from his conversation."[1]

Jim Thorpe had received a letter from Long Lance in mid-March, and Thorpe insisted later that his old Carlisle friend gave "no indication of worry or despondency." The instructor at the

Glendale flying school said that Long Lance appeared content in his work and very popular with his associates. Canon Middleton was convinced that Long Lance had been murdered, as was Dr. Clyde Fisher, who wrote Middleton on August 14, 1933: "I do not believe that Long Lance took his own life, and none of his close friends, that I know, believe it either." Even Irvin S. Cobb—perhaps ashamed of his earlier rejection of Long Lance—in replying to a letter from Emma Newashe said he did not "believe so gallant a man as he was ever deliberately took his own life." From information Cobb received, "no actual inquest was ever held, and no real investigation held, and . . . the so-called 'police inquiry' was a farce."[2]

Cobb was correct about the hasty nature of the investigation and inquest. Indeed, it was only because of a complaint by Irene Noonan, president of the American Indian Women's History and Art Club, and Mrs. Leta Myers Smart, an Omaha Indian, that a brief hearing was even held.[3] The inquest was conducted in Arcadia, an area carved out of Anita's father's huge estate and founded by him. Anita, who was assessed half the town's taxes, had enormous influence in Arcadia. Having been advised by her physician "to remain away from any further strain and take a complete rest," she did not even attend the inquest, and no steps were taken to force her to testify. She merely submitted a signed statement, telling what she knew of the events of the late evening and early morning of March 19 and 20.[4]

The compelling evidence came from the Arcadia and Los Angeles police, who reported at the hearing that no one but Long Lance himself could have fired the fatal shot. Frank Gompert, deputy sheriff of Los Angeles County, told the jury that he had arrived at Anoakia at about 2:45 A.M. on the morning of Sunday, March 20:

> After photographing the body, I removed the gun from
> the hands of the victim, and in removing it, the trigger

was released, so that it came forward and the hammer came back to its safety position. I examined the gun and found that only one cartridge had been exploded in the gun at any recent time. This proved to me conclusively that the case was a suicide, and that the gun could only be in that condition and that position by means of a self-inflicted wound.[5]

A more thorough and complete investigation might have revealed much more of the complex and introspective Long Lance, and the circumstances certainly would have justified it. Clearly Anita Baldwin, living in her heavily fortified estate, was a personality at least bordering on paranoid. She lived in fear and had spoken of the need in America for vigilante justice. She had become deeply suspicious of Long Lance and had engaged a private detective to track his movements. Long Lance had not made friends of a number of her guards. Those who had known Long Lance over the years believed the circumstances warranted the full investigation given to a murder. They would not get it. Such was the case of this man who, having been dogged by rumors his entire adult life, had rumors and suspicion attend even his final act.

Doubtless there was considerable evidence for the conclusion that Long Lance had taken his own life. He had spent most of his life covering his tracks, lying, then lying again to cover his lies. Clearly the rumors that circulated in New York upset him. Bessie's marriage wounded him badly, probably more than anything else, for Long Lance appears to have come close to committing himself to her. Years later, when she was living in Maine, Bessie remembered how caring and affectionate he was. She added that he was "the only man I ever really loved."[6]

In addition to having lost Bessie, Long Lance was in his forties, well past his "peak of prowess." Throughout his life he had worked hard to keep his body in perfect shape, swimming in icy lakes, running daily on the beach, boxing at the YMCA. Any decline would have been hard to accept. The frustrations and boredom of living off a wealthy heiress in a mansion on a fortified estate, being denied those things that he believed were firmly promised, and being followed everywhere by a hired detective would have contributed to Long Lance's unhappiness. His drinking, too, had become quite heavy.

Finally, the circumstances of Long Lance's life denied him any close, supportive friendships. He revealed parts of himself to some, parts to others, but no one person was truly a confidant. In cutting himself off from any deeply meaningful and sincere human contacts, Long Lance, in effect, shut himself up in a closet, but one whose door could not be securely locked. People and events intruded to challenge the self he had invented. He was among the most widely celebrated Indians of his time, yet he was truly known by no one.

Shortly after his death, Anita launched an investigation into Long Lance's life. She was sadly disillusioned, she said, that he was not the man he had claimed to be in his passport application or autobiography. In early May she bitterly told Susie Curtis that he had "kinky hair when he came to Carlisle—used grease on it to keep it down." She also said he "used makeup rouge on his cheekbones, dyed his hair, and used a straightening fluid on it." It was untrue, of course, for even his childhood friends in Winston remembered that his hair was black and straight.[7] Anita's initial esteem for Long Lance had finally turned to hatred.

She went so far as to solicit information from Edgar Miller, the Bureau of Indian Affairs superintendent at the Hopi agency in Arizona, who had been the printing instructor at Carlisle twenty years earlier. Anita had met him in the 1920s when she researched the music of the Hopi. Miller had kept track of Long Lance after leaving Carlisle, and he knew that he had fought in the Canadian army, that he called himself Chief Buffalo Child Long Lance and that he had published an autobiography. He remembered that Long Lance had registered at Carlisle as a Cherokee, although to Miller he had looked like a "half-blood [part Negro]."[8]

Anita commissioned a Pinkerton detective to investigate the Long family's racial origins. Without any qualifications or explanations the detective reported:

> Subject's father full-blooded negro. Joe S. Long, 95 Brookstown Avenue, Winston–Salem, North Carolina. Mother half Indian. Two brothers, one sister respected negros [sic]. One brother negro detective. Sister divorced from negro preacher. Father was janitor at high school for 25 years; now retired. Owns property. Subject's name Sylvester.[9]

Late Wednesday night, March 23, 1932, just after the last feature, the white manager of the Carolina Theater in Winston–Salem called Abe Long to his office. A few minutes later, Abe emerged shaken and went home. That night he wrote in his diary, "Mr. U.K. Rice related to me, or conveyed the most horrible news I have ever received. It was of my poor brother's death in California Sun. Mar. 20th 1932 by his own hands. May God have Mercy on his soul."

On March 24 Joe Long sent a telegram to the Los Angeles coroner explaining that he was the dead man's father and asking that funeral arrangements be deferred until he could send further details. The family wanted to bring the body back to Winston–Salem for burial but could not afford the expense. At three o'clock on the afternoon of March 30, 1932, Long Lance was buried by members of the British Benevolent Society in the British Empire War Veterans' section of the Inglewood Cemetery in Los Angeles.

Walter, curious about the circumstances of his brother's death, collected enough money to travel to Los Angeles and, in late April—one month after his brother's death—he met several of Anita's staff. He informed them that neither he nor Long Lance had any Negro blood.[10]

Jim Thorpe and Clyde Fisher at Long Lance's grave, Inglewood Cemetery, Los Angeles, California.

Walter learned from Anita's sympathetic employees that in the last year of his life Long Lance had associated with a disreputable crowd in Los Angeles, that he had been drinking too much and might even have been using drugs.[11] He was told that Long Lance had talked about suicide with his dentist the very day before his death.[12] At Anoakia, Walter observed the magnificent buildings, the lush gardens, the manicured lawns, the peacocks that ran loose on the estate. Had all this been worth the price of a man's pride and, ultimately, his very life?

After Long Lance's death, it was discovered that he had spent or given away nearly all that he owned. He had lent money to his friend Jim Thorpe, given a substantial amount to the endowment fund of St. John's Military School and sent nearly $500 — a hefty sum in the early years of the Depression — to his family. When his personal effects were sold and his bank account closed, only $740 remained.[14]

On April 18, 1932, his family contested his will, but their poverty defeated them. On May 18, 1933, the will produced by Canon Middleton was upheld. St. Paul's School on the Blood Reserve became Long Lance's sole beneficiary.[15] The money was used for scholarships for many years.

In the same year that Sallie Long lost her son Sylvester, she also lost her her husband and her mother, Adeline, who died at the age of eighty-three.[16] Supported by Abe and Walter, Sallie lived until 1942. When Walter died in March 1941, the *Winston–Salem Journal* published a lengthy obituary titled, "Walter L. Long, Widely Known Negro is Dead." Sallie's obituary a year later in the *Winston–Salem Twin City Sentinel* read, "The passing of Mrs. Long removes another member of one of the city's best-known Negro families." The respect in which the Long family was held is indicated by the reference to Sallie as "Mrs. Long."[17] In the South, Negro women were invariably referred to by their first names.

Abe Long's diaries record a life of quiet desperation, a life of struggle that led eventually to perhaps the very sense of despair that Sylvester had feared and fled from so many years before. Abe spent the thirties and forties directing the flow of traffic up the seventy-four steps to the colored gallery of the Carolina Theater.[18] He was never reported late, never took a vacation and only once missed a shift.[19] At work and in the community, he was constantly exposed to white bigotry. Gradually Abe came to see and accept himself as black. In one diary entry he commented on a public issue by writing, "We the better thinking negroes . . ."[20] Despite this, his last words on his death bed, uttered to a niece, were that the family had only white and Indian blood.[21]

Abe died in 1972, forty years after Sylvester. During a long and uneventful life, he witnessed many of the major changes that had affected African Americans in the United States. He often mentioned them in his diary, as he did on Friday, September 6, 1957, when he wrote, "Miss Gwendolyn Boily admitted to Reynolds high school — first Negro to attend white city school." After shopping in a Winston–Salem store on December 3, 1958, he wrote, "a colored man waited on me, something unusual." For October 16, 1961, the entry reads, "stated over television and radio tonight that 3 railroads of the South had integrated all its services.

Abe Long as an older man, probably taken in the 1940s.

The Rev. Martin Luther King, it is said, was the cause of the action—which resulted from a talk with President Kennedy." The next year, on October 1, 1962, he recorded, "Down in Mississippi last night was a big riot caused by a negro James Meredith attempting to enter the University of Missp." Two days later, without comment, Abe wrote in his diary, "Another man flew around the earth today 6 times in 9 hours. Schirra is his name."

In 1964, when Abe was eighty-three, the United States Congress passed the Civil Rights Bill. Further antisegregationist legislation followed with the Voting Rights Act of 1965 and the Civil

Rights Act of 1968. In his eighties, Abe witnessed the dismantling of the American apartheid system.[22]

Beyond the entry of March 23, 1932, made upon receiving news of his "poor brother's death," Abe's diaries revealed little of his thoughts of Sylvester. What is clear is that he loved and cherished Sylvester's memory and the scrapbook that carefully listed his accomplishments. Perhaps for Abe the scrapbook itself said it all. Nevertheless, his personal loss must have been deepened by his awareness that, in the new age dawning in America, Sylvester would never have felt compelled to leave home, would never have had to fear returning there. He would never have had to spend his life in the restless pursuit of the person he wanted to be.

Acknowledgments

My thanks to the following individuals for sharing with me their recollections of Long Lance and the stories they have heard about him.

Concerning Long Lance's family in Carson Town

Annie Blackburn, Carson Town, NC; Daisy Carson Blackburn, Carson Town, NC; Charles Carson, Carson Town, NC; Kalford Carson, Lexington, NC; Tracy Grose Caudle, Roaring River, NC; Newman Dalton, Mocksville, NC; Lillian Dalton Doulin, Mocksville, NC; Jency Carson Gaither, Carson Town, NC; Hamilton Horton, Sr., Winston–Salem, NC; Nannie Carson Lewis, Carson Town, NC; Jaspar S. Long, Yadkinville, NC; Mammie Carson Patterson, Carson Town, NC.

Concerning Long Lance's family in Winston–Salem

Joe Bradshaw, Winston–Salem, NC; Odell Clanton, Winston–Salem, NC; Arthur Williams, Winston–Salem, NC; Terrell Young, Winston–Salem, NC.

St. John's Military Institute

Robert Agne, New Hartford, NY; William M. Leffingwell, Washington, DC; Edmund C. Wall, Bronx, NY.

Long Lance's Years in Calgary

Hugh Dann, Calgary, AB; Margaret Vahey Eakin, Vancouver, BC; Maurice Fidler, Ottawa, ON; Harry Francis, Calgary, AB; Reg Hammond, Calgary, AB; Howard Kelly, Calgary, AB; Paul Thompson, Calgary, AB; Dorothy Wallace, Calgary, AB.

Long Lance's Indian Visits

Earl Calf Child, Blackfoot Reserve, Gleichen, AB; Joe Crowfoot, Blackfoot Reserve, Gleichen, AB; George Gooderham, Calgary, AB; Eli Taylor, Sioux Valley Reserve (Oak Lake Reserve), Griswold, MB.

The Blood Indians

Sophie Allison, Waterton, AB; Gordon Bird, Blood Reserve, Stand Off, AB; Mike Eagle Speaker, Blood Reserve, Stand Off, AB; Archdeacon Cecil Swanson, Calgary, AB; Dan Weasel Fat, Blood Reserve, Stand Off, AB.

Winnipeg

Allan Bill, Calgary, AB; Charles L'Ami, Winnipeg, MB; Pearl Driscoll L'Ami, Winnipeg, MB; Mrs. H. O'Malley, Winnipeg, MB.

West Point

R.A. Ericson, Oakland, CA; Dorothy Fellers, Washington, DC; F.B. Valentine, East Holden, ME.

The Silent Enemy

Douglas Burden, Charlotte, VT; S.C. Burden, Beverly Hills, CA; William C. Chanler, New York, NY; Wilfrid Eggleston, Ottawa, ON; Ted Hennessy, North Bay, ON; Agnes Lalonde, North Bay, ON; Sheila Burden Lawrence, Charlotte, VT; George McDougall, Cochrane, ON; Madeline Theriault, North Bay, ON.

New York

Lee Ash, Bethany, CT; Earl Parker Hanson, Santurce, Puerto Rico; Domenica Pallister, New York, NY; Elisabeth Randolph Clapp, York Village, ME; Te Ata, Oklahoma City, OK; Lowell Thomas, Pawling, NY.

Los Angeles

Roberta Forsberg, Whittier, CA; Ray Knisley, Boulder City, NV; Lowry McCaslin, Arcadia, CA.

Sources

The most important source is the Glenbow Archives in Calgary, Alberta. It contains Long Lance's two scrapbooks and some of his papers. I have placed photocopies of Long Lance's correspondence with Mike Eagle Speaker, Bonner Fellers, Commissioner Graham, Alice Tye, Howard Kelly, Canon S.H. Middleton and Emma Newashe McAllister in the Archives. Long Lance's correspondence with Vilhjalmur Stefansson is located in the Stefansson Collection, Dartmouth College Library, Dartmouth, Massachusetts. His correspondence with Bonner Fellers is contained in the Bonner Fellers Papers, Hoover Institute on War, Revolution and Peace, Stanford University, California. Several of Long Lance's letters are in the Carl Van Vechten Collection in the Beinecke Rare Book and Manuscript Library, Yale University Library, New Haven, Connecticut.

The National Archives in Washington, DC, has Sylvester Long's student record (R.G. 75, Office of Indian Affairs, Carlisle Student Record, file

5534), and the Office of Indian Affairs file on his true identity (R.G. 75, Office of Indian Affairs, General Service File, 1364–1925, 130). The Glenbow Archives has a copy of William Chanler's file on "Burden Pictures Inc. re — Joe S. Long (Long Lance) — Sylvester Long," 748–C10, the Archives of his law firm, Winthrop, Stimson, Putnam and Roberts of New York, NY.

Collections of Anita Baldwin's papers are held by the Rare Book Room of the Huntington Library, San Marino, California; and by the library of the Los Angeles State and County Arboretum, Arcadia, California.

The following newspapers and magazines were consulted for the dates indicated:

> *Winston–Salem Journal*, August–September 1909; July–October 1915.
> *Carlisle Arrow*, 1909–13.
> *Calgary Herald*, July 1919–March 1922.
> *Vancouver Sun*, May–August 1922.
> *Regina Leader*, October 1922–April 1923.
> *Winnipeg Tribune*, January 1923–May 1925.
> *Explorers Journal*, 1929–32.
> *Los Angeles Times*, March 16–31, 1932.
> *American Indian Magazine*, 1926–31.

Notes

PROLOGUE

[1]New York's weather on January 5, 1931, is described on the front page of the *New York Times* the following day. For the geographic setting see the pages on "Pennsylvania Station and Vicinity" in the Federal Writers' Project, *New York City Guide* (New York: Random House, 1976) 164–67. The *Guide* was first published in 1939.

[2]William T. Hagan, "Full Blood, Mixed Blood, Generic, and Ersatz: The Problem of Indian Identity," *Arizona and the West* 27 (Winter 1985): 309–26; reprinted in Roger L. Nichols, ed. *The American Indian Past and Present*, 4th ed. (New York: McGraw-Hill, 1992) 282.

[3]The best physical description of Long Lance appears in Beverly Smith's feature article, "One Hundred Per Cent American," *New York Herald Tribune* 19 Jan. 1930. He states his height in his letter to President Woodrow Wilson, March 8, 1915, in R.G. 75, Office of Indian Affairs, Carlisle Student Record, file 5534, National Archives, Washington, DC (hereafter cited as CARLISLE FILE). The description of Walter Long is taken from Ilia Tolstoy's report to William Chanler, April 14, 1930, in file 748–C10, "Burden Pictures Inc. re—Joe S. Long (Long Lance)—Sylvester Long," Winthrop, Stimson, Putnam and Roberts, 40 Wall Street, New York City (hereafter cited as CHANLER INVESTIGATION). For biographical details see "Walter L. Long, Widely Known Negro Is Dead," *Winston–Salem Journal* 28 March 1941.

[4]Long Lance's exact words were "Among themselves, Indians speak seldom and then only when they have something important to say." Long Lance, "My Trail Upward. I Took It Because I, a Blackfoot Indian, Wanted to Live Like a White Man," *Hearst's International–Cosmopolitan* June 1926: 138 (hereafter cited as "Trail Upward").

[5]Long Lance described the incident in a letter written to Walter the following day; see "Vester" to "My dear Brother," dated "Tuesday." The original copy of this letter (donated by Joe Bradshaw of Winston–Salem, NC) as well as copies of all of Long Lance's postcards and letters from 1911 to his death in 1932 are in the Glenbow Archives, Calgary, AB (hereafter cited as GLENBOW).

CHAPTER ONE: SYLVESTER CLARK LONG

[1]Sylvester was born on "December 1"; although he changed the year of his birth, he always held to the same day and month. The family Bible in the possession of the Dalton family, Mocksville, NC, gives this date. The year of

his birth is also given as 1890 in the 1900 Census, volume 25, ED 31, sheet 17, line 97, National Archives, Washington, DC. In his diary Abe Long also cites his brother's date of birth as December 1, 1890; see entries for December 30, 1961; November 28, 1965. Abe Long (1881–1972) was the eldest of Joe and Sallie Long's sons. Abe's diaries, written between his fifties and eighties, are now in the possession of Lillian Dalton Doulin, Mocksville, NC.

[2]Marriage of "S.D. Long" and "Lindy Carson," March 27, 1879 (both are registered as colored), Indexed Register of Marriages—Iredell County, NC, L to R Males, Iredell County, NC, p. 123. New Court House, Statesville, Iredell County, NC. Although there are discrepancies in Joe's initials and Sallie's name, other evidence suggests that this must be the correct entry.

[3]Birthdate: January 17, 1865. Sallie M. Long, Certificate of Death, February 8, 1942, Forsyth County Court House, Winston–Salem, NC. Her full name was "Sallie Malinda Long"; see her gravestone, Silver Hill Graveyard, Buena Vista, Winston–Salem, NC.

[4]Birthdate: February 14, 1853. Joe S. Long, Certificate of Death, November 14, 1932, Forsyth County Court House, Winston–Salem, NC. His full name was "Joseph Sylvester Long"; see his gravestone, Silver Hill Graveyard, Buena Vista, Winston–Salem, NC. In Carson Town he was called "Vet" (from Sylvester), but in Winston he went by the name of Joe. See also "Death Claims Uncle Joe Long," *Winston–Salem Sentinel* 16 Nov. 1932.

[5]Andrew Carson outlined his experience in the American Revolution in his application for a federal pension, August 22, 1832, in Walter Clark, ed., *The State Records of North Carolina*, vol. 22 (Goldsboro, NC: Nash Brothers, 1907). His family is listed in his will, Andrew Carson, April 18, 1836, and codicil, March 6, 1838, Iredell County Wills, Caldwell-Curry 1787–1890, 1915. C.R. 054 801.3, North Carolina Archives, Raleigh, NC. Andrew Carson's tombstone is still standing in the Young family cemetery near Houstonville. A photo of it appears in *Iredell County Landmarks* (Statesville: Iredell County American Revolution Bicentennial Commission, 1976) 61.

[6]It still stands there. His gravestone states that he was born January 5, 1792, and died August 29, 1865.

[7]Ilia Tolstoy's report, CHANLER INVESTIGATION.

[8]The number of Robert Carson's slaves appears in the Slave Schedule, 1860 Census, Iredell County, vol. 22, pp. 291–92. North Carolina State Archives, Raleigh, NC.

[9]Edward Byron Reuter, *The Mulatto in the United States* (Boston: The Gorham Press, 1918; reprinted New York: Johnson Reprint Company, 1970) 155; Angie Debo, *The Road to Disappearance* (Norman: University of Okla-

homa Press, 1941) 102; Kenneth Wiggins Porter, "Exploration, 1529–1909," *The Negro on the American Frontier* (New York: Arno Press and the *New York Times,* 1971) 7–137.

[10]Tracy Grose Caudle, *Memories from My Father's Trunk* (n.p.: Alpine Industries, 1970) 4. Interview with Tracy Grose Caudle, Roaring River, Wilkes County, NC, May 28, 1977.

[11]Birthdate: January 11, 1848. Adeline Lindsy, Certificate of Death, February 8, 1932, New Court House, Statesville, Iredell County, NC.

[12]John Hope Franklin, *The Free Negro in North Carolina, 1790–1860* (New York: W.W. Norton, 1971) 35.

[13]Slave Schedule, 1860 Census, Iredell County, vol. 22, p. 291. North Carolina State Archives, Raleigh, NC.

[14]Adeline Carson gave birth to Sallie, and Jincy Carson to Jim. Sallie recognized Jim as her brother (half-brother). On his death certificate Jim Carson's father is listed as Andrew Cowles. See Certificate of Death, October 16, 1917, New Court House, Statesville, NC. Jim Carson was born April 20, 1860. His son, Charles Carson, remembers him as a very fair-skinned man with blue eyes. Away from Carson Town, where he was classified as colored, he passed racially as white. Interview with Charles Carson, Carson Town, August 11, 1975.

[15]Andrew Carson Cowles' tombstone in the Flat Rock Cemetery, Hamptonville, Yadkin County, NC, reads, "born Jan. 12, 1833, died Jan. 5, 1881." He served first as Yadkin's member in the North Carolina House of Commons from 1860–65 and was elected to the state senate in late 1865, where he served 1865–67 and 1870–74. John L. Cheney, ed., *North Carolina Government, 1585–1974* (Raleigh, NC: North Carolina Department of the Secretary of State, 1975) 320, 328, 332, 334, 451, 454.

[16]Colonel Calvin Duvall Cowles, *Genealogy of the Cowles Families in America,* vol. 1 (New Haven, CT: Tuttle, Morehouse and Taylor, 1929) 743.

[17]William E. Rutledge, Jr., *An Illustrated History of Yadkin County, 1850–1965* (Yadkinville, NC: n.p., 1965) 23. A photo of the home appears on p. 20.

[18]His two sons by his white wife (whom he married in 1870), Hugh and Reuben, occasionally visited to see their colored first cousins. Interview with Jim Carson's daughters Daisy Blackburn, Mammie Patterson and Nannie Lewis, Carson Town, May 29, 1977.

[19]Joe's sister Lindy was married to Lee Carson, a cousin of Sallie's. According to the 1880 Census (Eagle Mills Township, Iredell County, NC, p. 198) Lindy was born in 1857 and was thus four years younger than Joe. As a young girl Lindy had been sold on a slave block. Interview with Daisy Blackburn, Carson Town, August 11, 1975.

[20]Joe Long to R. H. Latham, April 9, 1930, quoted in Ilia Tolstoy's report, CHANLER INVESTIGATION; Abe Long's diary, entry for December 12, 1939.

[21]Ilia Tolstoy wrote in his report, CHANLER INVESTIGATION, that Joe's father's name was John Weston, but he heard the name incorrectly. On Joe Long's death certificate, Walter Long lists his father's parents as John Vestal and Mary Long. Standard Certificate of Death, Forsyth County Court House, Winston–Salem, NC, November 14, 1932.

[22]"Death Claims Uncle Joe Long," *Winston–Salem Sentinel* 16 Nov. 1932. Joe's owner was Miles H. Long. A photo and short biography of Miles H. Long appear in Jaspar S. Long, *Long Family Records* (Winston–Salem, NC: Clay Printing Co., 1965) 175–78. See also Miles' obituary in the *Yadkin Ripple* 2 Sept. 1920.

[23]Joe Long to R. H. Latham, April 9, 1930, quoted in Ilia Tolstoy's report, CHANLER INVESTIGATION.

[24]Caudle, *Memories*, 4–5.

[25]In his diaries Abe Long gives March 1887 as the date on which the family moved to Winston; see entries of May 26, 1957, and March 1, 1970. Joe and Sallie's marriage went through a difficult period just before their move to Winston. Joe fathered a daughter, Lillie, by another woman in Carson Town in 1886. This possibly was a factor in their decision to move. Lillie lived separately from the family, but was always considered as a family member. She inherited many of her brothers' photos and manuscript materials, which her son, Newman Dalton (1919–1984), and daughter, Lillian Dalton Doulin, kindly showed me.

[26]Adelaide Fries, Stuart Thurman Wright, and J. Edwin Hendricks, *Forsyth: The History of a County on the March* (Chapel Hill: The University of North Carolina, 1976) 170 (electric lights and streetcars); 191 (telephones).

[27]The population statistic used here is that for Forsyth County, the county in which Winston is located. In 1900, out of a total population of 35,000, Forsyth had 10,543 blacks. Fries et al., *Forsyth*, 256. The effect of racial segregation was felt most after the turn of the century. In the 1890s "Jim Crow" laws were extended throughout the American South. The segregation of the races became complete in Winston in 1912 when the city council enacted an ordinance which made it unlawful for "any white person to occupy as a residence . . . any house upon any street . . . on which a greater number of houses are occupied as residences by colored than are occupied by white people." Anyone breaking this law faced a fine of $50 or thirty days in prison. Larry Edward Tise, *Winston–Salem in History. Volume 6: Government* (Winston–Salem, NC: Historic Winston, 1976) 40.

[28]Abe's birthdate was August 27, 1881. Abe Miles Long, Certificate of Death, July 28, 1972, Forsyth County Court House, Winston–Salem, NC. Walter was born on July 4, 1886. Walter Lee Long, Certificate of Death, March 27, 1941, Forsyth County Court House, Winston–Salem, NC. Katie was born July 29, 1899; see Abe's diary entry for July 29, 1958.

[29]For an understanding of the racial situation in the American South the following volumes proved extremely useful: C. Vann Woodward, *The Strange Career of Jim Crow* (New York: Oxford University Press, 1966), and John Hope Franklin, *From Slavery to Freedom: A History of Negro Americans*, 3rd ed. (New York: Vintage Books, 1967). For an understanding of the individual black's position, the two autobiographical works by black novelist Richard Wright, *Black Boy* (New York: Harper and Row, 1966; first published in 1937), and *American Hunger* (New York: Harper and Row, 1977), proved invaluable, as did white writer John Howard Griffin's *Black Like Me* (Bergenfield, N.J.: New American Library, 1976; first published in 1960). On racial "passing," see James Weldon Johnson, *The Autobiography of an Ex-Colored Man* (New York: Hill and Wang, 1960; first published in 1912). For an interesting novel about "growing up black" in Winston–Salem, NC, see Alfred W. Wilkes, *Little Black Boy* (New York: Charles Scribner's, 1971).

[30]Frank V. Tursi, *Winston–Salem: A History* (Winston–Salem: John F. Blair, 1994) 135. A wonderful source is Gunnar Myrdal's *An American Dilemma: The Negro Problem and Modern Democracy*, 2 vols. (New York: Harper and Row, 1962; first published in 1944).

[31]The best review of Kit Carson's link with Carson Town is found in Homer M. Keever's *Iredell: Piedmont County* (Statesville, NC: Iredell County Bicentennial Commission, 1976) 127–28. The anecdote of the oak Kit Carson topped appears in Caudle, *Memories*, 5. Mrs. Caudle's father, J.M. Grose, bought a portion of the old Robert Carson plantation and she grew up in the area.

[32]Sallie M. Long's book, May 10, 1907. In the possession of Lillian Dalton Doulin, Mocksville, NC.

[33]Anne R. Correll to Donald B. Smith, dated Winston–Salem, March 7, 1975.

[34]Interviews with Arthur Williams, January 6, 1977; and Terrill Young, August 22, 1976; both interviews in Winston–Salem, NC.

[35]Myrdal, *Dilemma*, vol. 1, 113.

[36]Affidavit prepared by William A. Blair, April 9, 1930, CHANLER INVESTIGATION; Abe Long's diaries, entries for May 5, 1939, and August 18, 1959; 1900 Census, National Archives, Washington, DC (vol. 25, ED 31, sheet 17, line 97).

[37]Interview with Terrell Young, Winston–Salem, NC, August 22, 1976. She was a student at the West End School at the time and remembers that Sylvester used to help his father clean the school.

[38]Interview with Odell Clanton, Winston–Salem, NC, January 7, 1977. Mr. Clanton was a student at the Depot School with Sylvester.

[39]Sylvester Clark Long's application to Carlisle, CARLISLE FILE.

[40]Abe Long's diary, entry for November 5, 1958.

[41]Application to Carlisle, CARLISLE FILE.

[42]George L. Chindahl, *A History of the Circus in America* (Caldwell, Idaho: Caxton Printers, 1959) 194.

[43]The library opened in February 1906. Fries et al., *Forsyth*, 199. He definitely was in Winston that year, for on May 7, 1906, he took out an insurance policy naming his mother as his beneficiary. N. D. Latrenta, Metropolitan Life Insurance Company, New York, to Donald B. Smith (hereafter cited as DBS), June 27, 1978.

[44]Colonel William Blair quoted in a letter to Canon Middleton, dated December 19, 1933. Letter in the possession of Sophie Allison.

[45]Charles Carson (1886–1978), Sylvester's first cousin (see footnote 14 of this chapter), told me that Sylvester and the Long family always returned to Carson Town for the Big Meeting. Interview with Charles Carson, Carson Town, August 11, 1975. This (1908) was the last year Sylvester attended.

[46]Application to Carlisle, CARLISLE FILE.

[47]Caudle, *Memories*, 4.

[48]Abe married Aurelia on January 6, 1908. See his diary entry for November 4, 1940. On his fiftieth wedding anniversary in 1958 he wrote that on January 6, 1908, he had married "the prettiest girl in Winston–Salem."

[49]Winston–Salem, NC, City and Suburban City Directory, editions for 1908 and 1910. Entries for Abraham, Joe and Walter Long.

[50]Interview with Odell Clanton, Winston–Salem, NC, January 7, 1977.

[51]Interview with Newman Dalton, Mocksville, NC, May 30, 1982.

[52]Interview with Tracy Grose Caudle, Roaring River, Wilkes County, NC, May 28, 1977.

[53]In early February 1930 Long Lance told William Chanler that he had been with Robinson's Circus. See William Chanler to Office of Indian Affairs Commissioner, February 14, 1930, CHANLER INVESTIGATION. While in Calgary, Alberta, in the early 1920s Long Lance had an excellent reputation as a rider. Interview with Howard Kelly, Calgary, March 9, 1975. Long Lance must have first learned about horses while with the Wild West Show.

[54]James Henderson to Office of Indian Affairs Commissioner, Novem-

ber 19, 1928, R.G. 75, Office of Indian Affairs, General Service File, 1364–1925. 130, National Archives, Washington, DC (hereafter cited as DIS-COVERY FILE). Allen Whipporwill, Application for share of money appropriated for the Eastern Cherokee Indians, March 4, 1907, Number 17856, National Archives, Washington, DC.

[55]The Cherokee words are from Mary Ulmer Chiltoskey, *Cherokee Words with Pictures* (Asheville, NC: Gilbert Printing Co., 1972) 14, 35.

[56]Tise, *Winston–Salem*, 36.

[57]Abe Long told his distant cousin, Joe Bradshaw, this story, and at the same time he gave Joe the clipping book of Long Lance's that Walter had brought back from Los Angeles (mentioned in the Preface). Joe recalls that the conversation took place shortly before Abe's death in 1972. Interview with Joe Bradshaw, Winston–Salem, July 13, 1975.

[58]Carmelita S. Ryan's PhD dissertation, "The Carlisle Indian Industrial School" (Diss. Georgetown University, 1962), provides an excellent overview of the school. Carlisle's enrollment for 1909 is given in the *Annual Report of the United States Indian School, Carlisle, Pennsylvania, for the year ending June 30, 1910*, p. 28. Their football record is given in Gene Schoor, *The Jim Thorpe Story* (New York: Pocket Books, 1967) 46, 51.

[59]Application to Carlisle, CARLISLE FILE.

[60]On mixed-blood Indian minorities in the Eastern United States see Brewton Berry, *Almost White* (Toronto: Collier Macmillan, 1969; first published 1963). For the Indian history of North Carolina see Douglas L. Rights, *The American Indian in North Carolina* (Winston–Salem: John F. Blair, 1957); on the Lumbees (formerly called Croatan) see Adolph L. Dial and David K. Eliades, *The Only Land I Know: A History of the Lumbee Indians* (San Francisco: The Indian Historian Press, 1975); Karen Blu, *The Lumbee Problem: The Making of an American Indian People* (Cambridge: Cambridge University Press, 1980); and W. McKee Evans, *To Die Game* (Baton Rouge: Louisiana State University Press, 1971) 19–34; on the Cherokees see Dale Van Every, *Disinherited: The Lost Birthright of the American Indian* (New York: William Morrow and Co., 1966). For a description of what might be described as an American equivalent of "ethnic cleansing" in the American South in the 1830s, see Anthony F.C. Wallace, *The Long Bitter Trail: Andrew Jackson and the Indians* (New York: Hill and Wang, 1993).

[61]A reference to Hamilton Willis and his school appears in Fries et al., *Forsyth*, 272.

[62]John D. Harrison to DBS, October 2, 1976. He enclosed his grandfather's obituary.

[63]Application to Carlisle, CARLISLE FILE.

[64]Lovie Galloway is mentioned in Abe Long's diary, entry for September 21, 1959.

[65]Richard B. Morris, ed., *Encyclopedia of American History* (New York: Harper & Brothers, 1953) 446.

[66]The above scene is based on the statement of James Henderson to the Commissioner of Indian Affairs, Washington, DC, dated Canton, NC, November 19, 1928, OIA DISCOVERY FILE: "One thing, however, we could not reconcile was the fact that he could speak some Cherokee. This fact bothered me some although I still believed him to be an impostor. This doubt was later cleared up by finding that for a year prior to his coming to Carlisle he had traveled with a sort of show all over the South and Cuba with a full blood longhaired Eastern Cherokee by the name of Whipporwill who taught him sufficient Cherokee to enable him to pass muster in enrolling at Carlisle." Apparently Henderson discovered in 1915 that Sylvester had learned his Cherokee from Whipporwill. See chapter 3, footnote 24.

[67]Wilfrid Eggleston, "Fastened Sleds Under Canoe in Mushing through Slush," *Toronto Star Weekly* 4 May 1929. His friend, Canon Middleton, also mentioned that he was "particularly fond" of *Ben Hur*, see Roberta Forsberg, ed., *Redman Echoes: Comprising the Writing of Chief Buffalo Child Long Lance and Biographical Sketches by His Friends* (Los Angeles: Frank Wiggins Trade School, Department of Printing, 1933) 185.

CHAPTER TWO: THE TRAIL UPWARD BEGINS

[1]M. Friedman, "The Carlisle Indian School: Its Foundation and Work," *The Red Man* 3, 3 November 1910: 119. A photo of Friedman appears in *The Indian Craftsman* 2, 2 (October 1909): 34.

[2]"Monthly Address to Students," *The Indian Craftsman* 2, 3 (November 1909): 37–38.

[3]For information on Pratt see Ryan, "Carlisle," 1–53. The quote by Booker T. Washington appears in his autobiography, *Up From Slavery*, reprinted in *Three Negro Classics* (New York: Avon Books, 1965) 80. Washington, of course, was unaware (see Chapter 2) that Indians had been enslaved in the American colonial period. Several North American Indian communities also had slaves, fellow Indian slaves, see Olive Patricia Dickason, *Canada's First Nations*, 2nd ed. (Toronto: Oxford University Press, 1997) 47. In the American south, slaveholding nations such as the Cherokees, Chickasaws and Choctaws, and Creeks had black slaves, see Kenneth Wiggins Porter, *The Negro on the American Frontier* (New York: Arno Press and the *New York Times*, 1971).

[4]Ryan, "Carlisle," 230–35. Good overviews of the school in the years Sylvester attended are Edward Thomas, "As Seen by a Foreigner," *The Indian Craftsman* 1, 3 (April 1909): 39–41; "Indians as Money Makers and Students at Carlisle," *New York Sun*, quoted in *The Red Man*, 4, 8 (April 1912): 330–39.

[5]Charles A. Eastman, *The Indian To-day* (Garden City: Doubleday, Page & Co., 1915) 69. G.A. Falk, "Missionary Education Work Amongst the Prairie Indian, 1870–1914" (M.A. thesis, University of Western Ontario, 1973) 16, footnote 1.

[6]James Henderson to Office of Indian Affairs Commissioner, November 19, 1928, DISCOVERY FILE. For an in-depth study of the Cherokees' attitudes toward blacks, see R. Halliburton, Jr., *Red Over Black: Black Slavery Among the Cherokee Indians* (Westport, Connecticut: Greenwood Press, 1977).

[7]Emma Newashe McAllister, "Chief Buffalo Child Long Lance," *Daily Oklahoman* 24 Mar. 1929. She incorrectly believed that James Henderson gave him the name. Henderson himself believed that it had been "Pop" Warner, Carlisle's football coach. See James Henderson to William Chanler, February 24, 1930, CHANLER INVESTIGATION. One can speculate that Sylvester picked up the name "Chahuska" from one of the many books on Indians that he read. There was an Osage chief named Pahusca, rhyming with Chahuska, and perhaps he simply wanted to keep his initials the same. Dr. Kenneth W. Porter to DBS, dated Eugene, Oregon, November 22, 1980.

[8]Emma Newashe recorded her reminiscences of her childhood and of Carlisle in an unpublished manuscript now in the Long Lance Papers, GLEN-BOW. Her comments on Sylvester at Carlisle are taken from her article, "Chief Buffalo Child Long Lance," and her Preface to Forsberg, ed., *Redman Echoes*.

[9]Mrs. E.H. Foster, "An Appreciation," in *Redman Echoes*, 71–72 (she mentions the birdcalls); Emma Newashe, "Chief Buffalo Child Long Lance" (his defence of weaker classmates).

[10]*Carlisle Arrow. (The Indian Craftsman* was renamed *The Carlisle Arrow* in 1910; hereafter the newspaper is cited as CA), November 11, 1910. It appeared in *The Red Man*, 3, 4 (December 1910): 173–75.

[11]February 9, 1912.

[12]Iva Miller's page in Sylvester Long's character book is pasted in the scrapbook donated to GLENBOW by Joe Bradshaw.

[13]Elizabeth Analla to C.L. Ellis, Superintendent, Mission Agency, Riverside, California, April 9, 1932, DISCOVERY FILE.

[14]Fannie Keokuk, "The Croatan Indians," CA 29 Oct. 1909.

[15]Edgar K. Miller, Superintendent, Hopi Indian Agency, to C.L. Ellis,

Superintendent, Mission Agency, Riverside, California, April 9, 1932, DISCOVERY FILE.

[16]Edgar K. Miller, "Trade Record" of Sylvester Long, CARLISLE FILE; *CA* 15 Sept. 1911.

[17]Carlisle's system of grades is explained in Ryan, "Carlisle," 134–41.

[18]Mrs. Foster's teaching posts are mentioned in the *CA* 5 Sept. 1913. Her reminiscences of Sylvester appear in Forsberg, ed., *Redman Echoes*, 71–72. For Emma Newashe's memories of Mrs. Foster, see her sketch of life at Carlisle in the Long Lance Papers, GLENBOW.

[19]Benjamin Franklin, *Autobiography* (Boston: The Riverside Press, 1958) 1.

[20]"Indians as Money Makers and Students at Carlisle," *New York Evening Sun*, quoted in *The Red Man*, 4, 8 (April 1912): 331.

[21]*CA* 12 Nov. 1909 (joined Invincibles); *CA* 23 Dec. 1910 (became secretary of the Invincibles); *CA* 25 Nov. 1910; 16 Dec. 1910; 3 and 17 Feb. 1911; 31 Mar. 1911 (mention of the debates); *CA* 7 Apr. 1911 (the hymns are listed).

[22]*CA* 7 Apr. 1911 (elected club president). Two of the postcards—one to his father and one to his mother—have survived. Both are dated December 12, 1911. The originals are in the possession of Lillian Doulin, Mocksville, NC, and copies of them are in GLENBOW.

[23]*CA* 26 Jan. 1912. Interview with Ed Wall, New York, May 23, 1977. Wall was the principal musician in Sylvester's next school band, at the St. John's Military Academy.

[24]See his "Outing Record" in the CARLISLE FILE. For information on Tyrone see Rev. W.H. Wilson, *Tyrone of To-day: The Gateway of the Alleghanies* (Tyrone: Herald, 1897); also Editing Committee, *Tyrone of To-day: Volume II, 1897–1976* (Tyrone: Tyrone Area Bicentennial Committee, 1976). Interview with Ed Wall, New York, May 23, 1977. Ed Wall to DBS, June 17, 1977.

[25]*The Carlisle Arrow* mentioned on July 30, 1915, that he had made the track team. A photo exists of him among the intramural football players. Jim Thorpe's photograph, donated by Joe Bradshaw, Winston–Salem, NC, is now at GLENBOW. See also Long Lance's article "Rise and Fall of Jim Thorpe," *Winnipeg Tribune* 1 Dec. 1923, and Thorpe's endorsement of Long Lance in Long Lance's pamphlet *How to Talk in the Indian Sign Language* (Akron, Ohio: B.F. Goodrich, 1930). For an excellent short summary of Jim Thorpe's career see Joseph D'O'Brian, "The Greatest Athlete in the World," *American Heritage*, July/August (1992): 93–100.

[26]For information on Joe Ross consult his student file, R.G. 75, Office

of Indian Affairs, Carlisle Student Record, file 3512, National Archives, Washington, DC. Four years after graduation Ross wrote Carlisle asking for Sylvester Long's address as he wanted to keep in touch with him. Long Lance mentioned "Joe Ross" to Frederick Griffin, a journalist. Ross's name appears in Griffin's sketch of Long Lance in the *Toronto Star Weekly* on January 10, 1925. Long Lance referred to Wesley Two Moons in his article "The Secret of the Sioux," *Cosmopolitan* June 1927: 208. Wesley Two Moons' student file number was 1325, and his file can be consulted in the National Archives. He attended Carlisle 1907–11 (he died at the school on September 15, 1911; pneumonia is listed as the cause of death). Robert Geronimo is mentioned as entering Carlisle in the fall of 1911; see the *CA* 22 Sept. 1911.

[27]Robert Gorman, "Indian Finds Blood on Trail of Lost Child," *Harrisburg Telegraph* 27 May 1911.

[28]An excellent review of a Carlisle commencement is J.M. Oskinson's article on that of 1910 in *Collier's,* reprinted in *The Red Man,* 3, 1 (September 1910): 18–22. The students' dress at the commencement exercises is described in *The Red Man,* 4, 9 (May 1912): 428.

[29]Sylvester's remarks are reprinted in the *CA* 19 Apr. 1912.

Chapter Three: Sylvester Chahuska Long Lance

[1]Arthur S. Link, *Woodrow Wilson and the Progressive Era, 1910–1917* (New York: Harper and Row, 1954) 63–66.

[2]Sylvester's application appears in the Conway Hall Registrar, kept in the Registrar's Office, Dickinson College, Carlisle, PA.

[3]James Henderson to the Office of Indian Affairs Commissioner, November 14, 1928, DISCOVERY FILE.

[4]YMCA cabinet, ed., *Students' Handbook of Conway Hall,* vol. 6 (1912–13) 59. A copy of the pamphlet is in the Dickinson College Archives.

[5]Long Lance (hereafter cited as LL), "Trail Upward," 138.

[6]His marks at Dickinson are included in the CARLISLE FILE. He appears in photos of the Hutchinson Society and the Conway Track Team. Dickinson College Archives.

[7]CA 6 June 1913.

[8]Leigh Kimball, Director, St. John's Cadet Band, to Moses Friedman, Superintendent of Carlisle, July 9, 1913; Moses Friedman to Leigh Kimball, July 11, 1913, CARLISLE FILE. CA 19 Sept. 1913.

[9]George S. Schuyler, *Black and Conservative* (New Rochelle, NY: Arlington House Publishers, 1966) 31.

[10]For information on St. John's Military Academy see C.P. Hurditch,

"Schools of America—St. John's, Manlius, NY," *The Illustrated Sporting News* (New York) 4 Feb. 1905: 12–14, 16; Ira L. Reeves, *Military Education in the United States* (Burlington: Free Press Printing Co., 1914) 175–76; Editorial, "End of a Great Tradition," *Syracuse Post-Standard* 24 Feb. 1973. The students' places of origin are given in the *Manlius Bulletin*, (March 1914): 35–8. Kenneth S. Latourette, "Guido Herman Fridolin Verbeck," *Dictionary of American Biography*, vol. 19 (New York: Charles Scribner's Sons, 1936) 248–49; H.C. Durston, "William Verbeck," *Manlius Thrift-News* 9 June 1938.

[11]Ryan, "Carlisle," 220–21, 226, 238–39.

[12]C.P. Hurditch, "St. John's," 14. The schedule is outlined in the *Manlius Bulletin*, (March 1914): 31. For his standing see *The Windmill* March 1915, April 1915 and June 1915. His membership in the drama society is mentioned in *The Windmill* July 1914, 86–87; and in the issue for September 1915, 64. He is listed as a member of the track team in *The Windmill* July 1914, 101. Interview with Ed Wall, New York, May 22, 1977.

[13]Interview with Ed Wall, New York, May 22, 1977; Ed Wall to DBS, June 17, 1977.

[14]*Syracuse Journal* 10 June 1914.

[15]Sylvester Long to Moses Friedman, November 15, 1913. CARLISLE FILE.

[16]War Department. Information Relative to the Appointment and Admission of Cadets to the United States Military Academy, *Official Register*, 1916, 68.

[17]"From 1802 to 1940, only four blacks were among the nearly 11,800 graduates of the Military Academy." Dr. Stephen B. Grove, USMA historian, to DBS, dated West Point, August 24, 1978. The four blacks graduated in 1877, 1887, 1889 and 1936.

[18]Sylvester Long Lance to President Woodrow Wilson, March 8, 1915, CARLISLE FILE. All correspondence relating to his request is contained in this file.

[19]Sylvester Long Lance to President Woodrow Wilson, dated May 14, 1915, Woodrow Wilson Papers, Series 4, no. 2281, one page. Manuscript Division, Reference Department, Library of Congress, Washington, DC.

[20]Actually David Moniac, a Creek, who graduated in 1822, was the first Indian appointed to West Point. He attained the rank of major and, ironically, was killed in battle with the Seminole Indians in 1836. Dr. Kenneth W. Porter to DBS, November 22, 1980.

[21]On April 9, 1930, the Longs told R.H. Latham that Long Lance "has

often sent clippings of his progress to the family." Ilia Tolstoy's report, CHAN-LER INVESTIGATION. For a previous reference to the postcards see chapter 2, footnote 22.

[22]Winston–Salem City Directories for 1913, 1915, 1916, 1918, 1920. Gravestone of Vivian Munita Long (1909–19), Silver Hill Graveyard, Buena Vista, Winston–Salem, NC.

[23]Lovie Galloway and her husband are mentioned in Abe Long's diary, entry for September 21, 1959.

[24]James Henderson to William Chanler, February 24, 1930, CHANLER INVESTIGATION: "Before Long graduated from Carlisle I went to Cherokee, North Carolina, where I was made superintendent and agent for the Eastern Band of Cherokee Indians. Soon after he was nominated by President Wilson for West Point I was called upon for the life history of this Indian. After diligent [sic] search I could find no one on the reservation who knew anything at all in regard to his life history." Conceivably, though, Henderson discovered at this time that Sylvester had learned some Cherokee language while traveling with the circus and working with Allen Whipporwill. See chapter 1, footnote 66.

CHAPTER FOUR: LIEUTENANT LONG LANCE, WAR HERO

[1]*New York Times* 21 Mar. 1916.

[2]For a description of Fort Slocum and the colored recruits there see George S. Schuyler, *Black and Conservative* (New Rochelle, NY: Arlington House Publishers, 1966) 33.

[3]Sylvester gave details of his weight and height in his letter to President Wilson, CARLISLE FILE. For the requirements for West Point consult "War Department. Information Relative to the Appointment and Admission of Cadets to the United States Military Academy," *Official Registrar*, 1916, 65–66.

[4]His marks are given in "Examination of Candidates for Admission to the United States Military Academy, March 1916," United States Military Academy Archives, West Point, NY. His standing at St. John's is given in his reports, copies of which are in the Long Lance Papers, GLENBOW.

[5]LL, "Trail Upward," 138.

[6]We know for certain that he wrote a letter to Superintendent Lips on March 17, 1914, CARLISLE FILE, and that he was in touch with a former teacher, Adelaide Belle Reichel. Miss Reichel later told the Commissioner of Indian Affairs that Long Lance had "refused an appointment to West Point." Adelaide Belle Reichel to the Office of Indian Affairs Commissioner, dated Tulsa, Oklahoma, November 20, 1928, DISCOVERY FILE.

[7]James Henderson to William Chanler, February 24, 1930, CHANLER INVESTIGATION.

[8]Frederick Griffin, "Redskin Extraordinary is this Indian Chief," *Toronto Star Weekly* 10 Jan. 1925. "Man Mountain Dean, 63, Dies in Georgia," *New York Times* 30 May 1953: 15, c. 5. Frank Leavitt's photo appears in Long Lance's large scrapbook, donated by Joe Bradshaw, GLENBOW. Who won the match? Long Lance, of course, claimed he did. Fred Griffin reports the Chief's version of the story: "In 1916, shortly before coming to Canada to enlist, he threw Frank Leavitt, heavyweight champion of the U.S. Army, four times at the West Side Athletic Club."

[9]*Montreal Star* 5 Aug. 1916: 8.

[10]LL, "Trail Upward," 138.

[11]G.W.L. Nicholson, *Canadian Expeditionary Force, 1914–1919* (Ottawa: Queen's Printer, 1964) 154 (Sanctuary Wood), 218 (recruits in July 1916) 213 (lowering of the medical).

[12]Mason Wade, *The French Canadians*, vol. 2 (Toronto: Macmillan, 1968) 661–67.

[13]Sylvester Long Lance, Attestation Paper, Canadian Over-seas Expeditionary Force, dated August 4, 1916. I am most grateful to W.A. MacIntosh, and to the staff of the Directorate of History, National Defence Headquarters, Ottawa, for their assistance in researching Long Lance's war record. The details of his service are contained in his service record and the "casualty form active service." The "Particulars of Service" prepared by the Canadian Forces Record Service, July 8, 1976, was also helpful.

[14]For a summary of the participation of the Canadian Indian in World War I see Duncan Campbell Scott, "The Canadian Indians and the Great World War," in *Canada in the Great World War*, vol. 3 (Toronto: United Publishers, 1919) 285–328. James Dempsey has written a biography of Henry Norwest, see the *Dictionary of Canadian Biography*, vol. 14: 1911–1920 (Toronto: University of Toronto Press, 1998) 786–87.

[15]The poem is in the CARLISLE FILE.

[16]John Swettenham, *To Seize the Victory* (Toronto: The Ryerson Press, 1965) 122–23.

[17]The respective positions at Vimy and the conflict itself are presented in Pierre Berton, *Vimy* (Toronto: McClelland and Stewart, 1986); Nicholson, *Canadian Expeditionary Force*, 233–68, and Swettenham, *To Seize the Victory*, 145–63; see particularly 146, 161.

[18]Swettenham, *To Seize the Victory*, 161.

[19]Long Lance quoted in the *New York World* 22 July 1917.

[20]In early 1925 Long Lance told Fred Griffin, the Toronto journalist, of this injury and his narrow escape. See Griffin, "Redskin Extraordinary," *Toronto Star Weekly* 10 Jan. 1925.

[21]The story appeared in the *New York World* on July 22 and in papers as far afield as the *Washington Post* and the *Seattle Post-Intelligencer* the following week.

[22]Thomas F. Gossett, *Race: The History of an Idea in America* (Dallas: Southern Methodist University Press, 1962) 269–73. John Hope Franklin, *From Slavery to Freedom*, 439–41, 454, 480–83.

[23]Fambrough L. Brownlee, *Winston–Salem: A Pictorial History* (Norfolk, Virginia: Donning Co., 1977) 148.

CHAPTER FIVE: LONG LANCE, JOURNALIST

[1]Long Lance's "Record of Service." W.A.B. Douglas, Directorate of History, National Defence Headquarters, Ottawa, to DBS, February 28, 1980.

[2]Anon., *Calgary* (London: Hodder and Stoughton, 1912) 1–12. The best history of Calgary is Max Foran, *Calgary: An Illustrated History* (Toronto: James Lorimer, 1978).

[3]Thorpe's batting average is given in the *Calgary Albertan* 12 July 1919: 16.

[4]Long Lance's style of dress is described in typewritten notes for an article by Walker, in the "Long Lance" file, news morgue, *Calgary Herald.* "His customary garb was a Palm Beach suit and soft hat." My thanks to the *Herald* for allowing me to use their news morgue.

[5]Walter McClintock, *The Old North Trail: Life, Legends and Religion of the Blackfeet Indians* (Lincoln: University of Nebraska Press, 1968; first published in 1910) 11.

[6]MacInnis is mentioned in H.G. Kennedy, *History of the 101st Regiment Edmonton Fusiliers* (1913), and is the subject of an article in the *Calgary Herald* 23 Aug. 1919: 11. Long Lance told this story in *Maclean's* magazine on May 15, 1926, and in *McClure's* of July 1927. The text of the *McClure's* article has been used. Throughout the 1920s the title of today's *Maclean's* magazine was written *MacLean's* with a capital *L*. Throughout this book I have followed the modern spelling.

[7]Diamond Jenness, "Canada's Indians Yesterday. What of Today?" *Canadian Journal of Economics and Political Science* 20 (1954): 97.

[8]Long Lance mentions their racial ancestry in "Indians of the Northwest and West Canada," *The Mentor* March 1924: 6.

[9]LL, "Trail Upward," 138. The Calgary Directory for 1919 mentions that the Soldiers Civil Re-establishment Office was in the Lancaster Building, 173.

[10]LL, "Trail Upward," 138.

[11]He is mentioned as helping coach the Calgary Canucks Football Team in October (*Calgary Herald*, hereafter cited as *CH*,) October 10 and 16, 1919). Long Lance is referred to as a reporter in the *CH* 21–23 Apr., 1920, and in the *Albertan* 23 Apr. 1920.

[12]*CH* 12 Nov. 1920: 18.

[13]Interview with Howard Kelly, Calgary, March 9, 1975. For a short biographical sketch of Howard Kelly, see Sheilagh S. Jameson, "John Howard Kelly, Q.C.," in *City Makers*, ed. Max Foran and Sheilagh S. Jameson (Calgary: The Historical Society of Alberta, 1987) 320–32. Interview with Reg Hammond, Calgary, May 5, 1976, and October 28, 1979. In the early 1920s he worked as the *Herald*'s office boy.

[14]Gerald Brawn, "A Veteran of Herald Staffers Traces Paper's Progress through the Years," *CH* 22 Oct. 1964: 64.

[15]Margaret Vahey Eakin to DBS, November 21, 1978.

[16]In 1924 he informed *The Mentor* (March 1924: 72) that he was "about thirty years of age."

[17]Ralph Wilson, "The Bombing of the City Hall," file D970.2.L845, GLENBOW.

[18]Walker, "Long Lance" file, news morgue, *Calgary Herald*.

[19]Interview with Hugh Dann, Calgary, February 21, 1975.

[20]Long Lance's militia commission as a lieutenant, dated September 1, 1921, is in GLENBOW (Long Lance papers donated by Joe Bradshaw). Canon Middleton's daughter, Mrs. Sophie Allison, has Long Lance's membership card in the Elks. W.B. Fraser mentions Fred McCall's flying record in *Calgary* (Montreal: Holt, Rinehart and Winston, 1967) 98. Maurice Fidler outlined Long Lance's boxing activities in Calgary in an interview in Ottawa, June 3, 1976. The *Calgary Eye-Opener*, 8 Oct. 1921, commented on his "unerring judgement" as a boxing referee. His election to the Canucks' executive is mentioned in the *CH* 22 Oct. 1920.

[21]Information on the "Human Spider" appears in *CH* 23 and 26 Sept. 1920. Two interesting articles on Bill Strother are H.G. Jones, "Was 'Human Fly' Tar Heel?" *News–Argus* (Goldsboro, North Carolina) 22 July 1982; and Michael Futch, "Fayetteville's Human Spider," *Observer–Times* (Fayetteville, North Carolina) 27 Dec. 1998.

[22]Interview with Howard Kelly, Calgary, March 9, 1975.

[23]Paul Senn, *The Lawless Decade* (New York: Bonanza Books, 1957) 56–60.

[24]Jack Dempsey quoted in Harry Scott, "Jack Dempsey," the *Albertan* 24 Mar. 1921.

[25]Long Lance's article on the Dempsey visit appeared in the *Winnipeg Tribune* (hereafter cited as *WT*) 19 June 1923. For details of Dempsey's activities in Calgary see *CH* 23–25 Mar., 1921. Jack Dempsey's comment on Long Lance is taken from his daughter's (Barbara Piattelli Dempsey) letter to DBS, August 19, 1977.

[26]Long Lance quotes Douglas Cunningham in "Coming East," *McClure's* July 1927: 122. For information on Cunningham see *CH* 13 Mar. 1926: 23, and *CH* 25 June 1955.

[27]LL "'Dare Devil' Locklear Falls to his Death," *CH* 3 Aug. 1920. See also *CH* 29 June 1920; *CH* 2 July 1920; and Long Lance's "Ormer Locklear, Air 'Daredevil,' Gentleman and Sportsman" in Long Lance's *Aviation Annual, 1921: Devoted to Flying in Alberta* in GLENBOW.

[28]"Nigger Humour," *The Beaver* March 1926: 74. My thanks to Jack Dunn of Calgary for this reference.

[29]"Rotary Minstrel Show One of the Year's Stage Treats," *CH* 21 Nov. 1919; Jack Peach, "Calgary Cut Its Cultural Teeth on Vaudeville," *CH* 11 Oct. 1986; *Calgary Rotary Minstrels, Grand Theatre, November 21, 22, 23, 1921,* program in the Glenbow Archives.

[30]Fred Kennedy, *Alberta Was My Beat* (Calgary: The *Albertan*, 1975) 65.

Chapter Six: Making a Name

[1]*CH* 27 May 1921.

[2]Copies of the original photos were donated to the Glenbow Archives by the late Newman Dalton of Mocksville, NC.

[3]My thanks to Donna Bloomfield of Calgary for her help with this description of Gleichen in the early 1920s.

[4]George Gooderham, "I Remember," George Gooderham Papers, GLENBOW; George Gooderham, diary entry for Friday, May 27, 1921, Gooderham Papers, GLENBOW; interview with George Gooderham, Calgary, February 7, 1975. The Department of Indian Affairs' ruling on school attendance is mentioned in Robert G. Moore, *The Historical Development of the Indian Act* (Ottawa: Treaties and Historical Research Centre, 1978) 115.

[5]George Gooderham, "Twenty-Five Years as an Indian Agent to the Blackfoot Band," 1. Gooderham Papers, GLENBOW. S.C. Long Lance, "Blackfoot Indians," *CH* 11 June 1921. L.M. Hanks and J.R. Hanks, *Tribe Under Trust* (Toronto: University of Toronto Press, 1950) 56. For details on Canadian Indian policy and the Indian Act see the appropriate sections in the following works: J.R. Miller, *Skyscrapers Hide the Heavens: A History of Indian–White Relations in Canada*, rev. ed. (Toronto: University of Toronto Press,

1991); Olive Patricia Dickason, *Canada's First Nations*, 2nd ed. (Toronto: Oxford University Press, 1997); and Arthur J. Ray, *I Have Lived Here Since the World Began: An Illustrated History of Canada's Native People* (Toronto: Key Porter, 1996).

[6]George Gooderham, "Autobiography," 5–14. Gooderham Papers, GLENBOW.

[7]Interview with George Gooderham, Calgary, February 7, 1975.

[8]Georgeen Barrass, Introduction to Canon H.W. Gibbon Stocken, *Among the Blackfoot and Sarcee* (Calgary: Glenbow Alberta Institute, 1976) iii–xv.

[9]Stocken, *Among the Blackfoot and Sarcee*, 12–13.

[10]LL, "Sarcee Indians," *CH* 23 July 1921.

[11]"Buffalo Child Long Lance Visits Ohio," *Ohio Archaeological and Historical Quarterly* 33 (1924): 523.

[12]*CH* 18 Nov. 1933.

[13]Winnifred A. Tims, "Life on an Indian Reservation," unpublished article, 1, Tims Papers, GLENBOW.

[14]Interview with Reginald Tims, Calgary, November 23, 1979 (son of Archdeacon Tims). *CH* 13 Oct. 1923; *CH* 18 Nov. 1933. The quotations are taken from Tims' manuscript, "Impressions Regarding Missionary Effort Amongst the Indians, January 6, 1919," Tims Papers, GLENBOW.

[15]LL, "Sarcee Indians," *CH* 23 July 1921. "Dr. T.F. Murray," *CH* 6 Feb. 1952. Jenness, "Canada's Indians," 99.

[16]For information on Jim Starlight see LL, "Sarcee Indians," *CH* 23 July 1921; Winnifred A. Tims, "Progressive Sarcee," *CH* 25 May 1929; George Gooderham, *Northern Plains Tribes*, vol. 5 (Sarcees), Gooderham Papers, GLENBOW; Stocken, *Among the Blackfoot and Sarcee*, 34 (Starlight's ability in chess); Long Lance to the Rev. S.H. Middleton (hereafter cited as SHM), October 12, 1924 (on the loan of Jim Starlight's buckskin suit).

[17]Nansi Swayze, *Canadian Portraits: Jenness, Barbeau, Wintemberg* (Toronto: Clarke, Irwin and Co., 1960) 83–85. Diamond Jenness, *The Sarcee Indians of Alberta* (Ottawa: National Museum of Canada, 1938).

[18]"Death of General Howard," *The Indian Craftsman* 2, 3 (November 1909): 37.

[19]Interview with George Gooderham, Calgary, February 7, 1975.

CHAPTER SEVEN: BUFFALO CHILD LONG LANCE

[1]For biographical information on S.H. Middleton see Roberta Forsberg, *Chief Mountain: The Story of Canon Middleton* (Whittier, California:

The Historical Society of Alberta, 1964); and S.H. Middleton, "Life of Service Among Indians," *Lethbridge Herald* 11 Dec. 1947. The Rev. S.H. Middleton became a canon in the Anglican Church in early November 1924 (*CH* 4 Nov. 1924), and after that date is referred to as Canon Middleton.

[2]For information on the Blackfoot Confederacy see Hugh A. Dempsey, *Crowfoot* (Edmonton: Hurtig, 1972) and his *Red Crow* (Saskatoon: Western Producer Prairie Books, 1980); and John C. Ewers, *The Blackfeet* (Norman: University of Oklahoma Press, 1958). In the United States, "Peigan" is spelled "Piegan."

[3]James G. MacGregor, *A History of Alberta* (Edmonton: Hurtig, 1972) 174, 177, 196.

[4]For Canon Middleton's reminiscences of his early years on the Blood Reserve see *Kainai Chieftainship* (Lethbridge: *Lethbridge Herald*, 1953) 57, 62; and his "Life of Service Among Indians," *Lethbridge Herald* 11 Dec. 1947.

[5]SHM to LL, August 22, 1922.

[6]Full descriptions of the school are found in Rev. Middleton's reports to the Department of Indian Affairs in the federal Sessional Papers for 1913 and 1914 and in his reports to the Anglican Church (those of 1913 and 1917 are in the Calgary Indian Mission Papers, GLENBOW).

[7]Report of J.A. Markle, Inspector of Indian Agencies, Report of the Superintendent of Indian Education, Department of Indian Affairs, Annual Report 1916, 217.

[8]Sophie Allison, "The Middleton Family," in *Fort Macleod: Our Colourful Past* (Fort Macleod: Fort Macleod History Book Committee, 1977) 369–71.

[9]Ken Liddell, "New Angle Found on Old School Tie," *CH* 15 Dec. 1951.

[10]LL, "Alberta's Most Progressive Indian Tribe," *CH* 27 Aug. 1921.

[11]SHM to Mrs. Edgar Pratt Hawkins, October 30, 1935.

[12]LL, "Alberta's Most Progressive Indian Tribe," *CH* 27 Aug. 1921.

[13]Canon Middleton in Forsberg, ed., *Redman Echoes*, 185.

[14]LL to SHM, dated Calgary, August 27, 1921.

[15]SHM to LL, January 12, 1922.

[16]My thanks to Sophie Middleton Allison (one of Canon Middleton's daughters) for confirming the details of an annual reunion of the Old Boys' and Girls' Association of St. Paul's.

[17]LL to SHM, dated Calgary, January 15, 1922. The Carlisle uniform is described in Ryan, "Carlisle," 42.

[18]Long Lance quoted in *CH* 15 Feb. 1922. Long Lance actually made these remarks in an afternoon address to the St. Paul's students, but no doubt he would have repeated the same themes to his older audience.

[19]For the background of the Mountain Horse family see Mike Moun-

tain Horse, *My People, The Bloods* (Calgary: Glenbow–Alberta Institute, 1979). Chief Mountain Horse's obituary appears in *CH* 15 Oct. 1937.

[20]The *Albertan* 7 Feb. 1936.

[21]Interview with Gordon Bird (who witnessed the ceremony), Stand Off, Blood Reserve, October 20, 1977. I have also relied on the description of the adoption ceremony given in Walter McClintock's *The Old North Trail* (1910) 31-35.

[22]Interview with Hugh Dempsey, Calgary, April 27, 1976.

[23]"Cherokee Given High Honor by Blood Indians," *CH* 14 Feb. 1922.

[24]The original Buffalo Child might well have been the Blackfoot that George Catlin, the American artist, met in 1832. At the mouth of the Yellowstone River he painted the portrait of "In-ne-o-cose (the buffalo's child)." See his *Letters and Notes on the Manners, Customs, and Condition of the North American Indians,* vol. 1 (London: Published by the Author, 1841) 30.

[25]"Buffalo Child Long Lance, a chief of the Bloods, in his official garb" in LL, "Before the Red Coats Came," *Maclean's* 15 Feb. 1923: 12.

CHAPTER EIGHT: LONG LANCE, PLAINS INDIAN

[1]The *Albertan* 30 Mar. 1922.

[2]F.G.E., "That Bogus Bomb!", the *Albertan* 31 Mar. 1922.

[3]"Tellum Bigley," "Slaps and Slams," the *Albertan* 30 Mar. 1922. "Tellum Bigley" was actually Harry Scott, the *Albertan's* sports editor.

[4]Nicholas K. Booth, "Biographical Account of Samuel H. Adams," chapter 8, p.6, GLENBOW (D920.B725A).

[5]He gives this as his address in his letter to the Rev. Middleton, dated Vancouver, May 11, 1922.

[6]Eric Nicol, *Vancouver* (Toronto: Doubleday, 1978) 146; Walter N. Sage, "Vancouver: The Rise of a City," *Dalhousie Review* 17 (1937): 47–54.

[7]Charles Bruce, *News and the Southams* (Toronto: Macmillan, 1968) 181.

[8]Stein was then the city editor. J. Swanson, Pacific Press Ltd., Vancouver, to DBS, December 14, 1979.

[9]Patricia Roy, Introduction to *The Writing on the Wall* (Toronto: University of Toronto Press, 1974) ix, xvii, xxvii. The quote from the *Sun* appears on p. vi.

[10]Diamond Jenness, "Canada's Indians Yesterday. What of Today?" *Canadian Journal of Economics and Political Science* 20 (1954): 95–100.

[11]Franz Boas, Diary entry for November 6, 1886, reprinted in Ronald P. Rohner, ed., *The Ethnography of Franz Boas* (Chicago: University of Chicago Press, 1969) 54.

[12]E. Palmer Patterson II, "Andrew Paull and Canadian Indian Resurgence" (PhD diss., University of Washington, 1962), 31–51.

[13]For the background to Indian land policy in British Columbia see Robin Fisher, *Contact and Conflict: Indian–European Relations in British Columbia, 1774–1890* (Vancouver: University of British Columbia Press, 1977) 146–211; and Paul Tennant, *Aboriginal Peoples and Politics: The Indian Land Question in British Columbia, 1849–1989* (Vancouver: University of British Columbia Press, 1994).

[14]Wilson Duff, *The Indian History of British Columbia. Volume 1: The Impact of the White Man* (Victoria: Provincial Museum of Natural History and Anthropology, 1964) 38–39. The Haidas' population dropped from an estimated 6000 in 1835 to 588 in 1915, the Bella Coola from an estimated 2000 in 1835 to 249 in 1929.

[15]Patterson, "Paull," 180–81.

[16]Kenneth E. Kidd, *Canadians of Long Ago* (Toronto: Longmans Canada, 1951) 52. Nicholson, *The Canadian Expeditionary Force*, 218.

[17]Patterson, "Paull," 43; E. Palmer Patterson II, "Andrew Paull (1892–1959)," *The Western Canadian Journal of Anthropology* 6, 2 (1976): 70–71.

[18]Elizabeth Bailey Price, "Magistrate Offended by Bitter Attack Sent Editor to Jail," *CH* 18 Nov. 1933.

[19]LL to SHM, dated Vancouver, May 11, 1922.

[20]Philip Drucker reviews the rise of native political organizations on the Pacific Coast in *The Native Brotherhoods: Modern Intertribal Organizations on the North West Coast* (Washington: United States Government Printing Office, 1958); and Paul Tennant, *Aboriginal Peoples and Politics: The Indian Land Question in British Columbia, 1849–1989* (Vancouver: University of British Columbia Press, 1994).

[21]LL to SHM, dated Vancouver, May 11, 1922.

[22]Forrest E. La Violette, "Missionaries and the Potlatch," *Queen's Quarterly* 58 (1951): 237–51; Chieftain, "Indians Persistent in Breaking Potlatch Law," *Vancouver Sun* 7 May 1922: 31. Forrest E. La Violette, *The Struggle for Survival* (Toronto: University of Toronto Press, 1961) 83–84, supplies slightly different figures for the total number imprisoned.

[23]LL, "Squamish," *Vancouver Sun* (hereafter cited as VS) 21 May 1922.

[24]In his article on the Kootenays in VS 25 June 1922, he cites both authorities, McLean and Boas.

[25]The dates of his articles on the Indians of British Columbia are May 21, 1922 (Squamish); May 28 (Musqueams); June 4 (Indians at Nanaimo); June 11 (Chilliwack Indians); June 18 (Haida); June 25 (Kootenays); July 2 (Lillooets); July 9 (Thompson Indians); July 16 (Shuswap); July 30 (Kwakiutl).

[26]LL to SHM, dated Vancouver, June 22, 1922.

[27]Alan Morley, *Roar of the Breakers: A Biography of Peter Kelly* (Toronto: The Ryerson Press, 1967).

[28]For Long Lance on Peter Kelly see LL, "Name of Haida Struck Panic to Indian Heart," VS 18 June 1922.

[29]LL, "What Indian Requests to Government Really Mean," VS 26 July 1922.

[30]LL to SHM, dated Muscowpetung Indian Reserve, Saskatchewan, September 10, 1922.

[31]LL, "Chief Long Lance takes his readers across Broad Plain," VS 27 Aug. 1922.

Chapter Nine: Talking to the Elders

[1]J. William Brennan, ed., *Regina Before Yesterday* (Regina: Historical Committee, 1978) 192.

[2]LL, "Where are Western Canada's Indians?" VS 7 June 1924.

[3]LL, "Before the Red Coats Came," *Maclean's* 15 Feb. 1923: 13.

[4]John Hawkes, "William Morris Graham," *Saskatchewan and Its People*, vol. 2 (Chicago: S.J. Clarke, 1924) 1196–97. "It is Fifty Years Since a Lasting Treaty was Made with Canada's Prairie Indians," *Saturday Night* 18 Oct. 1924: 3. "William Morris Graham," a short (one-page) sketch of his life in the possession of Bill Tye, Calgary. See also E. Brian Titley, "Chapter 10, The Ambitions of Commissioner Graham," in *A Narrow Vision: Duncan Campbell Scott and the Administration of Indian Affairs in Canada* (Vancouver: University of British Columbia Press, 1986) 184–99; and William M. Graham, *Treaty Days: Reflections of an Indian Commissioner*, ed. Hugh A. Dempsey (Calgary, Glenbow Museum, 1991), with introduction by James Dempsey.

[5]"Indians' Friend is Dead. Wife of Former Indian Official Passes Friday," *Regina Leader-Post* 16 Dec. 1939.

[6]W.M. Graham, "Report for South Saskatchewan Inspectorate," *Report of the Department of Indian Affairs*, 1910, 416–18; *Report of the Department of Indian Affairs*, 1914, 67–69; Eleanor Brass, "The File Hills Ex-Pupil Colony," *Saskatchewan History* 6, 2 (Spring 1953): 66–69.

[7]Charles Stewart speaking on April 24, 1923, in the House of Commons, Ottawa, House of Commons, *Debates*, 2146. Commissioner Graham felt vulnerable since he owed his appointment to the Conservative Arthur Meighen, who in 1918 had acted as Superintendent General of Indian Affairs. Meighen's wife was the stepdaughter of W.H.H. Wood, one of Mrs. Graham's brothers; hence Mrs. Arthur Meighen was Mrs. Graham's niece. When Mr. Meighen served as prime minister in 1920–21, it was reported in "Indians of

the Blood Reserve Make Allegations of Scandalous Treatment by the Government," *Ottawa Citizen* 6 May, 1921 that "a public official *Commissioner Graham* is well known to be a protege and relative by marriage of the leader of the present government." My thanks to Keith Wilson, secretary treasurer, Town of Birtle, Manitoba, for helping me to establish the family tie. Keith Wilson to DBS, December 11, 1980.

[8]Hugh A. Dempsey, "The Place of Indians in Western Canadian History," typed manuscript prepared in 1968, 12.

[9]Marius Barbeau, "Our Indians—Their Disappearance," *Queen's Quarterly* 38 (1931): 707.

[10]Jenness, "Canada's Indians Yesterday. What of Today?" 98–99. Charles E. Hendry, *Beyond Traplines* (Toronto: Ryerson, 1969) 13.

[11]"Charles Stewart," *Lethbridge Herald* 7 Dec. 1946. Ross Hamilton, ed., *Prominent Men of Canada, 1931–32* (Montreal: National Publishing Co., 1932) 456.

[12]LL to SHM, dated Muscowpetung Reserve, Saskatchewan, September 10, 1922.

[13]E.K. Brown, "Duncan Campbell Scott," in *Responses and Evaluations*, ed. David Staines (Toronto: McClelland and Stewart, 1977) 112–44. On Scott also see Brian Titley, *A Narrow Vision: Duncan Campbell Scott and the Administration of Indian Affairs in Canada* (Vancouver: University of British Columbia Press, 1986).

[14]Scott, "The Canadian Indians and the Great World War," 325–26.

[15]Charles Stewart speaking March 31, 1930, in the House of Commons, Ottawa, House of Commons, *Debates*, 1116.

[16]Edward Ahenakew, *Voices of the Plains Cree* (Toronto: McClelland and Stewart, 1973) 152. Long Lance's political activities are mentioned in a note from Mike Mountain Horse to J.T. Faunt, dated Cardston, November 22, 1924, R.G. 10, vol. 3233, file 600107, National Archives of Canada (my thanks to Bennett McCardle of Ottawa for this reference). Long Lance (presumably in early July 1924 at the Fort Macleod Jubilee) suggested that a meeting be organized "to get the sympathy of the public, in order that pressure be brought to bear on the Government with a view to having that section of the Indian Act which authorizes the Government to lease at will any portion of an Indian Reserve without the consent of the Indians, cut out of the Indian Act." The meeting was held at Fort Macleod in mid-November 1924, but Long Lance was not present.

[17]LL to Alice Tye, dated New York, April 24, 1930.

[18]Gooderham, "Twenty-Five Years as an Indian Agent," 2; Gooderham Papers, GLENBOW.

[19]"Red Men of the West—Yesterday and Today," *Regina Leader* 9 Dec. 1922.

[20]Chief Piapot's words are quoted in the rough notes of Long Lance, Canon Middleton Collection, GLENBOW. For a sketch of Piapot's life see John L. Tobias, "Payipot," *Dictionary of Canadian Biography*, vol. 13: 1901–1910 (Toronto: University of Toronto Press, 1994) 815–18.

[21]Dan Kennedy, *Recollections of an Assiniboine Chief* (Toronto: McClelland and Stewart, 1972) 54–56, 62.

[22]LL to SHM, dated Regina, November 11, 1922.

[23]Kennedy, *Recollections*, 87.

[24]LL to SHM, dated Regina, November 11, 1922.

[25]Wilfrid Eggleston, "Ottawa Supplies Clothing to Heads of Indian Tribes," *Toronto Star* 3 Mar. 1930.

[26]LL, *Long Lance* (New York: Cosmopolitan Book Corporation, 1928) 90–91.

[27]Hugh A. Dempsey, "Sylvester Long, Buffalo Child Long Lance," in *American Indian Intellectuals*, ed. Margot Liberty (St. Paul, MN: West Publishing Co., 1978) 202.

CHAPTER TEN: LONG LANCE, NATIVE RIGHTS ADVOCATE

[1]W.G.B. Kilroe, a photographer for the *Regina Leader*, took the photo which Long Lance signed and dated "Feb. 4, 1923."

[2]"The Author in Indian Garb," *WT* 10 Feb. 1923. He later used the second photo to illustrate his article in *The Mentor* March 1924: 3.

[3]Interview with Mike Eagle Speaker, Stirling, Alberta, January 16, 1976.

[4]LL to SHM, dated Regina, Saskatchewan, November 11, 1922.

[5]SHM to LL, February 3, 1923.

[6]LL to Alice Tye, dated New York, July 12, 1930.

[7]LL, "When the Indians Owned Manitoba," *WT* 12 Feb. 1923.

[8]"Indian Chief at Grace Ch. Forum," *WT* 5 May 1923. Garnet Clay Porter, "Long Lance, Indian Chief," *Saturday Night* 16 Aug. 1924. W.T. Allison, "Chief Buffalo Child Long Lance Writes Fascinating First Book," *WT* 27 Oct. 1928, magazine section, 6.

[9]"Chief Long Lance Tells of Indian History," *WT* 16 Jan. 1923; "Indian Chief at Grace Ch. Forum," *WT* 5 May 1923; "Predicts Redmen to Be Extinct in 200 Years," undated clipping about his talk to the Kiwanis Club at the Fort Garry Hotel, Winnipeg.

[10]W.L. Morton, *Manitoba: A History* 2nd ed. (Toronto: University of Toronto Press, 1967) 300, 321. Alan Ramsay, "Winnipeg! City of Contrast and

Beauty," *Canadian Geographical Journal* 26 (1943): 44–47. Robert Craig Brown and Ramsay Cook, *Canada, 1896–1921* (Toronto: McClelland and Stewart, 1974) 98.

[11]James H. Gray, *The Roar of the Twenties* (Toronto: Macmillan, 1975) 236.

[12]Interview with Charles L'Ami, Winnipeg, October 20, 1976.

[13]Interview with Allan Bill by Fran Fraser, May 11, 1962; a cassette of the recording is in GLENBOW.

[14]See the photo of Long Lance standing on his head in F.G. Griffin, "Redskin Extraordinary is this Indian Chief," *Toronto Star Weekly* 10 Jan. 1925.

[15]Interviews with Charles L'Ami and Pearl Driscoll L'Ami, Winnipeg, October 10, 1976.

[16]Mrs. H. O'Malley to DBS, June 6, 1980.

[17]Carlyle Allison, "The Corner Cupboard," *WT* 15 Dec. 1951: 6. Samuel Ichiye Hayakawa (1906–1992), then a young student at the University of Manitoba, who stayed at the Allisons', met Long Lance several times. Over half a century later he became a United States senator from California. Senator Hayakawa remembered the chief well. "In company he was perfectly charming—a good story-teller and conversationalist, gracious and flattering towards women, comradely with men." Senator Hayakawa to DBS, December 17, 1980.

[18]Vernon Knowles, "Buffalo Child Long Lance is Found Shot in White Girl's Home," *Toronto Daily Mail and Empire* 22 Mar. 1932.

[19]J.H. Cranston, *Ink on My Fingers* (Toronto: The Ryerson Press, 1953) 121.

[20]LL, "Canadian Sioux Chief Seeks $20,000,000 from U.S. Government," *Toronto Star Weekly* 31 Mar. 1923. LL, "Sioux Indians to Washington to Claim $20,394,951," *St. Paul Pioneer Press* 18 Mar. 1923. LL, "Custer Died by Own Hand, Say Indian Braves," *Chicago Herald and Examiner* 8 Apr. 1923.

[21]LL to SHM, dated St. Michael's Indian Boarding School, Duck Lake, May 17, 1923.

[22]Interview with Howard Kelly, Calgary, March 9, 1975.

[23]Mayor Webster's stampede costume is described in *CH* 9 July 1923.

[24]"Calgary Captured by Indians," *CH* 12 July 1923.

[25]The medal with Long Lance's name on it is engraved "Calgary Exhibition and Stampede 1923," Lilly E. Middleton to DBS, November 10, 1978. LL to Mr. and Mrs. Middleton, dated Calgary, June 27, 1924.

[26]Hector Crawler quoted in LL, "How do the Indians Regard the March of Civilisation?" *CH* 13 Oct. 1923. Marius Barbeau includes marvelous

stories about Hector Crawler and his family in his *Indian Days on the Western Prairies* (Ottawa: National Museum of Canada, 1960) 94–120.

[27]LL, "Secrets of the Forbidden Sun Dance Are Revealed," *Toronto Star Weekly* 17 Nov. 1923. The *Calgary Herald* also had a reporter at the Sun Dance camp, Dudley McClean. His article, "Sun Dance," appeared on August 25, 1923, in the *Herald*.

[28]Interview with Hugh Dempsey, Calgary, September 10, 1980.

[29]George H. Gooderham, "Chief Buffalo Child Long Lance," *Northern Plains Tribes*, vol. 2 (the Bloods), 10. Gooderham Papers, GLENBOW.

[30]Interview with George H. Gooderham, Calgary, February 7, 1975.

[31]Her name is given in Dudley McClean's article on the Sun Dance, *CH* 25 Aug. 1923.

[32]LL, "Secrets of the Forbidden Sun Dance Are Revealed," *Toronto Star Weekly* 17 Nov. 1923.

[33]LL, "The Sun Dance: A Chief of the Blackfoot Tribe Describes this Spectacular Ceremony of his People, in Which a Woman is the Central Figure," *Good Housekeeping* 85 August 1927: 64–65, 219–20. Mary's picture appears on p. 65.

[34]My thanks to Omer Lavallée, Supervisor, Special Projects and Corporate Archives, Canadian Pacific, Montreal, for supplying me with photocopies of four of Long Lance's menus. Omer Lavallée to DBS, April 22, 1975.

[35]T.N. Campbell and H.E. Ross, "The Battle of Duck Lake, The Star's Letterbox," *Saskatoon Daily Star* 3 Nov. 1923: 4. When Long Lance published an article in *Maclean's* 1 Feb. 1929 on Almighty Voice, his version of the facts was also contested. See "The Last Stand of Almighty Voice," *Maclean's* 15 June 1929.

[36]LL, "How do the Indians Regard the March of Civilisation?" *CH* 13 Oct. 1923. Grace Lee Nute, "Pierre-Esprit Radisson," *Dictionary of Canadian Biography*, vol. 2 (Toronto: University of Toronto Press, 1969) 535–40.

[37]LL, "Before the Red Coats Came," *Maclean's* 1 Mar. 1923: 50. Fran Fraser, "Blackfoot Chief Creates Legend," *CH* 19 May 1956. Interview with Earl Calf Child, Blackfoot Reserve, Gleichen, August 30, 1976. He recalls that Running Rabbit died in 1918.

[38]John Hawkes, *The Story of Saskatchewan and Its People* 3 vols. (Chicago: S.J. Clarke Pub. Co., 1924) vol. 2, 918.

[39]David Lee, "Almighty Voice and His Stories," *Native Studies Review* 10. 2 (1995): 57–76; see also Pierre Berton, "The Legend of Almighty Voice," *The Wild Frontier* (Toronto: McClelland and Stewart, 1978) 209–33, 239. His criticisms of Long Lance appear on 215–16.

[40]LL, "How Canada's Last Frontier Outlaw Died," *Maclean's* 1 Jan. 1924: 19–20, 42, 44; "Indian's Stand Against Mounted Police," *Family Herald and Weekly Star* 2 Jan. 1924; "When Almighty Voice Held the Mounties at Bay," *WT* 5 Jan. 1924.

[41]Here I am following Long Lance's version of the story as published in *Long Lance* (New York: Cosmopolitan Book Corporation, 1928) 247–75.

[42]Berton, "Legend of Almighty Voice," 215. Berton regrets this, claiming "the Long Lance narrative is studded with so many errors, easily established from the record, that it is not possible to give credence to his account."

[43]LL, *Long Lance*, 264–66.

[44]LL, *Long Lance*, 270, 272.

[45]LL, "Right to Jaw 'Kayoes' Firpo in 2nd Round," *WT* 15 Sept. 1923. Senn, *The Lawless Decade*, 89.

[46]LL, "Georges Carpentier Makes Poor Showing," *WT* 2 June 1924. LL to SHM, dated "en route Columbus–Winnipeg," October 12, 1924; F.G. Griffin, "Redskin Extraordinary," *Toronto Star Weekly* 10 Jan. 1925 (on LL's style as a boxing writer).

[47]Federal Writers' Project, *New York City Guide* (New York: Random House, 1976) 225.

[48]LL to SHM, dated "en route: Columbus–Winnipeg," October 12, 1924.

[49]W.D. Moffat in an editorial note, *The Mentor*, 12, 2 (March, 1924): 72.

[50]Herbert Cranston quoted in Wilfrid Eggleston, *While I Still Remember: A Personal Record* (Toronto: The Ryerson Press, 1968) 82.

[51]Ross Harkness, *J.E. Atkinson of the Star* (Toronto: University of Toronto Press, 1963) 179.

[52]Card announcing Chief Long Lance as a judge in the City Amateur Boxing and Wrestling Championships, in LL's scrapbook, donated by Joe Bradshaw, GLENBOW; George E. Johnston to DBS, February 7 and June 15, 1976 (on Long Lance's girlfriend, the music teacher).

[53]LL, "Ancient Days are Revived at Fort Macleod Festivities," *WT* 3 July 1924. C. Frank Steele, "Long Lance Speaks Again," *Winnipeg Free Press* 10 July 1937, magazine section.

[54]Interview with Mike Eagle Speaker, Stirling, Alberta, March 15, 1976, and at the old St. Paul's School, Old Agency, Blood Reserve, October 20, 1977.

[55]Long Lance quoted in Wilfrid Eggleston, "Fastened Sleds Under Canoe in Mushing Through Slush," *Toronto Star Weekly* 4 May 1929.

[56]"Soon I may stop writing about Indians altogether or trying to get

them together for their own good; for it is the most thankless, disheartening job anyone ever tackled." LL to Mrs. Ethel T. Feathers, dated Banff Springs Hotel, August 5, 1924 (a copy of this letter is in GLENBOW, and the original in Mrs. Sophie Middleton Allison's possession). LL to SHM, dated Banff Springs Hotel, August 5, 1924. See also footnote 16, chapter 9. After suggesting that the nations of the Blackfoot Confederacy meet together in the autumn of 1924, Long Lance did not appear at the meeting that November.

[57]*CH* 8 July 1924: 11.

[58]LL to SHM, dated Banff Springs Hotel, July 15, 1924.

[59]LL to SHM, dated "en route: Columbus–Winnipeg," October 12, 1924. "Buffalo Child Long Lance," *Ohio Archaeological and Historical Quarterly* 33 (1924): 516.

[60]Chief Logan quoted in Wilcomb E. Washburn, ed., *The Indian and the White Man* (Garden City, NY: Anchor Books, 1964) 427–28.

[61]Anna Church Colley, "At Logan's Elm, Where His Famous Speech Was Uttered," *The American Indian* March 1929: 8.

[62]"Ohio History Day at Logan Elm Park. Chief Buffalo Child Long Lance, Full Blooded Indian, was the Principal Orator," The *Circleville Herald* 6 Oct. 1924. LL to SHM, dated "en route: Columbus–Winnipeg," October 12, 1924.

[63]"Indian Chief on Unity of Dominion," *Montreal Gazette* 18 Nov. 1924. "Tells of Indian Life Before the White Man," *Hamilton Spectator* 3 Dec. 1924. "Says Indians Face Extinction Within Century and Half," *Toronto Daily Star* 11 Dec. 1924. "Indians Then and Now," *Edmonton Journal* 17 Dec. 1924. F.G. Griffin, "Redskin Extraordinary is this Indian Chief," *Toronto Star Weekly* 10 Jan. 1925.

[64]LL to SHM, dated Banff Springs Hotel, August 5, 1924; LL to SHM, dated Banff Winter Carnival, February 12, 1925.

CHAPTER ELEVEN: LONG LANCE, "REDSKIN EXTRAORDINARY"

[1]"Full Blooded Indian Chief Takes Up Newspaper Work. Chief Buffalo Child Long Lance Exchanges Tomahawk for Typewriter," unidentified clipping in LL scrapbook, donated by Joe Bradshaw, GLENBOW.

[2]LL, "Dempsey Remembers Little of Furious First Round," *WT* 6 Nov. 1923.

[3]LL to SHM, dated Winnipeg, January 7, 1925; LL to SHM, dated Banff Winter Carnival, February 12, 1925.

[4]"All Blacks Get Royal Welcome," *WT* 5 Feb. 1925; "Indian Chiefs Welcome Maoris," *WT* 7 Feb. 1925; "All Blacks First Time on Ice," the *Albertan* 9 Feb. 1925; "All Blacks take Banff by Storm," *CH* 9 Feb. 1925; Maurice Fidler to DBS, April 4, 1976.

[5]Eldred G.F. Walker, *Canadian Trails Re-Visited* (London: William Stevens, 1925) 97–99. A photo of Eldred Walker appears opposite the book's title page.

[6]Bart Robinson, *Banff Springs: The Story of a Hotel* (Banff: Summerthought, 1973) 80.

[7]"In the ballroom he is an imposing figure. Tall and stalwart his evening clothes seem to really belong to him. He has the ability that so many of us lack, the knack of fitting in, and is quite in demand as a dancing partner." Unidentified clipping, "Chief Buffalo Child Long Lance, Blackfoot, Carlyle graduate, press agent for the Canadian Pacific Railroad," LL scrapbook, donated by Joe Bradshaw, GLENBOW.

[8]"A Chief of Indians Invited to Britain," *Toronto Daily Star* 5 Sept. 1924. A short biography of Paget appears in *The Dictionary of National Biography, 1951–1960* (Oxford: Oxford University Press, 1971) 786–87.

[9]Griffin, "Redskin Extraordinary," *Toronto Star Weekly* 10 Jan. 1925.

[10]John Scott, "Three Cheers for Earl Haig: Canadian Veterans and the Visit of Field Marshall Sir Douglas Haig to Canada in the Summer of 1925," *Canadian Military History* 5.1 (Spring 1996): 35.

[11]Fred Jones, "Earl Haig," *CH* 8 July 1925.

[12]Long Lance quoted in "Haig is Made Indian Chief," the *Albertan* 11 July 1925.

[13]"Chief Bull Head of Sarcees Dead; Was Their Great Leader," *CH* 15 Mar. 1911. See also Hugh A. Dempsey, "Chula," *Dictionary of Canadian Biography*, vol. 14: 1911–1920 (Toronto: University of Toronto Press, 1998) 213–15.

[14]"Chief Akahtse (Field-Marshal Earl Haig) shaking hands with Chief Buffalo Child Long Lance, while Chief Big Plume of the Sarcees stands in the left foreground," *CH* 10 July 1925.

[15]*Providence Sunday Journal* 18 Oct. 1925. LL to SHM, dated Montreal, November 22, 1925.

[16]Ray Long quoted in a printed list of comments about Long Lance's lectures, prepared by the Bureau of Commercial Economics. Sophie Middleton Allison's copy has been photocopied and placed in GLENBOW.

[17]LL to SHM, dated Montreal, November 22, 1925.

[18]"The *Cosmopolitan* of Ray Long," *Fortune* 3 (March 1931): 49–55, particularly 54–55.

[19]LL to SHM, dated Montreal, November 22, 1925.

[20]The Bureau's objectives are outlined on the back of the Bureau's official letter-paper; see the letter of Randolph M. Boggs to LL, May 24, 1927,

GLENBOW. Long Lance's nineteen railway passes are all glued in his scrapbook, donated by Joe Bradshaw, GLENBOW.

[21]"American Blue Blood will Turn Red, Says Indian," *Chicago Tribune* 10 Jan. 1926. The comments of Dr. Bell and Charles MacConnell are listed in their printed endorsements of Long Lance's lectures, Bureau of Commercial Economics, GLENBOW.

[22]List of printed endorsements, Bureau of Commercial Economics, GLENBOW.

[23]LL, "I Wanted to Live Like the White Man," *Maclean's* 15 May 1926: 16, 60. LL, "Coming East," *McClure's* July 1927: 14–15, 121–22.

[24]LL to SHM, dated Winnipeg, May 7, 1926.

[25]LL to SHM, dated New York, November 2, 1926.

[26]My thanks to Peter Mirejovsky, Calgary, for the image of the pond.

[27]LL, "History of and Agricultural Work Among Indians in Western Canada," Proceedings of the Eighteenth Annual Meeting, American Railway Development Association, Hotel Vancouver, Vancouver, BC, Canada. June 23–26. (St. Paul, Minnesota: Riverside Press, 1926). pp. 25–27. "Parade Notes," *CH* 5 July 1926.

[28]Morley Roberts, *On the Old Trail: Through British Columbia After Forty Years* (London: Eveleigh Nash and Grayson Ltd., 1927) 68–69. My thanks to Don Bourdon, Archives of the Whyte Museum of the Canadian Rockies, Banff, for this reference.

[29]"John Jay Sheridan," *Who's Who in Chicago and Vicinity*, 1931 (Chicago: A.N. Marquis Company, 1931) 886. Marriage Certificate of John Jay Sheridan and Florence K. Donovan, September 10, 1924. Available from Grays Harbor County Auditor, 1708 Sumner, Montesana, Washington 98563. Interviews with Hugh Dann, Calgary, February 21, 1975, and December 18, 1979.

[30]Interview with Howard Kelly, Calgary, March 9, 1975.

[31]A full account of the incident appears in the *Banff Crag and Canyon* 10 Sept. 1926. Interviews with Howard Kelly, Calgary, March 9, 1975; and Hugh Dann, Calgary, February 21, 1975, and December 18, 1979.

[32]*Macleod Gazette* 24 Mar. 1932; *Banff Crag and Canyon* 10 Sept. 1926.

[33]"Victims of Banff Fray Recovering," *CH* 13 Sept. 1926. "Charge Against Long Lance First on Court Docket," *CH* 1 Oct. 1926. LL to SHM, dated Chicago, October 16, 1926.

[34]Fred Kennedy, *Alberta Was My Beat* (Calgary: The Albertan, 1975) 63. I have rearranged the quote slightly. In Fred Kennedy's book the statement reads: "Although Long Lance ultimately recovered, he confessed to me

later that he came close to losing his manhood, a condition [that,] so far as the gregarious Indian was concerned, would have been a fate worse than death."

[35]LL to SHM, dated Chicago, October 16, 1926.

[36]LL to Alice Tye, dated New York, July 17, 1930; John C. Ewers, *The Blackfeet* (Norman: University of Oklahoma Press, 1958) 3–5 (on Napi, the Old Man).

[37]LL, "Secret of the Sioux," *Hearst's International–Cosmopolitan* June 1927: 208. "Wesley Two Moons," R.G. 75, Office of Indian Affairs, Carlisle Student Record, file 1325, National Archives, Washington, DC.

[38]The comments of Bernard Clark of Didcot, Oxfordshire, England, on Long Lance's version of the Battle of Little Big Horn proved very helpful. Ted Blackmore of Eastbourne, Sussex, England, kindly forwarded them to me in early February 1976.

[39]*New York Times* 22 May 1927, Book Review Section.

[40]Mrs. Custer's threatened libel action is mentioned in the *CH* 21 Mar. 1932; *New York Times* 19 June 1927. The Frontiersmen declared that Custer was "the most gallant and bravest Indian fighter in history" and added that Long Lance's article was "nearly all fiction."

CHAPTER TWELVE: LONG LANCE, BIOGRAPHER

[1]"Farrar and Rinehart Buy Cosmopolitan," *New York Times* (hereafter cited as *NYT*), 24 Sept. 1931.

[2]A photo of Ray Long's office appears in "The *Cosmopolitan* of Ray Long," *Fortune* 3 (March 1931): 50.

[3]W.A. Swanberg, *Citizen Hearst: A Biography of William Randolph Hearst* (New York: Bantam Books, 1971) 436.

[4]The contract, signed March 30, 1927, was enclosed in a letter from Ellen Datlow, Holt, Rinehart and Winston, New York, to DBS, January 17, 1977.

[5]Mary Burnham, ed., *The Cumulative Book Index, 1926–1932* (New York: H.W. Wilson Co., 1933) 275.

[6]Frazier Hunt, *One American and His Attempt at Education* (New York: Simon and Schuster, 1938) 293.

[7]On the book's contract the typed title, "The Story of an Indian Boy," has been crossed out and "Long Lance" written above it. LL to SHM, dated New York, August 7, 1928.

[8]" . . . he met his brothers at least, in Philadelphia and elsewhere. . . ." Colonel William A. Blair quoted in a letter to Canon Middleton, dated Winston–Salem, January 27, 1934. Long Lance must have met Abe in Philadel-

phia, for he told Walter in 1931 how pleased he was to see him again—they had not met for twenty-two years. LL to Walter Long, January 6, 1931. The meeting with Abe can be dated from a letter in Lillian Doulin's possession (copy in GLENBOW). On January 30, 1935, U.K. Rice, the white manager of the Carolina Theatre in Winston–Salem, wrote John Kirby, a distributor for Paramount. He asked Kirby to send a print of *The Silent Enemy*, and added; "Chief Buffalo Longlance, a graduate of West Point who played the lead in this film was a brother of Abe Long, the manager of the colored section and he has not seen his brother for almost eight years."

[9]Vivian Munita Long (1909–19), Gravestone, Silver Hill Graveyard, Buena Vista, Winston–Salem. Interview with Joe Bradshaw, Winston–Salem, January 8, 1977.

[10]Abe Long's diary, entries for December 30, 1941, and March 14 and 17, 1946. Abe would become the manager of the all-Negro balcony of Winston–Salem's Carolina Theatre when it opened in 1929. See Robert Miller, "Sounds of Theater are Behind Him," *Twin City Sentinel*, September 16, 1967.

[11]"Walter L. Long, Widely Known Negro is Dead," *Winston–Salem Journal* 28 Mar. 1941. "Death Claims Uncle Joe Long," *Winston–Salem Sentinel* 16 Nov. 1932.

[12]LL, "Tunney," WT 12 Nov. 1926; LL, "Jack Sharkey," WT 21 May 1927.

[13]Interview with Maurice Fidler, Ottawa, June 3, 1976, and his letters of February 28, April 4 and May 17, 1976, and February 7, 1977.

[14]Interview with Maurice Fidler, Ottawa, June 3, 1976.

[15]Margaret Vahey Eakin to DBS, November 21, 1978.

[16]Interview with Maurice Fidler, June 3, 1976.

[17]Interview with Mike Eagle Speaker, Stirling, Alberta, January 16 and February 18, 1976; and at the old St. Paul's School, Old Agency, Blood Reserve, October 20, 1977.

[18]LL, *Long Lance* (New York: Cosmopolitan Book Corporation, 1928) 1–3.

[19]LL, *Long Lance*, 7, 11, 14, 35.

[20]LL, *Long Lance*, 7–8. Long Lance comments on the practice among the Lillooets in British Columbia in the VS 2 July 1922. Mike Eagle Speaker denied that whipping took place among the Blackfoot tribes, interview, February 18, 1976. For a summary of the "whipping complex" see Thomas R. Garth, "The Plateau Whipping Complex and its Relationship to Plateau–Southwest Contacts," *Ethnohistory* 12 (1965): 141–70.

[21]LL, *Long Lance*, 10. This practice was also denied by Mike Eagle Speaker, interview, February 18, 1976.

[22]*The Scotsman*, quoted on the back cover of the latest paperback British edition of *Long Lance* (London: Abacus, 1976).

[23]LL, *Long Lance*, 11.

[24]LL, *Long Lance*, 209, 243.

[25]LL, *Long Lance*, 277.

[26]LL, *Long Lance*, 247. See Hugh A. Dempsey, *Crowfoot* (Edmonton: Hurtig, 1972).

[27]LL to SHM, dated Calgary, November 21, 1927; LL to SHM, dated New York, February 11, 1928.

[28]Publicity circular prepared by Cosmopolitan Book Corporation, August 24, 1928, a photocopy is in GLENBOW. The book was published that day.

[29]LL to Howard Kelly, dated New York, February 2, 1928.

[30]The quotations from the *Public Ledger* and *Times-Picayune* are taken from the advertisement for *Long Lance* published in the book section of the *New York Herald Tribune* 28 Oct. 1928. *The New Statesman*, quoted on the back cover of the latest British paperback edition of *Long Lance* (London: Abacus, 1976). Ernest Thompson Seton, ed., *Famous Animal Stories* (New York: Brentano's Publishers, 1932) 327.

[31]Paul Radin, "An Indian's Own Story: *Long Lance* by Chief Buffalo Child Long Lance," *New York Herald Tribune* 14 Oct. 1928: 7. For information about Radin see Harry Hoijer, "Paul Radin, 1883–1959," *American Anthropologist* n.s. 61 (1959): 839–43.

[32]The translations of *Long Lance* and the various editions of the book are listed in *The National Union Catalog, Pre-1956 Imprints* (London, England: Mansell Information, 1970), vol. 83, 258, under "Buffalo Child Long Lance."

CHAPTER THIRTEEN: LONG LANCE, SOCIAL LION

[1]Long Lance describes the luncheon in a letter to Howard Kelly, dated New York, February 2, 1928. Ludwig's *Napoleon* was the number two nonfiction book in 1927 and number four in 1928. Alice Payne Hackett and James Henry Burke, *80 Years of Best Sellers* (New York: R.R. Bowker Company, 1977) 103, 105.

[2]Fred Gus Neuman, *Irvin S. Cobb: His Life and Achievements* (New York: Beekman Publishers, 1974; first published in 1934) 194. A picture of the house appears on p. 191.

[3]Irvin S. Cobb, quoted in the *Indianapolis Times* 14 May 1942.

[4]Neuman, *Cobb*, 107. A shorter account of Cobb's life is Irving Dilliard's sketch in the *Dictionary of American Biography*, supplement 3, 1941–1945 (New York: Charles Scribner's Sons, 1973) 170–71.

[5]"Bob Davis Recalls," *WT* 17 Oct. 1928.

[6]"Irvin S. Cobb to Receive File American Indian," *The American Indian* November 1927: 16.

[7]Neuman, *Cobb*, 50, 206, 225–28, 261; Elisabeth Cobb, *My Wayward Parent: A Book About Irvin S. Cobb* (Indianapolis: Bobbs-Merrill Company, 1945) 17; My thanks to Leo Fox for the spelling of the Blackfoot word, Oct. 16, 1981.

[8]Irvin S. Cobb, Foreword, *Long Lance*, vii–viii.

[9]LL to Howard Kelly, dated New York, February 2, 1928.

[10]A Norwegian journalist, Theodor Findahl, was present. He described Cobb's party in his book *Manhattan Babylon, en bok om New York idag* (Oslo, Norway: Gyldendal, 1928) 42–50. He gave Long Lance an English version of a draft of his chapter "An Indian Chief on Park Avenue." This is now at GLEN-BOW. Long Lance also describes the party in his letters to Howard Kelly (February 10, 1928) and to Canon Middleton (February 11, 1928). My thanks to Elise Corbet of Calgary for her comments on the dress of the late 1920s.

[11]The direct quotes have been taken from Long Lance's address to the Ohio State Archaeological and Historical Society on October 2, 1924. See "Buffalo Child Long Lance Visits Ohio," *Ohio Archaeological and Historical Society* 33 (1924): 519.

[12]*Ohio Archaeological and Historical Society*, 518.

[13]*Ohio Archaeological and Historical Society*, 520.

[14]*Ohio Archaeological and Historical Society*, 521–22.

[15]Findahl, "An Indian Chief," 4.

[16]For information on black New York in the 1920s see Gilbert Osofsky, *Harlem: The Making of a Ghetto: Negro New York, 1890–1930* (New York: Harper and Row, 1966); and the chapter "Africa" in Konrad Bercovici's *Around the World in New York* (New York: The Century Co., 1924) 211–48.

[17]Interview with Maurice Fidler, Ottawa, June 3, 1976.

[18]Findahl, "An Indian Chief," 7.

[19]LL to Howard Kelly, dated New York, June 8, 1928.

[20]O.O. McIntyre, a New York columnist, called Long Lance "a sepia edition of the late Valentino." O.O. McIntyre, "New York Day by Day," *Washington Herald* 22 May 1928.

[21]Each woman gave him her photograph. Mildred wrote on hers, "To Long Lance the Maker of Dreams," and Vivian, "To Chief Longlance with every good wish, Vivian Hart 1928." For press references to Vivian Hart see *NYT* 6 Dec. 1929: 26, c. 7; and to Mildred McCoy, *NYT* 4 Aug. 1929: section 8, 1.

²²Interview with Howard Kelly, Calgary, March 9, 1975. Long Lance wrote Howard telling him that Irvin S. Cobb had termed him "the Beau Brummel of Broadway."

²³Frederick Cunliffe-Owen, "Royalty in Jobs Doing Well," *NYT* 21 Oct. 1923: section 9, 4; "Princess Alexandra Seeks Citizenship Here," *NYT* 31 Jan. 1929: 27. Her sketch of Long Lance is dated 1930.

²⁴O.O. McIntyre, "New York Day by Day," *Washington Herald* 22 May 1928. For his readership see Charles B. Driscoll, *The Life of O.O. McIntyre* (New York: Beekman Publishers, 1974; first published 1938): 20, 35; "O.O. McIntyre is Dead," *NYT* 15 Feb. 1938: 25.

²⁵Interview (by telephone) with Dorothy Fellers, Washington, DC, May 26, 1977. For a short biography of General Bonner Fellers see *Association of Graduates* (United States Military Academy) 23, 3 (December 1974): 104–5.

²⁶"Cadet W.D. Moore" quoted in LL to Howard Kelly, dated New York, February 2, 1928. Kenneth W. Rapp, assistant archivist, USMA Archives to DBS, dated West Point, June 30, 1977.

²⁷LL to Howard Kelly, dated New York, February 2, 1928.

²⁸Gladys Baker, "Blackfeet Chief is Polished Man," *Birmingham News-Age-Herald.* 7 Oct. 1928; on Gladys Baker see Lily May Caldwell, "An Interviewer Who Understands," *Birmingham News-Age-Herald* 29 Sept. 1929.

²⁹LL to Howard Kelly, dated New York, February 10 and June 8, 1928; LL to Canon Middleton, dated New York, February 11 and August 7, 1928; LL to Bonner and Dorothy Fellers, dated New York, February 9 and June 4, 1928. Bonner Fellers Papers, Hoover Institute on War, Revolution and Peace, Stanford University, California (hereafter cited as HOOVER).

³⁰"Original Americans' First Vote," *Literary Digest* 22 Sept. 1928.

³¹Long Lance mentions his lecture fee in a letter to Vilhjalmur Stefansson, dated Calgary, July 5, 1927. Presumably his expenses were also paid. Stefansson Collection, Dartmouth College, Dartmouth, Mass. (hereafter cited as DARTMOUTH). "According to the Brookings estimates, even in this banner year of 1929 no less than seventy-eight per cent of the American population have family incomes of less than $3,000 or individual incomes of less than $1,500, and something like forty per cent have family incomes of less than $1,500 or individual incomes of less than $750." Frederick Lewis Allen, *Since Yesterday, 1929–1939* (New York: Bantam, 1965; first published 1940) 11.

³²LL to Bonner and Dorothy Fellers, dated New York, September 13, 1928, and dated Cleveland, October 18, 1928, HOOVER.

³³Kenneth Williams quoted in the Editor's Introduction, *How to Talk*

in the Indian Sign Language (Akron, Ohio: The B.F. Goodrich Rubber Co., 1930).

[34]Untitled manuscript written by Long Lance, GLENBOW (file AL856B f5). For a review of American Indian Policy in the 1920s, see Francis Paul Prucha, *The Great Father: The United States Government and the American Indians* abr. ed. (Lincoln: University of Nebraska Press, 1986) 272–310.

[35]The quotations are taken from Long Lance's untitled manuscript, 11, 13, 19, 23.

[36]Charles Burke quoted in Herbert Corey, "He Carries the White Man's Burden," *Colliers* 12 May 1923.

[37]Margaret Garretson Szasz, "Indian Reform in a Decade of Prosperity," *Montana: The Magazine of Western History* 20, 1 (January 1970): 20–21.

[38]Institute for Government Research, *The Problem of Indian Administration* (Baltimore: Johns Hopkins Press, 1928), termed the Meriam Report; D'Arcy McNickle, *Indian Man: A Life of Oliver LaFarge* (Bloomington: Indiana University Press, 1971) 50, 76.

[39]Bowles' letter (and all other correspondence relating to the inquiry) is in the DISCOVERY FILE.

[40]"Indian from Blood Reserve Shakes Hand of President. Also Meets Lindbergh, Dempsey and Ford," *Lethbridge Herald* 17 Nov. 1927.

[41]LL to Vilhjalmur Stefansson, dated New York, September 5, 1928, DARTMOUTH. " . . . my publishers want another book—an Indian novel of pre-white vintage; that is, a novel dealing entirely with Indians before the coming of European stock."

[42]LL to SHM, dated Rabbit Chutes, Temagami, December 24, 1928. "Do you know that you have written me a letter and I have not received it? Just before I left New York in late October I received a four line note from you, saying; 'Here are the letters that I mentioned in my letter.' Well, I never received that letter, and had been wondering all along why you had not answered my last letter nor written to tell me what you thought of the book which I sent you in August. And, if you will remember, I wired you from Cheyenne, Wyoming, asking you why you did not write."

[43]Interview (by telephone) with S.C. Burden, Los Angeles, June 20, 1977.

CHAPTER FOURTEEN: LONG LANCE, MOVIE STAR

[1]Interview with Douglas Burden, Charlotte, Vermont, May 4–5, 1977; *Who's Who in America*, 1976-1977, vol. 1 (Chicago: Marquis Who's Who, 1976) 446.

[2]Douglas Burden, "Autobiography: 'The Silent Enemy,'" 1. Manuscript shown to me, Charlotte, Vermont, May 4, 1977.

[3]Interview with William Chanler, New York, May 25, 1977.

[4]Douglas Burden quoted in William L. Laurence, "A Camera Record of the Indian," *New York World* (11 May 1930). Hearne's book is entitled *A Journey from Prince of Wales' Fort in Hudson's Bay to the Northern Ocean 1769, 1770, 1771, 1772.*

[5]Douglas Burden quoted in Kevin Brownlow, *The War, the West and the Wilderness* (New York: Alfred A. Knopf, 1979) 550.

[6]Interview with Douglas Burden, Charlotte, Vermont, May 4–5, 1977; "Film Depicts Tribal Life of the Ojibways," *Christian Science Monitor* 19 May 1930; interview with Madeline Theriault, an Ojibwa who appeared in the film, North Bay, Ontario, January 2, 1976; interviews with Ted Hennessy, who supplied the camps with wood, North Bay, Ontario, December 22, 1976, and May 12, 1977; and a visit with him to Rabbit Chutes, August 5, 1977. For information on the decline of the beaver in Northern Ontario and Quebec in the late 1920s see Grey Owl, *Pilgrims of the Wild* (Toronto: Macmillan, 1935) 47–48.

[7]John J. Rowlands, *Cache Lake Country* (New York: W.W. Norton, 1947) 211, 220.

[8]"Long Lance in Thrilling Movie," unidentified clipping, LL scrapbook, donated by Joe Bradshaw, GLENBOW; interview with Douglas Burden, Charlotte, Vermont, May 4, 1977.

[9]For details on the film and those who made it see the film's program, *How The Silent Enemy Was Made*, souvenir edition. The theme of the movie is outlined in Betty Shannon's article "The Silent Enemy," *Moving Picture Stories* 12 Aug. 1930: 10–11, 25–26.

[10]Interview with George McDougall, Cochrane, Ontario, May 11, 1977; interview with Douglas Burden, Charlotte, Vermont, May 4–5, 1977; Barbara Johnson, "Maine Indian Princess of Many Talents Wins Fame in Motion Pictures," *Portland Telegram* (Maine) 8 June 1930; Bunny McBride, *Molly Spotted Elk: A Penobscot in Paris* (Norman: University of Oklahoma Press, 1995).

[11]The sketch of Chauncey Yellow Robe is taken from three sources: his obituary in *NYT* 8 Apr. 1930; his article in *How The Silent Enemy Was Made*, 4, 17; Mildred Fielder, "Chauncey Yellow Robe, Bridge Between Two Cultures," *Sioux Indian Leaders* (Seattle: Superior Publishing Company, 1975).

[12]William Chanler, an expert archer, shot the arrows, but Douglas Burden was actually the one who killed the animal with a high-powered rifle. Interview with Ted Hennessy, North Bay, Ontario, December 12, 1976. Long

Lance mentions the slashes in his letter to Bonner Fellers, dated Rabbit Chutes, Temagami, January 27, 1929, HOOVER.

[13]LL to SHM, dated Rabbit Chutes, Temagami, January 24, 1929.

[14]LL to Bonner Fellers, dated Rabbit Chutes, Temagami, January 27, 1929, HOOVER.

[15]Brownlow, *The War*, 556.

[16]Interview with Douglas Burden, Charlotte, Vermont, May 4, 1977; Douglas Burden, "Autobiography: 'The Silent Enemy,'" manuscript shown to me May 4, 1977, Charlotte, Vermont; interview (by telephone) with S.C. Burden, Los Angeles, July 14, 1978; interview with Ted Hennessy, North Bay, Ontario, December 22, 1976.

[17]Interview with Agnes Belaney Lalonde, Temagami, Ontario, May 12, 1977.

[18]Grey Owl, *Men of the Last Frontier* (Toronto: Macmillan, 1972; first published in 1931) 210.

[19]LL to SHM, dated Rabbit Chutes, Temagami, December 24, 1928.

[20]Interview with Odell Clanton, Winston–Salem, January 7, 1977.

[21]Ted Hennessy to DBS, May 19, 1981. Long Lance did not kill it. Off-camera the moose was shot with the rifle—although it looks in the cleverly spliced film as if Long Lance killed it with his spear.

[22]County of Los Angeles, County Clerk's Office, Archives, Probate of Will, No. 126691, Longlance.

[23]The description of the funeral pyre sequence appears in *How the Silent Enemy Was Made*, souvenir edition, 7.

[24]Chauncey Yellow Robe quoted in Fielder, *Sioux Indian Leaders*, 118.

[25]William Chanler to Ilia Tolstoy, dated New York, March 26, 1930, CHANLER INVESTIGATION. Chanler mentions that Yellow Robe had told him that Long Lance "does not know the sign language as well as he pretends."

[26]Interview with Mike Eagle Speaker, Stirling, Alberta, January 16, 1976. He recalls that the Indians at Fort Macleod's Jubilee in 1924 were interested in watching Long Lance dance because he danced so "differently" from them.

[27]"Another Place for Burke," NYT 14 Mar. 1929: 17.

[28]Fielder, *Sioux Indian Leaders*, 124, mentions that he returned to Rapid City briefly in 1929.

[29]*How The Silent Enemy Was Made*, 5.

[30]Chauncey Yellow Robe quoted in *How The Silent Enemy Was Made*, 2.

[31]"Indians as Linguists," *Variety* 11 June 1930.

[32]"Society to Attend Indian Epic," *New York World* 19 May 1930. General Verbeck to LL, telegram, dated Manlius, May 19, 1930, in LL scrapbook, donated by Joe Bradshaw, GLENBOW; LL to W.M. Graham, dated New York, November 8, 1929; Anne Morgan to LL, dated New York, May 12, 1930, GLENBOW; LL to Vilhjalmur Stefansson, dated New York, May 24, 1930, DARTMOUTH.

[33]Robert E. Sherwood, "Motion Picture Album," *New York Post* 17 May 1930; *Time* 26 May 1930; *New Republic* 4 June 1930: 73; *Wall Street Journal* 20 May 1930.

[34]Irene Thirer, "'Silent Enemy,' Realistic Indian Epic," *Daily News* 19 May 1930; Regina Crewe, "'The Silent Enemy' Indian Epic Movie, Of Much Interest," *New York American* 20 May 1930, second section, 15; "The Silent Enemy," *Variety* 21 May 1930.

[35]For details on Grant's life see Fairfield Osborn, "Madison Grant (1865–1937)," *Dictionary of American Biography*, vol. 22, supplement 2 (New York: Charles Scribner's Sons, 1958) 256; and Thomas F. Gossett, *Race: The History of an Idea in America* (Dallas: Southern Methodist University Press, 1963) 353–64, 389–90, 396–98.

[36]Interview with Douglas Burden, Charlotte, Vermont, May 4, 1977.

[37]Gunnar Myrdal, *An American Dilemma: The Negro Problem and Modern Democracy* 2 vols. (New York: Harper and Row, 1962; first published in 1944) vol. 1, 114.

[38]Madison Grant, *The Conquest of a Continent* (New York: Charles Scribner's, 1933) 37, 285, 288.

[39]Grant's letter is printed in *How The Silent Enemy Was Made*, 5.

[40]Robert E. Sherwood, "Motion Picture Album," *New York Post* 17 May 1930.

[41]Brownlow, *The War*, 559–60.

[42]Kevin Brownlow in "The Silent Enemy: An Epic of the American Indian," *Blackhawk Films. Bulletin B-264* June 1975: 2.

CHAPTER FIFTEEN: THE TRAIL NARROWS

[1]Wilfrid Eggleston, "Fastened Sleds under Canoe in Mushing through Slush," *Toronto Star Weekly* 4 May 1929.

[2]Interview with Douglas Burden, Charlotte, Vermont, May 4–5, 1977.

[3]HM to LL, dated St. Paul's School, Blood Reserve, February 18, 1928.

[4]Long Lance quoted in *JWT Co. News Letter* 11, 33 (15 Apr. 1929): 1; Cynthia G. Swank, archivist, J. Walter Thompson Company, to DBS, dated June 13, 1980. She listed the publications in which the ads appeared.

[5]"Long Lance Frequent Visitor to NY Office," *JWT Co. News Letter* 11, 48 (March 1930): 2. Roland Cole, "Consumer's Suggestion Is Adopted as New Design for Product," *Printers' Ink* (29 Aug. 1929): 79–80.

[6]Gene Schoor, *The Jim Thorpe Story* (New York: Pocket Books, 1967; first published 1951) 160–64. See also Joseph D'O'Brian, "The Greatest Athlete in the World," *American Heritage* (July–August 1992): 99–100. Two of Thorpe's letters to Long Lance (in which he mentions his financial problems) are held in the U.S. Army Military History Research Collection, Carlisle, Pennsylvania. After Long Lance's death they were donated to the museum by his friend Clyde Fisher. The first letter is dated Las Vegas, Nevada, December 30, 1929, and the second, Hawthorne, California, January 3, 1930.

[7]Federal Writers' Project, *New York City Guide* (New York: Random House, 1976; first published 1939) 321.

[8]William Tomkins, *Universal American Indian Sign Language* (San Diego: Published by William Tomkins, 1970; first edition 1926). Seton's "Sign Talk," with about 1700 signs, appeared in 1918. See Tomkins, *Universal,* 7.

[9]LL, "West Point's Predicament. Why are there more than two hundred vacancies in its Corps of Cadets?" *Century* 117 (January 1929): 375–83.

[10]Interview (by telephone) with Dorothy Fellers, Washington, DC, May 26, 1977; Dorothy Fellers to DBS, August 12, 1980.

[11]*About the Explorers,* a recent booklet (eight pages long) which contains a short sketch of the club today and its past history (available from the club headquarters, 46 East 70 Street, New York, NY 10021). The price of the rooms is mentioned in the *Explorers Journal* 9, 3 (1930): 67.

[12]"Clyde Fisher," *Explorers Journal* 27 (1949): 29–30. Fisher's visit to, and his induction into, the Sioux nation is mentioned in *Explorers Journal* 6, 3 (1927): 13.

[13]On Seumas see "Chief Seumas is Dead," *NYT* 28 Mar. 1961; "Clan Chief's Death Sparks Will Dispute," *New York Post* 8 Sept. 1961; also "Descendant of Royal Scots Dwells in NY," *Brooklyn Daily Eagle* 13 Dec. 1931. My thanks to Marie E. Roy, executive secretary of the Explorers Club, for kindly allowing me to see Seumas's entrance form to the Explorers Club, dated 1921.

[14]Sergius Martin Riis, "In Memory: Seumas, the Chief of Clannfhearghuis of Stra-chur, C.M. etc.," *Explorers Journal* 39, 2 (1961): 50.

[15]Clyde Fisher's letter is dated October 2, 1929, and E.W. Deming's, September 28, 1929. My thanks to Marie Roy for allowing me to examine Long Lance's file at the Explorers Club. E.W. Deming quoted in "High

Ideals of American Indian Win Esteem of Author-Painter," *Christian Science Monitor* 20 Mar. 1931 (his comment on the Blackfoot). Clark Wissler quoted in Therese O. Deming, *E.W. Deming: His Work* (n.p.: T.O. Deming, 1925) 31.

[16]*Explorers Journal* 8, 3 (1929): 72. Minutes of the Membership Committee, October 11, 1929, Explorers Club.

[17]Federal Writers' Project, *New York City Guide*, 257, 266.

[18]For information on Hodge's life see Cole Fay-Cooper, "Frederick Webb Hodge, 1864–1956," *American Anthropologist* n.s. 59 (1957): 517–20. Lee Ash, who worked in the Explorers Club Library in 1929 and in the early 1930s, recalls that Dr. Hodge "always said good things about Long Lance." A short biography of George Heye appears in *Who Was Who in America*, vol. 3, 1951–1960 (Chicago: Marquis, 1960) 397. Long Lance claimed in a letter to Canon Middleton (January 10, 1930) that George Hyde wanted him "to teach him a little of the sign language." Clark Wissler's life is summarized in George Peter Murdoch's "Clark Wissler, 1870–1947," in the *American Anthropologist* n.s. 50 (1948): 292–304; and in George W. Stocking, Jr., "Clark Wissler," *Dictionary of American Biography*, supplement 4, 1946–1950 (New York: Charles Scribner's Sons, 1974) 906–9. Clyde Fisher's widow, Te Ata, showed me Long Lance's copy of *The American Indian* with the inscription, "With the compliments of Clark Wissler to Buffalo Child Long Lance." At the bottom Dr. Fisher wrote, "To Chief Buffalo Child Long Lance in appreciation of his writing *Long Lance*, Clyde Fisher, American Museum of Natural History, Sept. 12, 1929." She showed the book to me in Oklahoma City, March 13, 1976.

[19]Clyde Fisher mentioned that Dr. Wissler had read the book and noted Wissler's comment on it in his review of *Long Lance* in the *Explorers Journal* 8, 3 (1929): 74.

[20]As historian Ralph K. Andrist has written of Clark Wissler in his introduction to a re-edition of Wissler's *Red Man Reservations* (New York: Collier Books, 1971) viii: " . . . he was a fairer, more detached observer of the scene than most of his contemporaries. He saw Indians as human beings, in a time when far too many people still looked on them as little better than vermin."

[21]Jim Thorpe quoted in Schoor, *Thorpe*, 6; Etha Lawrence, "Mrs. Iva Thorpe Has Lived a Very Picturesque Life," *The American Indian* November 1926: 4; John C. Ewers, *The Blackfeet* (Norman: University of Oklahoma Press, 1958) 326; Hugh A. Dempsey, "Black White Man," *Alberta Historical Review* 6, 3 (1958): 7–11.

[22]Kathleen Jamieson, *Indian Women and the Law in Canada: Citizens Minus* (Ottawa: Ministry of Supply and Services, 1978).

[23]Frederick Lewis Allen, *Only Yesterday: An Informal History of the Nineteen–Twenties* (New York: Harper and Row, 1964; first published in 1931) 266–81.

[24]Circular advertising Chief Buffalo Child Long Lance's talk "An Indian's Story of his People," American Museum of Natural History, November 21, 1929, in LL scrapbook, donated by Joe Bradshaw, GLENBOW. *Explorers Journal* 8, 4 (1929): 97.

[25]"Fannie Hurst," *NYT* 24 Feb. 1968: 1, 29; Fannie Hurst to LL, December 30, 1929, GLENBOW.

[26]LL to SHM, dated New York, January 10, 1930.

[27]LL to Howard Kelly, dated New York, June 8, 1928; LL to Bonner and Dorothy Fellers, dated New York, October 5, 1929, HOOVER. On W.R. Edrington, see *Who Was Who in America*, vol. 1, 1897–1942 (Chicago: Marquis Who's Who, 1966) 359.

[28]LL to Carl Van Vechten, letter postmarked November 30, 1929, in Carl Van Vechten Papers, Beinecke Rare Book and Manuscript Library, Yale University, New Haven, Connecticut. Bruce Kellner, *Carl Van Vechten and the Irreverent Decades* (Norman: University of Oklahoma Press, 1968) 200.

[29]"Walter Winchell on Broadway," *New York Daily Mirror* 24 Dec. 1929 16. For background on Winchell see Neal Gabler, "Walter Winchell," *American Heritage* (November 1994): 97–105.

[30]Mrs. Domenica Pallister to DBS, dated New York, July 4, 1977. Mrs. Pallister's father was a close friend of Seumas's, and she served as his secretary in the 1940s and 1950s.

[31]Eleanor Ruggles, *The West-Going Heart: A Life of Vachel Lindsay* (New York: W.W. Norton, 1959) 398–99.

[32]Katharine Hale, "About Canadian Writers, Chief Buffalo Child Long Lance," *The Canadian Countryman* 14 June 1930: 8, 15. For a sketch of Katharine Hale's life see Lotta Dempsey, "Katharine Hale," in *Leading Canadian Poets*, ed. W.P. Percival (Toronto: The Ryerson Press, 1948) 79–87.

[33]The evening is described in *Poetry: A Magazine of Verse* 36, 1 (1930): 53. The quote is taken from the reference to Long Lance's contribution. The description of the Biltmore's ballroom is taken from the article "Open Big Biltmore on New Year's Eve," *NYT* 26 Dec. 1913; and from the pamphlet *The Biltmore* forwarded to me by Edwin Scalabrino, general manager, April 1, 1980.

[34]"The Death Song of Long Lance" printed in *Scholastic* 22, 1 (4 Feb. 1933): 11.

CHAPTER SIXTEEN: "HELLO, SYLVESTER"

[1]William Chanler to SHM, February 6, 1930, CHANLER INVESTI-
GATION.

[2]*NYT* 5 Feb. 1930. Lindbergh's birthday on the fourth was reported on
the fifth.

[3]"Yellow Robe called on me about three months ago and told me that
he had just discovered that Long Lance was not a Blackfoot and that he
understood he was really a negro." William Chanler to Ilia Tolstoy, dated
March 26, 1930, CHANLER INVESTIGATION.

[4]Interviews with William Chanler by telephone, New York, May 22,
May 25–26, 1977; William Chanler to Ilia Tolstoy, dated March 26, 1930,
CHANLER INVESTIGATION.

[5]William Chanler to the Commissioner of Indian Affairs, February 14,
1930, CHANLER INVESTIGATION.

[6]William Chanler to Ilia Tolstoy, dated March 26, 1930, CHANLER
INVESTIGATION.

[7]William Chanler to the Commissioner of Indian Affairs, February 14,
1930, CHANLER INVESTIGATION.

[8]Interview with William Chanler, New York, May 26, 1977. William
Chanler to Mr. Campbell, Blackfoot Indian Agency, Browning, Montana,
February 14, 1930, CHANLER INVESTIGATION.

[9]James Mooney, "Croatan Indians," *Handbook of American Indians
North of Mexico*, ed. Frederick Webb Hodge, 2 vols. (Washington, DC: Government Printing Office, 1907) 1: 365.

[10]William Chanler to Ilia Tolstoy, March 26, 1930, CHANLER
INVESTIGATION; "Jules S. Brulatour Dies in Hospital, 75," *NYT* 27 Oct.
1946: 62.

[11]SHM to William Chanler, March 3, 1930, CHANLER INVESTI-
GATION.

[12]William Chanler to Ilia Tolstoy, March 26, 1930, CHANLER
INVESTIGATION .

[13]Earl Parker Hanson to DBS, April 13, 1976, enclosing an excerpt from
chapter nine of his projected autobiography. In the late 1920s and early 1930s
Mr. Hanson was acting executive secretary of the Explorers Club. He heard
this story about Cobb from E.W. Deming's eldest daughter.

[14]Mrs. Domenica Pallister to DBS, August 5, 1977.

[15]I have no documentary proof that Long Lance actually confessed to
Yellow Robe. Some reconciliation, though, must have taken place as Yellow
Robe acquiesced in the decision to send Long Lance on the Hollywood trip.

See Chauncey Yellow Robe to William Chanler, dated March 31, 1930 (in the "Chauncey Yellow Robe" file, Winthrop, Stimson, Putnam and Roberts, 40 Wall Street, New York City). After Yellow Robe's death Long Lance mailed his letter to Rosebud Yellow Robe on April 23, 1930 (who kindly sent me a copy, which is now in GLENBOW). I learned that Long Lance offered to pay for Evelyn Yellow Robe's education in a letter from her, November 17, 1976.

[16]LL to Alice Tye, dated New York, April 24, 1930; Paul Senn, *The Lawless Decade* (New York: Bonanza Books, 1957) 136.

[17]LL to SHM, dated New York, April 23, 1930; LL to Alice Tye, dated New York, April 24, 1930.

[18]Lee Shippey, "The Lee Side o' L.A." *Los Angeles Times* 27 Mar. 1930.

[19]Anita Baldwin signed the sheet music for *My Blossom Bride (Hopi Indian Love Song). Text and Music by Anita Baldwin (Composer of "Omar — The Tentmaker") from The Romantic Play of the Southwest "His Blossom Bride" by Richard Walton Tully*. This is now in GLENBOW. The inscription reads, "For Chief Long Lance from Anita M. Baldwin, March 22 '30." The physical description of Anita Baldwin is from her passport issued January 22, 1926, Anita M. Baldwin Collection, Box 1, Huntington Library, San Marino, California.

[20]Details on Ilia Tolstoy's life are taken from his obituary in the *NYT* 30 Oct. 1970; a memorial address given at the Explorers Club; and his application for membership in the club, dated April 29, 1931. My thanks to Marie Roy of the Explorers Club for copies of these last two items.

[21]My thanks to Tom Flanagan of Calgary for the description of North Carolina in April.

[22]"Camels of Winston–Salem," *Fortune* 3, 1 (January 1931): 45, 48, 54.

[23]Ilia Tolstoy's report to William Chanler, April 14, 1930, CHANLER INVESTIGATION. The information on the Longs' home on Brookstown Avenue is taken from Abe's diaries, entries for August 28, 1946; March 11, 1959; April 15, 1959; September 1, 1959; November 17, 1964; March 9, 1965.

[24]Circular distributed by Abe Long, Carolina Theater, apparently prepared about 1930, in the volume of his diary for the years 1937–46.

[25]For a short biography of Latham, see "R.H. Latham, Educator, Dies at 67," *Winston–Salem Journal* 3 Apr. 1948.

[26]Ilia wrote in his report that his name was John Weston, but he heard the name incorrectly. On Joe Long's death certificate, Walter Long lists his father's parents as John Vestal and Mary Long. Standard Certificate of Death, Forsyth County Court House, Winston–Salem, NC, November 14, 1932.

[27]From 1913 to 1953 the North Carolina State Legislature redesignated

the "Croatans" as "Cherokees." Finally, in 1953, the Legislature changed their name to "Lumbees." Brewton Berry, *Almost White* (Toronto: Collier-Macmillan, 1969; first published 1963) 156.

[28]"Colonel William Allen Blair," in *North Carolina: The Old North State and the New*, vol. 3 (Chicago: The Lewis Publishing Company, 1941) 49–51; "Animate and Inanimate," *Winston–Salem Journal* 12 Aug. 1909: 6.

[29]"Pushkin . . . Negro according to American standards, i.e. has ancestor with mixture of Negro blood." M.N. Work, *A Bibliography of the Negro in Africa and America* (New York: H.W. Wilson, 1928) 456.

[30]William Blair's affidavit, dated April 9, 1930, CHANLER INVESTIGATION.

[31]Karen Blu, *The Lumbee Problem: The Making of an American Indian People* (Cambridge University Press, 1980) 67. People from groups similar to the Lumbee in North and South Carolina had been moving there since at least the early 1800s.

[32]Arlene Edwards, "First Poindexter Arrived 200 Years Ago. Man Married Granddaughter of Indian Chief," *Winston–Salem Journal* 11 Aug. 1975.

[33]Edith Bolling Wilson, *My Memoir* (Indianapolis: Bobbs-Merrill Company, 1938) 230. Concerning Charles Curtis's Indian background, see footnote 30, chapter 13.

[34]Colonel William A. Blair to SHM, dated Winston–Salem, January 27, 1934. Letter in the possession of Mrs. Sophie Middleton Allison, Fort Macleod, Alberta; copy in GLENBOW.

[35]Colonel William A. Blair to SHM, dated Winston–Salem, December 19, 1933, letter in the possession of Mrs. Sophie Middleton Allison, Fort Macleod, Alberta; copy in GLENBOW.

[36]William Chanler to Ilia Tolstoy, April 17, 1930; to R.H. Latham, April 17, 1930; to William A. Blair, April 17, 1930, CHANLER INVESTIGATION.

[37]They were married on March 27, 1879. New Court House, Statesville, Iredell County, NC.

[38]This last word, *Hanka-wanzi*, is his highest compliment. In his article on "The Secret of the Sioux," *Hearst's International-Cosmopolitan* June 1927: 41, he wrote of the *Weh-hunka-wanzi*, or blood-brother relationship: "When an Indian declares another man his *Weh-hunka-wanzi* it brings that man closer to him than his own consanguineous brother. On reaching manhood every Indian forms a 'blood brother' relationship with some particular member of his tribe whom he likes more than anyone else, and there can be no secrets between himself and this person. In battle and in peace they are Damon and Pythias for the rest of their mortal lives, and no one can come between them."

Netawa simply means "your" in Sioux (Dakota). Long Lance then would translate *Netawa Hanka-wanzi* as "your blood brother."

CHAPTER SEVENTEEN: THE LADY OF THE PEACOCKS

[1]LL to Alice Tye, dated New York, July 17, 1930.

[2]*Liberty* 20 Sept. 1930; Rose Reilly, "Long Lance, Chief of Heart-Breakers," *Screenland* October 1930: 114.

[3]"A Reporter meets Long Lance, Chief of the Blackfoot Indians, Writer, Actor, Explorer, a Modern Version of the American Tradition," *The Great Outdoors* August 1930.

[4]"Has Great Faith in Medicine Man," *NYT* 3 Oct. 1930.

[5]Dan Arapaho, student file, R.G. 75, Office of Indian Affairs, Carlisle Student Record, file 1325, National Archives, Washington, DC. LL to Emma Newashe McAllister, dated New York, July 13, 1930. Ramona Loman, daughter of Emma Newashe McAllister, kindly allowed me to make copies of her mother's letters from and about Long Lance. These are now in GLENBOW.

[6]Interview with Te Ata, Oklahoma City, March 13, 1976.

[7]Interview with Lee Ash, Edmonton, March 4, 1976.

[8]Mrs. Domenica Pallister to DBS, July 4, 1977.

[9]"Indian is Entered in Air Race Jump," *Trenton Evening Times* 16 Oct. 1930. "Indian Takes Course at Roosevelt Field," *Bridgehampton News* (NY) 10 Oct. 1930.

[10]"Jersey Guard Wins Roebling Air Race Prize," *Trenton Times-Advertiser* 19 Oct. 1930.

[11]"Indian Loops on First Solo Hop," *New York Sun* 29 Oct. 1930: 13.

[12]Interview with Te Ata, Oklahoma City, March 13, 1976. C.R. Roseberry, *The Challenging Skies: The Colorful Story of Aviation's Most Exciting Years, 1919–1939* (Garden City, NY: Doubleday, 1966) 244. "Buck and Woman Flier Set New Coast-to-Coast Records," *Trenton Sunday Times-Advertiser* 19 Oct. 1930.

[13]LL to Mike Eagle Speaker, sent from Roosevelt Field, no date (probably sent in March 1931); LL to Isabel Fellers Bush, dated Roosevelt Field, December 18, 1930 (a copy of the letter is in GLENBOW, supplied by Dorothy Fellers).

[14]Abe Long's diary, entries for January 11, July 26, November 3, 15, 23, 26, 1930 (about his parents' illnesses). On January 10, 1931, he recorded that Walter had left for New York on December 31 and had just returned that day.

[15]LL to Abe Long, dated "Tuesday" (January 5, 1931).

[16]The amounts sent home are listed in Abe Long's ledger, 1928–32, in

the possession of Lillian Doulin, Mocksville, NC. Long Lance's letter to Abe also is in Mrs. Doulin's possession; a copy of it and the ledger book are in GLENBOW.

[17]*New Hyde Park Herald* (NY) 16 Jan. 1931. "Labor Secretary to Speak at National Board Luncheon Next Saturday," unidentified clipping, LL scrapbook, donated by Joe Bradshaw, GLENBOW; "Doak Hails Movies as Force for Good," *NYT* 25 Jan. 1931: 19.

[18]Copy of a letter from Anita Baldwin to Susie B. Curtis, dated Santa Anita, California, May 10, 1932, enclosed in a letter from Susie B. Curtis to SHM, no date (probably late May 1932). This letter from Anita Baldwin is hereafter cited as BALDWIN LETTER. Copies of all of the correspondence between Susie B. Curtis and Canon Middleton are in GLENBOW. Statement of Anita Baldwin, dated March 23, 1932, read at the "Coroner's Inquest into death of Sylvester Long (also known as Sylvester Long Lance)," March 24, 1932, State of California, County of Los Angeles, no. 40150 (hereafter cited as BALDWIN STATEMENT).

[19]*New York Daily News* 14 May 1931; LL to Alice Tye, dated The Santa Fe Chief en route to California, May 19, 1931.

[20]Susie B. Curtis to SHM, dated Elmira, NY, May 8, 1932; Susie B. Curtis to SHM, no date (probably late May 1932).

[21]The information on Anoakia is taken from several sources: interview with Lowry McCaslin, Arcadia, October 16, 1980. Mr. McCaslin was Anita Baldwin's business manager in the early 1930s. Interview (by telephone) with Raymond Knisley, Logandale, Nevada, October 26, 1980. Mr. Knisley was the manager of Anita Baldwin's ranches in the early 1930s. Lavinia Griffin Graham, "Peacock used as Motif of Home of Mrs. M'Claughry," *Los Angeles Examiner* 30 June 1913. Anon., "Unique Among Homes of America's Rich," *Los Angeles Times* 21 Sept. 1913. The Editor, "The Building up of an Ideal California Ranch," *Outwest* May–June 1914. Porter Garnett, "Anoakia: Stately Homes of California," *Sunset: The Pacific Monthly* January 1914: 145–48. C.B. Glasscock, *Lucky Baldwin: The Story of an Unconventional Success* (Indianapolis: Bobbs-Merrill Company, 1933) 221. The value of Anoakia is given on a note in Box 1, Anita M. Baldwin Collection, Huntington Library, San Marino, California.

[22]"Tour Guide of Anoakia," prepared by Russell Chandler in 1976, 14. My thanks to Lowry McCaslin for giving me a tour of Anoakia, October 16, 1980.

[23]Edward B. Scott, "Tallac," *The Saga of Lake Tahoe* (Crystal Bay, Lake Tahoe, Nevada: Sierra-Tahoe Publishing Co., 1957) 151–65. Interview (by

telephone) with Raymond Knisley, Logandale, Nevada, October 26, 1980.

[24]Notes of an interview with Ralph Tweedle, Sierra Madre, California, May 26, 1976, conducted by Lucette Fogwill, volunteer, History Section, Los Angeles State and County Arboretum, Arcadia, California (hereafter cited as LASCA). Ralph Tweedle was a guard at Anoakia and Anita's home at Tallac from January 11, 1931, to February 28, 1933. The interview is in the Archives, LASCA.

[25]Glasscock, *Lucky Baldwin*, 15, 74, 100, 115, 206, 305.

[26]Glasscock, *Lucky Baldwin*, 221.

[27]Glasscock, *Lucky Baldwin*, 136.

[28]Sandra Lee Snider, "Elias 'Lucky' Baldwin: Southern California Rancher and Town Builder, 1875–1909," M.A. thesis, California State University, Los Angeles, 1979, 31–32.

[29]"A Millionaire's Third Marriage," *NYT* 1 June 1884: 4. "Mrs. Lily Howard Coast," *NYT* 10 Nov. 1938: 27. Genealogy of Anita Baldwin, Anita M. Baldwin Collection, Box 2, Huntington Library, San Marino, California.

[30]"Divorced in Twelve Hours," *NYT* 8 Oct. 1900: 1. "Anita Baldwin, Heiress of 'Lucky'," *NYT* 26 Oct. 1939: 23. For a short biography of Anita Baldwin see John Steven McGroarty, *The California Plutarch* 2 vols. (Los Angeles: J.R. Finnell, 1938) 2: 241–45.

[31]"Denial by Mrs. McClaughrey," *NYT* 6 May 1914: 5. "Dogs More Constant than Men Says Anita Baldwin," *San Francisco Chronicle* 27 Apr. 1916.

[32]Anita M. Baldwin to C.L. Lowman, Letterman Hospital, San Francisco, May 23, 1919, LASCA. Interview with Sandy Snider, historian, LASCA, October 17, 1980. As the arboretum is located on Lucky Baldwin's old Rancho Santa Anita, LASCA has collected a considerable amount of material on the history of the Baldwin family. Her comments on Long Lance appear in her statement dated March 23, 1932, BALDWIN STATEMENT; and her letter to Susie B. Curtis, written May 10, 1932, BALDWIN LETTER.

[33]Anita M. Baldwin Collection, LASCA. See Anita's letters to her son April 4, May 20 and December 16, 1930; the undated letter written in the spring of 1931; and the letter of July 6, 1931.

[34]Notes of an interview with Ralph Tweedle, May 26, 1976, LASCA. Anita Baldwin's letter to Baldwin, April 7, 1931, provides a good example of her fear of communists. "She'll Devote Life to Music," *Los Angeles Examiner* 23 Dec. 1929.

[35]Notes of an interview with Ralph Tweedle, May 26, 1976, LASCA.

[36]Passport Application (Form for Native Citizen). Edition of 1930, United States of America, State of California, County of San Francisco. The fol-

lowing quotations are all taken from the passport application and its supporting documents.

[37]LL to Emma Newashe McAllister, undated letter from Tallac, probably mailed in early June; and his second letter from Tallac, dated June 28, 1931.

[38]Elizabeth Analla to Rosebud Yellow Robe, dated Wagner, South Dakota, December 27, 1932; copy in GLENBOW.

[39]LL to Emma Newashe McAllister, dated Tallac, June 28, 1931; Anita Baldwin to Susie B. Curtis, May 12, 1932, BALDWIN LETTER. Anita Baldwin to Baldwin M. Baldwin, postmarked March 7, 1931, LASCA.

[40]Interview with Lowry McCaslin, Arcadia, October 16, 1980; the itinerary of the trip enclosed in a letter from Anita Baldwin to Baldwin M. Baldwin, early 1930, LASCA; LL to Alice Tye, dated Chicago–California, December 10, 1931.

[41]"Young Baldwin Goes to Work," *Hollywood Citizen* 28 Aug. 1930, clipping in LASCA. "Baldwin's Grandson Succumbs," *Arcadia Tribune* 27 Sept. 1970, clipping in LASCA.

[42]Wilfrid Eggleston, "Fastened Sleds under Canoe in Mushing through Slush," *Toronto Star Weekly* 4 May 1929.

[43]The itinerary of the trip enclosed in a letter from Anita Baldwin to Baldwin M. Baldwin, early 1930, LASCA; LL to Alice Tye, dated Chicago–California, December 10, 1931.

[44]John Toland, *Adolf Hitler* (New York: Ballantine Books, 1976) 329; *NYT* 18 June 1931: 5.

[45]Statement of Anita Baldwin, March 23, 1932, BALDWIN STATEMENT. Anita Baldwin to Susie B. Curtis, May 10, 1932, BALDWIN LETTER.

[46]Interview with Lowry McCaslin, Arcadia, October 16, 1980.

[47]Anita Baldwin to Susie B. Curtis, May 10, 1932, BALDWIN LETTER.

[48]"NY Society Girl Weds Japanese," *New York Sunday News* 6 Mar. 1932. "NY Society Girl, Forced to Leave U.S. for Wedding Japanese, Arrives Here," the *Japan Times and Mail* (Tokyo) 20 June 1932. "Japanese–American Couple Here Describe Their Romance and Troubles in New York," the *Japan Advertiser* (Tokyo), 19 June 1932. Interview (by telephone) with Elisabeth Randolph Clapp, York Village, Maine, October 19, 1980.

[49]Bessie Randolph Clapp Hayakawa to Lilly Sahlen, dated Osaka, Japan, September 23, 1932; copies of this correspondence in GLENBOW. As Elisabeth used the name "Bessie" in her letters to Lilly, this is the form followed in the text.

[50]Her uncle was C.E. Clapp. Through his obituary in the *NYT* 4 Jan. 1957, I was able to locate his widow in Virginia. (Anne Robinson, Research Librarian of the University of Virginia, Charlottesville, helped me locate her.) Mrs. C.E.

Clapp wrote back with the address of Bessie's stepmother, Mrs. Harold Clapp, in Oregon, who put me in touch with Bessie, then (1980) living in Maine.

[51]Philip B. McDonald, "Henry Clay Frick," *Dictionary of American Biography* vol. 7 (New York: Charles Scribner's, 1931) 29–31; and Oliver Jensen, "Essay: Filial Piety and the First Amendment," *American Heritage* 18, 6 (October 1967): 2–4.

[52]Bessie Randolph Clapp Hayakawa quoted in the *Japan Times and Mail* 20 June 1932.

[53]Bessie Randolph Clapp Hayakawa to Lilly Sahlen, dated Osaka, September 23, 1932.

[54]"Mary Rennels Says," *Cleveland Press* 16 Oct. 1928, second section, 25. LL to Mike Eagle Speaker dated New York, May 26, 1930; copies of Long Lance's letters to Mike Eagle Speaker in GLENBOW.

[55]Bessie Randolph Clapp Hayakawa to Lilly Sahlen, dated Osaka, September 23, 1932.

[56]Anita Baldwin to Susie B. Curtis, May 10, 1932, BALDWIN LETTER.

CHAPTER EIGHTEEN: THE TRAIL ENDS

[1]Susie B. Curtis to SHM, dated Elmira, NY, April 17, 1932.

[2]Louis Schellbach, assistant secretary, Explorers Club, to the Commissioner of the BIA, dated New York, December 7, 1931. Office of Indian Affairs Records, R.G. 75, file no. 1364–1925, 130 General Service, National Archives, Washington, DC.

[3]LL to Alice Tye, dated The Santa Fe Chief en route to California, May 19, 1931.

[4]Anita Baldwin to Baldwin M. Baldwin, postmarked December 28, 1931, Santa Anita, LASCA.

[5]"Mrs. Baldwin Quitting U.S.; Raps Regime," *Los Angeles Examiner* 5 Aug. 1932: section one, 3; interview with Lowry McCaslin, Arcadia, October 16, 1980.

[6]Statement of Anita Baldwin, March 23, 1932, BALDWIN STATEMENT. "Indian Chief Suicide on Eve of Air Survey," *Los Angeles Examiner* 22 Mar. 1932.

[7]Interview (by telephone) with Raymond Knisley, Logandale, Nevada, October 26, 1980.

[8]Iron Eyes Cody quoted in Kevin Brownlow, *The War, the West and the Wilderness* (New York: Alfred A. Knopf, 1979) 553. For a biographical sketch of Cody see Bill Richards, "A Couple of Old Timers' Slings and Arrows for the New Westerns," *Washington Post* 6 July 1976: B1, B6. "Iron Eyes Cody, Indian,

94, best known for a single tear. Starred in 100 Films," *National Post* 8 Jan. 1999.

[9]Anita Baldwin to Susie B. Curtis, May 10, 1932, BALDWIN LETTER.

[10]A copy of a letter sent by J.H. Williams, night clerk of the Glendale Hotel, to Susie B. Curtis, dated May 12, 1932, enclosed in letter of Susie B. Curtis to SHM, dated Elmira, NY, and probably sent in late May (hereafter cited as WILLIAMS LETTER).

[11]Notes of an interview with Ralph Tweedle, May 26, 1976, LASCA.

[12]Bessie Randolph Clapp Hayakawa to Lilly Sahlen, dated Osaka, September 23, 1932.

[13]G.C. Harrington to Edgar K. Miller, dated Los Angeles, April 15, 1932, DISCOVERY FILE. Harrington was an employee of Anita Baldwin. He reported to Edgar Miller at the Hopi Reservation in Arizona the "further information" that they had obtained about Long Lance's activities (immediately before the evening of March 19). The weather for March 19 is reported in the *Los Angeles Times* 19 Mar. 1932.

[14]J.H. Williams to Susie B. Curtis, dated May 12, 1932, WILLIAMS LETTER.

[15]Testimony of Joseph Hanna given at the "Coroner's Inquest into death of Sylvester Long (also known as Sylvester Long Lance)," March 24, 1932, State of California, County of Los Angeles, no. 40150, p. 15. The subsequent information is taken from the minutes of the inquest.

[16]Statement of Anita Baldwin, March 23, 1932, BALDWIN STATEMENT.

[17]LL, *Long Lance* (New York: Cosmopolitan Book Corporation, 1928) 277.

[18]ibid., 268–69.

[19]ibid., 268.

[20]ibid., 271.

Epilogue

[1]J.H. Williams to Susie B. Curtis, dated May 12, 1932, WILLIAMS LETTER. Mrs. Elizabeth Analla to Rosebud Yellow Robe, dated Wagner, South Dakota, December 27, 1932.

[2]"Chief Long Lance Ends His Life in California," *NYT* 22 Mar. 1932 (Jim Thorpe quoted). The manager of the Glendale Airport told Susie Curtis that Long Lance "was happy in his work and every one liked him." Susie B. Curtis to SHM, dated Elmira, NY, May 8, 1932. SHM to Mrs. Edgar M. Hawkins, dated October 30, 1935. Irvin S. Cobb to Emma Newashe McAllister, dated New York, April 4, 1932.

[3]"Indian's Death Calls Inquest," *Los Angeles Times* 24 Mar. 1932.

[4]C.B. Glasscock, *Lucky Baldwin: The Story of an Unconventional Success* (Indianapolis: Bobbs-Merrill Company, 1933) 242. "Anita Baldwin Pays Half Town's Taxes," *San Francisco News* 2 Sept. 1932, clipping in LASCA. Statement of Anita Baldwin, March 23, 1932, BALDWIN STATEMENT.

[5]Testimony of Frank Gompert given at the "Coroner's Inquest," March 24, 1932, p. 10.

[6]Interview (by telephone) with Bessie Randolph Clapp Hayakawa, York Village, Maine, October 19, 1980.

[7]Anita Baldwin to Susie B. Curtis, May 10, 1932, BALDWIN LETTER. Interview with Odell Clanton, Winston–Salem, January 7, 1977. Interview with Charles Carson, Carson Town, August 11, 1975.

[8]Miller told Emma Newashe McAllister in a letter dated May 19, 1932, that he knew Mrs. Baldwin "very well," and "there is no finer or better woman." Edgar K. Miller to C.L. Ellis, Mission Agency, Riverside, California, dated Hopi Indian Agency, April 9, 1932, DISCOVERY FILE.

[9]Pinkerton report enclosed in letter of Edgar K. Miller to Superintendent Ellis, dated Hopi Agency, April 26, 1932, DISCOVERY FILE. Anita Baldwin told Susie B. Curtis that she "requested information" from the Pinkerton Agency. See Susie B. Curtis to SHM, no date, probably sent in late May 1932.

[10]The family's wish to bring the body back to Winston is mentioned in "Sylvester Long Dies a Suicide. Native of this City Found Dead at Santa Anita, CA Well Known," *Winston–Salem Journal* 25 Mar. 1932. In his diary Abe mentions that Walter left for Los Angeles on April 24, 1932, returning on May 16, 1932. Walter's statement disclaiming negro blood is mentioned in a letter from Susie Curtis to SHM, no date, (probably sent in late May 1932). She quotes from one of Anita Baldwin's letters to her: "This brother Walter denies negro blood but the Pinkertons', of whom I requested information gave me an entirely different story."

[11]Raymond Knisley to DBS, January 28, 1980.

[12]G.C. Harrington to Edgar K. Miller, dated April 15, 1932, DISCOVERY FILE.

[13]Frank A. Nance, coroner, Los Angeles County, to Emma Newashe McAllister, dated March 30, 1932. Interview with Roberta Forsberg, Whittier, California, January 10, 1976. Although she never met Long Lance, Miss Forsberg was very fond of his writings, and with her mother's help printed a number of his articles and testimonials from his friends. This beautifully produced book, *Redman Echoes* (1933), is very useful for any study of Long Lance. Miss Forsberg was just completing high school when she finished the book.

[14]Jim Thorpe thanked Long Lance for a loan of $100 in his letter January 3, 1930. Original in the U.S. Army Military History Research Collection, Carlisle, Pennsylvania. The gift of $100 to St. John's (Manlius) was acknowledged by Walter R. Stone, December 24, 1928, GLENBOW. The value of Long Lance's estate is mentioned in County of Los Angeles County Clerk's Office Archives, Probate of Will, no. 126691, Longlance.

[15]The County of Los Angeles County Clerk's Office Archives, Probate of Will, no. 126691, Longlance. This file contains the judgment in favor of St. Paul's School, May 18, 1933, as well as Joe Long's affidavit of heirship, dated April 18, 1932.

[16]"Death Claims Uncle Joe Long," *Winston–Salem Journal* 16 Nov. 1932. Adeline died, according to her death certificate in the New Court House, Statesville, Iredell County, NC, on February 8, 1932.

[17]"Walter L. Long, Widely Known Negro is Dead," *Winston–Salem Journal* 28 Mar. 1941: 4. A.A. Mayfield, "Activities of Colored People," *Winston–Salem Twin City Sentinel* 9 Feb. 1942.

[18]Abe Long diary, entry for August 24, 1938.

[19]Abe Long diary, entry for April 1, 1939.

[20]Abe Long diary, entry for August 1, 1941.

[21]Interview with Annie Blackburn, Carson Town, August 11, 1975.

[22]A good review of racial legislation in the United States is Louis Claiborne, *Race and Law in Britain and the United States* (London: Minority Rights Group, 1974).

Bibliography

Ahenakew, Edward. *Voices of the Plains Cree.* Toronto: McClelland and Stewart, 1973.

Allen, Frederick Lewis. *Only Yesterday: An Informal History of the Nineteen-Twenties.* 1931. New York: Harper and Row, 1964.

——. *Since Yesterday, 1929–1939.* 1940. New York: Bantam, 1965.

Allison, Sophie. "The Middleton Family." *Fort Macleod: Our Colourful Past.* Fort Macleod: Fort Macleod History Book Committee, 1977. 369–71.

Barbeau, Marius. *Indian Days on the Western Prairies.* Ottawa: National Museum of Canada, 1960.

Barrass, Georgeen. Introduction. *Among the Blackfoot and Sarcee.* By Canon H.W. Gibbon Stocken. Calgary: Glenbow Alberta Institute, 1976. iii–xv.

Bercovici, Konrad. *Around the World in New York.* New York: The Century Co., 1924.

Berry, Brewton. *Almost White.* New York: Macmillan, 1963.

Berton, Pierre. "The Legend of Almighty Voice." *The Wild Frontier.* Toronto: McClelland and Stewart, 1978. 209–33, 239.

——. *Vimy.* Toronto: McClelland and Stewart, 1986.

Blu, Karen. *The Lumbee Problem: The Making of an American Indian People.* Cambridge: Cambridge University Press, 1980.

Brass, Eleanor. "The File Hills Ex-Pupil Colony." *Saskatchewan History* 6, 2 (Spring 1953): 66–69.

Brennan, J. William, ed. *Regina Before Yesterday.* Regina: Historical Committee, 1978.

Brown, E.K. "Duncan Campbell Scott." *Responses and Evaluations.* Ed. David Staines. Toronto: McClelland and Stewart, 1977. 112–44.

Brown, Robert Craig, and Ramsay Cook. *Canada, 1896–1921.* Toronto: McClelland and Stewart, 1974.

Brownlee, Fambrough L. *Winston–Salem: A Pictorial History.* Norfolk, Virginia: Donning Co., 1977.

Brownlow, Kevin. *The War, the West and the Wilderness.* New York: Alfred A. Knopf, 1979.

Bruce, Charles. *News and the Southams.* Toronto: Macmillan, 1968.

"Buffalo Child Long Lance." *The National Union Catalog, Pre-1956 Imprints.* Vol. 83. London, England: Mansell Information, 1970. 258.

"Buffalo Child Long Lance Visits Ohio." *Ohio Archaeological and Historical Society* 33 (1924): 516–26.

"The Building up of an Ideal California Ranch." *Outwest* May–June 1914: N. pag.

Burnham, Mary, ed. *The Cumulative Book Index, 1926–1932.* New York: H.W. Wilson Co., 1933.

Calgary. London: Hodder and Stoughton, 1912.

Catlin, George. *Letters and Notes on the Manners, Customs, and Condition of the North American Indians.* Vol. 1. London: Published by the Author, 1841.

Caudle, Tracy Grose. *Memories From My Father's Trunk.* N.p.: Alpine Industries, 1970.

Cheney, John L., ed. *North Carolina Government, 1585–1974.* Raleigh, NC: North Carolina Department of the Secretary of State, 1975. 320, 328, 332, 334, 451, 454.

Chindahl, George L. *A History of the Circus in America.* Caldwell, Idaho: Caxton Printers, 1959.

Claiborne, Louis. *Race and Law in Britain and the United States.* London: Minority Rights Group, 1974.

Clark, Walter, ed. *The State Records of North Carolina.* Vol. 22. Goldsboro, NC: Nash Brothers, 1907.

"Clyde Fisher." *Explorers Journal* 27 (1949): 29–30.

Cobb, Elisabeth. *My Wayward Parent: A Book About Irvin S. Cobb.* Indianapolis: Bobbs-Merrill Company, 1945.

Cobb, Irvin S. Foreword. *Long Lance.* By Long Lance. New York: Cosmopolitan Book Corporation, 1928. vii–viii.

Cole, Roland. "Consumer's Suggestion Is Adopted as New Design for Product." *Printers' Ink* (29 Aug. 1929): 79–80.

Colley, Anna Church. "At Logan's Elm, Where His Famous Speech Was Uttered." *The American Indian* (March 1929): 8.

"Colonel William Allen Blair." *North Carolina: The Old North State and the New.* Vol. 3. Chicago: The Lewis Publishing Company, 1941. 49–51.

Corey, Herbert. "He Carries the White Man's Burden." *Colliers* 12 May 1923: N. pag.

"The *Cosmopolitan* of Ray Long." *Fortune* 3 (March 1931): 49–55.

Cowles, Colonel Calvin Duvall. *Genealogy of the Cowles Families in America.* Vol. 1. New Haven, CT: Tuttle, Morehouse and Taylor, 1929.

Cranston, J.H. *Ink on My Fingers.* Toronto: The Ryerson Press, 1953.

"The Death Song of Long Lance." *Scholastic* 22, 1 (4 Feb. 1933): 11.

Debo, Angie. *The Road to Disappearance.* Norman: University of Oklahoma Press, 1941.

Deming, Therese O. *E.W. Deming: His Work.* N.p.: T.O. Deming, 1925.

Dempsey, Hugh A. "The Blackfoot Indians." *Native Peoples: The Canadian Experience.* Eds. R. Bruce Morrison and C. Roderick Wilson. 2nd ed. Toronto: Oxford University Press, 1995. 381–413.

——. "Black White Man." *Alberta Historical Review* 6, 3 (1958): 7–11.

——. "Chula." *Dictionary of Canadian Biography.* Vol. 14: 1911–1920. Toronto: University of Toronto Press, 1998. 213–15.

——. *Crowfoot.* Edmonton: Hurtig, 1972.

——. *Red Crow.* Saskatoon: Western Producer Prairie Books, 1980.

——. "Sylvester Long, Buffalo Child Long Lance." *American Indian Intel-*

lectuals. Ed. Margot Liberty. St. Paul, Minn.: West Publishing Co., 1978. 196–203.

Dempsey, Lotta. "Katharine Hale." *Leading Canadian Poets.* Ed. W.P. Percival. Toronto: The Ryerson Press, 1948. 79–87.

Dial, Adolph L., and David K. Eliades. *The Only Land I Know: A History of the Lumbee Indians.* San Francisco: The Indian Historian Press, 1975.

Dickason, Olive Patricia. *Canada's First Nations. A History of Founding Peoples from Earliest Times.* 2nd ed. Toronto: Oxford University Press, 1997.

D'O'Brian, Joseph. "The Greatest Athlete in the World." *American Heritage* (July–August 1992): 99–100.

Driscoll, Charles B. *The Life of O.O. McIntyre.* 1938. New York: Beekman Publishers, 1974.

Drucker, Philip. *The Native Brotherhoods: Modern Intertribal Organizations on the North West Coast.* Washington: United States Government Printing Office, 1958.

Duff, Wilson. *The Indian History of British Columbia. Volume 1: The Impact of the White Man.* Victoria: Provincial Museum of Natural History and Anthropology, 1964.

Eastman, Charles A. *The Indian To-day.* Garden City: Doubleday, Page & Co., 1915.

Editing Committee. *Tyrone of To-day: Volume II, 1897–1976.* Tyrone: Tyrone Area Bicentennial Committee, 1976.

Eggleston, Wilfrid. *While I Still Remember: A Personal Record.* Toronto: The Ryerson Press, 1968.

Ewers, John C. *The Blackfeet.* Norman: University of Oklahoma Press, 1958.

Fay-Cooper, Cole. "Frederick Webb Hodge, 1864–1956." *American Anthropologist* N.s. 59 (1957): 517–20.

Federal Writers' Project. *New York City Guide.* 1939. New York: Random House, 1976.

Fielder, Mildred. "Chauncey Yellow Robe, Bridge Between Two Cultures." *Sioux Indian Leaders.* Seattle: Superior Publishing Company, 1975. N. pag.

"Film Depicts Tribal Life of the Ojibways." *Christian Science Monitor* 19 May 1930: N. pag.

Findahl, Theodor. "An Indian Chief on Park Avenue." *Manhattan Babylon, en bok om New York idag.* Oslo, Norway: Gyldendal, 1928. 42–50.

Fisher, Robin. *Contact and Conflict: Indian–European Relations in British Columbia, 1774–1890.* Vancouver: University of British Columbia Press, 1977. 146–211.

Foran, Max. *Calgary: An Illustrated History.* Toronto: James Lorimer, 1978.

Forsberg, Roberta. *Chief Mountain: The Story of Canon Middleton.* Whittier, California: The Historical Society of Alberta, 1964.

Forsberg, Roberta, ed. *Redman Echoes. Comprising the Writings of Chief Buffalo Child Long Lance and Biographical Sketches by His Friends.*

Los Angeles: Frank Wiggins Trade School, Department of Printing, 1933. Peel Bibliography Microfiche Collection, National Library of Canada, no. 3328.

Franklin, Benjamin. *Autobiography.* Boston: The Riverside Press, 1958.

Franklin, John Hope. *The Free Negro in North Carolina, 1790–1860.* New York: W.W. Norton, 1971.

——. *From Slavery to Freedom: A History of Negro Americans.* 3rd ed. New York: Vintage Books, 1967.

Fraser, W.B. *Calgary.* Montreal: Holt, Rinehart and Winston, 1967.

Friedman, Moses. "The Carlisle Indian School: Its Foundation and Work." *The Red Man* 3, 3 (November 1910): 119.

Fries, Adelaide, Stuart Thurman Wright, and J. Edwin Hendricks. *Forsyth: The History of a County on the March.* Chapel Hill: The University of North Carolina, 1976.

Gabler, Neal. "Walter Winchell." *American Heritage* (November 1994): 97–105.

Garnett, Porter. "Anoakia: Stately Homes of California." *Sunset: The Pacific Monthly* January 1914: 145–48.

Garretson Szasz, Margaret. "Indian Reform in a Decade of Prosperity." *Montana: The Magazine of Western History* 20, 1 (January 1970): 20–21.

Garth, Thomas R. "The Plateau Whipping Complex and its Relationship to Plateau–Southwest Contacts." *Ethnohistory* 12 (1965): 141–70.

Glasscock, C.B. *Lucky Baldwin: The Story of an Unconventional Success.* Indianapolis: Bobbs-Merrill Company, 1933.

Gossett, Thomas F. *Race: The History of an Idea in America.* Dallas: Southern Methodist University Press, 1962.

Graham, William M. *Treaty Days: Reflections of an Indian Commissioner.* Ed. Hugh A. Dempsey. Calgary, Glenbow Museum, 1991.

Grant, Madison. *The Conquest of a Continent.* New York: Charles Scribner's, 1933.

Gray, James H. *The Roar of the Twenties.* Toronto: Macmillan, 1975.

Grey Owl. *Men of the Last Frontier.* 1931. Toronto: Macmillan, 1972.

——. *Pilgrims of the Wild.* Toronto: Macmillan, 1935.

Griffin, John Howard. *Black Like Me.* 1960. New York: New American Library, 1976.

Hackett, Alice Payne, and James Henry Burke. *80 Years of Best Sellers.* New York: R.R. Bowker Company, 1977.

Hagan, William T. "Full Blood, Mixed Blood, Generic, and Ersatz: The Problem of Indian Identity." *Arizona and the West* 27 (Winter 1985): 309–26. Rpt. in *The American Indian Past and Present.* Ed. Roger L. Nichols. 4th ed. New York: McGraw-Hill, 1992. 282.

Hale, Katharine. "About Canadian Writers, Chief Buffalo Child Long Lance." *The Canadian Countryman* (14 June 1930): 8, 15.

Halliburton, Jr., R. *Red Over Black: Black Slavery Among the Cherokee Indians.* Westport, Connecticut: Greenwood Press, 1977.

Hamilton, Ross, ed. *Prominent Men of Canada, 1931–32.* Montreal: National Publishing Co., 1932.

Hanks, L.M., and J.R. Hanks. *Tribe Under Trust.* Toronto: University of Toronto Press, 1950.

Harkness, Ross. *J.E. Atkinson of the Star.* Toronto: University of Toronto Press, 1963.

Hawkes, John. "William Morris Graham." *Saskatchewan and Its People.* Vol. 2. Chicago: S.J. Clarke, 1924. 1196–97.

Hearne, Samuel. *A Journey from Prince of Wales' Fort in Hudson's Bay to the Northern Ocean 1769, 1770, 1771, 1772.* N.p., 1795.

Hendry, Charles E. *Beyond Traplines.* Toronto: Ryerson, 1969.

"High Ideals of American Indian Win Esteem of Author-Painter." *Christian Science Monitor* 20 Mar. 1931: N. pag.

Hoijer, Harry. "Paul Radin, 1883–1959." *American Anthropologist* N.s. 61 (1959): 839–43.

Hunt, Frazier. *One American and His Attempt at Education.* New York: Simon and Schuster, 1938.

Hurditch, C.P. "Schools of America—St. John's, Manlius, NY." *The Illustrated Sporting News* (New York) 4 Feb. 1905: 12–14, 16.

"Indians as Linguists." *Variety* 11 June 1930: N. pag.

Iredell County Landmarks. Statesville: Iredell County American Revolution Bicentennial Commission, 1976.

"Irvin S. Cobb to Receive File American Indian." *The American Indian* November 1927: 16.

Jameson, Sheilagh S. "John Howard Kelly, Q.C." *City Makers.* Eds. Max Foran and Sheilagh S. Jameson. Calgary: The Historical Society of Alberta, 1987.

Jamieson, Kathleen. *Indian Women and the Law in Canada: Citizens Minus.* Ottawa: Ministry of Supply and Services, 1978.

Jenness, Diamond. "Canada's Indians Yesterday. What of Today?" *Canadian Journal of Economics and Political Science* 20 (1954): 95–100.

——. *The Sarcee Indians of Alberta.* Ottawa: National Museum of Canada, 1938.

Jensen, Oliver. "Essay: Filial Piety and the First Amendment." *American Heritage* 18, 6 (October 1967): 2–4.

Johnson, James Weldon. *The Autobiography of an Ex-Colored Man.* 1912. New York: Hill and Wang, 1960.

Kainai Chieftainship. Lethbridge: *Lethbridge Herald*, 1953.

Katz, William Loren. *Black Indians: A Hidden Heritage.* New York: Atheneum, 1991.

Keever, Homer M. *Iredell: Piedmont County.* Statesville, NC: Iredell County Bicentennial Commission, 1976.

Kellner, Bruce. *Carl Van Vechten and the Irreverent Decades.* Norman: University of Oklahoma Press, 1968.

Kennedy, Dan. *Recollections of an Assiniboine Chief.* Toronto: McClelland and Stewart, 1972.

Kennedy, Fred. *Alberta Was My Beat.* Calgary: The *Albertan*, 1975.

Kennedy, H.G. *History of the 101st Regiment Edmonton Fusiliers.* N.p.: n.p., 1913.

Kidd, Kenneth E. *Canadians of Long Ago.* Toronto: Longmans Canada, 1951.

Latourette, Kenneth S. "Guido Herman Fridolin Verbeck." *Dictionary of American Biography.* Vol. 19. New York: Charles Scribner's Sons, 1936. 248–49.

La Violette, Forrest E. "Missionaries and the Potlatch." *Queen's Quarterly* 58 (1951): 237–51.

——. *The Struggle for Survival.* Toronto: University of Toronto Press, 1961.

Lawrence, Etha. "Mrs. Iva Thorpe Has Lived a Very Picturesque Life." *The American Indian.* November 1926: 4.

Lee, David. "Almighty Voice and His Stories." *Native Studies Review* 10. 2 (1995): 57–76.

Link, Arthur S. *Woodrow Wilson and the Progressive Era, 1910–1917.* New York: Harper and Row, 1954.

Long, Jaspar S. *Long Family Records.* Winston–Salem, NC: Clay Printing Co., 1965.

Long Lance. "Before the Red Coats Came." *Maclean's* 1 Mar. 1923: 50.

——. "Coming East." *McClure's* July 1927: 14–15, 121–22.

——. "History of and Agricultural Work Among Indians in Western Canada." *Proceedings of the Eighteenth Annual Meeting. American Development Association. Hotel Vancouver, Vancouver, BC, Canada, June 23, 24, and 25, 1926.* St. Paul, MN: Riverside Press, 1926. 25–27.

——. "How Canada's Last Frontier Outlaw Died." *Maclean's* 1 Jan. 1924: 19–20, 42, 44.

——. *How to Talk in the Indian Sign Language.* Akron, Ohio: The B.F. Goodrich Rubber Co., 1930.

——. "Indians of the Northwest and West Canada." *The Mentor* March 1924: 6.

——. "I Wanted to Live Like the White Man." *Maclean's* 15 May 1926: 16, 60.

——. "The Last Stand of Almighty Voice." *Maclean's* 15 June 1929. N pag.

——. *Long Lance.* New York: Cosmopolitan Book Corporation, 1928.

——. "My Trail Upward. I Took It Because I, a Blackfoot Indian, Wanted to Live Like a White Man." *Hearst's International–Cosmopolitan* June 1926: 138.

——. "The Secret of the Sioux." *Hearst's International-Cosmopolitan* June 1927: 41.

——. "West Point's Predicament. Why are there more than two hundred vacancies in its Corps of Cadets?" *Century* 117 (January 1929): 375–83.

"Long Lance Frequent Visitor to NY Office." *JWT Co. News Letter* 11, 48 (March 1930): 2.

MacGregor, James G. *A History of Alberta*. Edmonton: Hurtig, 1972.

McBride, Bunny. *Molly Spotted Elk: A Penobscot in Paris*. Norman: University of Oklahoma Press, 1995.

McClintock, Walter. *The Old North Trail: Life, Legends and Religion of the Blackfeet Indians*. 1910. Lincoln: University of Nebraska Press, 1968.

McDonald, Philip B. "Henry Clay Frick." *Dictionary of American Biography*. Vol. 7. New York: Charles Scribner's, 1931. 29–31.

McGroarty, John Steven. *The California Plutarch*. 2 vols. Los Angeles: J.R. Finnell, 1938.

McKee Evans, W. *To Die Game*. Baton Rouge: Louisiana State University Press, 1971.

McNickle, D'Arcy. *Indian Man: A Life of Oliver LaFarge*. Bloomington: Indiana University Press, 1971.

Miller, J.R. *Skyscrapers Hide the Heavens: A History of Indian–White Relations in Canada*. Rev. ed. Toronto: University of Toronto Press, 1991.

Mooney, James. "Croatan Indians." *Handbook of American Indians North of Mexico*. Ed. Frederick Webb Hodge. Vol. 1. Washington, DC: Government Printing Office, 1907. 365. 2 vols.

Moore, Robert G. *The Historical Development of the Indian Act*. Ottawa: Treaties and Historical Research Centre, 1978.

Morley, Alan. *Roar of the Breakers: A Biography of Peter Kelly*. Toronto: The Ryerson Press, 1967.

Morris, Richard B., ed. *Encyclopedia of American History*. New York: Harper & Brothers, 1953.

Morton, W.L. *Manitoba: A History*. 2nd ed. Toronto: University of Toronto Press, 1967.

Mountain Horse, Mike. *My People, the Bloods*. Calgary: Glenbow–Alberta Institute, 1979.

Myrdal, Gunnar. *An American Dilemma: The Negro Problem and Modern Democracy*. 1944. 2 vols. New York: Harper and Row, 1962.

Neuman, Fred Gus. *Irvin S. Cobb: His Life and Achievements*. 1934. New York: Beekman Publishers, 1974. 194.

Nicol, Eric. *Vancouver*. Toronto: Doubleday, 1978.

Nicholson, G.W.L. *Canadian Expeditionary Force, 1914–1919*. Ottawa: Queen's Printer, 1964.

"Nigger Humour." *The Beaver* March 1926: 74.

Nute, Grace Lee. "Pierre-Esprit Radisson." *Dictionary of Canadian Biography*. Vol. 2. Toronto: University of Toronto Press, 1969. 535–40.

"Original Americans' First Vote." *Literary Digest* 22 Sept. 1928: N. pag.

Osborn, Fairfield. "Madison Grant (1865–1937)." *Dictionary of American Biography*. Vol. 22. Supplement 2. New York: Charles Scribner's Sons, 1958. 256.

Osofsky, Gilbert. *Harlem: The Making of a Ghetto: Negro New York, 1890–1930*. New York: Harper and Row, 1966.

Patterson, E. Palmer, II. "Andrew Paull and Canadian Indian Resurgence." Diss. University of Washington, 1962.

Patterson, E. Palmer, II. "Andrew Paull (1892–1959)." *The Western Canadian Journal of Anthropology* 6, 2 (1976): 70–71.

Poetry: A Magazine of Verse 36, 1 (1930). N. pag.

Porter, Kenneth Wiggins. *The Negro on the American Frontier*. New York: Arno Press and the *New York Times*, 1971.

Prucha, Francis Paul. *The Great Father: The United States Government and the American Indians*. Abr. ed. Lincoln: University of Nebraska Press, 1986.

Ramsay, Alan. "Winnipeg! City of Contrast and Beauty." *Canadian Geographical Journal* 26 (1943): 44–47.

Ray, Arthur J. *I Have Lived Here Since the World Began: An Illustrated History of Canada's Native People*. Toronto: Key Porter, 1996.

Reeves, Ira L. *Military Education in the United States*. Burlington: Free Press Printing Co., 1914.

Reilly, Rose. "Long Lance, Chief of Heart-Breakers." *Screenland* October 1930: 114.

"A Reporter meets Long Lance, Chief of the Blackfoot Indians, Writer, Actor, Explorer, a Modern Version of the American Tradition." *The Great Outdoors* August 1930. N. pag.

Reuter, Edward Byron. *The Mulatto in the United States*. Boston: The Gorham Press, 1918. New York: Johnson Reprint Company, 1970.

Rights, Douglas L. *The American Indian in North Carolina*. Winston–Salem: John F. Blair, 1957.

Riis, Sergius Martin. "In Memory: Seumas, the Chief of Clannfhearghuis of Stra-chur, C.M. etc." *Explorers Journal* 39, 2 (1961): 50.

Roberts, Morley. *On the Old Trail: Through British Columbia After Forty Years*. London: Eveleigh Nash and Grayson Ltd., 1927.

Robinson, Bart. *Banff Springs: The Story of a Hotel*. Banff: Summerthought, 1973.

Rohner, Ronald P., ed. *The Ethnography of Franz Boas*. Chicago: University of Chicago Press, 1969.

Roseberry, C.R. *The Challenging Skies: The Colorful Story of Aviation's Most Exciting Years, 1919–1939*. Garden City, NY: Doubleday, 1966.

Rowlands, John J. *Cache Lake Country*. New York: W.W. Norton, 1947.

Roy, Patricia. Introduction. *The Writing on the Wall*. By. Mrs. Glynn-Ward. Toronto: University of Toronto Press, 1974. ix, xvii, xxvii.

Ruggles, Eleanor. *The West-Going Heart: A Life of Vachel Lindsay*. New York: W.W. Norton, 1959.

Rutledge, William E., Jr. *An Illustrated History of Yadkin County, 1850–1965*. Yadkinville, NC: n.p., 1965.

Ryan, Carmelita S. "The Carlisle Indian Industrial School." Diss. Georgetown University, 1962.

Sage, Walter N. "Vancouver: The Rise of a City." *Dalhousie Review* 17 (1937): 47–54.

Senn, Paul. *The Lawless Decade. A Pictorial History of a Great American*

Transition: From the World War I Armistice and Prohibition to Repeal and the New Deal. New York: Bonanza Books, 1957.

Schoor, Gene. *The Jim Thorpe Story.* New York: Pocket Books, 1967.

Schuyler, George S. *Black and Conservative.* New Rochelle, NY: Arlington House Publishers, 1966.

Scott, Duncan Campbell. "The Canadian Indians and the Great World War." *Canada in the Great World War.* Vol. 3. Toronto: United Publishers, 1919.

Scott, Edward B. "Tallac." *The Saga of Lake Tahoe.* Crystal Bay, Lake Tahoe, Nevada: Sierra-Tahoe Publishing Co., 1957. 151–65.

Scott, John. "Three Cheers for Earl Haig: Canadian Veterans and the Visit of Field Marshall Sir Douglas Haig to Canada in the Summer of 1925." *Canadian Military History* 5. 1 (Spring 1996): 35.

Seton, Ernest Thompson, ed. *Famous Animal Stories.* New York: Brentano's Publishers, 1932.

Shannon, Betty. "The Silent Enemy." *Moving Picture Stories* 12 Aug. 1930: 10–11, 25–26.

"The Silent Enemy." *Variety* 21 May 1930. N. pag.

"The Silent Enemy: An Epic of the American Indian." *Blackhawk Films. Bulletin B-264* June 1975: 2.

Snider, Sandra Lee. "Elias 'Lucky' Baldwin: Southern California Rancher and Town Builder, 1875–1909." M.A. thesis, California State University, Los Angeles, 1979.Stocking, George W., Jr. "Clark Wissler." *Dictionary of American Biography.* Supplement 4, 1946–1950. New York: Charles Scribner's Sons, 1974.

Swanberg, W.A. *Citizen Hearst: A Biography of William Randolph Hearst.* New York: Bantam Books, 1971.

Swayze, Nansi. *Canadian Portraits: Jenness, Barbeau, Wintemberg.* Toronto: Clarke, Irwin and Co., 1960. 83–85.

Swettenham, John. *To Seize the Victory.* Toronto: The Ryerson Press, 1965.

Tennant, Paul. *Aboriginal Peoples and Politics: The Indian Land Question in British Columbia, 1849–1989.* Vancouver: University of British Columbia Press, 1994.

Tise, Larry Edward. *Winston–Salem in History. Volume 6: Government.* Winston–Salem, NC: Historic Winston, 1976.

Titley, E. Brian. "Chapter 10, The Ambitions of Commissioner Graham." *A Narrow Vision: Duncan Campbell Scott and the Administration of Indian Affairs in Canada.* Vancouver: University of British Columbia Press, 1986. 184–99.

Tobias, John L. "Payipot." *Dictionary of Canadian Biography* Vol. 13: 1901–1910. Toronto: University of Toronto Press, 1994. 815–18.

Toland, John. *Adolf Hitler.* New York: Ballantine Books, 1976.

Tomkins, William. *Universal American Indian Sign Language.* 1926. San Diego: William Tomkins, 1970.

Tursi, Frank V. *Winston–Salem: A History.* Winston–Salem: John F. Blair, 1994.

United States. Institute for Government Research. *The Problem of Indian Administration.* Baltimore: Johns Hopkins Press, 1928.

United States Military Academy. *Association of Graduates* 23, 3 (December 1974): 104–5.

Van Every, Dale. *Disinherited: The Lost Birthright of the American Indian.* New York: William Morrow and Co., 1966.

Wade, Mason. *The French Canadians.* Vol. 2. Toronto: Macmillan, 1968. 661–67.

Walker, Eldred G.F. *Canadian Trails Re-Visited.* London: William Stevens, 1925.

Wallace, Anthony F.C. *The Long Bitter Trail: Andrew Jackson and the Indians.* New York: Hill and Wang, 1993.

Washburn, Wilcomb E., ed. *The Indian and the White Man.* Garden City, NY: Anchor Books, 1964.

Washington, Booker T. *Up From Slavery. Three Negro Classics.* New York: Avon Books, 1965.

Who's Who in America, 1976–1977. Vol. 1. Chicago: Marquis Who's Who, 1976.

Who's Who in Chicago and Vicinity, 1931. Chicago: A.N. Marquis Company, 1931.

Who Was Who in America, 1897–1942. Vol. 1. Chicago: Marquis Who's Who, 1966.

Wilkes, Alfred W. *Little Black Boy.* New York: Charles Scribner's Sons, 1971.

Wilson, Rev. W.H. *Tyrone of To-day: The Gateway of the Alleghanies.* Tyrone: Herald, 1897.

Wilson, Edith Bolling. *My Memoir.* Indianapolis: Bobbs-Merrill Company, 1938.

Wissler, Clark. *Red Man Reservations.* New York: Collier Books, 1971.

Woodward, C. Vann. *The Strange Career of Jim Crow.* New York: Oxford University Press, 1966.

Work, M.N. *A Bibliography of the Negro in Africa and America.* New York: H.W. Wilson, 1928.

Wright, Richard. *American Hunger.* New York: Harper and Row, 1977.

——. *Black Boy: A Record of Childhood and Youth.* 1937. New York: Harper and Row, 1966.

Index

38th Battalion 76

97th Battalion 75

237th Battalion of the American Legion 75

Abitibi 231

Adams, Sam, Mayor (Calgary) 124, 125, 126

Age of Ballyhoo 193

Ahenakew, Edward, Reverend 142

Alberta, District of 113

Alberta Military District 85

Albertan 93, 125

Alexandra, Princess 215, 246, 263, 302

Allied Tribes 131, 133, 134 *see also* Pacific Coast Indians

Allison, Carlyle 153, 154

Allison, W.T., Professor 150

Almighty Voice 154, 162, 163–65, 201, 314

American Boy 251

American Bureau of Commerical Economics 182

American Indian, The: An Introduction to the Anthropology of the New World (Wissler) 260

An American Dilemma (Myrdal) 31–32

Analla, Elizabeth 300, 315

Anoakia 293–95, 298, 309

Anglican Residential School 98 *see also* Gooderham, George

Arapaho, Dan 286

Arras 77

Assiniboine Indians 144

August-Wilhelm, Prince 215, 302

Autobiogrpahy (Franklin) 54

B.F. Goodrich Company 221, 251, 252, 254

Babbitt (Lewis) 182

Back Street (Hurst) 263

Baker, Gladys 219–20

Baldwin, Anita 275, 292–303, 306–307, 310–11, 312, 316, 317, 318–19

Banff Crag and Canyon 190

Banff Springs Hotel 167, 169–70, 175, 176

Bankhead, Tallulah 292

Barbeau, Marius 140

Battle of Little Big Horn 57, 191–93

Beau Brummel of Broadway *see* Long Lance

Beaver magazine 95

Belaney, Agnes 237

Belaney, Archie 237–38

Bell, James Washington, Dr. 182

Ben Hur (Wallace) 45, 302

Bennett, Lilly 297

Benoit, Paul 233

Berlin, Irving 275

Big Island 114

Big Meeting 27, 29, 34, 35–36, 37–38, 55

Big Plume, Joe 178

Bill, Allan 152

"black bottom" rage 153

Black Panther *see* Willis, Harry

Blackfeet *see* Blackfoot

Blackfoot Confederacy 201, 225, 260

Blackfoot Indian Reserve 97, 98–101

Blackfoot Indians 100–105 (passim), 112, 114, 116, 121, 156, 158–59, 163, 167–69, 171, 191, 202

Blair, William, Colonel 279–83, 284

Blood Indian Council 224

Blood Indian Reserve 111, 113–17

Blood Indians 109, 111, 120, 168, 171, 201–204

Boaz, Franz 128, 133

Bonn, Charlie 240, 271

Bonneville Club 220

Borden, Robert 111

Boston Braves 82

Bow, Clara 275

boxing *see* Long Lance, boxing
Boy Scouts of America 68
Boy's Life 251
British Benevolent Society 319
British Columbia, racism in 128
British Empire Club 180
Brownlow, Kevin 249
Brulatour, Jules 271
buffalo 100, 102, 105, 141, 145, 158, 201,
    204, 234, 244, 251, 260
Buffalo Bill 243
Bull's Head, Chief 108, 179
Burden, Douglas 230–31, 235, 236, 237,
    240, 242, 244, 247, 248, 256, 268, 274
Burke, Charles 223–26, 244
cadet corps 117
Calf Child, Joe 159, 160
Calgary 81, 82–84
    annual minstrel show 95–96
    City Hall 123–25
    racial attitudes in 81
Calgary Canucks Football Club 91
Calgary Exhibition and Stampede
    155–57, 167, 168, 177, 178, 188
Calgary Herald 86–90, 103, 109, 125–
    26, 130, 156–57, 163, 166, 190, 163,
    190
Canadian Expeditionary Force 75
*Canadian Savage Folk: The Native
    Tribes of Canada* (McLean) 133
Canadian Trails Revisited (Walker)
    177
Canadians in World War I 74
Carlisle Arrow, The 51, 52, 64, 192
Carlisle Indian Residential School
    40, 73, 108, 116
    entrance requirements 42
    founder 48–49
    history 47–49
    mandate 47, 49
    racial tensions 50
    reputation 49
    student body 55, 58
    trades taught 49
    view of Indian identity 49

Carlisle Redskins 40
Carlisle YMCA 55
Carpentier, Georges 167
Carry-the-Kettle, Chief 144, 145–46,
    201
Carry-the-Kettle's Reserve 144
Carson, Adeline 24, 28, 37, 41, 321
Carson, Andrew 23
Carson, Kit 29–30
Carson, Lee 27
Carson, Robert 23–24, 25
Carson Town 29, 34
    race relations in 22–27
Carver, H.P. 230, 242, 244
Catlin, George 269
cayuses 101, 117
Centennial Railway Exhibition 225
Chang 228
Chanler, William 229, 235, 247, 248,
    267, 267–74, 275, 283, 284
Chaplin, Charlie 275
Cherokee 39, 50
Chevalier, Maurice 292
Chicago Herald 154
Civil Rights Act 323
Civil Rights Bill 322
"Cicero Sapp" 179–80
circus, heyday of 33–34
Clapp, Charles E., Mrs. 304
Clapp, Elizabeth Randolph 303–306,
    311
Cobb, Irvin S. 208–11, 212, 213, 214,
    224, 273, 317
Cobb, Laura 209
Cody "Iron Eyes" 275
Colbert, Claudette 292
Commodore Hotel 166
Conquest of a Continent, The (Grant)
    248
Coolidge, Calvin 235
Cooper, James Fenimore 213, 285
Cosmopolitan Book Corporation
    194, 205, 207, 223–24, 225, 226
Cosmopolitan magazine 180, 181,
    184, 185, 191–92, 226

Cosmopolitan Productions 230

Cowles, Andrew 25–27

Cranston, Herb 167

Crawler, Hector 157

Crewe, Regina 246

Croatan 41, 51–52, 270, 279, 281

Croix de Guerre 20, 86, 88, 127, 150, 289

Crowfoot, Chief 205

Cunnington, Douglas, Lieutenant 94

Curtis, Susie 293, 315, 318

Custer, George Armstrong, General 191–93

Damrosch, Walter 246

Dann, Hugh 91, 155, 198

Davis, Bob 209

Delmas, Henri, Father 154–55

Dempsey, Jack 20, 82, 92–94, 155, 165–66, 197, 155, 165, 166, 173–74, 196

Department of Indian Affairs 114, 116–17, 131, 134, 141 *see also* Indians

Depot Street School for Negroes 33, 109

Dexter, Jennie 297

Dixon, Maynard 295

Duck Lake 165

Dunkards 98

Dutch Treat Club 180

Eagle Speaker (edler) 168, 201

Eagle Speaker, Mike (son) 168, 201–04, 240, 262, 289, 300

Edrington, W.R. 263

Edward, Prince of Whales 120

Eggleston, Wilfred 250

emancipation 27

Empire State Building 254

Explorers Club 258, 257–60 (passim), 264, 287, 308

Explorers Journal 258–59

Fairbanks, Douglas 275

family tree, Joe Long 45

family tree, Sallie Carson Long 46

farmers, of Alberta 103

Federal Indian Residential School 243

Fellers, Bonner, Lieutenant 215, 221, 255

Fellers, Dorothy 215, 255

Ferdinand, Franz 68

Fidler, Maurice 198–200

File Hills 138–39

Firpo, Louis Angel 166, 173–74 *see also* Long Lance, boxing

Fisher, Clyde, Dr. 256–57, 259, 274, 287, 316

Flewellyn, Lester 288

Fort Gary Hotel 152

Fort Macleod Gazette 190

Fort Slocum 71

Foster, Emma 53

Franklin, William E. 43

French Canadians, views on WWI 74

Frick, Henry Clay 304, 305

Friday, Moses 192

Friedman, Moses 47–48, 64, 66

Galloway, Lovie 43, 59, 70

Garvin, John, Mrs. 264

"Genealogy" *see Beaver* magazine

German Baptist Brethern *see* Dunkards

Germany 68–69, 75

Geronimo, Robert 58

Gibbon, John Murray 162, 190

Gibbons, Tommy 155, 167

Gilbert, John 312

Gleichen 97–98 *see also* Blackfoot Indian Reserve

Glynn-Ward, Mrs. 127

Going-Up-to-Sky 165

Gompert, Frank 316

Good Housekeeping magazine 161–62, 198

Gooderham, George 98–102, 109, 142

Gooderham, Mary 101, 102, 159

Gorman, Robert 58

Graham, Bill 137, 140, 142, 149, 206, 224, 226, 246

Grant, Madison 247–48

Graves, Felix 33, 259
Great Depression 20, 262, 264, 286, 298
Great Production Movement 137
Great War Veteran's Association 84
Grey Owl *see* Belaney, Archie
Gyro Club 132
Haig, Douglas, Sir 78
Haig, Earl, Field Marshal 176–78
Hale, Katherine 264, 265
Halle Brothers Book Fair 220, 307
Hampton Institute 48
Handbook of American Indians (Hodge) 270
Handbook of American Sign Language (Hodge) 260
Hannah, Sargeant 312
Harding, Warren 111
Harrison, John Wesley 42
Hart, Vivian 215
Hawkes, John 163
Hayakawa, Tom 311
Hayden, Charlie 86, 125
Hearne, Samuel 230
Hearst, William Randolf 194, 230–31
Heidenreich, William, Dr. 313
Henderson, James 44, 70, 73, 225, 269, 270–71
Hiawatha (Longfellow) 213
Hitchcock, Thomas 246
Hitler, Adolf 302
Hodge, Frederick Webb 260
Howard, O.O., General 109
Human Spider *see* Strother, Bill
Hunt, Frazier 216
Hurst, Fannie 263, 275
Indian Act 101, 135, 141, 144
Indian agents 98–102, 106, 131, 137, 141
Indian Department 137, 138, 140
Indian ponies *see* cayuses
Indians
    adjustment to reserve life 99–100, 102, 105, 106, 112, 116, 130
    adoption ceremony 168, 178

agriculture 138
Canadian policy on 131
children 203
culture 203
difficulty of tracing ancestry 261–62
etiquette 159
federal franchise 220
fishing and hunting rights 129
land claims 129, 133
mortality rate 106, 223
population decline 113, 130, 140
reserve life 100–101, 133, 143, 222–23, 260
restrictions 141–42
Sun Dance 105, 111, 159–61, 204
susceptibility to disease 41, 106, 130
travel permits 101
treaties 142, 205, 225
tribal affiliations, difficulty proving 40–41
white attitudes toward 212
see also Cherokee; Croatan (Lumbee); Sarcee; Shuswap; Squamish; Stoney
Indians of Canada (Jenness) 140
Indians of Canada, The (McLean) 133
industrialization 43, 61
Ingalls, Laura 289
Inglewoord Cemetery 319
Invincibles 55
It Girl, The *see* Bow, Clara
Italian War Cross 150
J. Walter Thompson Advertising Agency 252
Jackson, Elias 293–94, 296–97
"Jefferson Exodus Poindexter" 209
    see also Cobb, Irvin S.
Jenness, Diamond 107–108, 109, 128, 140
Jesuit Relations (Thwaites) 230
Joseph, Chief 108–09, 209–10
"Judge Priest" 209 *see also* Cobb, Irvin S.

Kearns, Doc 93 *see also* Dempsey, Jack

Kelly, Howard 88, 91, 155, 193, 198, 215, 220

Kelly, Peter, Reverend 131, 133–34

Kennedy, Dan 144–45

Kennedy, Fred 96, 191

Keokuk, Fannie 51–52

kinnikinic 113

Kippewa 231

Knowles, Vernon 154

Kyne, Peter B. 182

L'Ami, Charles 153

Lady of the Peacocks, The *see* Baldwin, Anita

Lake Temagami 231

Lake Temiskaming 227, 231

Lasky, Jesse 229

Last of the Mohicans (Cooper) 285

Latham, R.H. 279, 283, 284

Leavitt, Frank 73

Lenglen, Suzanne 298

Lens 78–79, 101

Lewis, Sinclair 182

Liberty magazine 285

Lillooet Indians 204

Lindbergh, Charles 197–198, 259, 267

Lipps, Oscar H. 68, 70, 225

Little Black Bear Reserve 138

Little Dog, Percy 224–25

Lloyd, Harold 275

Locklear, Ormer 94

Logan, Chief 170

Logan Elm 170–71

Logan Park 170

Long, Abe 28, 30, 36, 43, 70, 196, 278–79, 281–82, 292, 319, 321, 322, 323

Long, Aurelia 36, 70, 196

Long, Joe 22–23, 26–28, 30, 31, 32–34, 36, 40, 41, 42, 43, 70, 196, 277–78, 279, 280–83, 291, 292, 319 *see also* family tree, Joe Long

Long, Katie 28, 30, 281–82

Long, Miles, Reverend 27

Long, Ray 180–81, 184, 190, 194–95, 208, 213, 227, 263, 281–82

Long, Sallie Carson 22–28, 30, 31, 32–33, 37, 40, 41, 277–78, 280–83, 291, 292, 321 *see also* family tree, Sallie Carson Long

Long, Sylvester Clark *see* Long Lance

Long, Walter 20–21, 28, 30, 36, 70, 196, 281–82, 291, 292, 319–20, 321

Long, Vivian 196

Long Lance

  academic aptitude 33, 53–54, 59, 65

  achievements 20, 55–56, 59

  adoption ceremony 168, 201

  affairs 90–91, 189–90

  alcohol and cigarette consumption 287, 303, 311, 318, 320

  ancestry 23–24, 30–31, 37, 43, 268

  application to Carlisle Indian Residential School 40–44, 73

  application to Dickson College 59

  application to St. John's Military Academy 64

  application to West Point 67–69

  appointment to West Point, media reports of 69

  at Blackfoot Sun Dance ceremony 158–61

  at *Calgary Herald* 86–90, 123

  at Carlisle 43–45, 47–59

  at Conway Hall 62–64

  at St. John's Military Academy 65–66, 70, 71

  attire 83–84, 175

  birth date 22

  birthplace 22

  boxing 82, 85, 88, 91, 93, 155, 165–66, 167, 173–74, 193, 197–198, 199, 289, 301, 318

  burial arrangements 319

  character 37, 38, 44, 45, 50–54, 81, 83–84, 90, 94, 104, 136, 153, 287, 288 correspondence 70, 76, 79, 97, 131, 133, 135, 139, 140, 142, 155, 167, 182, 184, 185–86, 215–16, 220, 238, 291–92, 300, 302, 306

CPR public relations representative 167, 175–76 *see also* Banff Springs Hotel

depression 302, 303, 308

dreams 30, 35, 38, 85, 169, 310, 313, 314

education in Indian ancestry 57–58

effects of discrimination 199

effects of lies 188

effects of segregation 33–34, 61–62

errors in articles 162–63

Explorers Club membership 259, 263

exposure as a fraud 273, 292

fear of discovery 73, 213, 234–35, 237–38, 251, 264, 287

film promotion tour 274–75

first by-line 86

flying lessons 287–88, 309

in Akron 220–21

in Banff 169–70, 174–76, 177, 179–80, 188–90

in Calgary 81–96, 155–57, 177–78, 188, 197–202

in Canadian armed forces 72–76, 78–80

in circus 33–34, 39

in England 75

in Europe 300–303

in Fort Macleod 167–68

in Gleichen 158–61, 199

in Long Island 287–92

in Montreal 74

in New York 20–21, 73, 165–66, 180–82, 191–93, 205, 208–16, 219–20, 226, 284; in social circles 208–16, 250, 251–66, 301

in Regina 136–46

in Santa Anita 293–301, 308

in Saskatchewan 154–55

in *Silent Enemy, The* 228–36, 240

in Tem-Kip Camp 231–32

in Toronto 177, 250

in Vancouver 127–35

in Winnipeg 149–54, 162

in Winston–Salem 28–29, 33

Indian rights advocate 141–43, 144, 157–58, 221–23, 313

injuries 76, 78, 79

interviews with Mike Eagle Speaker 201–204

investigations of background 70, 73, 223–26, 262, 267–74, 275–84, 308 *see also* suspicions about

knowledge of Cherokee language 39, 44

knowledge of Indian customs 211–12, 244

knowledge of Indian sign language 211, 244

lecture circuit 150, 170–71, 180, 182–84, 220, 262–63

lies about birth date 40, 62

lies about birthplace 62, 82

lies about name 127

lies about rank in Canadian military 76

lies to acquaintances and friends 150, 176, 185, 210, 213–14, 217–18, 239, 269, 299, 311

lies to Carlisle Indian Residential School 40, 43, 44

lies to media 59, 63, 79, 85, 86–88, 176–77, 184–85, 186–88, 192–93, 195, 250–51, 264

lies to President Woodrow Wilson 67

lies to recruitment office in Montreal 75

Long Lance 219, 223–24, 232, 238, 244, 260–61, 293, 303; international success of 207; lies in 199, 262; media response to 206–207, 275; public response

to 206–207; source material for 201–204; writing of 199–207
Long Lance running shoe 221, 251–52
media coverage 76, 79, 172, 173–74, 190, 215–16, 246, 263–64, 275
on Canada's Indian policy 102–103
origin of Long Lance name 50
origin of Buffalo Child name 120–21
passport application 299–300
pilot's license 290, 293
Plains Indian identity 147–48, 153
pranks 123–26, 155–56, 218–19, 255
publicity agent for Stampede 157
rank in Canadian military 75, 76, 80
scrapbook 59, 73, 79, 88, 122, 135, 174, 196, 219, 221, 264, 269, 323
schooling *see* Carlisle Indian Residential School; Conway Hall; Depot Street School for Negroes; Long Lance; St. John's Military Academy
speaking style 171
sportswriting 174
stunt flyer 288
suicide attempts 303
suicide 312–318, 320
suspicions about 44, 50, 51, 200, 242–44, 251, 260, 268, 311, 318 *see also* investigations of background
transition to Plains Indian 135
upbringing 28–29
valedictory address at Carlisle 59
views on Alberta politics 103–104
views on Canadian Indian policy 131
views on Indians' future 132
war dancing 153
West Point examinations 71–73
will 239–40, 320
works: *Carlisle Arrow* 51; *Cos-mopolitan* 63, 72, 74, 85, 181, 184–85, 186–88, 191–93, 198; CPR menu cards 162; *Devoted to Flying in Alberta* 91; *Good Houseleeping* 198; *How to Talk in Indian Sign Language* 252, 253–54; *Long Lance* 20, 195, 199–207; *Maclean's* 154, 163, 185; *McClure's* 185, 198; *Mentor* 167, 180; *Red Man* 51; newspaper articles: *Calgary Herald* 102–103, 106–107, 108–09, 116–17, 157, 161, 163, 166; *Chicago Herald* 154; *Montreal Family Herald* 164; *Regina Leader* 146, 154, 166; *St. Paul Pioneer Press* 154; *Saskatoon Daily Star* 162–63, 166; *Toronto Star Weekly* 154, 167, 198; *Vancouver Sun* 131, 132, 133, 134, 135; *Winnipeg Tribune* 164, 166
writing process 199
writing style 108, 154, 164
Los Angeles Times 275
Lougheed, James, Senator Sir 85
Lougheed, Lady 85
Ludwig, Emil 208
Lusitania 69
lynchings (1917–19) 80
MacConnell, Charles 182
MacDonald, H.F., Brigadier General 85
MacFarlane, Athay 189–90
MacInnis, Carlyle William, Major 84
Maclean's magazine 154, 163, 164, 185, 188
Macleod Jubilee 167
MacTavish, Wilfred 153
Main Street (Lewis) 182
Man Mountain *see* Leavitt, Frank
Manassa Mauler *see* Dempsey, Jack
March, Frederick 292
Matawa 231

Mathias, Chief 131

McCall, Fred 91

McCaslin, Lowry 301, 303

McClaughrey, Hull 297

McCoy, Mildred 215

McDougall, George 233, 235

McIntyre, O.O. 215

McKay, James 85

Meighen, Arthur 110

Merchant of Venice, The (Shakespeare) 53

Meriam report *see Problem of Indian Administration, The*

Middleton, Samuel Henry ("S.H."), Reverend 109, 110–118, 120, 121, 148, 149, 168, 169, 205, 207, 220, 225, 226, 238–39, 240, 251, 269, 271, 272, 274, 316, 320

Miller, Edgar 52–53

Miller, Iva 51, 253, 261

Mills, Henry 261

Minneapolis Sunday Tribune 184

Mission, British Columbia 130

missionaries 104, 105, 131 *see also* Tims, John; Stocken, Canon; Middleton, Samuel Henry

Montreal 74

Moore, W.D. 217, 218

Morgan, Anne 246

Morning Bird 168

Mountain Horse 117, 119

Mountain Horse, Mike 119

Murray, Thomas F., Doctor 106

Napolean (Ludwig) 208

National Socialists 302

Nelson, Molly *see* Spotted Elk, Molly

New Orleans Times–Picayune 206

New Republic 246

New Statesman 206

New York American 246

New York Daily News 246

"New York Day by Day" (McIntyre) 215

New York Herald Tribune 206, 263

New York National Guard 68

New York Post 246

New York Sun 76, 246–47, 288

New York Times 193, 267, 286

New York World 79, 179–80

New York Zoological Society 248

New Zealand "All Blacks" 174–75

Newashe, Emma 50–51, 55, 299, 300, 316

News-Age-Herald 219

Nez Percé Indians 108–09, 210

Night Owl 142

Nina, Princess of Russia 263

Noonan, Irene 316

Norris, Kathleen 182

North Peigan Indians 112

Norwest, Henry 75

Office of Indian Affairs 221, 222–23, 225

Oka, Mike 168

Oakalla Prison 132

Ohio History Day 170–71, 180, 220

Ojibwa Indians 230–31

Okanese Reserve 138

Old Boys and Girls Association, Re-Union of 118–21, 225

Old Mountain Horse 119–21, 168

Olympic 75

On the Old Trail: Through British Columbia After Forty Years (Roberts) 188–89

Only Owl, Mary 160–62 *see also* Indians, Sun Dance

Oregon Trail (Parkman) 269

Overseas Military Forces of Canada 79–80

Pacific Coast Indians 129–30, 131, 133

Paducah Daily News 209

Paget, Richard, Sir 176–77

Palliser Hotel 82, 91, 93, 96

Pantages Vaudeville Circuit 93

Paramount 229, 249

Pardue, Captain 313

Parkman, Francis 230

Passchendaele 101

Passing of the Great Race, The (Grant) 249

Paull, Andy 128–29, 130–31, 132, 134

Peace Day 84

Peepeewesis Reserve 138

Pennsylvania Railroad Band 55

Philadelphia Public Ledger 206

Piapot, Chief 143–44

Piapot's Reserve 101

Pickford, Mary 275

Pinkham, Bishop 115

Poetry Society of America, dinner of 264–66

Polo Grounds 166, 173

Poor Man's Reserve 101

Popular Mechanics 251

Porter, Garnett Clay 150

potlatch 131–32

Pratt, Richard Henry 48–49, 116, 243

Prince Albert Historical Society 162

Problem of Indian Administration, The (Meriam) 223

Prohibition 84

R.B. Bennett Shield Trophy 116

R.J. Reynolds Tobacco Company 277

Rabbit Chutes 231, 251

race relations 23–24, 27–33, 37, 50, 61, 80, 91, 95–96, 127–28 *see also* segregation; slave ownership; slaves; slavery

racial incidents 29, 80 *see also* segregation

Radin, Paul, Dr. 206

Raleigh, Walter, Sir 281

Rambova, Natacha 214–15

Rebellion of 1885 *see* Riel Rebellion (1885)

Red Gun, Harry 100

Red Man, The 51, 52

Regina Leader 138, 139

Rhoads, Charles 268, 269, 270

Richards, Louis, Police Chief 313

Rice, Grantland 246–47

Riel Rebellion (1885) 154, 162

Roberts, Morley 188

Robinson's Circus 39

Rocky Mountains 84, 113

Rogers, Will 281

Roosevelt, Franklin D., Governor 267

Roosevelt, Kermit 246

Ross, Joe 57

Running Rabbit (father) 156, 163

Running Rabbit (son) 163

San Francisco Chronicle 297

Sanctuary Wood 75

Sarajevo 68

Sarcee Indians 84, 106, 107–08

Sarcee Reserve 104

Saskatchewan and Its People (Hawkes) 163

Saskatoon Daily Star 162

Scott, Duncan Campbell 134, 135, 140, 141, 206

Screenland 285

scrofula 102

Seamus 257–59, 263, 273–74, 287

segregation 61

   African American 212

   in Carson Town 27–28

   in Washington 61

   in Winston–Salem 27–28

Seton, Ernest Thompson 206

settlers, prairie 163

Sheridan, Florence 189–90, 191

Sheridan, John Jay 189–90

Sherman, W.T., General 210

Sherwood, George 246

Sherwood, Robert 246

Shorncliffe training camp 75

Shuswap Reserve 133

Sign Talk (Seton) 255

Silent Enemy, The 20, 229, 292; critical response to 246, 285; distribution of 229, 245–46; failure of at box office 249; filming of 228–36, 240–42, 244; investors 229; opening night of 246; promotion tour 274–75; screening of 247; stars of 232–33, 243

silent movies 249
Sitting Bull, Chief 57, 191–93, 234
slave hunts 41
slave ownership 23, 50
slaves
    African American 23, 50
    children of 24
    Indian 23
slavery 23–24
smallpox 40
Smart, Leta Myers 316
Smith, Beverly 263
Smith, C.O. 125
Soldiers Civil Re-establishment
    Office 85, 86
Somme offensive 77
Sounding Sky 163
Spear Chief 168
Spirit of St. Louis, The 197–198
Spotted Calf 163, 314
Spotted Elk, Molly 233
Squamish Indian reserves 127, 128
Squamish Indians 127, 128, 131
St. John's Military Academy 64–65,
    66, 72, 320
St. Paul Pioneer Press 154
St. Paul's Blood Indian School 110,
    113, 114, 320
Star Blanket Reserve 138
Starlight, Jim, Chief 106–107
Stefansson, Vilhjalmur 182
Stein, Bert 126–27
Stewart, Charles 134, 135, 139–40, 141
stock market crask (1929) 262
Stocken, Canon 102–105 (passim)
Stoney Indian Reserve 157
Stoney Indians 163
Story of an Indian Boy, The see Long
    Lance, works: Long Lance
Story of the American Indian, The
    (Radin) 206
Strother, Bill 91–92, 153
Sun Dance *see* Indians, Sun Dance
Taft, William Howard 61–62, 267
talking pictures 249

Te Ata 286–87
Tem-Kip Camp 231, 240
Thirer, Irene 246
Thompson, Mary *see* Te Ata
Thorpe, Jim 20, 40, 51, 55–56, 82,
    100, 252–53, 261, 264, 315, 320
Thunder Dance 107
Time magazine 246
Tims, John, Archdeacon 104–106, 111
Tims, Winnifred 106
Tolstoy, Ilia 236–37, 240, 251, 272,
    275–84
Tolstoy, Leo 280
Topean 165
Toronto Star Weekly 154, 167, 172,
    176–77, 181, 198, 250, 251
trachoma 222
Trail of Tears 41
treaties *see* Indians, treaties
Truant Act 99
Tsuu T'ina *see* Sarcee
tuberculosis 102, 106, 223
Tunney, Gene 197
Tweedle, Ralph 296
Twin City Daily Sentinel 69, 321
Two Moons, Wesley 57, 192
Tye, Alice 137, 308
typhus 40
Underwood, Katherine 115
Underwood Tariff 61
United Farmers of Alberta 103
*Universal American Indian Sign
    Language* (Tomkins) 255
University Club 182
Vahey, Jean 199
Vaheys, the 90, 198
Valentino, Rudolph 214, 215
Van Vechten, Carl 263
Vancouver 126, 127, 132
Vancouver Province 126
Vancouver Sun 124–27, 128, 132
Vanderbilt, William K. 246
Variety magazine 246
Verbeck, William, General 64, 68,
    246

Vestal, John 27, 279
Vimy Ridge 77–78, 101
Voting Rights Act 322
Wahl, Major General 224
Waldorf-Astoria Hotel 254
Walker, Eldred 175–76
Walker, Jimmy 225
Wall, E.A. 64
Wall, Edmund 66
Wall Street Journal 246
War Department 68, 70, 73, 224
Washington, Booker T. 48–49
Washington Post 69
Wayne, John 301
Webster, George, Mayor (Calgary)
    155–56
West End School 32, 33, 40, 277
West Point 216, 224, 255, 271
    entrance requirements 67
    racial policies 67
Western Canadian Ranching Com-
    pany 133
Whipporwill, Allen 39
Wild Bull of the Pampas *see* Firpo,
    Louis Angel
Wild West Show 33–34, 37, 38
Willard, Jess 82
Williams, J.H. 311, 315
Willis, G. Hamilton 42, 43
Willis, Harry 166 *see also* Long
    Lance, boxing
Wills, Harry 93
Wilson, Ralph 90
Wilson, Woodrow 61–62, 67–68, 271,
    281
Winchell, Walter 263
Windmill 74
Winnipeg 150–51; racial tensions in
    151
Winnipeg Tribune 149, 150, 152, 154,
    165, 174, 191, 197
Winston Clothing Company 42
Winston Realty Company 43
Winston–Salem 20, 277
    city directories 30

prosperity of 27, 39
race relations in 22, 27–33
race riot in 80
Winston–Salem Journal 278
Wissler, Clark 261, 260–61
Wolf Leg, Mary *see also* Indians,
    Sun Dance 161
Woods, Colonel 89, 125, 126 *see also*
    Calgary Herald
World War I 68–69, 71–72, 74, 76–78
Wounded Knee, massacre at 57–58,
    243
*Writing on the Wall, The (Vancouver
    Sun)* 127
Xenia, Princess of Greece 263
Yellow Robe, Chauncey 234–35, 237,
    242–45, 251, 268, 274, 300
Youth's Companion 251
Ypres 74